THE TERROR CONSPIRACY

© 2006 Jim Marrs

Published by The Disinformation Company Ltd.
163 Third Avenue, Suite 108
New York, NY 10003
Tel.: +1.212.691.1605
Fax: +1.212.691.1606
www.disinfo.com

Design: raisedBarb Graphics
Cover design: anlända
Editor: Byron Belitsos

Library of Congress Control Number: 2006929813

ISBN-13: 978-1-932857-43-6
ISBN-10: 1-932857-43-5

Printed in USA

10 9 8 7 6 5 4 3 2

Distributed in the USA and Canada by:
Consortium Book Sales and Distribution
1045 Westgate Drive, Suite 90
St Paul, MN 55114
Toll Free: +1.800.283.3572 Local: +1.651.221.9035
Fax: +1.651.221.0124
www.cbsd.com

Distributed in the United Kingdom and Eire by:
Virgin Books
Thames Wharf Studios, Rainville Road
London W6 9HA
Tel.: +44.(0)20.7386.3300 Fax: +44.(0)20.7386.3360
E-Mail: sales@virgin-books.co.uk

Distributed in Australia by:
Tower Books
Unit 2/17 Rodborough Road
Frenchs Forest NSW 2086
Tel.: +61.2.9975.5566 Fax: +61.2.9975.5599
Email: towerbks@zip.com.au

THE TERROR CONSPIRACY

Deception, 9/11 and the Loss of Liberty

Jim Marrs

disinformation®

TABLE OF CONTENTS

INTRODUCTION

"Quis custodiet ipsos custodies?"

(Who will guard the guards themselves?)

— Roman poet Juvenal, *Satires*, VI. 347

There is a conspiracy among us, one that is poisoning our nation. No one can doubt that the tragic attacks of 9/11 were the result of a conspiracy, heretofore a term disparaged by the mass media when connected to any past event in America—whether the JFK assassination, CIA drug running, or the deaths of church members in Waco.

On September 11, 2001, widespread contempt for the word conspiracy was swept away in the attacks on the United States. No longer could a major tragic event be blamed on a lone deranged individual. The question now became who precisely was behind this conspiracy to kill Americans, a question that the US Government has so far failed to provide an adequate answer.

According to official pronouncements, the 9/11 conspiracy involved 19 suicidal Middle Eastern Muslim terrorists—their hearts full of hatred for American freedom and democracy—who used small box cutters to hijack four airliners, crashing two into the Twin Towers of New York City's World Trade Center and a third into the Pentagon, near Washington, D.C.

The fourth airliner reportedly crashed in western Pennsylvania after passengers attempted to overcome the hijackers. To add insult to injury, this whole incredible "Mission Impossible" operation, which defeated a $400 billion defense system, was under the direction of a devout Muslim cleric from Saudi Arabia using cell phones and a portable computer in a cave in Afghanistan.

If this conspiracy theory sounds far-fetched or just too convenient, a closer look at the events of 9/11 reveals a huge number of disturbing and unanswered questions. This also holds true for the aftermath of the event, in which the Bush administration used their customized 9/11 conspiracy theory as a pretext for curtailing the cherished liberties of Americans.

As pointed out by thoughtful students of history, one must not be distracted by the *how* of an event but instead should focus on the *who* and the *why*. Accumulate the facts, though often contradictory, then concentrate on the overall process by which these events transpired. In other words, consider the overview and try to think like a good police detective: Who benefited from this crime? Who had the means, the motive, and the opportunity—not only to devise such attacks, but to circumvent normal security measures and hinder any objective investigation?

Such reasoning brings knowledge, and it is said that knowledge is power.

While many ardent 9/11 researchers have focused on specific and even technical aspects of that event—the melting temperature of structural steel, the size of the Pentagon's hole, etc.—at some point one must back off and look at a broad overview and search for deeper meanings.

The information within this book should empower Americans who long for such a wider framework and who are ready for some straight talk about the many factual anomalies, conflicting claims, and unanswered questions that still surround the horrific attacks of September 11, 2001 as well as its aftermath.

Indeed, it was the provocation of the attacks of 9/11 that provided the underlying justification for all that followed—the hurried passage of The PATRIOT Act, increases in the defense and intelligence budgets, the invasion and occupation of Afghanistan and Iraq, the creation of the Department of Homeland Security, the justifications for torture at secret prisons, the warrantless wiretapping of Americans, the centralization of power around the Presidency, and the general stifling of dissent in a nation that claims to be free.

A wider framework for understanding the post-9/11 era is also offered by the Bush administration. It's called the "War on Terrorism," yet the dictionary definition of terrorism is "organized intimidation," simply a tactic of terrorists. Following the Japanese attack on Pearl Harbor, what if President Roosevelt had declared a "War on Naval Aviation"? Yet Americans have been warned by Vice President Dick Cheney and others that this global war against a vague concept will last for many years, even decades.

Knowledge of the facts about 9/11 should have been available in print within months of the 9/11 tragedies—but it seems that freedom of the press, at least within the United States, belongs only to those who own the presses.

To those of us who follow the shadowy side of America's national life, the events of 9/11 immediately raised red flags of warning. Just one day after 9/11, I posted my initial thoughts in a piece on the Internet. Here are some excerpts:

WHO'S TRULY BEHIND THE ATTACK ON AMERICA?

Many people have compared the horrendous terrorist attack on New York's World Trade Center and the Pentagon in Washington to the attack on Pearl Harbor in 1941. It is an apt comparison, though not for the reasons most people think.

For true students of history, it is now beyond dispute that certain high-ranking officials in Washington, D.C. knew in advance of the Japanese intention to attack the US fleet in Hawaii, yet did nothing to prevent it.

Must the citizens of the United States wait another 50 years to learn that the 9/11 terrorist attack was allowed to take place just like Pearl Harbor? Could such an appalling scenario possibly be true?

Simple countermeasures against such an attack now seem apparent. For example, if the airlines would assign just one armed plainclothes security man to each flight, this tragedy may have been averted since apparently the hijackers were armed only with knives or other type blades. So, how were they able to overpower a plane load of people and, more importantly, gain access to the cockpits? Who taught them to fly jumbo jets?

As in the case of the assassination of President John F. Kennedy, the key to understanding the event lies not in who actually committed the violence but rather who was able to strip away the normal security protection.

Government and airline officials knew immediately that planes had been hijacked, yet no interceptors appeared in the air until after the attacks were completed. Who stripped away the normal security protection of America on 9/11?

At least in this most recent case, the government cannot blame the attack on a lone deranged individual, some Lee Harvey McVeigh. They must deal with a full-blown conspiracy, even though authorities were quick to point the finger at Osama bin Laden. Any investigation of bin Laden must look beyond the man, to his backers and financiers.

The trail of the terrorists will most probably become murky, with plenty of accusations for all concerned. But one thing appears quite clear, the tragic events of 9/11 play right into the hands of persons with an agenda aimed at eroding American liberties and sovereignty.

After decades of bloated and misused defense budgets, there are now calls for doubling our defense allocation. In a time of rising recognition that the CIA is an agency never sought by the public and one which has brought so much condemnation on this nation, there are now cries for doubling its size and budget. If the chief security officer for a large company fails to protect one of its most prized assets, is he more likely to be fired or have his pay doubled?

Watch for more anti-terrorist legislation to further shred the US Constitution.

As we all scramble to deal with the effects of terrorism, are we in danger of losing our few remaining individual liberties?

Also, consider that we are distracted from a faltering econ-

omy (the current crisis may require more federal financial controls), a plummeting public opinion of George W. Bush and
surging energy prices.

Would leaders allow a public disaster to happen with an
eye toward advancing their agendas? It's happened before...
in Nero's burning Rome, Germany's gutted Reichstag, at Pearl
Harbor and again at the Gulf of Tonkin.

While we should grieve for our losses, we must keep our
heads. When the emotions of the moment run hot, we must
remain cool and thoughtful so that we can find who is truly
behind this attack on America.

I believe the basic questions and issues I raised in this posting are as
valid today as in September, 2001.

And I didn't stop there. Within two months of 9/11, I had gathered a
vast amount of material, much of which appears in this book (along with
lots of new information) and presented it as a proposal to my publisher,
HarperCollins of New York, under the title, *The War on Freedom*.

I was told that emotions were too high and the content too "hot" for
immediate publication. Foot dragging on the book deal continued until
mid-2002. At that time, several employees of the FBI and CIA had come
forward to testify that they had tried to warn superiors of an impending
terrorist attack. The attitude toward my book proposal softened and I
signed a contract to publish the book, along with a sizeable advance.

Working feverishly throughout the summer of 2002, I produced a
manuscript by my October deadline. My editor was elated with the work
and predicted it would sell more than a million copies (not to brag, but
based on sales of my earlier books, this was not at all implausible).

The wheels of major publishing grind slowly and it was not until
March of 2003 that the book received a legal review. I had already been
sent a copy of the cover and publication was just a few weeks away. The
legal review, or vetting, is a process in which legal counsel verifies the
source material and checks for anything that might cause a legal problem. This hurdle was passed and the last words from the attorney were,
"You have satisfied me."

Within two days, however, I was informed that a senior officer who had not even read it had canceled the book. The only justification given was that the officer "did not want to upset the families of 9/11 victims." This was a dubious argument as by today more than 600 families have filed lawsuits and complaints against either Saudi Arabia or senior members of the Bush administration.

Under normal circumstances, if a book must be cancelled for legal reasons, the author is required to return any payments made in advance. In this case, I was paid the remainder of the entire advance. To me, this was an indication that the cancellation of the book was nothing less than sheer censorship, although the identity and motivation of the censor was not clear.

"Why would they want to prevent people from learning truths about 9/11 even if those truths were discomfiting to the public and embarrassing to government authorities?" I asked myself, still believing that I lived in a nation which valued free speech.

I proceeded to self-publish *The War on Freedom*, albeit with very limited distribution, and the book's reception was uniformly good despite the small circulation. Part I of that book was later published and distributed by a small California press under the title of *Inside Job*. *The Terror Conspiracy* expands, updates and replaces *Inside Job* and includes the three additional parts of the original *War on Freedom*, also greatly updated and expanded in the light of events and discoveries since 2002.

As readers kept expressing astonishment at these earlier books, I realized that the knowledge gleaned from a study of published matter, both in print and on the Internet, was indeed painting a dark picture of the persons and forces behind today's current events. I came to see that some force existed which did not want this information available to the general public. It would certainly upset the carefully constructed "official" explanations for the horrors of 9/11.

Today is a new day. The authorized story of 9/11 has been all but discredited in the eyes of an increasingly aware population, thanks to the dedicated work of scores of journalists and researchers, the rapidly growing "9/11 truth" movement, courageous government whistleblowers and even revelations from official inquiries.

As of this writing, we now know that:

- A wide variety of standard defense mechanisms designed to

prevent such an attack systematically failed on 9/11. Especially notable are the atypical failures which occurred simultaneously within the Federal Aviation Administration (FAA), the National Military Command Center (NMCC) and the North American Aerospace Defense Command (NORAD), all charged with protecting US airspace.

- Interceptor jets were not scrambled for more than 30 minutes after it was obvious that four airliners had gone off course and were presumably hijacked. In the case of Flight 77, which reportedly slammed into the Pentagon, an hour and 45 minutes elapsed with no interception.

- Missile batteries designed to protect Washington, D.C. failed to stop the strike on the Pentagon, one of the world's most protected structures; and fighter jets on constant alert at Andrews Air Force Base just 12 miles away were never scrambled.

- Several war game exercises, involving both the FAA and NORAD, were being played out on the morning of September 11, 2001, which may have facilitated the attacks. Yet, there has been little or no mention of these exercises by either the major media or the 9/11 Commission.

- President Bush proceeded with a "photo op" at a Florida elementary school even after he and his aides knew that three planes had been hijacked. He lingered in and around the classroom for nearly 20 minutes after being informed that a second plane had struck the World Trade Center (WTC).

- Not one steel-framed building in history has collapsed solely due to fire. The free-fall speed collapse of the Trade Center towers, with attendant melted steel and powdery dust, exhibited all the characteristics of a controlled demolition.

- Just such a controlled demolition apparently occurred about 5 pm that same day when, according to the owner of the WTC complex, the 47-story Building 7 was "pulled," collapsing in only eight seconds into its foundation.

- Vital evidence, including the buildings' structural steel, was destroyed through rapid removal and destruction by US

Government officials with no investigation.

■ An 8-mile-long debris trail indicated that Flight 93 was destroyed in the air rather than in the Pennsylvania crash reportedly caused by an onboard struggle between the hijackers and passengers.

■ More than a dozen countries tried to warn US authorities that an attack on American soil was imminent, some only days before the events.

■ A growing number of whistleblowers within the federal government have pointed to evidence that various agencies were well aware of the possibility of attack but were prevented from mounting investigations by senior officials.

■ In 2005, the public learned of a secret Pentagon intelligence operation codenamed "Able Danger." The officers within this unit had identified Mohamed Atta as a potentially dangerous member of al Qaeda a full year before the 9/11 attacks.

■ Far from being a reaction to 9/11, the US invasions of Afghanistan and Iraq were the culmination of longstanding plans, which only awaited a provocation such as 9/11.

■ The official explanations for the invasion of Iraq, such as the need to capture weapons of mass destruction, have proven false while the public release of the Downing Street memo proved that officials were well aware of the weakness of this argument more than six months prior to hostilities in Iraq.

■ Within a few hours after the 9/11 events, the FBI released names and photos of the suspected hijackers although later many of those named turned up alive in the Middle East.

■ Also within hours of the attacks, FBI agents were scouring the houses, restaurants and flight schools the alleged perpetrators had frequented. If no one had foreknowledge of the hijackers or their activities, how did the FBI know where to look?

■ Far from ordering a full and objective investigation to determine who was responsible for the 9/11 tragedies, the Bush administration dragged their feet and actually took actions to impede a swift and truthful probe into the events of that day. It was nearly two years after the events that mounting pressure from the public led by the families of 9/11 victims finally forced the creation of an investigatory commission. But this commission's final report left most of the questions of these 9/11 families unanswered.

■ No one in government has been reprimanded or even scolded for what we are told was the greatest intelligence failure in US history. In fact, the very agencies which failed the nation watched their budgets increase dramatically.

■ No person in government, except former National Security Council counterterrorism chief Richard A. Clarke, has felt the need to apologize to the American people for the 9/11 security failure.

■ President Bush himself declined to apologize for the 9/11 tragedy to either the American public or to victim's families during an April, 2004, press conference despite being presented with the opportunity to do so at least four times.

This is merely a short list of unanswered questions, anomalies and puzzles concerning the 2001 attacks.

The paucity of answers to these questions coming from official sources has prompted the growth of a nationwide 9/11 truth movement that has resulted in hundreds of websites, dozens of books and films, and numerous citizens' inquiry conferences. More recently, a group of academics came together in early 2006 to form Scholars for 9/11 Truth. This collection of more than 50 credentialed scholars and experts was spearheaded by Brigham Young University physics professor Steven E. Jones, who made headlines when he charged that the World Trade Center collapsed because of "pre-positioned explosives."

"We believe that senior government officials have covered up crucial facts about what really happened on 9/11," the group says in a statement announcing its formation. "We believe these events may have been orchestrated by the administration in order to manipulate the American people into supporting policies at home and abroad."

Key members of the group include Jones, University of Minnesota Duluth distinguished McKnight professor of philosophy Jim Fetzer, former director of the US "Star Wars" space defense program Robert M. Bowman and Texas A&M Professor Emeritus Morgan Reynolds.

Morgan Reynolds, former director of the Criminal Justice Center at the National Center for Policy Analysis headquartered in Dallas, was also the chief economist for the Labor Department during the first George W. Bush administration. In mid-2005, Reynolds undoubtedly shocked his former Bush associates when he publicly declared the official story of the collapse of the World Trade Center towers "bogus" and said evidence more clearly indicated that the buildings were brought down by controlled demolition.

A collective paper by these scholars asked, "Did the Bush administration know in advance about the impending attacks that occurred on 9/11, and allow these to happen, to provoke pre-planned wars against Afghanistan and Iraq? These questions demand immediate answers."

They went on to declare that they were stunned to learn that the government has brought but one indictment against an alleged perpetrator and, to the best of their knowledge, has not reprimanded anyone in positions of responsibility for incompetence or dereliction of duty. They also concluded the official conspiracy theory—that nineteen Arab hijackers under control of one man in the wilds of Afghanistan brought this about—is unsupportable by the evidential data. They even indicated that there are good reasons for suspecting that video tapes officially attributed to Osama bin Laden are not genuine. The group also found the government's own investigations of 9/11 to be "severely flawed." For example, they pointed out that the 9/11 Commission was directed by Philip Zelikow, who had served on the National Security Council's team for the transition between the Clinton and Bush II administrations, and was the co-author of a book with then National Security Advisor Condoleezza Rice. A man with close ties to the White House and a senior member of the administration's foreign policy team could hardly be expected to conduct an objective and impartial investigation. Their studies further pointed out that that *The 9/11 Commission Report* is filled with omissions, distortions, and factual errors. The official report, for example, entirely ignored the collapse of WTC7, a 47-story building, which was hit by no airplanes, was only damaged by a few small fires, and collapsed seven hours after the attack.

In 2006, yet another former government official broke ranks by questioning the collapse of the Twin Towers and WTC7. Paul Craig Roberts served as former Assistant of the Treasury in the Reagan administration and was the man credited with the success of "Reaganomics."

A former *Wall Street Journal* editor and currently an Internet columnist, Roberts wrote, "Many patriotic readers have written to me expressing their frustration that fact and common sense cannot gain a toehold in a debate guided by hysteria and disinformation. Other readers write that 9/11 shields Bush from accountability. They challenge me to explain why three World Trade Center buildings on one day collapsed into their own footprints at free fall speed, an event outside the laws of physics except under conditions of controlled demolition. They insist that there is no stopping war and a police state as long as the government's story on 9/11 remains unchallenged.

"They could be right. There are not many editors eager for writers to explore the glaring defects of *The 9/11 Commission Report*. One would think that if the report could stand analysis, there would not be a taboo against calling attention to the inadequacy of its explanations. We know the government lied about Iraqi WMD, but we believe the government told the truth about 9/11."

Other concerned citizens went so far as to file lawsuits against the Bush administration for complicity in the 9/11 attacks.

One was attorney Stanley G. Hilton, a Republican who had served as chief of staff to Senator Robert Dole (R-KS), who in late 2004 filed a suit on behalf of 400 9/11 victims' family members against top administration officials, including President Bush.

The suit charges that administration officials "all conspired with the government of Saudi Arabia prior to 9/11/01 to knowingly finance, encourage, recruit, permit, and aid and abet, certain individuals to carry out the 9/11/01 attacks on the World Trade Center and Pentagon, in order to orchestrate a contrived, stylized and artificial second Pearl Harbor event for the purpose of galvanizing public support for their military adventure agenda in the Middle East, and in order to persuade congress to enact their repressive patriot acts I and II for the purpose of suppressing political dissent inside the US."

To newsmen, Hilton was even more to the point, stating that al Qaeda is simply a CIA creation and that "[t]his was a government-ordered operation." Citing documents in his possession, Hilton said, "[Bush] personally authorized the attacks. He is guilty of treason and mass murder."

Hilton claimed he had gained information from top military officers, FBI agents and others who asserted that high-ranking government officials were complicit in the attacks of 9/11, which were carried out under the cover of disaster drills and war games, code named "Tripod," under the command of Vice President Cheney. He said participants were bound by official gag orders but indicated they would testify if subpoenaed.

Despite what Hilton claimed was a threat by a federal judge, he persisted in prosecuting the $7 billion suit. The was dismissed in January, 2005, by US District Court of Northern California Judge Susan Illston under an unusual ruling citing the "Doctrine of Sovereign Immunity," which has nothing whatsoever to do with the facts of a case but rather the old English contention that the "sovereign [King]" is exempt from lawsuits.

Critics of this ruling said apparently the judge reasoned that US citizens do not have the right to hold a sitting President accountable for anything, even if the charges include premeditated mass murder and premeditated acts of high treason.

A California appeals court refused to hear Hilton's case and even refused to allow him to file a brief outlining the case for government complicity in the 9/11 attacks.

Such serious accusations coupled with the ever-growing wealth of information pertaining to 9/11 has prompted many honest people from all across the political spectrum to conclude that the tragic attacks of 9/11 were indeed an *inside job*. Indeed, one professional poll in 2004 showed that nearly 50 percent of New Yorkers believe this to be the case.

You see, one does not have to actively participate in a crime to be part of it. The employee who knowingly unlocks the rear door to a business is just as guilty as the burglars who loot the building later that night

This is called an *inside job*. It happens all the time in criminal activity.

At a minimum, 9/11 was criminal activity that officials at the highest level allowed to happen on purpose. Far worse, the evidence in the record provided here can lead to the conclusion that an element within the US government actually orchestrated the 9/11 attacks.

Whatever the case, the attacks of 9/11 were without doubt some of the most monstrous crimes in history. It is my hope that this book will motivate the American public to seek out and bring to justice the real perpetrators behind the horrors that chilled the world on September 11, 2001, and which have led to an aftermath that is putting the future freedom of America in jeopardy.

Jim Marrs

PART I – THE EVENTS OF SEPTEMBER 11, 2001

"Let me just be very clear about this.

Had we had the information that was necessary to

stop an attack, I'd have stopped the attack...

if we'd known that the enemy was going to fly airplanes

into our buildings, we would have

done everything in our power to stop it."

— President George W. Bush to reporters, April 5, 2004

Bearing in mind the many unanswered questions concerning 9/11 and its aftermath, this inquiry begins with a brief look at the timeline of these tragic events.

This independent timeline is based on the best factual information now available, not on the "official" timeline that has been shown to be inaccurate and even misleading.

A CHRONOLOGY OF EVENTS

At 6:30 am on September 11, 2001, employees at the North American Aerospace Defense Command (NORAD) begin work, already alerted that a week-long series of war game exercises with the overall title "Vigilant Guardian" would command their attention that day. The event was designed to pose an "imaginary crisis" in the form of an "air defense exercise simulating an attack on the United States," according to later news reports. But we now know that these exercises provided the distraction and confusion necessary for the real air attacks of that day to succeed.

Sometime between 7:45 am and 8:10 am that day, American Airlines Flight 11 and United Airlines Flight 175 were hijacked. By 8:15, air traffic controllers knew that they were obviously off course. Flight 11, a Boeing 767 with 92 persons on board out of a possible 351, had taken off from Boston's Logan International Airport en route to Los Angeles. Flight 175, another Boeing 767 carrying 65 passengers out of a possible 351, also departed from Logan to Los Angeles.

During that same time frame, American Flight 77, a Boeing 757 with 64 passengers out of a possible 289, took off from Dulles International Airport in Washington destined for Los Angeles, while United Flight 93, a Boeing 757 with 45 passengers out of a possible 289, headed for San Francisco from Newark Airport at 8:42 am, after a long delay.

According to the independent timeline presented here, at about 8:40 am, the Northeast Air Defense Sector (NEADS) of NORAD was alerted to the hijackings of Flights 11 and 175 by the Federal Aviation Administration (FAA) and, according to a NORAD statement, two F-15 jet fighters were scrambled from the Otis Air National Guard Base in Falmouth, Massachusetts. Taking the initial call was Tech. Sgt. Jeremy Powell, a member of the Air National Guard at NEADS. "Hi. Boston [controller here], we have a problem here," Powell was told by Boston Flight Control. "We have a hijacked aircraft headed toward New York, and we need you guys to, we need someone to scramble some F-16s or something up there, help us out." Powell's reply was: "Is this real-world or exercise?"

Moments after 8:45 am, it was known to the FAA that four airliners had been hijacked, an unprecedented occurrence.

At 8:46 am, Flight 11 struck the north face of the 110-story North Tower of the World Trade Center (WTC) at the 96th floor. Also at this time, the two F-15s from Otis took to the air, after earlier warnings of a hijacking and waiting for several critical minutes for take-off orders. They quickly were redirected to New York City.

At 8:47 am, despite having its tracking beacon turned off by the hijackers, air traffic controllers could see that American Flight 77 had reversed course somewhere over West Virginia and was moving back toward the East Coast.

At 9:03 am, with the evacuation of the WTC towers proceeding amidst fear and confusion, United Flight 175 careened into the southeast corner of the South Tower at the 80th floor, sending a massive ball of burning fuel into the air over lower New York City. The F-15s were reported as being seventy-one miles away. According to official sources, the jets arrived over New York City at 9:10 am, seven minutes too late.

A short time after 9:03 am, Secretary of Defense Rumsfeld joined in on an emergency teleconference of top government officials being run out of the White House that included counterterrorism chief Richard A. Clarke, acting chairman of the joint chiefs Richard Myers, and FAA head Jane Garvey. Despite the 9/11 Commission's claim that no one could locate Rumsfeld until approximately 10:30 am that morning, the record shows that Rumsfeld—the military's top civilian official—was on the teleconference by as early as 9:05 am, along with the top official of the FAA. (See appendix for further details on this point.)

Nonetheless, according to the timeline presented in *The 9/11 Commission Report*, FAA authorities failed to the inform NORAD and NEADS about three of the four hijackings until *after* these planes had crashed (i.e., Flight 175 into the second World Trade Center tower at 9:03 am, Flight 77 into the Pentagon at 9:32 am, and Flight 93 into the ground in Pennsylvania at 10:06 am).

At 9:06 am, President Bush is attending a photo op in Sarasota, Florida at Booker Elementary School in a second grade classroom. His chief of staff, Andrew Card, enters the room and whispers into his ear, "A second plane hit the other tower, and America's under attack."

Between 9:06 and 9:16 am, with both WTC towers burning and terrified occupants leaping to their deaths, President Bush reads *My Pet Goat* to second graders for nearly ten minutes.

By 9:20 am, Transportation Secretary Norman Mineta arrives at the emergency operations bunker under the east wing of the White House. Vice President Cheney had already been rushed to this location by the Secret Service, according to several witnesses. When Mineta arrives, Cheney and others are engaged in the emergency teleconference indicated above. He witnesses Vice President Cheney being told by an aide that an airplane is headed toward Washington from only 50 miles away.

The 9/11 Commission Report ignores this eyewitness account by Mineta and others, and instead asserts that Cheney did not reach the White House bunker until about 10 am.

At 9:30 am, two F-16 fighters are scrambled from Langley Air Force Base (AFB) in Hampton, Virginia, heading toward Washington, D.C., in an attempt to intercept incoming Flight 77. But according to numerous authoritative sources, this pair of interceptors is ordered to fly at about a quarter of its top speed, as were the F-15s dispatched from Otis.

At 9:31 am, President Bush, speaking from the schoolhouse in Florida, declared the disaster in New York an apparent terrorist attack.

At 9:32 am rather that at the official time of 9:37 am—according to veteran military journalist Barbara Honegger, author of the special Appendix in this book—a flying object crashes into the west side of the steel-reinforced concrete and limestone Pentagon, penetrating three of its five rings of offices. A hot debate continues over what actually struck the Pentagon and exactly when.

If it is true that Flight 77 actually did hit the Pentagon at 9:32 am, anyone concerned with the fact that their tax money supports a half trillion yearly defense budget should be appalled that this flight was allowed to wander over northeastern airspace unmolested for over an hour.

Also at about this moment, a bomb or bombs reportedly go off at the same location in the west side of the Pentagon as the location of the crash of a flying object. (See also the Appendix.)

At 9:35 am, what official sources claim to be American Flight 77, but which may have been a reconnaissance fighter jet that was dispatched just after the impact on the Pentagon, begins making a complicated 270-degree spiral turn while descending seven thousand feet in the direction of the Pentagon.

By 9:48 am, key officials of the White House and the Capitol were evacuated and taken to secure but undisclosed locations. One minute later, in an unprecedented action, the FAA ordered all airline flights across the nation grounded. Air traffic controllers, who moments before seemed paralyzed by the confusion over the hijacked planes, were able to accomplish this nationwide grounding activity with unprecedented alacrity.

As early as 9:50 and no later than 10:00 am, according to numerous mainstream sources, President Bush had issued a shoot-down order that was transmitted to the military and was intended to apply to any remaining hijacked planes. This would have included Flight 93. With no supporting evidence, the 9/11 Commission claims that this order was not given until 10:25 am.

Shortly after 10 am, the South Tower of the World Trade Center collapsed, covering lower Manhattan with tons of asbestos-filled ash, dust, smoke, and debris.

At 10:06 am, United Flight 93, also with transponder turned off or disabled, crashed in western Pennsylvania about eighty miles southeast of Pittsburgh near Shanksville after passengers reportedly used back-of-the-seat radio phones to report that they intended to fight the hijackers.

This event was followed about twenty-three minutes later by the collapse of the WTC North Tower, the upper floors of which had been burning for about an hour and a half.

By noon, there were closings at the United Nations, Securities and Exchange Commission, the stock markets, some skyscrapers in several cities and even some large tourist attractions such as Walt Disney World, Mount Rushmore, the Seattle Space Needle, and St. Louis's Gateway Arch.

At 1:04 pm, speaking from Barksdale Air Force Base in Louisiana, President Bush proclaimed, "Make no mistake, the United States will hunt down and punish those responsible for these cowardly acts." But as of April, 2006, there had been no convictions of any terrorist involved in the 9/11 attacks nor had the proclaimed culprit, Osama bin Laden, been located or captured.

At 5:25 pm the 47-story Building 7 of the WTC suddenly collapsed despite the fact it was not hit by aircraft nor suffered major fire—a rather strange occurrence usually ignored in the official accounts until brought to the attention of the public by independent researchers.

After about an hour and a half, disaster relief crews began moving into the area searching for survivors and removing debris.

It should be noted that this timeline is not sacrosanct as there are unresolved conflicts between times reported by the Federal Aviation Administration (FAA), North American Aerospace Defense Command (NORAD), *The 9/11 Commission Report*, and the independent research cited in this book.

Only a truly independent inquiry possessing subpoena power will ever be able to resolve these and a myriad of other factual discrepancies. This book provides essential support to such an effort still to come.

[*Editor's note to researchers:* very detailed timeline information may be found at www.cooperativeresearch.org. Also, for a useful graphic depiction of some of the various 9/11 issues covered in this book, watch the movie *Loose Change* at www.loosechange911.com.]

UNRESOLVED QUESTIONS ABOUND

As previously noted, the 9/11 attacks have prompted a lengthy list of disturbing questions, most of which have never been satisfactorily answered despite several official government inquiries.

For example, the "New Jersey widows" who co-founded the 9/11 Family Steering Committee (FSC), along with many other 9/11 family members, made this clear at a July 21, 2005 press conference convened at the National Press Club on the occasion of the first anniversary of the 9/11 Commission's final report. In their opening statement, they declared that the Commission had ignored "approximately 70 percent" of their concerns, while also suppressing important evidence and whistleblower testimony that challenged the official story. It will be remembered that the 9/11 Commission was formed only after 18 months of intense lobbying by the FSC, and that the FSC's list of questions were initially considered to be the "road map" for the work of the Commission.

Many unanswered questions concern the collapses of the towers at the World Trade Center (WTC). But due to the premature and illegal cleansing of Ground Zero, these crucial issues may never be definitively answered. These questions include the controversy concerning how relatively minor fires could have brought down steel-frame buildings; the unprecedented speed of their collapse; the cause of their apparent pulverization into fine dust; multiple reports of bombs in the buildings; and the mystery surrounding the collapse of Building 7, which was not hit by hijacked planes nor subjected to intense fires.

In the course of this inquiry, it will become clear that many other pieces of evidence have been systematically withheld, ignored, or even destroyed, raising additional unanswered questions.

Years of foot-dragging and unnecessary secrecy by the Bush administration, widely documented in the mainstream press, also hampered independent and official inquiries into unanswered questions.

Throughout this difficult process, unanswered questions about the failure of US intelligence also linger in the minds of critics of the official story. How could an obviously sophisticated terrorist plan that likely involved scores of persons collaborating over many years escape the notice of our intelligence services, especially the FBI and CIA? The fact is, it didn't. Following 9/11, the American public was to learn again and again that a great deal was already known about the alleged plot within the intelligence community—but simply not acted upon, or directly suppressed. Mild admissions of incompetence have been made in official hearings, but a great deal of additional evidence of wrongdoing and missteps by these agencies has still not entered mainstream discourse.

And what about the question of accountability? Was 9/11 simply a case of bungling incompetence, as the official account claims? To many thoughtful people, it is unsettling that *not one* individual within the federal government or military has been fired or even reprimanded for the many obvious government missteps of that day. Indeed, many of those responsible for failures were actually promoted. Many have interpreted this lack of discipline as evidence that government actions on 9/11 were not missteps at all.

And perhaps most important of all is this crucial question: Why did there appear to be such a systematic failure of response on the part of our air defense authorities?

Both American Flight 11 and United Flight 175 were known to be off course by 8:15 am, yet NORAD was not notified for almost twenty minutes. Why the long delay? It then required another fifteen minutes before jet interceptors were ordered off the ground at Otis AFB, entailing a total delay of more than thirty minutes—according to independent chronologies. Even so, we now know that the F-15s still had enough time to reach the World Trade Center in time to intercept Flight 175 before it hit the second tower. Simple calculations using NORAD's own numbers reveal that the fighters were flying at far less than their top speeds.

The fighter jets scrambled on 9/11 did not arrive in time for a visual check of the hijacked planes' cockpits, even though such jet intercepts of wayward flights are a routine occurrence. For example, in October 1999, when golf pro Payne Stewart's Learjet went off course due to a failure of the plane's oxygen system, the Air Force announced that two F-15s from Eglin Air Force Base, Florida, intercepted the plane within twenty-four minutes after it had lost contact with air traffic controllers, and followed it until it crashed after running out of fuel. In 2001, a private plane that merely passed too close to the Bush ranch in Texas was immediately ordered to land.

"It happens all the time," noted investigative journalist William Thomas in a definitive essay on the issue of the 9/11 interceptors. "Between September 2000 and June 2001, the Pentagon launched fighters on sixty-seven occasions to escort wayward aircraft."

The air traffic controllers who actually handled the hijacked flights on 9/11 may have been able to give a clearer picture of what really happened in the hand off to NORAD and other authorities. In fact, according to the inspector general of the Department of Transportation, at least six of the controllers had made tape recordings that day describing their experiences. Incredibly, an FAA quality-assurance manager destroyed these tapes, without making any copies or even a transcript. According to an article in the May 6, 2004, *New York Times*, the manager told investigators he had destroyed the tape because he thought its production was contrary to FAA policy, which calls for written statements, and because he felt that the controllers "were not in the correct frame of mind to have properly consented to the taping" due to stress.

But even more disconcerting than the aforementioned fatal delays, and the intended or unintended destruction of evidence, is this disturbing fact previously noted: The US military had almost *an hour and a half* lead time to protect Washington after learning that four airliners had been hijacked. Yet no jet interceptors were launched from nearby Andrews AFB where two squadrons of jet fighters are specifically assigned to protect the Pentagon and the White House. Instead, F-16s were dispatched from the more distant Langley AFB, and for some reason flew at an estimated one-fourth of their top speed of 1875 mph, as had also occurred with the F-15s earlier dispatched toward New York. Curiously, none of the sophisticated anti-aircraft batteries adjacent to the Pentagon or in the Washington area were activated. These installations are set to fire automatically if any aircraft approaches the Pentagon that is not sending out a "friendly" signal from its transponder.

What could explain such failures? "It seems evident that…the Commission has not succeeded in removing grounds for suspicion that the US military had issued stand-down orders for 9/11," concluded author David Ray Griffin in his landmark analysis of the 9/11 Commission's report. Griffin is a distinguished author, philosopher, and theologian who taught at California's Claremont School of Theology until his retirement.

And what about the war game exercises on that day? The indisputable record shows that multiple war games and exercises were underway simultaneously with the attacks, and thus might have been the true cause of failure of our air defenses. This case is argued in convincing detail by researcher Michael Ruppert, author of another lengthy study of 9/11 entitled *Crossing the Rubicon*.

And there are more questions:

What are the odds that four transcontinental flights on two major airlines—American Flights 77 and 11 and United Flights 175 and 93—would have 78, 74, 81, and 84 percent of their seats empty, respectively, on September 11, 2001? This came at a time when many airlines were trying to save money by overbooking and canceling flights that were not full.

And how did the terrorists obtain top-secret White House and *Air Force One* codes and signals, one of the excuses for hustling President Bush from Florida to Louisiana and finally to Nebraska on September 11?

At 9:00 am on September 11, just about the time Flight 175 slammed into the South Tower of the WTC, Secret Service agents in Washington received this chilling message: "*Air Force One* is next." Within minutes Vice

President Dick Cheney was hustled from his seat in front of a television down to the president's nuclear-bombproof emergency operations center, while the White House was evacuated.

The warning was transmitted in that day's top-secret White House code, indicating that whoever was behind the ongoing attacks had access to the highest level of security codes, only known to the Secret Service. It meant that whoever had the codes could track and accurately pinpoint the president's plane.

After several days of investigation, the picture grew even darker. Someone had penetrated the National Security Agency's (NSA) Echelon surveillance system. In fact, the perpetrators appeared to have more electronic capability than even the NSA, including the use of "steganography," technology that allows its user to bypass Echelon and other electronic monitoring by hiding messages randomly in otherwise innocent digital files such as music, online advertisements, email headers or even Internet pornography. Such buried messages leave no trace of their presence. The idea that someone had access to such high-level codes provoked speculation that there were "moles," deep-cover secret agents, within the US government. It also meant that whoever was behind the attacks had access to our latest and most sophisticated electronic technology. Was this evidence of an inside job?

Access to high-level secret codes; "moles" within the government; foreknowledge of war-game exercises which disrupted normal air defenses; the lack of a rapid and decisive response to the hijackings; a systemic lack of response to numerous pre-9/11 warnings; no one fired or reprimanded over the series of security failures. Could all this be attributed to simple bad luck?

A key member of the 9/11 Family Steering Committee, Mindy Kleinberg, summed up the frustration of many about so many unanswered questions in her testimony before the 9/11 Commission during its first public proceedings in early 2003.

"Is it luck that aberrant stock trades were not monitored?" Kleinberg asked, referring to the widespread reports of possible insider trading in the week leading up to September 11 indicating specific prior knowledge of the attacks.

"Is it luck when 15 visas are awarded based on incomplete forms? Is it luck when Airline Security screenings allow hijackers to board planes with box cutters and pepper spray? Is it luck when Emergency FAA and NORAD protocols are not followed? Is it luck when a national emergency is not reported to top government officials on a timely basis?

"To me luck is something that happens once. When you have this repeated pattern of broken protocols, broken laws, broken communication, one cannot still call it luck..."

WHAT DID PRESIDENT BUSH KNOW, AND WHEN?

Despite the government's systematic failure to respond to the 9/11 attacks themselves, reaction *after the fact* came so swiftly that it lent support to the disconcerting idea that planning for such a reaction had been made months before. Perhaps the most remarkable and puzzling instance of this apparent foreknowledge is the actual behavior of President Bush himself.

About ten minutes after the North Tower of the WTC was struck, Bush arrived at an elementary school in Sarasota, Florida, for a photo op with grade school kids. CNN had already interrupted broadcasting to tell of the strike two minutes after it happened, yet reportedly Bush remained unaware until he was briefed shortly after arriving at the school. Or was he?

On more than one occasion Bush said he saw the first plane strike the WTC North Tower. "I was sitting outside the classroom waiting to go in and I saw an airplane hit the tower—the TV was obviously on, and I used to fly myself, and I said, 'There's one terrible pilot.'" The oddity here is that no video of the strike on the North Tower was available until that evening, when a French camera team revealed that they had accidentally filmed the hit while shooting a documentary in Manhattan.

Could Bush have seen the hit via an unannounced private broadcast? This possibility was hinted at when Vice President Cheney, during an interview with *Meet the Press* on September 16, 2001, said, "The Secret Service has an arrangement with the FAA. They had open lines after the World Trade Center was..." He ended his statement and moved on to other matters. If Bush indeed witnessed the first strike, why have all later official versions of the school events stated otherwise?

Bush told the school principal that "a commercial plane has hit the World Trade Center and we're going ahead and...do the reading thing anyway." Bush then entered the classroom at about the same time as the second plane struck the WTC South Tower. Moments later, then Chief of Staff Andrew Card entered the front of the room and whispered to Bush, alerting him that a second plane had struck and that this was clearly a terrorist attack. To the later amazement of many, Bush calmly continued his interaction with the second-graders—even as the rest of country watched terrorist mayhem consume lower Manhattan, and while two additional hijacked planes remained in the air over American territory.

In an effort to address criticism of Bush's lack of immediate action, Card later altered the time frame by telling newsmen that after he informed the president of the second strike, "Not that many seconds later the president excused himself from the classroom." It is now known, however, and supported by video tapes of the photo op, that Bush remained in the classroom until 9:16 am, more than *seven hundred* seconds after Card's notification.

Adding to this puzzling behavior on the part of the nation's commander-in-chief is the fact that his Secret Service detail surely must have realized the danger to the president inherent in a large-scale terrorist attack. Yet, Bush was allowed to finish his chat with the elementary students and calmly leave the school after making general comments to the media. He also left by the same motorcade and along the originally planned route even after officials were alerted that White House security codes had been compromised. *Air Force One* then left Florida with no military jet escort—disconcertingly odd behavior considering the potential danger to the president.

What did the president know, and when? Was the threat to *Air Force One* an attempt to terrorize the president himself? "The guess here is that Bush knew far less than many of his most severe critics might surmise," wrote Webster Griffin Tarpley, a veteran journalist, lecturer, and author of *9/11 Synthetic Terror*. "Bush's crime was not the crime of knowing everything in advance; it was rather the crime of not knowing what he should have known, and then compounding that by capitulating, by turning the US Government and policy in the direction demanded by the terror plotters…Students who build their work around the thesis that 'Bush Knew' are on treacherous ground."

DID WAR GAMES AID THE TERRORISTS?

U S military war games did take place on the very day—in fact the very hour—of the actual 9/11 attacks. Indeed, it appears likely that plans for staging a variety of war game exercises were designed to be so distracting that they may well have contributed to the success of the actual strikes.

Equally startling has been the revelation that some of these exercises involved scenarios in which terrorists fly hijacked planes into buildings.

The existence of such exercises remained a secret for nearly a year after 9/11 and then was dismissed as an Internet hoax for several more months. But as many as a half-dozen 9/11 war game exercises have since been acknowledged by the government.

To begin with, the powerful but little publicized National Reconnaissance Office (NRO) had scheduled a test exercise for the morning of September 11, 2001. The scenario was that of a corporate jet, crippled by mechanical failure, crashing into one of the four towers of the NRO headquarters building in Chantilly, VA, which is about four miles from Washington's Dulles International Airport. No actual planes were to be used in the exercise, but plans called for evacuating most of the three thousand NRO employees.

The exercise, later described as a "bizarre coincidence," was the brainchild of CIA officer John Fulton, chief of the NRO's strategic gaming division. In 2002, an announcement for a Department of Homeland Security conference noted the exercise with the comment, "On the morning of September 11, 2001, Mr. Fulton and his team…were running a pre-planned simulation to explore the emergency response issues that would be created if a plane were to strike a building. Little did they know that the scenario would come true in a dramatic way that day."

The exercise was cancelled when the first plane struck the World Trade Center less than an hour before the test was to begin. All NRO employees, except for certain essential personnel, were sent home for the day, according to NRO officials.

The NRO exercise, astounding in its timing, apparently was either part of—or concurrent with—*an even larger* set of war games being played out by NORAD's northeast sector, the region that included the three 9/11 crash sites in New York, Washington, D.C., and Pennsylvania. This was confirmed by then-NSC counterterrorism chief Richard A. Clarke. In his 2004 book *Against All Enemies*, while narrating his experiences during a video teleconference in the White House Situation Room on the morning of 9/11, Clarke writes: "I turned to the Pentagon screen. 'JCS, JCS [Joint Chiefs of Staff]. I assume NORAD has scrambled fighters and AWACS. How many? Where?'"

Acting chairman of the joint chiefs Richard Myers then responded, "We're in the middle of Vigilant Warrior, a NORAD exercise, but…Otis has launched two birds toward New York. Langley is trying to get two up now. The AWACS [Airborne Warning and Control System aircraft] are at Tinker [AFB] and not on alert."

Lt. Col. Robert Marr, commanding the Northeast Air Defense Sector (NEADS), upon also receiving notification from Boston regarding the possible hijacking of American Flight 11, asked: "Part of the exercise?" He was then told the hijacking was real. Lt. Col. Dawne Deskins, a NORAD airborne control and warning officer, also received word from Boston regarding the possible hijacking. She immediately thought, "It must be part of the exercise."

It has also been reliably reported that the war game exercises included not only real military aircraft posing as hijacked planes but that perhaps as many as two dozen "inserts"—false aircraft images placed in the FAA's monitors—were in use. Such false images may account for the rumors that day that as many as eight or more aircraft were hijacked.

"In essence, [FAA] technicians were half-blind," explained journalist William B. Scott, "trying to separate hijacked airliners from thousands of skin-paint returns. At the time, more than 4,000 aircraft were airborne over the nation, most in the northeast sector, which monitors half a million square miles of airspace."

In addition to the NRO, the Pentagon drills and the "inserts," by several reliable accounts these war game exercises also included "Northern

Vigilance," which sent fighter interceptors deep into Canada in response to a Russian exercise in the arctic and northern Pacific; "Vigilant Guardian," which may have included scenarios based on a hijacked airplane; "Vigilant Warrior," believed to have been the "aggressor" component of Vigilant Guardian; "Northern Guardian," another portion of the Vigilant Guardian exercise; and "Tripod II," a biological warfare exercise mentioned by Mayor Rudolph Giuliani that may explain the arrival of FEMA's National Urban Search and Rescue Team in New York the night before the 9/11 attacks and confusion in New York on the day of the attacks.

Author Barbara Honegger, noting the obvious lack of timely response to the 9/11 attacks—especially at the Pentagon—suggested, "This is beyond comprehension over the nation's capital unless some previous piece of information or mental set led them to assume the Pentagon plane could not be a terrorist vehicle, or at least confuse them as to whether it was or not. If those looking on from inside the Pentagon as 9/11 unfolded believed Flight 77 was, or might be, part of a counter-terror exercise set for that very morning, it would explain the otherwise incomprehensible delay, almost to the point of paralysis, in effectively scrambling interceptors."

Honegger, well-known for her 1989 book *October Surprise* that revealed the elder Bush's role in a covert deal with Iranian terrorists that ensured the election of Ronald Reagan in 1980, noted that if in fact the 9/11 attacks were enabled by homegrown war games, this might explain why the leak by a congressional investigation (to be examined later) of a September 10, 2001, NSA intercept message is reported to have upset Vice President Cheney so much.

That message reportedly was between hijack leader Mohamed Atta and the purported attack mastermind, Khalid Sheikh Mohammed. It stated, "The Match is about to begin. Tomorrow is zero hour."

"'Match,' of course, is what you would expect if the speakers were referring to his discovery of the date that the US government had selected to conduct its counter-terror exercises—one that was about to turn very real when the terrorists piggybacked their long-planned plot onto it," said Honegger. "[G]iven the context in which all this finally begins to make sense, Atta was merely communicating to his boss, or vice versa, the date that the US government exercise was to take place. Bin al-Shibh, Atta, and Mohammed didn't choose the date. The US government did."

The NSA phone intercept makes it clear that the hijackers knew when to coordinate their attack with the war games. How could they have obtained this vital yet top-secret information unless through some source within the government? In the Appendix to this book, Honegger provides a detailed scenario for how the hand-off of the "match" information to Atta may have taken place.

The release of news concerning such exercises also certainly gives lie to the numerous public statements of President Bush, National Security Adviser Condoleezza Rice, FBI Director Robert Mueller, and others who stated, at times under oath, that the government never considered that terrorists might use airplanes as weapons.

If the idea that war game exercises both explained the lack of initial response on 9/11 as well as put to lie the oft-stated question by Bush administration officials that they could not have known terrorists might use aircraft as weapons, in early 2005 this issue grew even hotter. The *American Free Press* reported that the US Army had planned just such a scenario—in 1976!

Timothy McNiven, a US Defense Dept. contract operative, revealed that his military unit conceived of a mock terrorist attack on the World Trade Center as part of a 1976 exercise. "[A]s I watched the twin towers really collapse on the morning of September 11, I realized I was watching the very same thing we devised in 1976," McNiven said.

McNiven, who successfully passed a polygraph "lie detector" test in regard to his story as well as naming about 40 individuals who took part in the planning, said in 1976 he was with C Battery, 2/81st Field Artillery stationed in Strasbourg, Germany, when the unit was ordered to concoct the "perfect terrorist plan" using the World Trade Center towers as their target. The congressionally commissioned project reportedly was to identify security lapses and alert lawmakers to needed legislation. McNiven's group came up with a plan in which Middle Eastern terrorists would hijack commercial airliners using plastic box cutters to bypass security, then level the towers by crashing the planes into them. He said the team's leader, Lt. Michael Teague, was specifically ordered by his superiors to use the World Trade Center towers as the terrorist target.

"Why have I spent every waking hour trying to bring this story to the American people?" McNiven asked during an interview. He said he told his superior officer that if the towers were ever brought down in the manner in which his group had foreseen, he would go public with the story. Initially, he said he was ordered never to talk about the 1976 plan and was even physically beaten for speaking about it. He said a week or so later, in a strange turn of events, he was given a direct order that if the twin towers were every attacked as in the 1976 study, he was to do everything he could to bring this story to the public. "I have no idea why they changed their minds," he said, "but I was then emphatically told that this order was never to be rescinded—never—because those who would rescind it, would be the very same people who turned against the American people."

Do the war games provide sufficient evidence of an inside job? "I think the people who planned and carried out those exercises, they're the ones that should be the object of investigation," said Dr. Robert M. Bowman, Lt. Col., USAF (ret.). Bowman flew 101 combat missions in Vietnam and was a recipient of the Eisenhower Medal, the George F. Kennan Peace Prize, the President's Medal of Veterans for Peace, the Society of Military Engineers Gold Medal (twice), six Air Medals, and dozens of other awards and honors. His Ph.D. is in Aeronautics and Nuclear Engineering from Caltech and he is considered one of the country's foremost experts on National Security. In the 1970s, Bowman worked on the then-secret Star Wars space defense system but left the program when he realized it was designed for offensive warfare against the old Soviet Union.

Bowman said that the entire chain of military command may have been unaware of what was taking place and were used as tools by the people pulling the strings behind the attack. "If I had to narrow it [a 9/11 conspiracy] down to one person...I think my prime suspect would be Dick Cheney," said Bowman in an April, 2006, radio interview. He added that reaction to the 9/11 attacks, such as the PATRIOT Act has "...done more to destroy the rights of Americans than all of our enemies combined."

But if Cheney is a key conspirator as Bowman claims, how was the apparent subterfuge of the war game exercises put into place?

One speculation points to yet another piece of evidence of gaming scenarios. It was learned that as far back as November 3, 2000, the Military District of Washington's Command Emergency Response Training unit conducted a scenario entitled The Pentagon Mass Casualty Exercise, which simulated the crash of an airliner into the courtyard of the Pentagon.

According to an email message sent by a NORAD officer in September 2001, and published by the nonprofit watchdog group, Project Government Oversight, "The NORAD exercise developers wanted an event having a terrorist group hijack a commercial airliner (foreign carrier) and fly it into the Pentagon. Joint Staff action officers rejected it as unrealistic."

"What do you want to bet that, when the April, 2001, hijacked-plane-into-Pentagon NORAD war game script writer was turned down, that he took his idea to Cheney or one of Cheney's people, who then took it as their own..." mused Honegger, "...and on September 11, the same scenario that had been turned down in April was embedded in NORAD's own game, 'Vigilant Guardian'?"

Few people realize to what extent Cheney was in a commanding position to know all aspects of the international terrorist structure and particularly America's terrorist attack planning scenarios. On May 9, 2001, four months prior to the attacks, the Bush administration had launched an effort to address the problem of terrorism. President Bush created a new Office of National Preparedness (ONP) within the Federal Emergency Management Agency (FEMA) and named Vice President Dick Cheney to head a special task force to study terrorism and guide FEMA's anti-terrorism operations. His position in the counterterrorism effort of the federal government was therefore central—especially so if one considers his previous experience as Secretary of Defense during the first Bush administration.

Practically speaking, Dick Cheney was in a virtual command-and-control position during the actual events of 9/11, argues Mike Ruppert in *Crossing the Rubicon*. We've already noted that Cheney was rushed to the White House Presidential Emergency Operations Center, (located in a bunker under the east wing of the White House) just after the second plane had hit the WTC, and was directing activities of the government from this secure location while President Bush was being whisked around the country on *Air Force One*.

Cheney's terrorism task force was scheduled to produce antiterrorism recommendations for Congress by October 1, 2001, too late to make a difference. Of course, by that time, the nation was well into the new War on Terrorism.

During much of 2001 prior to 9/11, Cheney also was in charge of another crucial task force, this one reviewing national energy policy. This panel later became the center of controversy, when California's power woes indicated that corporate energy executives had unduly influenced national policies. Cheney's task force never turned over its internal papers, despite a lawsuit over this refusal that made its way up to the Supreme Court. Some observers have argued that smoking-gun documents related to 9/11—and revealing a motive involving an invasion of Iraq for the sake of oil—may be hidden in the records that Cheney has refused to make public. But what *has* been revealed is the fact that Cheney met at least six times with officials of the failed energy company Enron.

WHO AUTHORIZED THE BIN LADEN EVACUATION?

While hundreds of people around the world were rounded up by national authorities in the wake of the 9/11 attacks and the public denied the right to fly, about 140 Saudis—including two dozen members of Osama bin Laden's own family—were allowed to fly by private jet to a reunion in Washington and then on to Boston. According to the *New Yorker*, the bin Ladens grouped in Boston, from where they eventually were flown out of the country once the FAA reinstated overseas flights. And this curious operation was carried out even as Osama bin Laden was being fingered as the undoubted perpetrator of the attacks.

Initially dismissed as an Internet rumor or an urban legend, the reports of the bin Laden family flight were confirmed in an October 2003 *Vanity Fair* interview with Richard A. Clarke, who had resigned earlier that year as chief of the Counterterrorism Security Group of the NSC. Clarke said that he did not recall who requested approval for the flight, but thought it was either the FBI or the State Department. "Someone brought to us for approval the decision to let an airplane filled with Saudis, including members of the bin Laden family, leave the country," he said. "So I said, 'Fine, let it happen.'"

Although both the *Tampa Tribune* and the *New York Times* reported that the Saudis were shepherded to their flights by FBI agents, bureau officials denied such reports. The Saudi flights, which came from ten American cities, including Los Angeles, Washington, D.C., and Houston, ended up in Boston where two jumbo jets flew the group to Saudi Arabia in mid-September 2001.

None of the Saudis was seriously interrogated by anyone.

"We were in the midst of the worst terrorist act in history and here we were seeing an evacuation of the bin Ladens..." groused Tom Kinton, director of aviation at Boston's Logan International Airport. "I wanted to go to the highest levels in Washington," he told *Vanity Fair* but realized that the operation had the blessing of top federal officials.

"How was it possible that, just as President Bush declared a no-holds-barred global war on terrorism that would send hundreds of thousands of US troops to Afghanistan and Iraq, and just as Osama bin Laden became Public Enemy No. 1 and the target of a worldwide manhunt, the White House would expedite the departure of so many potential witnesses, including two dozen relatives of the man behind the attack itself?" asked *Vanity Fair* writer Craig Unger.

Numerous bin Laden family members flew out of the US from Logan International on September 18, 2001. The very next day, White House speech writers were formulating President Bush's stirring call for a war on terrorism while at the Pentagon plans were being drawn up for this war to include Iraq. No one yet has pinpointed the authority behind this incredible evacuation, although it is clear this authority must have had control over both the FBI and the FAA.

WHAT ABOUT THE HIJACKERS THEMSELVES?

Lending support to the contention that al Qaeda has been overblown as a monolithic terrorist network is a lengthy series of disturbing questions concerning the 9/11 hijackers themselves, as well as the apparent obfuscation of the facts in the official government account.

The day following 9/11, FBI director Robert Mueller announced some astonishingly swift police work. "We have, in the last twenty-four hours, taken the [passenger] manifests and used them in an evidentiary manner. And have successfully, I believe, identified many of the hijackers on each of the four flights that went down," he told newsmen. Sounding like a 1940s police detective, Mueller added, "We will leave no stone unturned to find those responsible for the tragedies."

Yet, at the same time, Mueller acknowledged that the list of named hijackers might not contain their real names.

An obvious set of questions arises from this scenario: If they used aliases, how did the FBI identify them so quickly? How did the FBI learn the names of five of the hijackers and obtain their photographs the day of the attacks? And where did agents obtain the names and locations of businesses and restaurants used by the hijackers by that same afternoon?

Not one of the accused hijackers' names appeared on the passenger lists made public by American or United airlines. In fact, as many as seven of those named as the culprits in the attacks were soon found alive and well in the Middle East.

Saudi pilot Waleed al-Shehri was identified by the US Justice Department as one of the men who crashed American Flight 11 into the WTC. But a few days later, Waleed al-Shehri contacted authorities in Casablanca, Morocco, to proclaim that he was very much alive and played no part in the attacks. He said he did train as a pilot in the United States but left the country in September 2000, to become a pilot with Saudi Arabian Airlines. Strangely, *The 9/11 Commission Report* speculates in its opening pages that al-Shehri must have been the man responsible for stabbing one of the flight attendants on Flight 11.

Another man identified as one of the hijackers of Flight 11, Abdulaziz al-Omari, also turned up alive in the Middle East, telling BBC News that he lost his passport while visiting Denver, Colorado. Actually two turned up, as yet another Abdulaziz al-Omari surfaced in Saudi Arabia very much alive and telling newsmen, "I couldn't believe the FBI put me on their list. They gave my name and my date of birth, but I am not a suicide bomber. I am here. I am alive. I have no idea how to fly a plane. I had nothing to do with this."

Yet another man identified as one of the hijackers of United Flight

93, Saeed al-Ghamdi, was reported alive and well and working as a pilot in Saudi Arabia. "You cannot imagine what it is like to be described as a terrorist—and a dead man—when you are innocent and alive," said al-Ghamdi, who was given a holiday by his airline in Saudi Arabia to avoid arrest.

There were even reports that another identified hijacker, Khalid al-Midhar, might also be alive.

"It was proved that five of the names included in the FBI list had nothing to do with what happened," announced Saudi Arabia's foreign minister Prince Saud al-Faisal, after meeting with President Bush on September 20, 2001.

Mueller acknowledged within days of the attacks that the identities of the hijackers were in doubt but this gained little notice in the rush to publicize the culprits. Despite initially saying he was "fairly confident" that the published names of the hijackers were correct, Mueller later admitted, "The identification process has been complicated by the fact that many Arab family names are similar. It is also possible that the hijackers used false identities."

Since Saudi Arabia's foreign minister claimed five of the proclaimed hijackers were not aboard the death planes and in fact are still alive, and a sixth man on that list was reported to be alive and well in Tunisia, why are these names still on the FBI list? These same names were used in the final report of the 9/11 Commission with no attempt to clarify the name confusion. In fact, its report goes into considerable detail throughout its pages about the supposed sinister activities of these men, apparently oblivious that numerous mainstream media sources such as the Associated Press and the BBC had long ago established that they were not on the flights.

Very soon after the attacks, the stunning news that many of the accused hijackers were in training at American flight schools hit the headlines.

In September 2002, during testimony before a joint congressional committee, Kristin Breitweiser, whose husband, Ronald, died at the WTC, asked a most pertinent question about this admitted fact, a question that continues to go unanswered. She cited a *New York Times* article the day after the strikes stating that FBI agents arrived at flight schools within hours to gather biographies on the terrorists. "How did the FBI know where to go a few hours after the attacks?...Were any of the hijackers already under surveillance?"

One obvious lead ignored by the FBI but pursued by investigative reporter Daniel Hopsicker concerns two flight schools at the tiny Venice Airport at the retirement community of Venice, Florida, where three of the four accused 9/11 pilots learned to fly. "Florida is the biggest 9/11 crime scene that wasn't reduced to rubble," noted Hopsicker. "But it hasn't been treated that way. And no one has offered any reason why.

"Both flight schools were owned by Dutch nationals. Both had been recently purchased, at about the same time. A year later terrorists began to arrive, in numbers greater than we have so far been told. All of this must be just a freak coincidence, according to the FBI."

Hopsicker also noted that government officials claimed that the Arab terrorists came to the United States for flight training because it was less expensive, yet, according to aviation experts, they actually paid more than double the cost of training elsewhere.

Hopsicker said he confirmed that within hours of the 9/11 attacks, a military C-130 Hercules transport plane arrived at the Venice airport where a rental truck loaded with the records of Huffman Aviation—one of the flight schools reportedly used by the hijackers—was driven onto the craft and airlifted to Washington escorted by Florida Gov. Jeb Bush.

We've noted that none of the accused hijackers' names appear on any of the passenger lists. Additionally, there was also a discrepancy of thirty-five names between the published passenger lists and the official death toll on all four of the ill-fated flights. The published names—none with Arabic-sounding names—did not match the total listed for the number of people on board. Why the discrepancy?

To add to this mystery, Dr. Thomas R. Olmsted, a psychiatrist and former navy line officer, filed a Freedom of Information Act request with the Armed Forces Institute of Pathology (AFIP), which had responsibility for identifying all victims in the Pentagon reportedly killed by the crash of Flight 77. Only after the start of the Iraq invasion did Dr. Olmsted finally receive his accounting. "No Arabs wound up on the morgue slab," noted Dr. Olmsted. "However...*additional* [emphasis in the original] people not listed by American Airlines sneaked in. I have seen no explanation for

WHAT ABOUT THE HIJACKERS THEMSELVES?

these extras."

The airline listed fifty-six persons on Flight 77 yet the AFIP listed sixty-four bodies as passengers on the plane. "And they did not explain how they were able to tell 'victims' bodies from 'hijacker' bodies," added Dr. Olmsted.

Plenty of disturbing questions surround the story of alleged Flight 77 pilot, Hani Hanjour. It is widely known that this young Saudi had a history of great difficulties in his efforts to learn to fly. As late as August 2001, he was unable to demonstrate enough piloting skills to even rent a Cessna 172.

Among other news sources on this subject, *Newsday* revealed the following remarkable facts about Hanjour: "At Freeway Airport in Bowie, MD, 20 miles west of Washington, flight instructor Sheri Baxter instantly recognized the name of alleged hijacker Hani Hanjour when the FBI released a list of 19 suspects in the four hijackings. Hanjour, the only suspect on Flight 77 the FBI listed as a pilot, had come to the airport one month earlier seeking to rent a small plane.

"However, when Baxter and fellow instructor Ben Conner took the slender, soft-spoken Hanjour on three test runs during the second week of August, they found he had trouble controlling and landing the single-engine Cessna 172. Even though Hanjour showed a federal pilot's license and a log book cataloging six hundred hours of flying experience, chief flight instructor Marcel Bernard declined to rent him a plane without more lessons."

Yet, Hanjour, who was not permitted to rent a Cessna, according to the official story, piloted a huge Boeing 757 in a 7,000-feet spiraling dive within two minutes, leveled the craft at tree-top level and smashed into the west wall of the Pentagon.

Danielle O'Brien, one of the Dulles air traffic controllers, said, "The speed, the maneuverability, the way [the pilot] turned, we all thought in the radar room, all of us experienced air traffic controllers, that it was a military plane." This assessment may indeed have been correct, as is revealed in the Appendix to this book.

Numerous puzzling stories have also emerged about the so-called mastermind of the hijackers, Mohamed Atta.

Atta reportedly left behind in his parked car two suitcases containing incriminating documents, including Atta's passport, driver's license, his last will, a copy of the Koran, flight simulation manuals for Boeing aircraft and a note to other hijackers. But why even take suitcases on a suicide mission? And if the suitcases were camouflage to present the appearance of a normal tourist, why did he leave them behind?

CNN reported on September 16, 2001 "In New York, several blocks from the ruins of the World Trade Center, a passport authorities said belonged to one of the hijackers was discovered a few days ago, according to city Police Commissioner Bernard Kerik. That has prompted the FBI and police to widen the search area beyond the immediate crash site." What happened to the passport and this story? Both seemed to have disappeared.

The discovered passport has been widely reported to have belonged to Mohamed Atta but actually was said to have been in the name of Satam al Suqami, supposedly the pilot of Flight 11 which reportedly was consumed within the North Tower after striking it dead on. The "black box" flight recorders on both WTC planes, designed to withstand crashes, were said to have been damaged beyond recognition, yet all of the concrete of the actual buildings was reduced to very fine dust. So how is that a paper passport can be fortuitously found intact on the ground blocks from the WTC? Some suspicious researchers smelled planted evidence.

Author David Ray Griffin quoted an unnamed high-level intelligence source as saying what was on many people's minds, "Whatever trail was left was left deliberately—for the FBI to chase."

Furthermore, in light of media stories concerning the discovered passport, a Koran left behind, flight school materials, and even "suicide notes," why did FBI director Robert Mueller in an April 19, 2002, speech before the Commonwealth Club in San Francisco declare that the hijackers "left no paper trail"?

Further suspicions were aroused concerning how the WTC fires could destroy airliner "black boxes" yet leave a paper passport undamaged in mid-2003 when two New York firefighters, Nicholas DeMasi and Mike Bellone self-published a book in which they contradicted the official announcement that no flight or cockpit recorder "black boxes" were found at the WTC.

Footnote 76 of *The 9/11 Commission Report*, states, "The CVR's [Cockpit Voice Recorders] and FDR's [Flight Data Recorders] from American 11 and United 175 were not found…"

A spokesman for the National Transportation Safety Board, Ted Lopatkiewicz told the *American Free Press* that such recorders are designed to withstand the tremendous impact and heat of plane crashes. "I can't remember another case [in] which we did not recover the recorders."

DeMasi and Bellone, both now retired from the NYFD, claimed to have found three of the four reddish-orange white-striped boxes while riding an All Terrain Vehicle at Ground Zero with three federal agents. Bellone said federal agents were adamant about not talking about their find. "They confronted me and told me not to say anything," he recalled. "I said, 'Give me one good reason.' When they couldn't, I told them I wouldn't shut up about it…I can tell you this, though, it was all very strange. I worked on the spaceship *Columbia* cleanup, and you known when something important is found and when something is not." He added that he did not catch the FBI agents' names but added, "They had on their FBI jackets [and] I'm sure I could pick them out of a lineup or recognize their pictures."

Both firemen said several other firefighters witnessed the recovery of the data recorders but were ordered into silence by federal agents. DeMasi and Bellone published their story in a book entitled *Behind the Scene: Ground Zero* in August 2003, but no one contacted them about their claims except reporter William Bunch of the *Philadelphia Daily*.

Questions also arose regarding the behavior of the identified hijackers. On the night before the attacks, according to the *Boston Globe*, four of the suspected hijackers called several escort services asking how much it would cost to acquire prostitutes for the night. Other news sources stated that other suspects spent time in bars and strip clubs in Florida, New Jersey, and Las Vegas. Heavy drinking and a search for hookers by some of the hijackers sound more like mercenaries carousing before a mission than pious religious fundamentalists about to meet their maker.

According to journalist Daniel Hopsicker, stripper Amanda Keller was the girlfriend of Mohamed Atta while he was in the USA. She told of Atta's cocaine use as well as shadowy contacts with foreign nationals while living in Florida. Hopsicker was amazed that Keller's tale of sex, drugs and hijackers was not picked up and ballyhooed by the sensation-seeking mass media.

Hopsicker also was astounded that no one in government seemed concerned or interested in facts he discovered linking Atta and other 9/11 hijackers in Florida to an underworld of international drug smuggling. In his book *Welcome to Terrorland: Mohamed Atta & the 9-11 Cover-Up in Florida*, Hopsicker quoted former Assistant Attorney General Michael Chertoff as telling a Senate Banking Committee, "Frankly, we can't differentiate between terrorism and organized crime and drug dealing."

More discrepancies: Why did the seat numbers of hijackers given by a phone call from flight attendant Madeline Amy Sweeney to Boston air traffic control not match the seats occupied by the men the FBI claimed were responsible?

And why did news outlets describe the throat cutting and mutilation of passengers on Flight 93 with box cutters when *Time* magazine on September 24 reported that one of the passengers called home on a cell phone to report, "We have been hijacked. They are being kind."?

In the days following September 11, many major media pundits correctly pointed out that a ragtag bunch of fanatics could not have successfully pulled off the large-scale and well-coordinated attacks by themselves. They must have had the sponsorship of some state, they argued. It was this rationale that provided the foundation argument for the subsequent attacks on Afghanistan and Iraq.

One captured al Qaeda chief may have provided a startling answer to the question of who actually provided state sponsorship for the 9/11 attacks—most likely working hand-in-hand with cosponsors in the US as well as other US-connected foreign intelligence agencies including the Israeli Mossad and/or the Pakistani ISI (i.e., the Mossad and the ISI being the central intelligence agency equivalent in each country).

This "smoking gun" case links al Qaeda directly to Saudi Arabia. It came to light in late March 2002, with the capture of Abu Zubaydah in a middle-class suburb of the Pakistani city of Faisalabad. On April 2, 2002, White House spokesman Ari Fleischer described Zubaydah as the most senior member of al Qaeda captured to that point and stated, "He will be interrogated about his knowledge of ongoing plans to conduct terrorist activities. This represents a serious blow to al Qaeda."

But instead it appears to have been a serious blow to the Saudis.

WHAT ABOUT THE HIJACKERS THEMSELVES?

According to a new book by Gerald Posner entitled *Why America Slept*, Zubaydah turned out to be tightly connected with ranking Saudis, including members of the royal family.

Posner, a noted debunker of JFK assassination conspiracies, supported the official version of pre-9/11 intelligence failures in this new book, arguing that despite all the tax dollars spent, federal agencies simply couldn't connect the dots. Posner has admitted being close to friendly CIA sources, which make his ensuing revelations that much more shocking.

According to Posner, when attempts to pry information out of Zubaydah with drugs failed, the al Qaeda chief was flown to an Afghan facility remodeled to look like a Saudi jail cell. Two Arab American Special Forces operatives, disguised as Saudis, then confronted Zubaydah. The idea was to scare him into revealing al Qaeda secrets. Recall that al Qaeda reportedly detests the Saudi royalty.

Yet, when faced by the faked Saudi interrogators, Zubaydah expressed relief rather than fear, according to Posner. He seemed genuinely happy to see them and offered them telephone numbers for ranking Saudi officials. One number was for Saudi Prince Ahmed bin Salman bin Abdul Aziz, a westernized nephew of Saudi King Fahd and a equestrian whose horse, War Emblem, won the 2002 Kentucky Derby. Zubaydah said Prince Aziz would vouch for him and give the interrogators instructions. The disguised Americans were shocked to find the unlisted Saudi numbers valid.

The Saudi Arabian-born al Qaeda leader then proceeded to outline his Saudi connections. He explained that one such contact in Saudi Arabia was intelligence chief Prince Turki al-Faisal bin Abdul Aziz, who met with Osama bin Laden in 1991 and agreed to provide bin Laden with funds in exchange for his pledge not to promote a jihad war in Saudi Arabia. He said his royal Saudi contacts operated through Pakistani Air Marshal Mushaf Ali Mir, a man with close ties to Muslims inside Pakistan's Inter-Services Intelligence (ISI). The ISI has long been suspected of providing al Qaeda with arms and supplies. And according to Posner, this convoluted pipeline was blessed by the Saudis. Zubaydah went on to claim that 9/11 did nothing to change the relationships between the Saudis, Pakistanis, and al Qaeda. He claimed that while both Prince Ahmed and Mir knew in advance of the attacks, they did not know the specific targets. They also would have been hesitant to reveal their secret agreements.

Posner also noted that not long after Zubaydah's revelations were passed along to the Saudis, the men mentioned by Zubaydah all died within days of each other. Prince Ahmed died of a heart attack at age 43 on July 22, 2002, while two princes, Sultan bin Faisal bin Turki al-Saud and Fahd bin Turki bin Saud al Kabir both were killed in car wrecks within a week of each other. Pakistani Air Marshal Mir died in a plane crash during clear weather. Posner told *Time* the deaths, most convenient to anyone desiring to keep the Saudi–Pakistani–al Qaeda axis hidden, "may in fact be coincidences."

Despite this remarkable information tying al Qaeda to Saudi royals and Pakistani intelligence published in a major US news magazine, very little of such coverage has made its way to the American public.

Bin Laden even had followers within the US military, as evidenced by court records of a former Fort Bragg, North Carolina, sergeant who gathered top-secret materials for more than two years.

Ali A. Mohamed, from 1987 until his arrest in 1989, served for a time at the John F. Kennedy Special Warfare Center and School. Mohamed, who once served as a major in the Egyptian army's special operations forces, was trained at the officer's course for Green Berets at Fort Bragg in 1981. At about that same time, he joined the terrorist group Islamic Jihad, responsible for the 1981 assassination of Egyptian president Anwar Sadat and later became a close adviser to bin Laden. He also tried unsuccessfully to join the CIA but did become a source of information for the FBI, according to Larry Johnson, a former CIA agent and director of counterterrorism at the State Department during the first Bush administration.

The FBI found documents, believed to have come from Mohamed, in the possession of one of the men convicted in the 1993 WTC bombing. Included were top secret papers belonging to the Joint Chiefs of Staff and the commander in chief of the army's Central Command.

One former Special Forces officer said, "There is no doubt that his proximity, in hindsight, was very harmful," adding, "Does this hurt our efforts now? Absolutely."

It must be recalled that Osama bin Laden as well as many of his al Qa-

WHAT ABOUT THE HIJACKERS THEMSELVES?

eda operatives are Saudis. And this makes for a very troublesome aspect to the War on Terrorism.

To understand the problem, one must bear in mind the fact that the United States, and perhaps most of the industrialized world, is immeasurably dependent on the eight major oil fields of Saudi Arabia. Loss of even a significant portion of this petroleum could mean unthinkable consequences to the economy of both America and the world. And control over this crucial strategic resource is concentrated in one ruling family, a family line with longstanding and well-documented ties to major players in the oil industry, notably the Bush family.

Contradicting widely circulated news reports, *The 9/11 Commission Report* acknowledged, "...Bin Laden did not fund al Qaeda through a personal fortune and a network of businesses in Sudan. Instead, al Qaeda relied primarily on a fund-raising network developed over time...particularly in Saudi Arabia."

WHAT REALLY HAPPENED AT THE PENTAGON?

At the Pentagon, again the official story initially seemed plausible—a third hijacked airliner, Flight 77, was flown into America's military command center creating a fire that killed more than 185 persons and caused a section of the west wall to collapse. But, as with the rest of the 9/11 account, the closer one looks, the more mysterious becomes the event.

Even the exact time of the attack has been modified several times. Pentagon spokespersons first reported the explosion at 9:48 am. Over the intervening months, this time was lowered to 9:37 am, as stated in *The 9/11 Commission Report.*

Neither of these times comes close to what appears to be the correct time of 9:32 am, as determined by witnesses at the scene. Multiple battery-operated wall clocks in the west corridors of the Pentagon, including the heliport near the west wall, were stopped by a violent event between 9:31 and 9:32 am. Military affairs journalist Barbara Honegger taped a 2002 statement from then-White House Counsel Alberto Gonzales in which he stated, "The Pentagon was attacked at 9:32." This timing is critical because it appears that some events connected to the Pentagon strike occurred both before and after the now-official time of 9:37 am.

The continuing controversy over the Pentagon attack is the result of a simple lack of decisive evidence. One can hardly doubt that there must have been ample evidence at the actual crime scene, and so, the primary problem is that most of this evidence was removed by a variety of suspicious official actions in the wake of the attack. These include the seizing of security videos that have never been made public, the immediate and rapid mop-up of the crime scene and the destruction of, or suppression of, nearly all the physical evidence inside the building in the days and weeks following the attack. These "pre-emptive" actions left researchers with only two types of evidence: a small number of eyewitness accounts, and post-crash photographs taken by witnesses by happenstance. Thus, although the best current theories of what happened at the Pentagon are not entirely reliable, the preponderance of the remaining evidence still casts grave doubt on the official story.

Take the case of April Gallop, who was at work inside the Pentagon's west side when it was struck on 9/11. Gallop was preparing to take her infant son to day care when an explosion rocked the building. "I thought it was a bomb," Gallop recalled. "I was buried in rubble and my first thought was for my son. I crawled around until I found his stroller. It was all crumpled up into a ball and I was then very afraid. But then I heard his voice and managed to locate him. We crawled out through a hole in the side of the building. Outside they were treating survivors on the grassy lawn. But all the ambulances had left, so a man who was near the scene stepped up, put us in his private car, and drove us to the hospital. The images are burned into my brain."

Gallop said while in the hospital, men in suits visited her more than once. "They never identified themselves or even said which agency they worked for. But I know they were not newsmen because I learned that the Pentagon told news reporters not to cover survivors' stories or they would not get any more stories out of there. The men who visited all said they couldn't tell me what to say, they only wanted to make suggestions. But then they told me what to do, which was to take the [Victim Compensation Fund] money and shut up. They also kept insisting that a plane hit the building. They repeated this over and over. But I was there and I never saw a plane or even debris from a plane. I figure the plane story is there to brainwash people."

Adding support to Gallop's account of no all-consuming fire at the Pentagon are photographs taken at the scene which clearly show undamaged computers, chairs, tables and filing cabinets exposed at the location of the west wall's collapse. Yet, according to the official account, the fire was so intense that it completely melted the Boeing 757 aircraft, in an immense fireball rising through the debris adjacent to this exposed office material.

Eyewitness accounts still emerging give credence to the idea that several bombs may have gone off at the Pentagon around the same time that some sort of flying vehicle slammed into the same part of the building.

"A bomb had gone off. I could smell the cordite. I knew explosives had been set off somewhere," stated witness Don Perkal. Another witness, John Bowman, said, "Most people knew it was a bomb." "It smelled like cordite, or gun smoke," recalled Gilah Goldsmith while Mike Slater said, "I knew it was a bomb or something."

As reported by Honegger, many people in the Pentagon at the time of the attack believed a bomb or bombs had exploded inside the building. She reported that, oddly enough, multiple teams of K-9 bomb-sniffing dogs with handlers in camouflage were seen just outside the Pentagon about at 7:30 am on September 11, 2001. One Army officer said he had never seen the bomb dogs there before or since 9/11.

In addition, an initial Associated Press story stated that the Pentagon had been attacked by a "booby-trapped truck."

The idea of bombs placed in the Pentagon also brings into focus the objectives of the attack. An explosion destroyed the Secretary of Defense's hardened basement Counterterrorism Command Center. "Did the attackers know where the [war game] exercises were being run and intentionally took it out?" questioned Honegger. "If so, they would have eliminated the one place frantic officials could call to ask details of the 'game' scenarios, to try to find out what was real and what was just the games that morning."

To paint a better overall picture of what may have happened inside the Pentagon, one can join the photographic evidence by those who happened to be near the event. Unlike the World Trade Center, unaffected witnesses were around the Pentagon, some with digital cameras. One such was Steve Riskus, a 24-year-old computer worker, who said he saw the craft pass over him and strike a lamppost before plunging into the Pentagon. He immediately began snapping photographs from less than 200 yards away and later that day posted his photos on a newly acquired website. His photos, along with others not controlled by the government, caused major problems for the later official version of the Pentagon crash.

They depicted a clean green lawn in front of the damaged wall, which contradicted the official claim that the plane hit the ground before entering the building. They also showed one highway lamppost knocked down but not others nearby it within range of the plane's wingspan.

One website even posted numerous official photos of the Pentagon crash and challenged viewers to find any trace of the aircraft. Interestingly enough, years after 9/11 neither the mass media nor the FBI had taken any notice of Riskus's pictures or the questions being raised. It is well worth noting here that the FBI confiscated all the security videos in the vicinity of the crash within minutes; somewhat later, the Pentagon released a mere five frames from one of these videos, which show a barely discernable object slamming into the building followed by a huge fireball.

The major mystery in regard to the Pentagon crash centers on what exactly happened to American Flight 77, a Boeing 757 carrying a mere 64 passengers. According to official sources, the entire plane was consumed inside the walls of the Pentagon.

To date, no one had produced any photographs of Boeing 757 fuselage, jet engines, seats, luggage, or other recognizable debris. Even the familiar photo of a small piece of red and white painted fuselage on the Pentagon lawn has been called into question because it does not appear in the very first photos of that area. This one small piece of red, white, and silver metal widely distributed by the major news media has never been firmly identified as coming from a Boeing 757. This now-famous mystery item, categorized as a fake by some foreign press, simply does not appear in any of the pictures taken within the first half hour of the Pentagon attack. Many researchers believe this evidence was planted at a later time.

WHAT REALLY HAPPENED AT THE PENTAGON?

Several photos of what appears to be part of a jet engine cannot be matched with the 757 engine, but more like that of a missile jet engine.

The initial version of the official story claimed that Flight 77 was entirely consumed by fires raging inside the Pentagon. But this version was called into question when the FBI announced it was able to identify passengers by their fingerprints. The fires were hot enough to incinerate metal airplane parts but not hot enough to destroy human tissue?

This non sequitur resulted in FBI spokesman Chris Murray later announcing, "The pieces of the plane are stocked in a warehouse and they are marked with the serial numbers of Flight 77."

Murray's announcement seemed reasonable, as after any major air disaster, every fragment of the aircraft is re-assembled to learn the cause and prevent any reoccurrence. But then this prompts the question: In addition to all the other suppressed evidence at the scene, why has no one within the government produced any photograph of the wreckage of Flight 77? Although such photographs could not prove where the wreckage came from, wouldn't this put an end to the theories regarding no plane hitting the Pentagon?

Then there are the startling problems with the holes in the Pentagon. The Boeing 757 has a normal wingspan of 124 feet, 10 inches. The official version of the Pentagon crash states that a 757 entered the building at a 45-degree angle. This angle would increase the wingspan to 177 feet. Note that the overall height of a 757 is 44 feet, 6 inches and the exterior body width is 12 feet, 6 inches. Yet the hole in the Pentagon cited as the entry point, photographed before the walls collapsed, was only between 15 and 20 feet wide, barely enough to accommodate the width of the craft's body. And the hole's height was less then two stories or about 20 feet, *less than half the height of the 757.*

Even after the walls collapsed shortly after 10 am, the gaping hole in the building was still not large enough to accommodate the Boeing 757's wingspan. Oddly, no evidence of any kind of the plane's wings or tail were found outside the building, other than the small piece of metal mentioned earlier.

Francois Grangier, a French aviation accident investigator, hoping to defend the official version, studied the Pentagon crash carefully but was forced to conclude, "I think the trajectory as far as one can make it out today rules out an impact against the façade…What is certain when one looks at the photo of this façade that remains intact is that it's obvious the plane did not go through there. It's like imagining that a plane of this size could pass through a window and leave the frame still standing."

Just as strange were photographs depicting what officials said was the exit hole caused by the plane as it completed its penetration of the Pentagon. This hole, located on the inside of the building's fourth ring, is barely more than eight feet high; it shows only slight scorching at the top and even unbroken window panes immediately above it. It is most peculiar that the front of a Boeing 757, lacking density in its aluminum-sheathed nose, could have survived the penetration of four hardened concrete walls, while leaving no known remnants behind. The official story claims that 1500-degree heat caused by the crash was intense enough to immolate the entire plane and occupants. One wonders why the walls to either side of this exit hole are not scorched.

While several witnesses, such as Army Captain Lincoln Liebner, said they distinctly saw an American Airlines jetliner coming toward the Pentagon swiftly and at low altitude, others were not so certain. Steve Patterson told the *Washington Post* that day, "The airplane seemed to be able to hold between eight or twelve persons." Tom Seibert said, "We heard something that made the sound of a missile, then we heard a powerful boom." Mike Walter excitedly told CNN, "A plane, a plane from American Airlines. I thought, 'That's not right, it's really low.' And I saw it. I mean, it was like a cruise missile with wings." Danielle O'Brien told ABC News, "The speed, the maneuverability, the way that he turned, we all thought in the radar room, all of us experienced air traffic controllers, that that was a military plane. You don't fly a 757 in that manner. It's unsafe."

O'Brien's perceptions were accurate. For whatever plunged toward the Pentagon—reportedly starting 7,000 feet above the ground—was piloted in such a way that it dropped in a downward spiral, forming an almost complete circle in just more than two minutes. This is an extremely difficult maneuver for the even the most experienced pilot. We've already noted that it is exceedingly unlikely that the Haji Hanjour, the alleged hijacker pilot of Flight 77, could have accomplished this miracle of piloting.

The speed, maneuverability, and the high-pitched scream of the jet coupled with the smallness of the hole prompted many researchers to suggest that what struck the Pentagon was nothing less than some sort of winged missile painted to resemble an American Airlines plane.

Could this be why Defense Secretary Donald Rumsfeld inadvertently mentioned a "missile" when describing the Pentagon attack to *Parade* magazine?

Supporting the hypothesis of a missile attack are the recent discoveries by Honegger that NORAD commander, Maj. Gen. Larry Arnold, had ordered one of his jet fighters to fly low over the west side of the Pentagon moments after the attack. The pilot reported, according to Arnold, that there was no evidence a plane had struck the building.

"The likely reason the Pentagon has refused to lower the currently-official time of Flight 77 impact from 9:37 to 9:32—the actual time of the first explosions there—is that they decided to pretend the blip represented by Arnold's surveillance jet approaching just before 9:37 was Flight 77," Honegger concluded. "As the Official Cover Story claims that the alleged 9:37 impact was the only Pentagon attack that morning, and by the time Arnold's surveillance jet arrived on the scene the violent event had already happened, the Pentagon cannot acknowledge the earlier 9:32 attack time without revealing that there was an attack on the building prior to impact."(See Appendix for more details.)

Then there are the disturbing statements, noted earlier, of another high government official. Testifying under oath before the 9/11 Commission in mid-2003, Transportation Secretary Norman Mineta gave a revealing account of his experiences on the morning of 9/11. After joining Vice President Cheney and others in the White House Presidential Emergency Operating Center shortly after the South Tower of the WTC had been struck, at about 9:20 am, Mineta recalled: "During the time that the airplane was coming in to the Pentagon, there was a young man who would come in and say to the Vice President, 'The plane is 50 miles out.' 'The plane is 30 miles out.' And when it got down to 'the plane is 10 miles out,' the young man also said to the Vice President, 'Do the orders still stand?' And the Vice President turned and whipped his neck around and said, 'Of course the orders still stand! Have you heard anything to the contrary?' Well at the time, I didn't know what all that meant...[This was the] flight that came into the Pentagon..."

Asked if these "orders" were to shoot down the errant airliners, Mineta responded, "Well, I don't know that specifically. I do know that the [interceptor] airplanes were scrambled from Langley or from Norfolk, the Norfolk area, and so I did not know about the order specifically other than to listen to that other conversation…Subsequently, I found that out."

Commission vice chairman Lee Hamilton then asked, "But there were military planes in the air in position to shoot down commercial aircraft?" "That's right," replied Mineta. "The planes had been scrambled, I believe from Otis, at that point."

The strange conversation between Cheney and the "young man" as related by Mineta prompts several puzzling questions. What were these orders? And if the orders were to shoot down captured airliners as later stated by the White House, why weren't they carried out?

And, if fighter jets could not reach the Pentagon in time, what about the antiaircraft missile batteries in place around Washington—indeed, just adjacent to the Pentagon itself?

Amazingly enough, the final report of the Commission, in order to construct its official story, entirely omitted Secretary of Transportation Norman Mineta's testimony given to the Commission itself that Cheney and others in the underground shelter were aware at least by 9:20 am that an aircraft was approaching the Pentagon. Despite evidence to the contrary from Mineta and other eyewitnesses, the Commission would have us believe that no one in the US military knew that Flight 77 was incoming toward the Pentagon until a few minutes before the official time of the impact, 9:37 am. Even this time is under dispute. (Please see Appendix for details).

In fact, the Commission goes further, even claiming against all the evidence that Cheney did not reach this underground shelter until nearly 10 am that morning. In his study of *The 9/11 Commission Report*, David Ray Griffin states that this denial "is probably the feature of the 9/11 Commission's case that is the most patently false."

While researchers have hunted fruitlessly for a stand-down order issue from within the administration to explain the lack of effective response on 9/11, it may be that such orders were much more mundane—a simple matter of slightly changing standard NORAD procedures.

Prior to June 2001, under Department of Defense directives, while the Secretary of Defense retained approval authority for the release of military jets to support civil air authorities, they also provided that "Nothing in this Directive prevents a commander from exercising his or her immediate emergency response authority…" and that "Requests for an immediate response (i.e., any form of immediate action taken by a DoD Component or military commander to save lives, prevent human suffering, or mitigate great property damage under imminently serious conditions) may be made to any Component or Command. The DoD Components…may initiate informal planning and, if required, immediately respond as authorized in DoD Directive 3025.1 (reference (g))." In other words, in the event of an air emergency, local commanders could initiate a response pending later approval of the Secretary of Defense.

This all changed on June 1, 2001, with the issuance of Chairman of the Joint Chiefs of Staff Instruction [CJCSI] 3610.01A. This document states, under the heading, "Aircraft Piracy (Hijacking) of Civil and Military Aircraft," that, "the NMCC [National Military Command Center] is the focal point within the Department of Defense for providing assistance. In the event of a hijacking, the NMCC will, with the exception of immediate responses as authorized by reference 'd,' forward requests for DoD assistance to the Secretary of Defense for approval."

"Secretary of Defense [Donald] Rumsfeld is personally responsible for issuing intercept orders," surmised Internet writer Jerry Russell. "Commanders in the field are stripped of all authority to act…it is now clear that [any 'Stand Down' order] was implemented through a routine administrative memo."

Of course, if Flight 77 did not hit the Pentagon, even more questions arise. What happened to the plane and its passengers? Did it cross into Washington air space before a missile was sent into the Pentagon? Was it ditched into the Atlantic as suggested by some? Was a missile or plane guided from an external location as will be discussed later?

Simply showing the public the wreckage of the aircraft could end all such conjecture. But five years on, such photos still had not been forthcoming.

Finally, there is the question of motive. Why would anyone want to risk attacking the Pentagon, undoubtedly the world's strongest and most protected structure?

Unanswered questions continued to grow in the wake of the 9/11 tragedies, and the strange case of the Pentagon crash is among the most puzzling of all. Even many researchers within the 9/11 truth community continue to disagree on the interpretations of the few useful facts we have.

EXPLOSIONS AT THE WORLD TRADE CENTER

Why, according to several experts and numerous independent observers, did the destruction of the World Trade Center towers appear more like a controlled implosion than terrorist-caused destruction?

Both North and South Towers had 47 core columns made of steel with 236 steel columns around the outer perimeter, for a total of 566 columns. Explosives would have been required at each column to bring down the building by controlled demolition. This would not have been a small undertaking.

Experts in demolition and firefighting immediately advanced such questions concerning the collapse of the towers, only to die away in the subsequent media blitz of "official" pronouncements. Many people, experts and laymen alike, also asked why the South Tower collapsed first when it was not as extensively damaged as the North Tower, which burned for almost an hour and a half before its collapse?

Numerous sources have claimed that bombs rather than the planes caused the collapse of the World Trade Center towers.

Van Romero, vice president for research at the New Mexico Institute of Mining and Technology and a former director of the Energetic Materials Research and Testing Center said televised images of the collapse of the WTC towers suggested that explosives were used to create a controlled demolition.

"My opinion is, based on the videotapes, that after the airplanes hit the World Trade Center there were some explosive devices inside the buildings that caused the towers to collapse," Romero told the *Albuquerque Journal* on September 11, 2001.

Romero, who ironically was in the Washington area during the 9/11 attacks attempting to gain government funding for defense research at his school, said the collapse of the WTC was "too methodical" to be the chance result of airplanes colliding with the structures. He said it appeared more like the controlled implosions used to demolish old buildings.

"It could have been a relatively small amount of explosives placed in strategic points," he said, adding that the detonation of bombs within towers is consistent with common terrorist strategy. "One of the things terrorist events are noted for is a diversionary attack and secondary device. Attackers detonate an initial, diversionary explosion that attracts emergency personnel to the scene, then detonate a second explosion," he explained.

Within 10 days, Romero reversed himself, telling the *Albuquerque Journal* that following conversations with "other experts" he came to understand that "Certainly the fire is what caused the building to fail." He did concede that the final collapse may have been caused when fire reached an electrical transformer or other source of combustion within the building, leaving open the question of explosions. There was no word of whether or not New Mexico Tech received its federal funding requests although it was learned that the school does provide counterterrorism training to firemen, policemen, and first responders.

Many have wondered about the witnesses who claimed to have heard multiple explosions within the buildings. One such witness was the head of WTC security, John O'Neill, who stated shortly before he himself became a victim that he had helped dig out survivors on the 27th floor before the building collapsed. Since the aircraft crashed into the 80th floor, what heavily damaged the 27th floor?

Another of those mentioning bombs was Louie Cacchioli, a fifty-one-year-old fireman assigned to Engine 47 in Harlem. "We were the first ones in the second tower after the plane struck," recalled Cacchioli. "I was taking firefighters up in the elevator to the twenty-fourth floor to get in position to evacuate workers. On the last trip up a bomb went off. We think there were bombs set in the building." The fireman became trapped in an elevator but managed to escape with the use of tools.

Auxiliary Fire Lt. Paul Isaac, Jr. also mentioned bombs, telling Internet reporter Randy Lavello that New York firemen were very upset by what they considered a cover-up in the WTC destruction. "Many other firemen know there were bombs in the buildings," he said, "but they are afraid for their jobs to admit it because the higher-ups forbid discussion of this fact." Isaac, who was stationed at Engine 10 near the WTC in the late 1990s, said the higher-ups included the NYFD's antiterrorism consultant, James Woolsey, a former CIA director. "There were definitely bombs in those buildings," Isaac added.

Survivor Teresa Veliz, manager for a software development company, was on the 47th floor of the North Tower when it was struck. "I got off [the elevator], turned the corner and opened the door to the ladies' room. I said good morning to a lady sitting at a mirror when the whole building shook. I thought it was an earthquake. Then I heard those banging noises on the other side of the wall. It sounded like someone had cut the elevator cables. It just fell and fell and fell."

Veliz reached ground level with a coworker when the South Tower collapsed, knocking them down. In near total darkness, she and the co-worker followed someone with a flashlight. "The flashlight led us into Borders bookstore, up an escalator and out to Church Street. There were explosions going off everywhere. I was convinced that there were bombs planted all over the place and someone was sitting at a control panel pushing detonator buttons. I was afraid to go down Church Street toward Broadway, but I had to do it. I ended up on Vesey Street. There was another explosion. And another. I didn't know which way to run."

Ross Milanytch watched the horror at the WTC from his office window on the 22nd floor of a building a couple of blocks away. "[I saw] small explosions on each floor. And after it all cleared, all that was left of the buildings, you could just see the steel girders in like a triangular sail shape. The structure was just completely gone," he said.

John Bussey, a reporter for the *Wall Street Journal*, watched the collapse of the South Tower from the ninth floor of the newspaper's office building. "I...looked up out of the office window to see what seemed like perfectly synchronized explosions coming from each floor.... One after the other. From top to bottom, with a fraction of a second between, the floors flew to pieces."

Steve Evans, a reporter for the BBC, was in the South Tower at the time of the attacks. "I was at the base of the second tower, the second tower that

EXPLOSIONS AT THE WORLD TRADE CENTER

was hit," he recalled. "There was an explosion—I didn't think it was an explosion—but the base of the building shook. I felt it shake…then when we were outside, the second explosion happened and then there was a series of explosions…. We can only wonder at the kind of damage—the kind of human damage—which was caused by those explosions, those series of explosions."

Fox 5 News in New York City, shortly after 10 am on September 11, videotaped a large white cloud of smoke billowing near the base of the South Tower. The commentator exclaimed, "There is an explosion at the base of the building…white smoke from the bottom…something has happened at the base of the building…then, another explosion. Another building in the World Trade Center complex…"

The most compelling testimony came from Tom Elliott, who was already in his office at Aon Corp. on the 103rd floor of the WTC South Tower before the planes struck.

Elliott said he was at his computer answering emails when a bright light startled him shortly before 9 am. A rumble shook the building and he could see flames accompanied by dark smoke that appeared to be crawling up the outside of the building. He also felt heat coming through the windows. Strangely, there were no alarms.

"I don't know what's happening, but I think I need to be out of here," Elliott recalled thinking to himself.

Elliott and two others began walking down the building's stairwell when they ran into a few others. The absence of more people and the lack of alarms made them feel they had prematurely panicked.

He recalled that as his small group reached the 70th floor, they heard the announcement that the building was secure and there was no need to evacuate. "Do you want to believe them?" one woman said to Elliott. "Let's go!" He followed the woman down the stairs.

After descending three more floors, Flight 175 crashed into the South Tower. An article in the *Christian Science Monitor* described what happened next:

"Although its spectacularly televised impact was above Elliott, at first he and those around him thought an explosion had come from below. An incredible sound—he calls it an 'exploding sound'—shook the building, and a tornado of hot air and smoke and ceiling tiles and bits of drywall came flying up the stairwell."

"In front of me, the wall split from the bottom up," Elliott said. He said people in the stairwell panicked and tried to flee upward until some men pointed out that the only escape was downstairs. By about 9:40 am, Elliott managed to stumble out of the South Tower and make his way to his roommate's office in Midtown, where he broke down sobbing upon learning of the tower's collapse.

Elliot's description of explosions below the buildings are supported by accounts of engineers working below ground level. Mike Pecoraro told *The Chief Engineer* magazine he was working in the 6th sub-basement of the North Tower when the lights flickered. This was followed by a loud explosion. Pecoraro and a coworker made their way up to a C level machine shop but found it "gone." "There was nothing there but rubble," recalled Pecoraro. "We're talking about a 50-ton hydraulic press—gone!"

Working their way upwards to a parking garage, the pair found it too was destroyed. "There were no walls, there was rubble on the floor, and you can't see anything," Pecoraro recalled. Ascending two more levels to the tower's lobby, they were astonished to find more debris including a 300-pound steel and concrete fire door wrinkled up "like a piece of aluminum foil." By now, Pecoraro was convinced that a bomb had gone off in the building.

"When I walked out into the lobby, it was incredible," Pecoraro recalled. "The whole lobby was soot and black, elevator doors were missing. The marble was missing off some of the walls. 20-foot section of marble, 20 by 10 foot sections of marble, gone from the walls." The west windows were all gone. They were missing. These are tremendous windows. They were just gone. Broken glass everywhere, the revolving doors were all broken and their glass was gone. Every sprinkler head was going off. I am thinking to myself, how are these sprinkler heads going off? It takes a lot of heat to set off a sprinkler head. It never dawned on me that there was a giant fireball that came through the air of the lobby." He said much later he heard the accounts of jet fuel spilling down the elevator shaft, blowing off all the elevator doors and flames rolling through the lobby.

The lobby of the North Tower was so unrecognizable that many people streaming down the stairs seeking to escape the building bypassed the lobby and had to be directed back up. After moving with other building personnel to the South Tower where he helped evacuate the building, Pecoraro made a dramatic and hazardous escape when the tower collapsed.

Pecoraro's experiences in the basement all occurred prior to the tower's collapse. Yet, according to the official story, there had been only the airplane strike about 95 floors above them.

Adding details that support Pecoraro's account of explosions in the basement was William Rodriguez. President Bush and others hailed him as a hero at the time for his rescue efforts on 9/11. It was widely reported that Rodriguez had adeptly guided rescue workers and had single-handedly saved a number of lives. He was the last person to escape as the North Tower collapsed. But when Rodriguez later went public, it was with a very different account of the WTC tragedy.

Rodriguez had worked for the New York and New Jersey Port Authority for about twenty years. In 2001, he was in charge of maintenance for three stairwells in the North Tower.

Arriving at 8:30 am on September 11, Rodriguez went to the maintenance office located on the first sublevel, one of six sub-basements beneath ground level. There were a total of fourteen people in the office at this time. As he was talking with others, there was a very loud, massive explosion that seemed to emanate from between sub-basements B2 and B3. There were twenty-two people on B2 sub-basement who also felt and heard that first explosion.

At first he thought it was a generator that had exploded. "When I heard the sound of the explosion, the floor beneath my feet vibrated, the walls started cracking and everything started shaking," said Rodriguez. Seconds later there was another explosion way above, which made the building oscillate momentarily. This, he was later told, was a plane hitting the 90th floor.

Upon hearing about the plane, Rodriguez started heading for the loading dock to escape the explosion's fire. When asked later about those first explosions he said: "I would know if an explosion was from the bottom or the top of the building." He was clear about hearing explosions both before and after the plane hit the tower.

Rodriguez said a fellow worker, Felipe David, came into the office. "He had been standing in front of a freight elevator on sub-level 1 about

400 feet from the office when fire burst out of the elevator shaft, causing his injuries. He was burned so badly from the basement explosion that flesh was hanging from his face and both arms." Rodriguez led David outside to safety but returned to the building after hearing screaming inside.

Water from the fire sprinklers from all of the floors had gone into the elevator shaft and there were people trapped below who were in danger of drowning. Rodriguez was able to lower a long ladder into the shaft to enable their escape.

Rodriguez held one of the five master keys that opened all of the stairwell doors at each of the floors in the 110-story building. The other four key holders, though trained for emergencies, had already left the building. Firemen from New York City Unit Six arrived. Each fireman, in addition to protective clothing, had about 70 pounds of equipment. Rodriguez led the firemen up stairwell B.

Reaching the 27th floor, firemen were becoming exhausted from the weight of their equipment. Ascending the stairs, Rodriguez as well as the firemen heard explosions from the 20th through the 30th floor. Chunks of the building fell around them and they could literally hear the building coming down. The firemen continued to climb and give aid.

On the 33rd floor, Rodriguez found the air thick with smoke. Grabbing some dust masks from a maintenance office, he was able to help a woman to evacuate. While on that floor, Rodriguez said he heard what sounded like the movement of heavy equipment and furniture on the 34th floor. This puzzled him because he knew that floor had been closed due to a construction project.

Rodriguez accompanied firefighter to the 39th floor where he was told to turn back. As he began his descent he heard the plane hit the South Tower.

Racing through the wrecked lobby, Rodriguez took cover under a fire truck where he was later discovered. After receiving first aid, he joined the effort to find survivors. Rodriguez spent hours giving closed-door testimony before the 9/11 Commission, yet his eyewitness account does not appear anywhere in the 576 page report. He also tried to talk to investigators for the National Institute of Standards and Technology (NIST) but was ignored. "I contacted NIST…four times without a response," he recalled. "Finally, [at a public hearing] I asked them before they came up with their conclusion…if they ever considered my statements or the statements of any of the other survivors who heard the explosions. They just stared at me with blank faces."

He also said he contacted the FBI but they never followed up. The media also seemed uninterested. Rodriguez said CNN spent most of a day filming and interviewing him at his home but, when the interview aired, it was severely edited. Rodriguez said one reporter not so subtly warned him to keep quiet or he could be in jeopardy. "You do not know who you are dealing with!" he was told. His response was, "I am living on borrowed time since I probably should be dead anyway."

In late 2004, Rodriguez filed suit in a Philadelphia federal court under the provisions of the Racketeer Influenced and Corrupt Organizations (RICO) Act, naming George Bush, Dick Cheney, Donald Rumsfeld and others as being complicit in the 9/11 attacks. Rodriguez claims that top officials either planned the attacks or had foreknowledge of the attacks and permitted them to succeed for the purpose of exploiting a "New Pearl Harbor" in order to launch wars against Afghanistan and Iraq. The lawsuit entitled *Rodriguez v. Bush, et al.,* Civil Action No. 04 CV 4952, was filed in the US District Court in Philadelphia on October 22. (For details on the lawsuit, see www.911forthetruth.com)

"If what the government has told us about 9/11 is a lie," said Rodriguez explaining why he chose to file suit against government officials, "somebody has to take action to reveal the truth. If suing President Bush is what I have to do to accomplish that, so be it."

Rodriguez's account has been corroborated by José Sanchez, who was in the workshop on the fourth sub-level. Sanchez said that he and a co-worker heard a big blast that "sounded like a bomb," after which "a huge ball of fire went through the freight elevator."

By mid-2005 even more accounts of multiple explosions at the World Trade Center were being made public. Perhaps the most significant were 503 oral histories of 9/11 recorded near the end of 2001 by the New York Fire Department. The tapes were of both fire personnel and emergency medical workers. The city had refused to release the tapes until ordered to do so by the New York Court of Appeals acting on a suit filed jointly by the *New York Times* and several 9/11 victims' families. Although some were edited, the tapes became public on August 12, 2005.

Comments in these tapes relating to the possibility of controlled demolitions in the WTC, include:

Fire Captain Dennis Tardio: "I hear an explosion and I look up [at the South Tower]. It is as if the building is being imploded from the top floor down, one after another, boom, boom, boom."

New Jersey Fire Officer Sue Keane: "[I]t sounded like bombs going off [in the South Tower]. That's when the explosions happened...I knew something was going to happen.... It started to get dark, then all of a sudden there was this massive explosion.... [In the North Tower] another explosion. That sent me and the two firefighters [with her] down the stairs...I can't tell you how many times I got banged around. Each one of those explosions picked me up and threw me...There was another explosion and I got thrown with two firefighters out onto the street."

Fire Battalion Chief John Sudnik: "[W]e heard a loud explosion or what sounded like a loud explosion and looked up and I saw Tower Two start coming down."

Paramedic Daniel Rivera, "At first I thought it was—do you ever see professional demolition where they set the charges on certain floors and then you hear, 'Pop, pop, pop, pop, pop'? That's exactly what—because I thought it was that. When I heard that frigging noise, that's when I saw the building coming down."

Assistant Commissioner Stephen Gregory: "I thought...before... [Tower] No. 2 came down that I saw low-level flashes...Lieutenant Evangelista...asked me if I saw low-level flashes in front of the building and I agreed with him because I...saw a flash, flash, flash...[at] the lower level of the building. You know, like when they demolish a building, how when they blow up a building, when it falls down? That what I thought I saw."

Captain Karin Deshore: "Somewhere around the middle of the World Trade Center, there was this orange and red flash coming out. Initially, it was just one flash...Then this flash just kept popping all the way around the building and that building had started to explode. The popping sound and with each popping sound it was initially an orange and then a red flash came out of the building and then it would just go all around the building on both sides as far as I could see. These popping sounds and the explosions were getting bigger, going both up and down and then all around the building."

Deputy Commissioner Thomas Fitzpatrick: "We looked up at the [South Tower]…All we saw was a puff of smoke coming from about two-thirds of the way up…It looked like sparkling around one specific layer of the building…My initial reaction was that this was exactly the way it looks when they show you those [building] implosions on TV."

Firefighter Christopher Fenyo: "At that point [the collapse of the South Tower], a debate began to rage because many people had felt that possible explosives had taken out 2 World Trade and officers were gathering companies together and the officers were debating whether or not to go immediately back in or to see what was going to happen with 1 World Trade [the North Tower] at that point. The debate ended pretty quickly because 1 World Trade came down."

Auxiliary Lieutenant Fireman Paul Isaac: "…[T]here were definitely bombs in those buildings, many other firemen know there were bombs in the buildings, but they're afraid for their jobs to admit because the higher-ups forbid discussion of this fact."

Foreign news accounts also noted testimony regarding explosions. A story in the London *Guardian* said that, "police and fire officials were carrying out the first wave of evacuations when the first of the World Trade Centre towers collapsed. Some eyewitnesses reported hearing another explosion just before the structure crumbled. Police said that it looked almost like a 'planned implosion.'"

A CNN video of the scene at the WTC showed smoke boiling up from the street level prior to the collapse of the towers, apparently from the eight-story WTC Building 6, more popularly known as the Customs House building. Nothing of significance had struck street level at that time. Did the billowing smoke come from a premature detonation?

Due to a delayed broadcast, there was some initial confusion about just when the smoke began. However, CNN's Public Affairs Department confirmed that the video footage of an apparent explosion at ground level was made at 9:04 am, just one minute after Flight 175 struck the South Tower and long before either tower collapsed.

Asked what might have caused the smoke seen in the video, the CNN archivist replied, "We can't figure it out." Later, arguments were made that CNN's time code was wrong and that the billowing smoke was simply dust from the collapsing South Tower.

Lending support to the idea that Building 6 was ravaged by a separate explosion were photos depicting a very noticeable huge circular hole with deep crater blasted from this building which was not hit by airplanes and still standing after the towers collapsed.

According to news reports, the FEMA team of engineers commissioned to investigate the WTC tragedy was barred from entering the Customs House building. FEMA officials reported that because the structure was considered "very dangerous," there was "no data collection" from Building 6. Yet, the FEMA report blithely stated, "Building Five was the only building accessible for observation [by the team of engineers]...the observations, findings and recommendations are assumed to be applicable to all three buildings."

A spokesman for the Export-Import Bank of the United States confirmed the 9:04 time of the blast but said all of the eight hundred or so employees of the Customs House building had already been evacuated after the WTC North Tower was struck.

Other occupants of the building, which included the Customs Service, the Departments of Commerce, Labor, and Agriculture and the Bureau of Alcohol, Tobacco and Firearms, declined to explain either the early blast or the massive crater at the center of the Customs House ruins.

No explanation for this explosion or crater has been forthcoming.

But if there were bombs in the towers, how did they get there?

With the buildings turned to powdered ash and the metal quickly hauled away, no one will ever be certain but some interesting theories have been advanced.

One is that charges were placed in the towers at the time of their construction to prevent a catastrophe such as 9/11 from causing them to fall over on neighboring buildings, magnifying the destruction. No proof of this has been established. Explosive experts discount this theory, stating that explosives could not have remained effective after an extended period of time. A similar theory postulates that charges were placed in the buildings following the 1993 bombing for the reason stated above.

Yet another theory emerged after Ben Fountain, a financial analyst who worked on the 47th floor of the South Tower, told *People* magazine that in the weeks preceding 9/11 there were numerous unusual and un-announced "drills" in which sections of both towers as well as Building 7 were evacuated for "security reasons." These drills could have provided a perfect cover for persons planting explosives.

Reporting in *The American Reporter*, an electronic daily newspaper, Margie Burns cited President Bush's younger brother, Marvin P. Bush, as a principal in a company called Securacom that provided security for the World Trade Center, United Airlines, and Dulles International Airport. The company, Burns noted, was backed by KuwAm, a Kuwaiti-American investment firm.

Securacom has since changed its name to Stratesec, but is still backed by KuwAm. Marvin Bush, who did not respond to repeated interview requests from *The American Reporter*, is no longer on the board of either company and has not been linked with any terrorist activities. According to its present CEO, Barry McDaniel, the company had an ongoing contract to handle security at the World Trade Center "up to the day the buildings fell down."

Many people lost their lives in the collapse of the Twin Towers because the public address system advised workers to return to their desks. Who exactly ordered that broadcast over the loudspeakers in the South Tower as workers were trying to evacuate, "Remain calm, damage is in Tower One. Return to your desks."? Many people lost their lives because of these announcements. Minutes later the towers collapsed unexpectedly.

Yet, apparently New York Mayor Rudolph Giuliani did get word of what was coming. The next morning, he explained to ABC's Peter Jennings that he was in the Mayor's Emergency Management Command Center on the 23rd floor of Building 7 at the WTC. He said, "We were operating out of there when we were told that the World Trade Center was going to collapse and it did collapse before we could get out of the building." Giuliani's recollection of advanced warning was echoed in the testimony of New York Emergency Medical Technician Richard Zarrillo, who provided an oral account of his actions on 9/11 on October 25, 2001.

After rushing into Manhattan after the North Tower was struck, Zarrillo found himself running down Vesey Street "stepping over airplane pieces, several bodies and what not."

Less than 10 minutes after entering WTC Building 7 at the location of the Mayor's Office of Emergency Management (OEM) Command Center, Zarrillo said a representative from OEM came into the main room and said they needed to evacuate the building; that a third plane was inbound and the buildings might collapse.

After leaving the building, Zarrillo met a fire chief who told him there was no third plane but that they needed to re-establish their OEM site. Zarrillo soon found himself alone on Vesey Street. He tried to warn some responders to get out, that the buildings might collapse.

"As I was walking towards the fire command post, I found Steve Mosiello. I said, 'Steve, where's the boss? I have to give him a message.' He said, 'What's the message?' I said the buildings are going to collapse; we need to evac everybody out. With a very confused look, he said, 'Who told you that?' I said I was just…at OEM. OEM says the buildings are going to collapse; we need to get out.

"He [Mosiello] escorted me over to Chief [Peter] Ganci. He said, 'Hey, Pete, we got a message that the buildings are going to collapse. His reply was, 'Who the fuck told you that?' Then Steve brought me in with Chief Ganci, Commissioner Feehan, Steve…I believe Chief Turi was initially there. I said, 'Listen, I was just at OEM. The message I was given was that the buildings are going to collapse; we need to get our people out. At that moment, this thunderous, rolling roar came down and that's when the building came down, the first tower came down"

But how could anyone have known about the collapse in advance? Who warned Giuliani of the impending collapse and who warned EMT Zarrillo? What exactly was going on at the OEM such that one of its representatives knew such information?

FIREFIGHTERS THOUGHT THE FIRES WERE CONTROLLABLE

An audiotape of New York firefighters at the scene, unpublicized until mid-2002, indicated that fire officials managed to reach the 78th floor of the South Tower—very near the crash scene, which was at the 80th floor—and seemed convinced that the fire was controllable.

The tape was briefly mentioned by the *New York Times* but was kept from the public by the US Justice Department, which claimed it might be needed in the trial of the "twentieth hijacker," Zacarias Moussaoui, even though Moussaoui was in custody at the time of the attacks.

The audiotape was a recording of radio transmissions made on the morning of September 11, 2001. The tape reportedly was discovered two or three weeks after 9/11 in offices of the Port Authority of New York and New Jersey at WTC Building 5. Apparently, Port Authority personnel were monitoring and recording the New York Fire Department (NYFD) channel.

Two fire officials mentioned by name in the tape were Battalion Chief Orio J. Palmer and Fire Marshal Ronald P. Bucca, both of whom perished when the South Tower collapsed along with 343 other firefighters, the greatest single loss of firefighters in one incident in history.

According to the *Times* article, both firemen "showed no panic, no sense that events were racing beyond their control....At that point, the building would be standing for just a few more minutes, as the fire was weakening the structure on the floors above him. Even so, Chief Palmer could see only two pockets of fire and called for a pair of engine companies to fight them."

Transcripts released on the Internet provided this statement, "Battalion Seven...Ladder 15, we've got two isolated pockets of fire. We should be able to knock it down with two lines. Radio that, 78th floor numerous 10-45 Code Ones."

As noted by reporter Christopher Bollyn, "The fact that veteran firefighters had a 'coherent plan for putting out' the 'two pockets of fire,' indicates they judged the blazes to be manageable. These reports from the scene of the crash provide crucial evidence debunking the government's claim that a raging steel-melting inferno led to the tower's collapse."

Supporting Chief Palmer's description of only small fires in the South Tower are survivors Stanley Praimnath, Donovan Cowen and Ling Young. Praimnath, on the 81st floor, recalled, "The plane impacts. I try to get up and then I realize that I'm covered up to my shoulder in debris. And when I'm digging through under all this rubble, I can see the bottom wing starting to burn, and that wing is wedged 20 feet in my office doorway." Cowan was in an open elevator at the 78th floor sky-lobby. She recalled, "We went into the elevator. As soon as I hit the button, that's when there was a big boom. We both got knocked down. I remember feeling this intense heat. The doors were still open. The heat lasted for maybe 15 to 20 seconds I guess. Then it stopped." Young was in her 78th floor office and related, "Only in my area were people alive, and the people alive were from my office. I figured that out later because I sat around in there for 10 or 15 minutes. That's how I got so burned."

Government pronouncements and hired experts claimed temperatures in the area of these three witnesses were hot enough to cause the trusses of the south tower to fail, yet these eye-witnesses stated temperatures were cool enough for them to walk away.

A number of experts have disputed the claim that melting structural steel brought down the Twin Towers.

Kevin R. Ryan was a site manager for Environmental Health Laboratories in South Bend, IN, a subsidiary of Underwriters Laboratories Inc. (UL), the giant product safety testing firm. In 2003, Ryan wrote to Frank Gayle, deputy chief of the Metallurgy Division of the National Institute of Standards and Technology's (NIST) Material Science and Engineering Laboratory, challenging the theory that burning jet fuel weakened the towers' structural steel causing them to fall.

In this communication, Ryan wrote, "As I'm sure you know, the company I work for certified the steel components used in the construction of the WTC buildings…the samples we certified met all requirements…the results of these tests appear to indicate that the buildings should have easily withstood the thermal stress caused by pools of burning jet fuel."

Ryan went on to question the conclusions of "experts," including Dr. Hyman Brown, who have claimed that the towers collapse was caused by structural steel melting at temperatures of 2,000 degrees Fahrenheit.

Reiterating that his company had certified the steel to withstand temperatures of 2,000 degrees for several hours, Ryan wrote, "I think we can all agree that even un-fireproofed steel will not melt until reaching red-hot temperatures of nearly 3,000°F. Why Dr. Brown would imply that 2,000°F would melt the high-grade steel used in those buildings makes no sense at all."

"This story just does not add up," Ryan concluded. "If steel from those buildings did soften or melt, I'm sure we can all agree that this was certainly not due to jet fuel fires of any kind, let alone the briefly burning

FIREFIGHTERS THOUGHT THE FIRES WERE CONTROLLABLE

fires in those towers. That fact should be a great concern to all Americans. Alternatively, the contention that this steel did fail at temperatures around 250°C suggests that the majority of deaths on 9/11 were due to a safety-related failure. That suggestion should be of great concern to my company."

Although Ryan made it clear that he was speaking only for himself, not his company, his employers' reaction was decisive. On November 22, 2004, the *South Bend Tribune* carried this headline, "South Bend firm's lab director fired after questioning federal probe." UL officials denied any testing of the WTC steel and said Ryan was terminated because his letter was written "without UL's knowledge or authorization."

But the cat was out of the bag as Ryan's letter had reached the hands of several organizations questioning the official 9/11 story. Dan Kubiak, then-executive director of 911truth.org, a national organization of activists and researchers, said Ryan's firing was "unfortunate for the country and it's particularly tragic for him, but inspiring as hell."

"The way things are working in the country right now, it's only going to be citizens like this who take their professional knowledge and sense of personal integrity and put it ahead of the strange status quo, that we will see truth and justice [come] out of the system."

Another puzzling anomaly of the World Trade Center building collapses concerns pools of molten steel, which were recorded under the towers as well as Building 6 up to five weeks after September 11, 2001. Thermal imaging aerial photos showed large pools of hot molten steel in the basement of the three buildings, indicating temperatures of up to 2,000 degrees Fahrenheit.

Mark Loizeaux, president of Controlled Demolition, Inc., of Phoenix, Arizona, who consulted on removing the WTC debris, confirmed that these "hot spots" of molten steel were found as many as five weeks after the collapse when rubble was removed from the elevator shafts seven levels down. These pools of melted metal were also mentioned by Peter Tully, president of Tully Construction, one of four contractors hired to remove debris. Interestingly enough, WTC Building 7, which may have been brought down by explosives, does not show any heat signatures in the thermal imaging photos.

Loizeaux speculated that steel-melting fires were generated by "paper, carpet and other combustibles packed down the elevator shafts by the towers as they 'pancaked' into the basement." Since construction steel's melting point is about 2,800 degrees Fahrenheit, other experts disputed this idea, saying that due to the lack of oxygen, such debris would have been only a smoldering pile.

Speculating further, Loizeaux told the *American Free Press*, "If I were to bring the towers down, I would put explosives in the basement to get the weight of the building to help collapse the structure." Subterranean explosives could explain the "hot spots" discovered under the rubble. Considering the total destruction, reports from survivors and firemen, and the seismic shocks just prior to the collapse, many people believed that Loizeaux's description was exactly what happened on September 11, 2001.

It is worth noting that Controlled Demolition, Inc. is the same company that hurriedly removed the rubble of the Murrah Federal Building in Oklahoma City following the explosion there in 1996. Both there and at the WTC, crucial structural evidence was removed before any independent examination or investigation.

Further strong evidence of ground explosions causing the WTC collapses came from seismographs at Columbia University's Lamont-Doherty Earth Observatory in Palisades, New York, twenty-one miles north of the WTC. Just prior to the collapse of the twin towers, seismic equipment recorded two "spikes," indicating large bursts of energy that shook the ground beneath the WTC towers just before their collapse.

Columbia's seismic equipment recorded a 2.1-magnitude ground shock during the ten-second collapse of the South Tower and a 2.3 quake during the eight-second collapse of the North Tower. However, the strongest shocks, or "spikes," on the data recorder both occurred at the beginning of the tower's collapse, well before falling material struck the ground. The two spikes were more than twenty times the amplitude of the other seismic shock waves associated with the falling buildings. One seismologist said the 1993 truck bomb at the WTC did not even register on seismographs; that massive explosion did not cause detectable shock waves through the ground.

"New York seismometers recorded huge bursts of energy, which caused unexpected seismic 'spikes' at the beginning of each [tower] collapse. These spikes suggest that massive underground explosions may have literally knocked the towers off their foundations, causing them to collapse," reported the *American Free Press* in September, 2002.

Seismologist Arthur Lerner-Lam, director of Columbia's Center for Hazards and Risk Research, added to this by saying, "During the collapse, most of the energy of the falling debris was absorbed by the towers and the neighboring structures, converting them into rubble and dust or causing other damage—but not causing significant ground shaking." Asked about the two unusual shocks, Lerner-Lam was noncommittal. "This is an element of current research and discussion. It is still being investigated," he told the media.

Compounding the mystery of the seismic spikes and the witnesses who claimed to have heard multiple explosions prior to the fall of the towers is the question of the free-fall speed of the collapse. The South Tower, which was struck second but fell first, collapsed within 10 seconds. The North Tower collapsed in only eight seconds. It has been estimated that any object, a hammer for example, dropped from the roof of either tower would free fall to the ground in 9 seconds. It should also be noted that the collapse of WTC Building 7, which according to much evidence was brought down by a controlled demolition, took 8 seconds, approximately the same time as both towers.

Noting the near free-fall speed of the towers' collapse, many researchers have asked, "How could the debris crush one hundred steel and concrete floors while falling as fast as objects fall through the air?"

Pools of molten steel still registering intense heat weeks after the incident, seismic "spikes" just prior to the collapse of the buildings, the free-fall speed of the buildings' collapse, the pulverization of cement walls—none of this can be adequately explained by airplane crashes and fires alone, much less falling masonry and steel.

So the public was left with the official explanation that high-temperature fires caused by burning jet fuel melted structural steel beams, causing the towers to fall. No one will ever know for certain since none of the engineers hired by FEMA inspected or tested the steel before it was hauled away for salvage.

"I am not a metallurgist," explained Dr. W. Gene Corley, head of the FEMA engineer team, who admitted his group was not allowed to make a close study of the WTC steel girders.

Corley himself seemed unconvinced that burning jet fuel was the sole cause of the towers' collapse. In the executive summary of the "World Trade Center Building Performance Study," he wrote, "...absent other severe loading events such as a windstorm or earthquake, the buildings could have remained standing in their damaged states until subjected to some significant additional load." He then explained that fires must have constituted this "significant additional load."

"The large quantity of jet fuel carried by each aircraft ignited upon impact into each building. A significant portion of this fuel was consumed immediately in the ensuing fireballs. The remaining fuel is believed either to have flowed down through the buildings or to have burned off within a few minutes of the aircraft impact. The heat produced by this burning jet fuel does not by itself appear to have been sufficient to initiate the structural collapses," he stated.

But Corley explained that secondary fires, involving office supplies and furniture ignited by the burning jet fuel "induced additional stresses into the damaged structural frames while simultaneously softening and weakening these frames."

"This additional loading and the resulting damage were sufficient to induce the collapse of both structures," the FEMA-sponsored study concluded.

But a growing number of people, including experts, have questioned this conclusion.

After all, it has been pointed out, no independent investigation was funded and the $600,000 allocated by FEMA for the WTC study included the cost of hiring their selected experts plus the cost of printing their report. Additionally, Corley and his group were barred from independent visits to Ground Zero and were not able to examine any steel for almost a month after 9/11. Even then, they only examined 150 pieces of steel out of millions, with no way of knowing where they came from.

By the time the FEMA team called for "further investigation and analysis" in its report of May 2002, Ground Zero had been scraped clean of all debris.

According to FEMA's "Building Performance Assessment," temperatures at the crash site—only two floors above Chief Palmer and Marshal

Bucca—were as high as 1,700–2,000 degrees Fahrenheit, so intense as to melt the structure's steel frame girders.

Assuming FEMA's temperature estimates are correct, the interiors of the towers became furnaces capable of casting aluminum and glazing pottery. Yet the firemen were able to work for an extended period of time in close proximity and believed the fires they encountered were manageable. Furthermore, photographic blowups depicting the jagged gash in the North Tower just before its collapse clearly show survivors peering out through the hole made by the airplane.

"The sooty smoke and the black holes [seen in photographs of the towers prior to their collapse] cannot be dismissed as interesting aspects of the fires, nor as problems with the photography," said researcher and author Eric Hufschmid. "Rather, they are signs that the air flow was so restricted that the only significant fires were near broken windows. The fires in both towers were probably coating the [structural] columns with soot rather than heating the columns to a high temperature."

Citing a severe fire in Philadelphia's Meridian Plaza in 1991, Hufschmid noted, "The Meridian Plaza fire was extreme, but it did not cause the building to collapse.

"The fire in the South Tower seems insignificant by comparison to both the Meridian Plaza fire and the fire in the North Tower. How could the tiny fire in the South Tower cause the entire structure to shatter into dust after fifty-six minutes while much more extreme fires did not cause the Meridian Plaza building to even crack into two pieces?" The fact still remains that no other high-rise buildings have ever collapsed due to a fire of any size, or of any length—let alone in under one hour.

"The official theory of the collapse, therefore, is essentially a fire theory, so it cannot be emphasized too much that fire has *never* caused large steel-frame buildings to collapse—never, whether *before* 9/11, or *after* 9/11, or anywhere in the world *on* 9/11 except allegedly New York City—*never*," declared David Ray Griffin.

To see how ludicrous is the claim that the short-lived fires in the towers could have induced structural collapse, we can compare them with some other fires. In 1988, a fire in the First Interstate Bank Building in Los Angeles raged for 3.5 hours and gutted 5 of this building's 62 floors, but there was no significant structural damage. In 1991, a huge fire in

Philadelphia's One Meridian Plaza lasted for 18 hours and gutted 8 of the building's 38 floors, but, said the FEMA report in 1991, although "[b]eams and girders sagged and twisted...under severe fire exposures..., the columns continued to support their loads without obvious damage." In Caracas in 2004, a fire in a 50-story building raged for 17 hours, completely gutting the building's top 20 floors, and yet it did not collapse. And yet we are supposed to believe that a 56-minute fire caused the WTC south tower to collapse. Unlike the fires in the towers, moreover, the fires in Los Angeles, Philadelphia, and Caracas were hot enough to break windows.

Another important comparison is afforded by a series of experiments run in Great Britain in the mid-1990s to see what kind of damage could be done to steel-frame buildings by subjecting them to extremely hot, all-consuming fires that lasted for many hours. FEMA, having reviewed those experiments, said: "Despite the temperature of the steel beams reaching 800-900°C (1,500-1,700°F) in three of the tests..., no collapse was observed in any of the six experiments"

These comparisons bring out the absurdity of NIST's claim that the towers collapsed because the planes knocked the fireproofing off the steel columns. Fireproofing provides protection for only a few hours, so the steel in the buildings in Philadelphia and Caracas would have been directly exposed to raging fires for 14 or more hours, and yet this steel did not buckle. NIST claims, nevertheless, that the steel in the south tower buckled because it was directly exposed to flames for 56 minutes.

It was also considered peculiar that both towers dropped within fifteen seconds, essentially free-fall speed. Wouldn't the lower floors have held the weight even if only momentarily?

Massachusetts Institute of Technology Materials Professor Thomas Eager explained to PBS's *NOVA* that the WTC fires were so massive that they caused the total collapse of 47 core steel-reinforced columns as well as 236 exterior columns. "If it [fire] had only occurred in one small corner, such as a trashcan caught on fire, you might have had to repair that corner, but the whole building wouldn't have come crashing down," explained Eager. "The problem was, it was such a widely distributed fire, and then you got this domino effect."

He described this domino effect as caused by the failure of angle clips,

FIREFIGHTERS THOUGHT THE FIRES WERE CONTROLLABLE

steel brackets that held the floor trusses between the inner core columns and the exterior columns. "Once you started to get angle clips to fail in one area, it put extra load on the other clips, and then it unzipped around the building on that floor in a matter of seconds," said Eager.

Eager's explanation suffers from the fact that neither tower had fires covering the entire floor and the fact that cross trusses would have prevented, or at least slowed, the "unzipping" effect of the angle clips. His explanation also fails to address the speed of the towers' collapse. Even if one can accept that each floor did not impede the collapsing ones above it, there is no explanation for what shattered the outer walls and inner core columns, threw debris hundreds of feet away from the buildings, and turned most of the concrete to pulverized dust.

Rather than come up with an explanation of how a limited hydrocarbon fire that burned for a short time could have weakened the 47 core steel-reinforced columns in each of the two towers sufficiently for a free-fall collapse, *The 9/11 Commission Report* simply omitted this fact, and instead depicts the interior of the towers as "a hollow steel shaft, in which elevators and stairwells were grouped."

According to David Ray Griffin, the Commission avoided the "embarrassing problem" of the massive steel interior columns by simply denying their existence, "thereby demonstrating enormous ignorance or telling an enormous lie."

Even more peculiar than the rapid collapse of the twin towers was the sudden and unexplained collapse of WTC Building 7, which apparently had suffered damage only from falling debris that caused minor fires.

WHAT CAUSED THE COLLAPSE OF WTC BUILDING 7?

The 47-story Building 7 was an oddity to begin with, as it housed two New York electrical substations, which existed there prior to construction of the building. These substations housed ten transformers, 35 feet tall by 40 feet wide. Additionally, as noted, Mayor Giuliani's Emergency Command Center was located there along with three 500 kW generators for emergency power. Both the command center and other operations in the building stored an estimated 42,000 gallons of diesel fuel for auxiliary generators. Of special interest is the fact that some of that power may have been used by the CIA, Department of Defense, or Secret Service, all of which had offices in Building 7.

Shortly after 4 pm on September 11, six hours after the collapse of the South Tower, firemen turned their attention to Building 7 after someone reported small fires. But firemen who were allowed to enter the building as they had in the towers were ordered out at 11:30 am. At 5:25 pm the 47-story structure suddenly collapsed into its footprint, causing very little damage to adjacent structures—the Verizon Building and the US Post Office.

Although no real explanation of the collapse has been offered, it has been reported that the small fires grew larger, reached the stored fuel and started a conflagration so intense it melted the steel frame of the building causing it to crumple. Hufschmid dismissed this version by noting, "Every photo taken of Building 7 shows only a few tiny fires in only a few windows, and only tiny amounts of smoke were produced," he said. "I would think that a fire of the magnitude necessary to collapse a steel building would have set fire to a lot of the office furniture, carpeting, and other flammable objects. This in turn would have caused a lot of flames to be visible in a lot of windows. I also suspect that such a large fire would have caused many windows to shatter. How could an incredible fire burn in the building without any photos showing evidence of large flames or tremendous plumes of smoke?"

Unlike the twin towers, which collapsed from the top down, Building 7 collapsed from the bottom up, the classic form of a typical building demolition. In fact, this might have indeed been the case.

In September 2002, during a PBS documentary entitled *America Rebuilds*, WTC leaseholder Larry Silverstein had this to say about Building 7: "I remember getting a call from the, er, fire department commander, telling me that they were not sure they were going to be able to contain the fire, and I said, 'We've had such terrible loss of life, maybe the smartest thing to do is pull it. And they made that decision to pull and we watched the building collapse."

The term "pull" is industry slang for the controlled demolition of a structure as voiced by a New York fire commander who told TV news of "pulling" the heavily damaged WTC Building 6.

The idea that a modern 47-story steel building can totally collapse strictly due to fire is something outside of normal experience, yet no serious investigation was undertaken. If Building 7 was "pulled" by demolition, why is it so far-fetched to consider that the towers were felled the same way? Perhaps there are more reasonable explanations for modern buildings to collapse into nothing but dust, but no one will ever know for certain due to the destruction of evidence and lack of a rigorous investigation.

Perhaps the most expedient way to deal with the mystery of the loss of WTC7 was exemplified by the government's 9/11 Commission. Its final report deals with the collapse by simply omitting any mention of it.

FEMA'S REPORT: CAUSE OF WTC COLLAPSES UNKNOWN

The public might know more of what really happened to the WTC if the New York Police Department and New York Fire Department had been allowed to do their jobs. But, as with the JFK assassination, their work was taken from them by federal officials, who immediately closed doors and shut out the public from their consultations. People were even arrested for taking photographs of Ground Zero.

The FBI took charge of the criminal investigation while the little-understood Federal Emergency Management Agency took responsibility for determining what happened to cause the collapse of the twin towers. FEMA seemed determined to haul away the evidence, even before a full and impartial investigation could be made. Such premature destruction of evidence was called into question by Bill Manning, editor of the 125-year-old firemen's publication *Fire Engineering* in its January 2002 issue.

"For more than three months, structural steel from the World Trade Center has been and continues to be cut up and sold for scrap," wrote Manning. "Did they throw away the locked doors from the Triangle Shirtwaist Fire? Did they throw away the gas can used at the Happyland Social Club Fire? Did they cast aside the pressure-regulating valves at the Meridian Plaza Fire? Of course not. But essentially, that's what they're doing at the World Trade Center.

"For more than three months, structural steel from the World Trade Center has been and continues to be cut up and sold for scrap. Crucial evidence that could answer many questions about high-rise building design practices and performance under fire conditions is on the slow boat to China, perhaps never to be seen again in America until you buy your next car."

Challenging the theory that the twin towers collapsed as a result of crashed airplanes and fires, Manning added, "*Fire Engineering* has good reason to believe that the 'official investigation' blessed by FEMA and run by the American Society of Civil Engineers (ASCE) is a half-baked farce that may already have been commandeered by political forces whose primary interests, to put it mildly, lie far afield of full disclosure.

"Except for the marginal benefit obtained from a three-day, visual walk-through of evidence sites conducted by the ASCE investigation committee members—described by one close source as a 'tourist trip'—no one's checking the evidence for anything.

"The destruction and removal of evidence must stop immediately," Manning declared.

In that same issue, a number of fire officials, including a retired deputy chief from New York's fire department, called on FEMA to "immediately impanel a 'World Trade Center Disaster Review Panel' to coordinate a complete review of all aspects of the World Trade Center incident."

These fire officials noted that the WTC disaster was the largest loss of firefighters ever at one incident; the second largest loss of life on American soil; the first total collapse of a high-rise during a fire in United States history; and the largest structural collapse in recorded history.

"Now, with that understanding, you would think we would have the largest fire investigation in world history," they wrote. "You would be wrong. Instead, we have a series of unconnected and uncoordinated superficial inquiries…Ironically, we will probably gain more detailed information about the destruction of the planes than we will about the destruction of the towers. We are literally treating the steel removed from the site like garbage, not like crucial fire scene evidence."

Complaints from the federal investigating team of engineers supported these accusations.

FEMA'S REPORT: CAUSE OF WTC COLLAPSES UNKNOWN

Citing delays by federal agencies and incomplete information, the twenty-six-member team of ASCE engineers that was formed to study the collapse of the WTC towers finally produced a 296-page report by early May 2002.

But even as the report was issued, team leader and structural engineer Dr. W. Gene Corley told Congress there were still many questions left unanswered by his study.

"We didn't have time and resources," Corley complained. It should be noted that in 1995, Corley was selected to lead a Building Performance Assessment Team investigating the bombing of the Alfred P. Murrah Federal Building in Oklahoma City, a tragedy, which has also generated much controversy and speculation among conspiracy researchers.

Corley said his team didn't have enough data to create a computer model of the interior damage caused by the aircraft, nor could they model the spread of the fires. The team also griped that federal agencies feuded over funding and to whom the team should be reporting.

The team never had access to 911 emergency calls, which could have helped determine exactly what happened in the minutes prior to the collapse of the buildings, and—this can not be emphasized enough—they confirmed reports that much of the structural steel was removed from the site, cut up, and sold as scrap before they had a chance to examine it.

The team could not even obtain a complete set of building plans until early in 2002. Then they found that floor supports were attached to exterior columns by strong welds and not, as widely believed, relatively small bolts.

The hurried and superficial nature of the FEMA inquiry was evident in the conclusion of its report: "With the information and time available, the sequence of events leading to the collapse of each tower could not be definitively determined."

Corley did say the team learned just enough to know that more answers were desperately needed to design protective measures for similar structures that might be future terrorist targets.

His quest for more answers coupled with congressional outrage over the obstacles thrown in front of the engineering team prompted President Bush to pledge $16 million for a follow-up study by the National Institute of Standards and Technology (NIST).

NIST's National Construction Safety Team (NCST), after more than a year of administrative and organizational activity, finally announced in early 2004 that a draft report on the World Trade Center disaster might be "realistic and achievable" by September 2004.

A goodly portion of the NIST team's effort went to study the February 20, 2003, West Warwick, Rhode Island, nightclub fire, which claimed one hundred lives and apparently their $16 million budget was taxed. In an initial report to Congress in December 2003, the group complained of the "recurring problem" of insufficient staff for on-site inspections and subsequent research and tests. "The scale and complexity of the current World Trade Center disaster has strained NIST's existing resources," they reported.

They did, however, recommend the creation of a NIST Building and Fire Research Laboratory with a permanent staff funded for $2 million, the establishment of a safety team investigation reserve fund for another $2 million, the establishment of a program to "familiarize local and state investigating authorities about the NCST Act, and a "research program investigating the factors affecting human decision making and evacuation behavior during emergencies in buildings."

The report echoed complaints from the FEMA engineering team by stating the group's major challenges were lack of data ("through most of 2003, significant gaps existed in the data collection related to almost all of the project areas.") and the future need to deploy safety teams immediately to an incident for the collection of physical evidence and witness testimony.

The NIST inquiry also declined to hear testimony from New York firemen or building engineers despite repeated efforts on their part to contact the panel.

In light of the time lapsed and lack of hard evidence as well as considering the track record of such investigatory panels in the past, many researchers are not holding their breath in expectation of real answers.

As we have seen, the large gaps left by the dismal official record of reporting on the WTC collapses has been filled by others. Perhaps the best information that we now have about the collapses of the towers comes from independent researchers—most notably from a growing list of courageous scientists and academics noted earlier, whose names can be found listed at the website scholarsfor911truth.org.

Observers have long noted that the physical characteristics of the collapses of the two towers were almost identical. That has permitted one physicist and pioneer critic of the official story, Jim Hoffman, of 911research.wtc7.net, to compile the list below that describes principal features of the destruction of both towers. These observations are based on intensive independent study of the surviving evidence, as contrasted with the "official" explanation—although, as we have seen, in truth there is none—of a gravity collapse caused by fire. One can easily see that critical mysteries about the towers' collapse remain unsolved, in large part due to the destruction of evidence and the underfunded investigations earlier noted.

1. *The cores of the towers were obliterated and the perimeter walls were shredded.* According to Hoffman, "there is no gravity collapse scenario" or probable explanation by fire that can account for the complete leveling of the massive columns that comprised the towers' cores, or the ripping apart of their sturdy perimeter walls. But if not, what scenario does explain this?

2. *Nearly all the concrete was pulverized in the air,* so finely that it blanketed parts of lower Manhattan with inches of dust. In a gravity collapse, according to Hoffman, "there would not have been enough energy to pulverize the concrete until it hit the ground, if then." With regard to this observation, the crucial unanswered question becomes: How then was it possible for the non-metallic components of the buildings to turn to dust as fine as flour—and further, to begin to appear so massively at the very outset of the collapse? Independent scientists cited by Hoffman in a highly technical paper have shown that the energy required for the pulverization of this much concrete and for the stupendous expansion of the dust clouds is as much as "100 times greater than could have been produced from each tower's gravitational potential energy" (i.e., mass times gravitational acceleration times height).

3. *Parts of the towers were thrown up to 500 feet laterally* (as dis-

cussed earlier). Hoffman: "The downward forces of a gravity collapse cannot account for the energetic lateral ejection of pieces." But what forces caused these lateral explosions?

4. *Explosions were visible before many floors had collapsed.* "But in the South Tower collapse," writes Hoffman, "energetic dust ejections are first seen while the top is only slightly tipping, not falling." There is no known source of the dense powder in these clouds of ejected dust. We have also cited numerous eye-witness reports of explosions in the buildings.

5. *The towers' tops mushroomed into thick dust clouds much larger than the original volumes of the buildings.* "Without the addition of large sources of pressure beyond the collapse itself," claims Hoffman, "the falling building and its debris should have occupied about the same volume as the intact building."

6. *The tops fell at nearly the rate of free fall, in less than fifteen seconds.* We've examined this previously. These astounding rates of fall, according to Hoffman's technical explanation, "indicate that nearly all resistance to the downward acceleration of the tops had been eliminated ahead of them. The forms of resistance, had the collapses been gravity-driven, would include: the destruction of the structural integrity of each storey; the pulverization of the concrete in the floor slabs of each storey, and other non-metallic objects; and the acceleration of the remains of each storey encountered either outward or downward. There would have to be enough energy to overcome all of these forms of resistance and do it rapidly enough to keep up with the near free-fall acceleration of the top."

The issue of the cause of the collapse of the towers has become so salient that one wealthy American activist, Jimmy Walter, has offered a one million dollar reward to anyone who can prove that explosives were not used in the World Trade Center. Walter has gained notoriety and headlines by his efforts—costing him millions—to educate ordinary Americans and Europeans about the possibility that 9/11 is an inside job. Details of his work can be found at reopen911.org.

FEMA'S REPORT: CAUSE OF WTC COLLAPSES UNKNOWN

An equally detailed and shocking analysis of the collapses of all three buildings came recently from an unexpected quarter—Brigham Young University, in the heart of the conservative state of Utah.

Professor Steven E. Jones of the department of physics and astronomy at Brigham Young University, in a paper accepted for peer review, stated, "It is quite plausible that explosives were pre-planted in all three buildings and set off after the two plane crashes —which were actually a diversion tactic. Muslims are (probably) not to blame for bringing down the WTC buildings after all."

Jones acknowledged that there have been many "junk science" conspiracy theories about what happened on 9/11, but concluded, "I have called attention to glaring inadequacies in the 'final' reports funded by the US government. I have also presented multiple evidences for an alternative hypothesis. In particular, the official theory lacks repeatability in that no actual models or buildings (before or since 9-11-01) have been observed to completely collapse due to the proposed fire-based mechanisms. On the other hand, dozens of buildings have been completely and symmetrically demolished through the use of pre-positioned explosives. And high-temperature chemical reactions can account for the observed large pools of molten metal, under both Towers and WTC7, and the sulfidation of structural steel. The controlled-demolition hypothesis cannot be dismissed as "junk science" because it better satisfies tests of repeatability and parsimony. It ought to be seriously (scientifically) investigated and debated."

Asked by one news reporter, "Who set the explosives?" Jones replied, "I try not to go there because we have to answer the first question first— the scientific issue first. We need to consider all options for the collapse of these buildings. Let the chips fall where they may."

As noted earlier, in 2006, Jones teamed with James H. Fetzer, the Distinguished McKnight University Professor of Philosophy at the University of Minnesota, Duluth, a former Marine Corps officer, to found the organization scholarsfor911truth.org. The two co-chairs and their nationwide membership have brought a new credibility to the rapidly expanding movement for the truth about 9/11.

Concerns over the validity of the free-fall scenario based on fires in the buildings were echoed by former Bush I administration official Morgan Reynolds, a Texas A & M Professor Emeritus of Economics who was also former chief economist for the Department of Labor and former director of the Criminal Justice Center at the National Center for Policy Analysis. Reynolds is also a leading member of scholarsfor911truth.org.

"Only professional demolition appears to account for the full range of facts associated with the collapses of WTC 1 (North Tower), WTC 2 (South Tower), and the much-overlooked collapse of the 47-story WTC building 7 at 5:21 pm on that fateful day," wrote Reynolds.

He added, "Controlled demolition would have required unimpeded access to the WTC, access to explosives, avoiding detection, and the expertise to orchestrate the deadly destruction from a nearby secure location. Such access before 9/11 likely depended on complicity by one or more WTC security companies."

His detailed analysis of both the World Trade Center collapses and the Pentagon strike may be found at www.lewrockwell.com/reynolds/reynolds12.html.

Reynolds also speculated on why WTC7 was brought down later on 9/11. "Why would the killers destroy WTC7, especially since a collapse would arouse suspicion in some quarters?" he asked. "A logical if unproven theory is that the perpetrators used Mayor Giuliani's sealed OEM 'bunker' on the 23rd story of WTC7 to conduct the twin tower implosions and then destroyed the building and evidence to cover up their crimes, just as a murderer might set his victim's dwelling ablaze to cover up the crime (one in four fires is arson). Giuliani's 'undisclosed secret location' was perfect because it had been evacuated by 9:45 am on 9/11, it enabled unmolested work, provided a ringside seat, was bullet- and bomb-resistant, had its own secure air and water supply, and could withstand winds of 160 mph, necessary protection from the wind blasts generated by collapsing skyscrapers."

The professor also joined the chorus of criticism leveled at FEMA officials for the rapid removal of WTC debris, which prevented later study. "The criminal code requires that crime scene evidence be saved for forensic analysis but FEMA had it destroyed before anyone could seriously investigate it," stated Reynolds. "FEMA was in position to take command because it had arrived the day before the attacks at New York's Pier 29 to conduct a war game exercise, 'Tripod II,' quite a coincidence. The authorities apparently considered the rubble quite valuable: New York City officials had every debris truck tracked on GPS and had one truck driver who took an unauthorized 1 ½ hour lunch fired."

Responding to the question of why controlled demolitions have never been considered by the official government investigations of 9/11, Reynolds said, "If demolition destroyed three steel skyscrapers at the World Trade Center on 9/11, then the case for an 'inside job' and a government attack on America would be compelling."

Military affairs journalist Barbara Honegger honed this argument to an even sharper point by offering the chilling conclusion that if bombs were planted inside both the Pentagon and the WTC buildings, it would have been difficult—if not impossible—for foreign terrorists to have the opportunity to plant and detonate such bombs.

"...[B]ecause the true *modus operandi* of the WTC and Pentagon attacks are so similar, a single group of US/domestic conspirators almost certainly planned both the WTC and Pentagon attacks and controlled both the approaching planes and inside-the-building explosions in real time on 9/11 and, thus, neither attack could have been executed by al Qaeda." (See Appendix for details.)

TRACKS OF FOREKNOWLEDGE

F ollowing the devastating attacks of 9/11, US leaders said we should avoid "finger pointing" to place blame, yet advance warnings were too numerous and specific to do otherwise.

During 2001, the United States spent $30 billion on intelligence gathering plus an additional $12 billion aimed specifically at counterterrorism. This total of $42 billion exceeds most nations' total gross national product, yet Americans were told that none of its two-dozen alphabet intelligence agencies had any inkling that we were about to be attacked.

Information available today seriously disputes this claim. It was in fact disputed within days of the attacks by people both in and outside the government.

Questions as to why there had been no warning came quickly. The day after the attacks, Congressional Research Service antiterrorism expert Kenneth Katzman was quoted as saying, "How nothing could have been picked up is beyond me."

But something must have been picked up. How else to explain the fact that the State Department on September 7, 2001, issued a worldwide caution to Americans that they "may be the target of a terrorist threat from extremist groups with links to Osama bin Laden's al Qaeda organization…Such individuals have not distinguished between official and civilian targets. As always, we take this information seriously. US government facilities worldwide remain on heightened alert."

As months passed, more and more evidence accumulated until it became overwhelmingly clear that persons within the federal government were warned of terrorist attacks, including the use of airplanes against buildings. Even congressional researchers determined that US intelligence agencies had received at least twelve warnings of coming offensive action by terrorists. And, as will be seen, this is a low figure.

By April 2002, leaks in the news media damaging to the official explanation, plus public clamor for an investigation of the 9/11 attacks, prompted congressional leaders to agree to a joint investigation by both the Senate and House Intelligence committees. The charter of the Joint Inquiry into Intelligence Community Activities before and after September 11, 2001—known as the JICI—was to be limited in scope, with authorization only to review intelligence failures and recommend corrections.

The JICI got off to a rocky start when retired CIA Inspector General Britt Snider, the staff director for the JICI, resigned under pressure from committee members who believed his close connection to CIA director George Tenet might interfere with an impartial investigation.

Amid numerous difficulties and delays, the unusual joint hearings that were scheduled for June 2002 did not convene until late September. "Are we getting the cooperation we need? Absolutely not," charged the senior Republican on the Senate Intelligence Committee, Senator Richard Shelby of Alabama.

Florida Democratic Senator Bob Graham echoed Shelby's complaint, saying the Bush administration told them they can "only talk to the top of the pyramid."

"Well, the problem is, the top of the pyramid has a general awareness of what's going on in the organization, but if you want to know why Malaysian plotters were not put on a watch list...you've got to talk to somebody at the level where those kinds of decisions were made." Graham referred to a preliminary report, which pointed out that two of the hijacking suspects, Khalid al-Midhar and Nawaf al-Hazmi, lived openly in San Diego even after being observed in a Malaysia meeting with known terrorists.

Bush and Cheney had long opposed any independent investigation of the 9/11 attacks, claiming it would impede the War on Terrorism by leading to leaks of security measures and tying up personnel needed in the war.

But with the revelations of irregularities in investigations by government agencies that came to light in the spring and summer of 2002, Congress was finally moved to get the JICI funded and operational. "The attacks of September 11...highlighted a failure of national policy to respond to the developments of a global terror network implacably hostile to American interests," thundered Senator John McCain, who, along with Senator Joseph Lieberman, cosponsored the bill to fund the independent commission. Legislation authorizing the creation of the ten-person panel, armed with subpoena power and a $3 million budget, was approved by the Senate in a 90/8 vote late in September 2002.

The run-up to the actual hearings illustrated the need to strengthen the JICI's charter, including the need for subpoena power.

According to a story in the *Los Angeles Times* in May 2002, "Small teams of investigators have been at the Justice Department and the CIA, gathering documents and conducting interviews. They have come back with a litany of complaints about tactics they say are designed to slow their progress and restrict their access to documents and potential informants, sources said."

Research was quickly coming to light making it clear that from 1998 onward, both the CIA and FBI had received ever-increasing warnings concerning al Qaeda using hijacked aircraft to attack targets within the United States. Despite the serious nature of this evidence, the Bush administration continued to stonewall and hamper the congressional investigation, even launching an investigation of the investigators.

This occurred after word leaked to the public in June 2002 that communications in Arabic intercepted by the National Security Agency on

September 10, 2001 contained phrases such as "Tomorrow is zero hour" and "The match is about to begin." As noted earlier, this made it seem likely that the hijackers were privy to the war game exercises scheduled for the following day, evidence of an inside job.

The FBI swung into action.

But instead of going after the authors of the notes indicating foreknowledge, they went after the persons on the joint committee who leaked the information.

Even as White House spokesman Ari Fleischer was calling the notes "alarmingly specific," bureau agents were asking committee members to take lie detector tests regarding the leaks. The *Washington Post* reported that nearly all of the thirty-seven members of the joint committee were questioned. Some members declined to take the lie detector tests, citing constitutional separation of powers and the unreliability of such tests.

Eleanor Hill, the new staff director of the JICI, spoke out about advance notice of the attacks passed to ranking leaders. She noted that a briefing for "senior government officials" in July 2001 specifically warned that Osama bin Laden "will launch a significant terrorist attack against US and/or Israeli interests in the coming weeks. The attack will be spectacular and designed to inflict mass casualties against US facilities or interests. Attack preparations have been made. Attack will occur with little or no warning." She said it was unknown if President Bush received specific information regarding the possibility of airliners being used as flying bombs because the director of the CIA would not declassify the information.

Hill, who wrote a report described as preliminary, said it was based on a review of 400,000 government documents and testimony taken during four months of closed-door hearings. Hill stated that while investigators found no specific warning of the 9/11 attacks, collectively the warnings "reiterated a consistent and critically important theme: Osama bin Laden's intent to launch terrorist attacks inside the United States."

Even a survey of mainstream sources shows that warnings of a domestic attack had been coming in for some time—and with increasing frequency right up to 9/11.

For example, in December 2000, the Congressional Advisory Panel to Assess Domestic Response Capabilities for Terrorism Involving Weapons of Mass Destruction issued a report stating, "We are impelled by the stark realization that a terrorist attack on some level within our borders is inevitable."

One clear warning came as early as eight years before the 9/11 attacks in the form of a book written by Yossef Bodansky, director of the US House Task Force on Terrorism and Unconventional Warfare.

In his book, *Target America: Terrorism in the US Today*, Bodansky detailed the airfields in Iran and North Korea where Muslim terrorists trained and noted, "According to a former trainee in Wakiland [Iran], one of the exercises included having an Islamic Jihad detachment seize (or hijack) a transport aircraft. Then, trained air crews from among the terrorists would crash the airliner with its passengers into a selected target."

Wiretaps on suspected al Qaeda terrorists in Italy as far back as 2000 also gave indications of plans for a major attack on the United States involving airplanes and airports. "This will be one of those strikes that will never be forgotten..." was the comment recorded from Abdelkader Mahmoud Es Sayed, an Egyptian accused of being a ranking al Qaeda member in Italy and a man convicted of the 1997 massacre of fifty-eight tourists at Luxor, Egypt. Es Sayed also mentioned danger in airports and flying.

In another taped conversation on January 24, 2001, a Tunisian terrorist spoke about fake identification papers to Es Sayed and asked, "Will these work for the brothers who are going to the United States?" Es Sayed also stated the war against the enemies of Islam would be fought "with any means we can combat them, using...airplanes. They won't be able to stop us even with their heaviest weapons."

According to the *Los Angeles Times*, several US officials said they were unfamiliar with the wiretap messages but "one Justice Department official noted that a small cadre of US intelligence agents might have been privy to them." What is most enlightening about these Italian wiretaps is not that they evinced foreknowledge—they were too vague to be considered a precise warning—but that they gave indication of the many and varied alerts coming into the United States as well as the fact that many foreign intelligence services were monitoring al Qaeda cells.

Spain got in on the act. In August 2001, the voice of an unidentified man in London was taped speaking with the head of a Madrid terrorist cell. The man said he had entered the field of aviation and was taking flying lessons.

Such warnings were not lost on the British. It was revealed in June, 2002, that British intelligence chiefs warned the Prime Minister less than two months before September 11 that Osama bin Laden and al Qaeda were in "the final stages" of preparing a terrorist attack in the West. It was stated that this prediction was based not only on reports from MI6 but also from the Cabinet Office Joint Intelligence Committee, which included representatives from the American CIA and NSA.

According to a report on MSNBC, just two weeks before the 9/11 attacks, a radio station in the Cayman Islands received an unsigned letter warning of a major attack against the United States involving airliners. It was reported that US government officials went to investigate but no further information was forthcoming. As will be seen, the Cayman Islands are an offshore banking haven to many factions, including the CIA and international bankers.

Even the much-disparaged Taliban apparently tried to give us warning. According to a story posted September 7, 2002, by Independent Digital, an aide to then Taliban foreign minister Wakil Ahmed Muttawakil tried to warn US authorities weeks prior to the 9/11 attacks. Muttawakil, unhappy with the glut of foreign Arab militants in Afghanistan, told his aide he was concerned over the prospect of US military action against his country. He was quoted as saying, "The guests are going to destroy the guesthouse."

The aide, unidentified for his own safety by the British publication, said Muttawakil was shocked in the summer of 2001 to learn of a coming attack from fundamentalist Islamic leader Tahir Yildash. "At first, Muttawakil wouldn't say why he was so upset," explained the aide. "Then it all came out. Yildash had revealed that Osama bin Laden was going to launch an attack on the United States. It would take place on American soil and it was imminent. Yildash said Osama hoped to kill thousands of Americans."

The aide said he first traveled across the Pakistan border to meet with American consul general David Katz late in July 2001. "They met in a safe house belonging to an old Mujahideen leader who has confirmed to the

Independent that the meeting took place," reported the news outlet. Katz declined to discuss the matter.

Next, Muttawakil sent the aide to the Kabul offices of the United Nations, where he again issued his warning.

Apparently, since the aide failed to make it clear that he was sent by Foreign Minister Muttawakil, both American and United Nations officials thought his warning more propaganda from the warring factions within Afghanistan and did nothing.

Similar warning signs came from the Far East. In 1995, when Manila authorities answered a fire call they discovered bomb-making materials in the apartment of Ramzi Yousef, later convicted for his role in the 1993 WTC bombing. Yousef escaped but another suspected al Qaeda member, Abdul Hakim Murad, was taken into custody.

Murad told his interrogators that Ramzi had a plan to hijack a commercial airliner in the United States and crash it into CIA Headquarters or the Pentagon. Philippine investigators also found evidence that Ramzi's plan, code-named "Project Bojinka," also involved targeting the White House, the Sears Tower in Chicago, the Transamerica Tower in San Francisco, and the World Trade Center. The plans for Bojinka must have been known at the highest levels of government, which makes a mockery of later claims that no one could have imagined that hijacked airliners could be used as deadly missiles.

Apparently Muslim fanatics had already attempted to put Ramzi's plan into effect. On Christmas Eve 1994, four men thought to be connected to bin Laden's terrorist network hijacked Air France Flight 8969 bound from Algiers to Paris. The plane landed in Marseilles, where the hijackers demanded that it be loaded with explosives and extra fuel. Their plan, apparently to crash the craft into the Eiffel Tower, was derailed when commandos stormed the plane and killed all four hijackers.

Warnings had continued to pour in from the Philippines, a hotbed of terrorist activity. According to the *Manila Times*, Philippine defense and police intelligence officers warned American authorities of an alliance between Abu Sayyaf (ASG) terrorists there and the al Qaeda network. The paper said American officials ignored the warnings until September 11, 2001.

The report went on to describe a 1994 meeting between ASG co-founder Edwin Angeles and WTC bombing mastermind Ramzi Yousef that included convicted Oklahoma City bombing accomplice Terry Nichols, who was married to a Philippine national. The topics of discussion were terrorist targets. The Murrah Federal Building in Oklahoma City was mentioned as well as another attack on the World Trade Center.

It seemed everyone from the Chinese to our own FBI tried to warn Washington authorities that an attack was imminent, yet nothing was done.

Chinese military officers wrote about just such an attack as occurred on 9/11 three years before the fact. In a military manual entitled "Unrestricted Warfare," People's Liberation Army colonels Qiao Liang and Wang Xiangsui noted, "Whether it be the intrusions of [computer] hackers, *a major explosion at the World Trade Center, or a bombing attack by bin Laden* [emphasis added], all of these greatly exceed the frequency bandwidth understood by the American military..."

A CIA translation of this Chinese manual was published on September 11, 2002, the one-year anniversary of the attacks. The manual is a recipe book of unorthodox methods for weaker nations to humble America. It discusses multilevel attacks on America's social, political, and economic systems using strategies involving computer hackers, the infiltration of illegal immigrants, stock market manipulation, and even the use of weapons of mass destruction.

The Chinese leadership, and particularly its military chiefs, has long viewed the United States as their principal enemy, a fact that has been marginalized by both the US Congress and the corporate mass media due to the close business and trade relations between the nations.

Exactly one month following the 9/11 attacks, China was quietly approved as a member of the World Trade Organization after fifteen years of negotiation. It was a move that had previously prompted many and widespread protests due to that Asian nation's abysmal human rights record. This time, with Americans in shock over the 9/11 attacks, little notice was given to this action.

With the heightened security resulting from the attacks, there was no opportunity for demonstrations against this WTO action. According to CNN, WTO ministers meeting in the Persian Gulf state of Qatar were protected by a US helicopter gunship and naval vessels, and were inside a cordon that included more than two thousand US Marines.

WTO director general Mike Moore declared China's entry into the trade organization "a major historic event," yet there was minimal publicity in the United States.

Even the Russians seemed to be aware that something big was coming.

Dr. Tatyana Koryagina, a senior research fellow for the Institute of Macroeconomic Research under the Russian Ministry of Economic Development and reportedly close to President Putin's inner circle, predicted that an "unusual catastrophe" would strike the United States in late August 2001. Her prediction appeared in a *Pravda* story published on July 12, 2001.

"The US has been chosen as the object of financial attack because the financial center of the planet is located there. The effect will be maximal. The strike waves of economic crisis will spread over the planet instantly and will remind us of the blast of a huge nuclear bomb."

Asked about the discrepancy of dates in a later interview, Dr. Koryagina explained, "I did not make a serious mistake. Indeed, between 15 and 20 August, the dollar started trembling under the pressure of multiple bad news about the US and economy. And within weeks, the Manhattan skyscrapers fell down.

"As a result, a significant part of the world financial network was paralyzed. This strike was aimed at destabilization and destruction of America and (in domino fashion) all the countries making countless billions of dollars." She advised Russian citizens not to invest in American dollars.

She also said the 9/11 attacks were not the work of nineteen terrorists but a group of extremely powerful private persons seeking to reshape the world. This group, she added, has assets of about $300 trillion, which it will use to legitimize its power and create a new world government.

Many persons have taken Dr. Koryagina's comments very seriously when considering both her credentials and her knowledge of Russia's close contacts with nations identified with terrorism, such as Iraq, Iran, Syria, Libya, and North Korea.

As reported by the *Washington Times* on September 28, 2001, "US intelligence agencies have uncovered information that Russian criminal groups have been supplying Osama bin Laden and his al Qaeda terrorist network with components for chemical, biological and nuclear weapons."

Arabic sources too seemed to have been able to discern that bin Laden was preparing to launch a major attack.

In mid-2002, Egyptian president Hosni Mubarak revealed that his intelligence service warned US officials about a week before the 9/11 attacks that bin Laden's organization was in the last stages of preparing a major operation against an American target.

Mubarak said Egyptian intelligence chiefs tried unsuccessfully to thwart the operation using an unnamed agent who had penetrated the al Qaeda network. They passed the information regarding this penetration to US intelligence between March and May 2001, he said, adding, "We informed them about everything."

An American intelligence official told the *New York Times* that they had received no such warning but Mubarak said he was informed that security at the US embassy in Cairo was tightened just before the attacks. Mubarak's interview with the *Times* apparently was the first time that a foreign leader admitted that an intelligence service had penetrated the al Qaeda terrorist network.

The *Times* writers noted dryly, "At a minimum, Mr. Mubarak's account adds detail and drama to a list of warnings about potential terrorist attacks that American intelligence fielded in the days, weeks and months before September 11."

Within hours of the attacks Abdel-Barri Atwan, editor of the London newspaper *al-Quds al-Arabi*, told Reuters News Service, "Osama bin Laden warned three weeks ago that he would attack American interests in an unprecedented attack, a big one... Personally we received information that he planned very, very big attacks against American interests. We received several warnings like this."

Although Atwan said he did not notify the authorities of this warning because he did not take it seriously, it begs the question: if a London newspaper knew of impending attacks, why not the American intelligence services?

An article in the June 23, 2001, issue of *Airjet Airline World News* noted another Arabic source as claiming that "a big surprise" was expected in coming weeks.

A reporter from Arabic satellite television channel MBC who had recently met with bin Laden was quoted as saying, "A severe blow is expected against US and Israeli interests worldwide...There is a mobilization among the Osama bin Laden forces. It seems that there is a race of who will strike first. Will it be the United States or Osama bin Laden?"

Another source for a warning may have been an Iranian being held in Germany at the time of the 9/11 attacks. According to the German newspaper *Neue Presse*, prior to 9/11 the man asked to contact American authorities to warn them of an imminent attack. It was reported that when the man told the Secret Service that he was facing deportation from Germany, they hung up on him. On September 14, 2001 US agents finally interrogated the man.

Closer to home, in a 1993 letter to the *New York Times*, the Middle Easterners who bombed the World Trade Center in that year made it plain that they would try again. Their letter read:

> We, the fifth battalion in the LIBERATION ARMY, declare our responsibility for the explosion on the mentioned building. This action was done in response for the American political, economical, and military support to Israel the state of terrorism and to the rest of the dictator countries in the region.
>
> Our demands are:
> 1. Stop all military, economical, and political aid to Israel.
> 2. All diplomatic relations with Israel must stop.
> 3. Not to interfere with any of the Middle East countries' interior affairs.
>
> If our demands are not met, all of our functional groups in the army will continue to execute our missions against the military and civilian targets in and out the United States.
> For your own information, our army has more than hundred and fifty suicidal soldiers ready to go ahead.
>
> The terrorism that Israel practices (which is supported by America) must be faced with a similar one. The dictatorship and terrorism (also supported by America) that some countries are practicing against their own people must also be faced with terrorism.

The American people must know that their civilians who got killed are not better than those who are getting killed by the American weapons and support.

The American people are responsible for the actions of their government and they must question all of the crimes that their government is committing against other people. Or they—Americans—will be the targets of our operations that could diminish them.

The conspirators also drafted a second letter, which was later recovered from an erased file on a computer disc seized from Ayyad's office. This second letter, which the conspirators apparently did not send, proclaimed that the World Trade Center bomb did not do as much damage as had been intended, because their "calculations were not very accurate this time." They warned, however, that they would be more precise in the future and would continue to target the World Trade Center if their demands were not met.

Following his 1995 arrest in Pakistan, Ramzi Yousef was more specific. He clearly stated that the conspirators had intended for the bomb to topple one of the towers and hoped that it would crash into the other, bringing them both down and killing one quarter of a million people.

One of the strangest items indicating foreknowledge of the attacks came in the form of registered Internet domain names.

Two highly suggestive domain names—attackontwintowers.com and worldtradetowerattack.com—were registered more than a year before the 9/11 attacks. Since the registration was allowed to elapse, no one knows who registered the names.

Neil Livingston, who heads Global Options LLC, a Washington-based investigation and counterterrorism firm, said, "It's unbelievable that they [the registration company whose name was withheld] would register these domain names, probably without any comment to the FBI. If they did make a comment to the FBI, it's unbelievable that the FBI didn't react to it."

Incredibly, other domain names registered prior to the 9/11 tragedy included attackamerica.com, horrorinamerica.com, horrorinnewyork.com, nycterroriststrike.com, pearlharborinmanhattan.com, worldtradecenter929.com, worldtradetowerstrike.com, and terroristattack2001.com.

Even from a cursory search of September 11 reports, it would appear as though many people had some inkling of what was to come.

As recounted by Russ Kick, author and columnist for the *Village Voice*, a veteran New York police investigator said that numerous Arab Americans in New York heard about the coming attacks. The officer said the number of leads were so overwhelming that it was difficult to tell who had heard about the attacks from a secondhand source and who had heard it from someone who may have been a participant. A Brooklyn detective was quoted as saying that "a serious and major priority" investigation was made into why so many Middle Easterners failed to show up for work at the World Trade Center on September 11. According to a former US military intelligence officer who arrived in New York on the morning of September 11, 2001, just prior to the attacks he had difficulty in getting a taxi. Once he found one, his driver told him that most of the Arab cab drivers had called in sick that day and that the taxi system was down to nearly half strength.

Even certain school kids seemed to have foreknowledge, according to Kick. A Dallas suburb fifth-grader told his teacher on September 10, "Tomorrow, World War III will begin. It will begin in the United States and the United States will lose."

Another school kid in Jersey City, home of several of the accused hijackers, told friends to stay away from lower Manhattan on the morning of September 11. One week before the attacks, a Brooklyn high school freshman pointed at the WTC towers and told his class, "Do you see those two buildings? They won't be standing there next week."

There are even telltale signs that some prominent politicians and government officials within the United States had some warning of the September atrocities.

San Francisco mayor Willie Brown was scheduled to fly to New York on the morning of September 11, 2001. But at about 10 pm the evening of September 10, he received a phone call at home advising him to be cautious about traveling by air. Brown would only say that the call came from "my security people at the airport," but the warning was clear: don't travel by air. He said the call "didn't come in any alarming fashion, which is why I'm hesitant to make an alarming statement." Brown was preparing to leave for the airport the next morning when instead he joined millions of other Americans in viewing the destruction on TV.

One San Francisco official noted that the FAA routinely issues security notices but added that none had been received in the days before September 11. No one has yet discovered who sent the after-hours warning to Brown.

Newsweek reported on September 24, 2001, that on September 10 "a group of top Pentagon officials suddenly canceled travel plans for the next morning, apparently because of security concerns."

On July 28, 2001, then Attorney General John Ashcroft left Washington on a fishing trip to Missouri but it was not on a commercial airliner. CBS news correspondent Jim Stewart reported that Ashcroft had suddenly begun flying only on government-chartered jets in response to what an FBI spokesman called a "threat assessment" by the bureau. Ashcroft was advised to travel only by private jet for the remainder of his term under FBI guidelines.

Former Attorney General Janet Reno and all but the Secretaries of Interior and Energy in the Bush administration had flown by commercial airliners. Asked about this sudden change in policy, Ashcroft said, "I don't do threat assessments myself and I rely on those whose responsibility it is in the law enforcement community, particularly the FBI. And I try to stay within the guidelines that they've suggested I should stay within for those purposes."

But perhaps most extraordinary was a comment attributed to a member of Congress. During live coverage of the 9/11 attacks, National Public Radio congressional correspondent David Welna was describing the evacuation of the Capitol.

He reported, "I spoke with Congressman Ike Shelton—a Democrat from Missouri and a member of the Armed Services Committee—who said that just recently the director of the CIA warned that there could be an attack—an imminent attack—on the United States of this nature. So this is not entirely unexpected."

All of the above information stands in sharp contrast to often-repeated Bush administration assertions that no one in government could have imagined an attack such as that on 9/11.

Secretary of Defense Donald Rumsfeld himself admitted, "there were lots of warnings" in an interview with *Parade* magazine. A transcript of his interview was released by the Department of Defense on October 12, 2001.

And even then-CIA Director George Tenet had testified to the JICI that by the end of summer, 2001, "the system was blinking red."

As if all of this was not enough, it is now also clear that the Federal Bureau of Investigation itself had numerous advance warnings of what was to come.

THE FBI COULDN'T, OR WOULDN'T, CONNECT THE DOTS

Even with its extensive use of an electronic eavesdropping system originally named "Carnivore," and despite specific reports from FBI field offices that directly pointed to the imminent attacks, the top tier of the FBI couldn't seem to piece together the available information. In some cases "probable cause" data was presented to FBI Headquarters (FBIHQ) that would have led any reasonable person to conclude that Middle Eastern terrorists were working diligently on plans to attack the United States by hijacking airplanes. Or, perhaps reasonable persons at the FBI weren't allowed come to such conclusions.

Just six days after the 9/11 tragedy, FBI director Robert Mueller stated, "There were no warning signs that I'm aware of that would indicate this type of operation in the country." Clearly contradicting his statement is the suppressed evidence from FBI investigations held at the Phoenix, Minneapolis, Oklahoma City, and Chicago field offices that came to light in the mainstream media in the months following the attacks, not to mention the reports cited in the last section of this book. One can add to this the August 6, 2001, Presidential Daily Brief report, soon to be examined, that was revealed during the hearings of the 9/11 Commission.

The Carnivore electronic monitoring system created so much consternation from persons concerned with individual rights and privacy that it is now called simply DCS-1000. In at least one instance, Carnivore actually prevented the bureau from gaining information on a suspected terrorist.

In May 2002, the Electronic Privacy Information Center acquired FBI memos under the Freedom of Information Act, which showed that a bureau wiretap in the year 2000 aimed at an unnamed suspect was ineffective because a low-level FBI technical person destroyed the information.

According to David Sobel, general counsel for the center, "The FBI software not only picked up the emails under the electronic surveillance of the FBI's target...but also picked up emails on non-covered targets." One of the obtained memos showed that an FBI supervisor explained, "The FBI technical person was apparently so upset [about intercepting unauthorized emails] that he destroyed all the email take."

The FBI had previously issued assurances that Carnivore could only capture a narrow field of information authorized by a court order. "This shows that the FBI has been misleading Congress and the public about the extent to which Carnivore is capable of collecting only authorized information," Sobel said.

Sobel also discovered that, when Chief Judge Royce Lamberth—heading the special, and mostly secret, Foreign Intelligence Surveillance Court (FISC), which reviews national security wiretaps—found out that in 2000 the FBI had been misrepresenting information in their requests for eavesdropping, an investigation was ordered forcing many FBI wiretaps to be shut down. This disciplinary action foreshadowed the Bush administration's later use of warrantless NSA wiretaps that entirely bypassed the FISC, which came to light in 2006.

Despite the problems with their Carnivore system and bungled wiretaps, many agents within the bureau were actively working on the problem of terrorism by other means.

Perhaps the most knowledgeable person within the FBI on Middle Eastern terrorism in general and Osama bin Laden in particular was John O'Neill.

In 1995 O'Neill was promoted to head the FBI's counterterrorism section and began working out of FBI headquarters in Washington, D.C. One of his initial jobs was the capture of Ramzi Yousef, then a key suspect in several acts of terror including the 1993 bombing of the World Trade Center.

Through the late 1990s, O'Neill, according to Lawrence Wright writing in the *New Yorker*, became "the bureau's most committed tracker of Osama bin Laden and his al Qaeda network of terrorists."

THE FBI COULDN'T, OR WOULDN'T, CONNECT THE DOTS

But O'Neill came to believe that his superiors did not carry the same zeal against terrorism as he did. "John had the same problems with bureaucracy as I had," said Richard A. Clarke in a 2002 magazine interview. Clarke had served as White House coordinator for counterterrorism since the George H. W. Bush administration in the late 1980s. "The impatience really grew in us as we dealt with the dolts who didn't understand."

Despite the 1996 defection of Jamal Ahmed al-Fadl, a long-sought al Qaeda terrorist, and his subsequent detailing of the network to both the CIA and FBI, the State Department refused to list al Qaeda as a terrorist network.

Despite O'Neill's growing ire over perceived indulgence of terrorists by higher authorities and his contentious personality, he accepted the post of special agent in charge of the National Security Division in New York City. Here he created a special "al Qaeda desk" and worked doggedly to pinpoint Osama bin Laden. O'Neill, one of the top-level terrorism experts within the FBI, knew well who and what he was up against.

"Almost all of the groups today, if they choose to, have the ability to strike us here in the United States," O'Neill said in a 1997 Chicago speech.

By the summer of 2001, O'Neill had been passed over for promotion and was growing weary of fighting his superiors on the issue of terrorism. Adding to his disillusionment was O'Neill's experience trying to conduct an investigation of the bombing of the US destroyer Cole, which had been severely damaged by a small boat filled with explosives operated by two suicide bombers.

O'Neill, commanding about three hundred heavily armed FBI agents, claimed his investigation was being hampered by everyone from Yemen president Ali Abdullah Saleh to US ambassador Barbara Bodine. The FBI force believed they were never given the authority they required to conduct a strenuous investigation.

"... O'Neill came home feeling that he was fighting the counterterrorism battle without support from his own government," noted Wright in the *New Yorker*. When he tried to return to Yemen in early 2001, O'Neill was refused entry.

"The last two years of his life, he got very paranoid," writer Lawrence Wright was told by Valerie James, a close friend of O'Neill's. "He was convinced there were people out to get him."

In the end, it appears it was his old archenemy, Osama bin Laden—or perhaps more precisely bin Laden's covert handlers in the US government—who got him.

By the summer of 2001, events and O'Neill's career were coming to a head. Someone had leaked information on some of O'Neill's bureau gaffes to the *New York Times* and information on terrorism was pouring into government agencies. "Something big is going to happen," he told a friend.

"It all came together in the third week of June," recalled Clarke. "The CIA's view was that a major terrorist attack was coming in the next several weeks." Clarke said orders to beef up security were passed to the FAA, the Coast Guard, Customs, the INS, and the FBI.

But O'Neill had had enough. By August 23, he had retired from the FBI and accepted a job paying twice his bureau pay—as chief of security for the World Trade Center.

When the first tower was struck, O'Neill ordered the building evacuated but stayed behind to help others in the North Tower. He used a cell phone to speak to a few friends and relatives. He assured them he was okay. He was last seen alive walking toward the tunnel that led to the South Tower.

John O'Neill was not the only FBI agent to see definite warning signs.

In mid-2002 twelve-year FBI veteran Robert G. Wright Jr. charged the bureau's counterterrorism efforts were ineffective and "not protecting the American people." Going further, Wright charged that FBI superiors had derailed investigations that could have prevented the 9/11 attacks, saying the bureau had evidence that the World Trade Center was a possible target.

Wright already had excellent credentials as an FBI agent fighting terrorists. His own investigation initiated in 1998 resulted in the seizure of financial assets of one Yassin Kadi of Chicago, who has since been identified as one of the chief money launderers connected to Osama bin Laden. He then launched an investigation into money laundering by other terrorists within the United States only to have his probe terminated by higher authorities.

THE FBI COULDN'T, OR WOULDN'T, CONNECT THE DOTS

On May 9, 2002, Wright, who worked out of Chicago, called a news conference in Washington to publicly accuse the bureau of gross negligence in investigating terrorists in America, despite orders from FBI director Robert Mueller for him to stay home and stay quiet. At the same time he filed a lawsuit against the bureau in Washington's US District Court accusing the bureau of violating his First Amendment rights by prohibiting him from speaking out about FBI wrongdoing.

He charged senior bureau officials "intentionally and repeatedly thwarted and obstructed" his own efforts to root out terrorists and that they prevented his attempts to file cases that could have broken up their operations.

In the press conference, Wright revealed that he has been given written orders not to disclose what he knew—either in speech or in writing—and that he was threatened in writing with disciplinary action, civil suits, revocation of security clearances, and even criminal prosecution.

"I love America, and likewise I love the FBI, particularly its purpose and mission," agent Wright told newsmen, echoing the thoughts of many bureau personnel. "However, the mission has been seriously jeopardized to the point where American lives have been needlessly lost." "Knowing what I know," Wright added, "I can confidently say that until the investigative responsibilities for terrorism are transferred from the FBI, I will not feel safe."

As might be expected by now, *The 9/11 Commission Report* makes no mention of Wright and his attempt to reveal the truth about Bureau officials blocking terrorist investigations.

Wright's suit was filed just one day after Congress berated the FBI for failing to vigorously act on a July 2001 recommendation from its Phoenix field office that aviation schools should be checked for Middle Easterners seeking flight training.

Counterterrorism experts in Phoenix were concerned after noting that several Middle Eastern men were seeking information on airport operations, security, and flight training. One wrote in a memo to Washington, "FBIHQ should discuss this matter with other elements of the US intelligence community and task the community for any information that supports Phoenix's suspicions."

The memo was written by Phoenix Special Agent Kenneth J. Williams and noted, "Osama bin Laden and Al-Muhjiroun supporters [were] attending civil aviation universities/colleges in Arizona."

FBI officials merely passed the memo, which actually pointed to bin Laden by name, along to about a dozen of its offices for "analysis." There was no follow up on this lapse by the 9/11 Commission.

A much more serious issue concerning the FBI arose when five people, including a former and a current agent, were charged in May, 2002, with using confidential government information to manipulate stock prices and extort money from businesses.

In indictments brought in Brooklyn, San Diego stock adviser Amr Ibrahim Elgindy was accused of bribing FBI agent Jeffrey A. Royer to give him information on publicly traded companies. Royer, who had worked for the FBI between 1996 and 2000, subsequently left the bureau and went to work for Elgindy's firm, Pacific Equity Investigations. Another FBI agent, Lynn Wingate, was also indicted, accused of passing information to Royer and helping to track investigations of Elgindy through FBI computers. Elgindy reportedly supported Muslim refugees in Kosovo.

According to Assistant US Attorney Kenneth Breen, Elgindy tried to sell $300,000 in stock on September 10, 2001, and told his broker the market was about to drop. Breen saw this as evidence of foreknowledge of the 9/11 attacks. However, higher officials claimed there was no hard evidence of such foreknowledge or that Elgindy had obtained insider information from his FBI contacts.

Elgindy's father, Ibrahim Elgindy, founded a consortium of Muslim organizations in Chicago and spearheaded a 1998 protest on behalf of Muhammad A. Salah, whose assets were seized after US investigators linked Salah to Palestine's radical Hamas organization.

Former FBI agent Gary Aldrich described the bureau's top management as "incompetent lunkheads and deadheads." Aldrich too said many opportunities to stop the attack were missed.

Aldrich blamed Bill and Hillary Clinton for the breakdown of the FBI as well as other federal agencies. He said the Clintons' blatant disregard for national security procedures made the government weak and vulnerable and that they showed more concern for political opponents than foreign enemies.

According to several FBI sources, when the Clinton administration ar-

THE FBI COULDN'T, OR WOULDN'T, CONNECT THE DOTS

rived, emphasis in the bureau shifted from antiterrorism to investigating militias, white supremacists, anti-abortion groups and other "right-wing" extremists.

"When I left [the FBI] in 1998, domestic terrorism was the number one priority," said retired agent Ivan C. Smith, former head of the analysis, budget, and training sections of the FBI's National Security Division. "And as far as I know, it was still a higher priority than foreign terrorism on September 11."

With the arrival of the Clintons, FBI probes were aimed everywhere except at foreign terrorists. Veteran agents said some forty boxes of evidence gathered in the 1993 World Trade Center bombing were never analyzed, including almost ten boxes of material from the Philippine side of the investigation.

The Clinton-era disinterest in foreign terrorism was not limited to the FBI. Commerce Department officials told reporter Paul Sperry they were ordered to "sanitize" a Y2K counterterrorism report by removing mention of Islamic threats. Only "right-wing" groups were included in the report.

But on March 23, 2004, Richard A. Clarke, former counterterrorism czar under Clinton and Bush, told CNN's *Inside Politics* a different story about the Clinton administration's terrorism strategy. "I would argue that for what had actually happened prior to 9/11, the Clinton administration was doing a great deal," Clarke said. "In fact, so much that when the Bush people came into office, they thought I was a little crazy, a little obsessed with this little terrorist bin Laden. Why wasn't I focused on Iraqi-sponsored terrorism?" In their appearances before the 9/11 Commission in March 2004, Clarke and former Clinton-era officials defended the Clinton record on al Qaeda, claiming that it was the Bush people and especially Bush's FBI and CIA that dropped the ball immediately after the new administration entered the White House.

Mere negligence or incompetence cannot explain the obvious moves by both the Clinton and early Bush administrations to block any meaningful investigations into foreign terrorism. Many theories have been advanced for this odd behavior, including an argument that no one in high authority wanted to incur the anger of the oil-producing states or even that deep probes might have brought to light deep-rooted business and banking connections. It should also be noted that many of the officials within both the Clinton and early Bush administrations were ranking members of globalist organizations such as the Council on Foreign Relations. These high-level connections have prompted some researchers to suspect that overlapping conspiracies may have taken place regardless of party affiliation.

By mid-2002, even FBI director Robert Mueller was forced to acknowledge that the FBI had missed many "red flags," including the Chicago investigations and the Phoenix memos as well as two from the Oklahoma City office. There, FBI agents and one FBI pilot reported "large numbers" of Middle Eastern men receiving flight training at local airports and warned this activity might be related to "planned terrorist activity."

The revelations of FBI misconduct prompted an unusual two-hour press conference in late May 2002 in which a defensive Mueller told reporters, "There was not a specific warning about an attack on a particular day. But that doesn't mean there weren't red flags out there, there weren't dots that should have been connected to the extent possible." Mueller even admitted that he had misspoken in fall 2001 when he denied the existence of any pre-9/11 attack warnings.

Mueller outlined his plan to reorganize the FBI, which consisted primarily of shifting agents from the War on Drugs to the War on Terrorism and to create a new Office of Intelligence headed by a CIA analyst. Many observers saw this plan as an attempt to merge the FBI and CIA into a terrorist-fighting force that would only bring more centralized authority to Washington. This same plan—to combine the worst of two worlds—was later echoed in the Homeland Security Department legislation.

One government informant, a self-confessed Florida con man named Randy Glass, said he worked undercover for the bureau for more than two years and learned specifically that the World Trade Center twin towers were to be the target of terrorists.

Hoping to lessen a prison term for a conviction of defrauding jewelry wholesalers out of $6 million, in 1998 Glass contacted federal agents and said he could set up illegal arms deals. Aided by veteran Bureau of Alcohol, Tobacco and Firearms agent Dick Stoltz, Glass began to arrange deals with a variety of persons. He claimed he had acquired heavy weapons such as Stinger and TOW missiles stolen from military facilities.

THE FBI COULDN'T, OR WOULDN'T, CONNECT THE DOTS

Business was good but none of the deals seemed to work out until Glass contacted a Pakistani-born New Jersey deli owner. This man helped arrange arms deals with Pakistanis who claimed contacts to Pakistani intelligence, the Taliban, and even Osama bin Laden. Many hours of tapes were made of their meetings.

However, during the lengthy and detailed maneuvering to arrange the financing in early 2001, the Pakistanis grew suspicious and left the country. Only the deli owner and one other man were arrested. The other man pled guilty to trying to sell weaponry and was sentenced to thirty months in jail, while the deli owner went free and his court records were sealed from the public.

ATF agent Stoltz said cases against the men were hampered by the fact that government prosecutors had to remove references to Pakistan in court filings because of diplomatic concerns.

Internet Commentator Allan P. Duncan took note of this case and wrote:

"Between the Fall of 1998 and June 2001, a group of Middle Eastern men living in New Jersey is caught on tape in an ATF weapons sting conspiring to buy millions of dollars of weapons including components for nuclear bombs. Three years after the operation ended, all of the people involved in the deal are free.

"Federal agents who worked on the case were frustrated because it was handled as a criminal case instead of a counterterrorism case. In an in depth look at 'Operation Diamondback' I reveal that one of the suspects who was accused of skimming millions of dollars from a fraudulent HMO to offshore accounts where the money allegedly went to finance terrorism, was defended in the HMO case by a lawyer who later became the Assistant Attorney General in charge of the Criminal Division, under John Ashcroft. The lawyer, Michael Chertoff, was in his position as Assistant Attorney General when Operation Diamondback ended and his client was never arrested even though an intelligence document claimed he and his brother in Egypt had links to Osama Bin Laden.

"Is this why the ATF operation was handled as a criminal case and not a terrorism case by the federal government?"

One of the men Glass taped was the brother of New Jersey neurologist Dr. Magdy Elamir [real name: Magdy El Sayed El Amir] who also said he wanted radioactive materials. Dr. Elamir owned an HMO which was under investigation following a foreign intelligence source accusation that more than $15 million had been siphoned from Elamir's HMO and sent to bin Laden's al Qaeda terrorist network.

"So at this point we now have information that Dr. Magdy Elamir along with his brother Mohamed El Amir have ties to Osama Bin Laden and yet neither one of them is arrested. Randy Glass says in fact that federal agents told him to drop the matter," wrote Duncan.

Chertoff, who participated as a lawyer in two of the investigations into the death of Clinton administration official Vincent Foster, was named in 2005 by President Bush to head the Department of Homeland Security, an odd choice considering Chertoff's actions in the Diamondback operation.

This case took a step closer to the 9/11 attacks when Glass told news reporters that on one occasion in 1999 he met with one of the Pakistanis in the Tribeca Grill in Manhattan. "At the meeting, [he] said Americans are the enemy and they would have no problem blowing up this entire restaurant because it is full of Americans," Glass recounted. "As we left the restaurant, [he] turns and says, 'those towers are coming down.'" The man was indicating the World Trade Center.

But perhaps the most provocative evidence of governmental foreknowledge came from the man who led the prosecution in President Bill Clinton's 1998 impeachment in 1998 as the chief investigative counsel for the judiciary committee in the US House of Representatives.

Chicago attorney David Schippers, who by mid-2002 was representing Wright and other disgruntled FBI employees, said in a late October 2001 interview that he had been approached by FBI agents a month and a half prior to the 9/11 attacks. The agents revealed that they had knowledge that lower Manhattan was to be the object of a terrorist attack using airplanes as flying bombs and they wanted to prevent this.

They were seeking legal advice because their FBI superiors had ordered them off the case and threatened them with the National Security Act if they spoke out. Schippers said he tried in vain to warn Attorney General John Ashcroft.

"[A]gain I used people who were personal friends of John Ashcroft to try to get him. One of them called me back and said, 'All right, I have talked to him. He will call you tomorrow morning.' This was like a month before the bombing. The next morning I got a call. It wasn't from Ashcroft. It was from somebody in the Justice Department...He said, 'We don't start our investigations at the top. Let me look into this and I will get back to you.' As I sit here today [October 10, 2001], I have never heard from him."

Once again, no mention of this incident or even the name of David Schippers, a very prominent Republican attorney, can be found anywhere in *The 9/11 Commission Report*.

Shippers echoed FBI Agent Aldrich's charge that national security precautions were stripped away during the Clinton administration. Speaking of his attempts to warn authorities, Schippers said, "I tried the House, I tried the Senate, I tried the Department of Justice. I didn't go to the FBI because I know there is a roadblock there and I didn't go to the Justice Department until Ashcroft got in there because I know there are roadblocks out there. These are the very same people who put up roadblocks on the attack against the terrorists under Clinton, they are still there. They still constitute, almost like a moat, between the people with the information and the people who should hear the information..."

One particularly damning indictment of both the bureau and the Bush administration came in 2004 when a woman hired as a translator for the FBI revealed that senior US officials knew of al Qaeda's plans to attack targets with aircraft months in advance of 9/11. She claimed that the proper handling of intelligence flowing into the FBI could have prevented the 9/11 attacks and that Condoleezza Rice's statement to the 9/11 Commission regarding no foreknowledge of the attacks was an "outrageous lie."

Sibel Edmonds, a Turkish-American, then 32, explained in a 2004 radio interview, "I started working for the Bureau immediately after 9/11 and I was performing translations for several languages: Farsi, Turkish, and Azerbaijani. And I do have top-secret clearance. And after I started working for the Bureau, most of my translation duties included translations of documents and investigations that actually started way before 9/11.

"The most significant information that we were receiving did not come from counter-terrorism investigations, and I want to emphasize this. It came from counter-intelligence, and certain criminal investigations, and issues that have to do with money laundering operations.

"During my work there I came across some very significant issues that I started reporting in December of 2001 to the mid-level management within the FBI. They said to basically leave it alone, because if they were to get into those issues it would end up being a can of worms. And after I didn't see any response from this mid-level bureaucratic management I took it to higher levels all the way up to [Assistant Director] Dale Watson and Director Mueller. And, again, I was asked not to take this any further and just let it be. And if I didn't do that they would retaliate against me.

"At that point, which would be around February 2002, they came and they confiscated my computer, because, they said, they were suspecting that I was communicating with certain Senate members and taking this issue outside the Bureau. And, at that point, I was not. They did not find anything in my computer after they confiscated it. And they asked me to take a polygraph as to the allegations and reports I'd made. I volunteered and I took the polygraph and passed it without a glitch. They have already confirmed this publicly."

In March 2002, Edmonds was fired by the FBI for reporting shoddy work and security breaches to her supervisors that could have prevented those attacks. She remains under two court gag orders that forbid her from testifying in court or mentioning the names of the people or the countries involved. After her firing, Edmonds took her information to the Senate Judiciary Committee, which requested an investigation by the Department of Justice Inspector General's office. Today, the findings of this investigation have not been made public, citing concerns of "national security." Furthermore, at least four attempts to bring Edmonds' gag order into court were rejected with no explanation.

Finally, on Tuesday, July 6, 2004, Judge Reggie Walton dismissed her case. "Under his ruling, I, an American citizen, am not entitled to pursue my 1st and 5th Amendment rights guaranteed under the Constitution of the United States," lamented Edmonds. "The vague reasoning cited, without any explanation, is to protect 'certain diplomatic relations for national security.' Judge Walton reached this decision after sitting on this case with no activity for almost two years. He arrived at this decision without allowing my attorney and I any due process: NO status hearing,

NO briefings, NO oral argument, and NO discovery [emphasis in the original]. He made his decision after allowing the government attorneys to present their case to him, privately, in camera, ex parte; we were not allowed to participate in these cozy sessions. Is this the American system of justice we believe in? Is this the due process we read about in our civics 101 courses? Is this the judicial branch of our government that is supposed to be separate from the other two branches in order to protect the people's rights and freedom?

"This court decision by itself would have been appalling and alarming enough, but in light of all other actions taken against my case for the past two years it demonstrates a broken system, a system abused and corrupted by the current executive, a system badly in need of repair."

"This [suppression of her case] was mainly for the reason of accountability," Edmonds said. "As you know... to this day, not a single person has been held accountable [for the failures of 9/11]. And certain issues, yes, they were due to a certain level of incompetence. But there were certain other issues—you know they keep talking about this 'wall,' and not having communication. I beg to differ on that, because there are certain instances where the Bureau is being asked by the State Department not to pursue certain investigations or certain people or certain targets of an investigation—simply citing 'diplomatic relations.' And what happens is, instead of targeting those people who are directly related to these illegal terrorist activities, they just let them walk free."

It should be pointed out in this connection that according to multiple knowledgeable sources, the State Department has been under the control of the Council on Foreign Relations (CFR) since before World War II. Ranking CFR members filled both the Clinton and Bush administrations.

"I have seen several top targets for these investigations of these terrorist activities that were allowed to leave the country," Edmonds continued. "I'm not talking about weeks, I'm talking about months after 9/11...I can tell you that there is so much involvement, that if they did let this information out, and if they were to hold real investigations...we would see several significant high level criminal prosecutions in this country. And that is something that they are not going to let out. And, believe me; they will do everything to cover this up."

It would appear that Edmonds' words were prophetic. Despite her three and a half hours of testimony to the 9/11 Commission, there was only one reference to her in a footnote buried on page 473 of their 567-page report. Far from mentioning any of her serious charges, the note merely indicated the need for "quality control" of FBI translations.

In a scathing letter to 9/11 Commission Chairman Thomas Kean after the report was issued, Edmonds noted several incidents that indicated advance knowledge of the 9/11 attack within the FBI and added, "...I must assume that other serious issues I am not aware of were in the same manner [as her testimony] omitted from your report. These omissions cast doubt on the validity of your report and therefore on its conclusions and recommendations."

The muzzling of Sibel Edmonds at the highest levels of the federal government prompted US Senators Patrick Leahy (D-VT) and Charles Grassley (R-IA) to write then Attorney General John Ashcroft stating, "...we fear that the designation of information as classified in some cases [such as Sibel Edmonds] serves to protect the executive branch against embarrassing revelations and full accountability...Releasing declassified versions of these reports, or at least portions or summaries, would serve the public's interest, increase transparency, promote effectiveness and efficiency at the FBI, and facilitate Congressional oversight."

It is now clear that still other bureau employees also tried to send warnings upstairs regarding the flight training of terrorists but got nowhere. In August 2001, the FBI arrested Zacarias Moussaoui, the so-called 20th hijacker, after a Minnesota flight school warned the bureau that Moussaoui appeared to be the type of person who might fly a plane loaded with fuel into a building.

FBI Special Agent Harry Samit followed up by writing more than one memo to superiors stating that Moussaoui, a French citizen of Moroccan descent, was the type of individual to take a plane and hijack it, perhaps even fly it into the World Trade Center. He also noted that Moussaoui told a flight instructor that he only wanted to learn to maneuver a Boeing 747 but did not need to learn how to land it.

CBS's *60 Minutes II* reported on May 8, 2002, that a ranking French jurist and terrorist expert had also sent a report on Moussaoui, a French citizen, to the FBI weeks before 9/11.

THE FBI COULDN'T, OR WOULDN'T, CONNECT THE DOTS

US authorities denied there was anything in the report to alert them. One FBI supervisor even questioned the French report, asking how many men named Zacarias Moussaoui must live in France. When informed that there was only one listed in Paris, the supervisory special agent continued to stall any action.

Meanwhile, FBI attorneys turned down or blocked repeated requests from their agents in the Minneapolis field office to search Moussaoui's computer and apartment. If they had, they would have found numerous small knives, jumbo-jet pilot manuals, the names of flight schools and other clues that might have sounded an alarm.

As a result of all this inaction, Moussaoui was simply held on immigration charges until after 9/11 when FBI agents finally were able to make their search. They recovered incriminating financial records linking Moussaoui to al Qaeda, flight simulators, and information on crop dusters.

Moussaoui, whose trial was postponed until early 2003, was known as the "twentieth hijacker" based on the theory that he was to replace an original "twentieth hijacker," Ramzi bin al-Shibh, a former roommate of Mohamed Atta, who reportedly sent $14,000 to Moussaoui. Al-Shibh, who also was unable to gain entry into the United States, was arrested in Pakistan in late September 2002. Moussaoui and al-Shibh were the only two men in custody believed to be directly involved in the 9/11 attacks.

The feds were further embarrassed in 2002 when government prosecutors left forty-eight classified documents, summaries of FBI interviews, with Moussaoui. They were later found in searches of Moussaoui's Alexandria, Virginia, jail cell.

Moussaoui eventually pled guilty to six charges in connection with the 9/11 attacks and was sentenced to life in a maximum security prison in 2006, to the disappointment of prosecutors seeking the death penalty. Previously, he had been thrown out of court more than once for creating a scene and reportedly shouting, "I am al Qaeda!"

FBI Special Agent Hamit, who arrested Moussaoui prior to the 9/11 attacks, caused a brief sensation during the penalty phase of the trial when he stated in court that his superiors in the bureau were guilty of "criminal negligence and obstruction" for blocking his attempts to learn if Moussaoui was part of a group planning to hijack aircraft in the

United States.

Samit said under cross-examination, "They [FBI superiors] obstructed it." He said this was a calculated management decision "that cost us the opportunity to stop the attacks."

Such top-side interference in the Moussaoui case briefly made headlines in the late spring of 2002 with the publication of a scathing thirteen-page letter from FBI special agent and Minneapolis chief division counsel Coleen M. Rowley to Director Robert Mueller. In her May 21 letter, Rowley, a twenty-one-year veteran of the bureau, described a top-heavy FBI management bureaucracy riddled with "many who were failures as street agents" and "careerists" who placed advancing their own careers over integrity and truth.

"I know I shouldn't be flippant about this, but jokes were actually made that the key FBIHQ personnel had to be spies or moles like Robert Hanssen, who were actually working for Osama bin Laden, to have so undercut Minneapolis's effort...

"I have deep concerns that a delicate and subtle shading/skewing of facts by you and others at the highest levels of FBI management has occurred and is occurring in an effort to avoid or minimize personal and/or institutional embarrassment on the part of the FBI and/or perhaps even for improper political reasons," she told Mueller. She added, "I'm hard pressed to think of any case which has been solved by FBIHQ personnel and I can name several that have been screwed up!"

Rowley, after hearing the news media continually quote Director Mueller as saying the bureau would have taken action if only they had had advance warning of the attacks, sent a message informing him of the intelligence sitting in the Minneapolis files. She said when the same denials of knowledge continued, she and other agents again attempted to inform Mueller of the facts.

"Finally, when similar comments were made weeks later we faced the sad realization that the remarks indicated someone, possibly with your approval, had decided to circle the wagons at FBIHQ in an apparent effort to protect the FBI from embarrassment and the relevant FBI officials from scrutiny," Rowley wrote the director.

She also pointed out that the only difference between incidents when informed FBI agents were denied a search warrant on Moussaoui and when one was approved was the fact of the 9/11 attacks, events that certainly could not be swept under the rug.

Rowley was one of many persons who pointed out the fact that FBI headquarters personnel "were privy to many more sources of intelligence information than field division agents." Despite this fact, she said, "key FBIHQ personnel whose job it was to assist and coordinate with field division agents on terrorism investigations continued to, almost inexplicably, throw up roadblocks and undermine Minneapolis's by-now desperate efforts to obtain a FISA [Foreign Intelligence Surveillance Act] search warrant, long after the French Intelligence Service provided its information and probable cause became clear."

Even after the 9/11 attacks had occurred, Rowley said higher authorities still would not untie their hands. Taking a call from a bureau superior just after the attacks had begun, Rowley said she told him in light of the attacks it would be the "hugest coincidence" if Moussaoui were not involved with the terrorists. Her superior replied that coincidence was the right term; it was just that and the Minneapolis office should not do anything without headquarters' permission because "we might 'screw up' something else going on elsewhere in the country."

Rowley's insightful and damning critique of FBI inefficiency in light of the 9/11 attacks prompted widespread, though brief, mass media coverage. Now a well-known federal whistleblower, Rowley was selected as a "person of the year" by *Time* magazine in 2002. Yet, her testimony to the 9/11 Commission was not made public, and she was relegated to one fleeting footnote on page 557 in its report.

One Internet columnist noted that the Bush administration took advantage of the cover of the "Rowley firestorm" to announce a reversal of some of the government's meager rules against indiscriminate domestic spying, rules prompted by the many abuses of the FBI during the 1960s.

Steve Perry with *CounterPunch*, a biweekly newsletter, commented that the Bush team defused Rowley's revelations by choosing that time to announce plans to reorganize the entire intelligence apparatus. Such a move would be time consuming and require much preparation, yet the administration requested no funding for its proposal. According to Perry, this tactic indicated that the timing of the announcement may indeed have been meant to distract attention from Rowley's accusations.

It might also be added that any failures at the FBI cannot be laid off on lower level agents and supervisors. In August 2001, Attorney General Ashcroft, apparently more concerned with the long-lost War on Drugs and pornography, had turned down a bureau request for $50 million to beef up its counterterrorism efforts. All critical information flowing upward within the FBI routinely ended at the desks of Director Mueller and his boss, Ashcroft, both of whom worked closely with President Bush in the period up to the events of 9/11.

MISSED OPPORTUNITIES AT THE CIA

By all accounts the CIA also received a large share of the pre-attack warnings. By some accounts the agency intentionally blocked access to critical information—or worse, may have been covertly setting up "terrorist" patsies for later service in false-flag activities.

Like the FBI, the CIA has its own electronic eavesdropping satellite and computer system, noted earlier, called "Echelon." This system tracks international telephone calls, faxes and email messages all around the world. It was so secret that the government would neither confirm nor deny its existence until 2001. According to a study by the European Union, Echelon accumulates electronic transmissions like a vacuum cleaner using keyword search software in conjunction with massive computer data banks.

The Echelon system, headquartered in the United States with the National Security Agency at Fort Meade, Maryland, has caused protests in several nations, excluding the United States whose population rarely sees any news concerning this powerful global wiretapping system.

In 2000, French prosecutor Jean-Pierre Dintilhac ordered his country's counterintelligence agency to see if Echelon was being used to steal foreign business secrets, to spy on citizens, and to see if it was "harmful to the vital interests of the nation." The Italian Parliament also opened inquiries into Echelon, saying, "The scope is not military." According to a German newspaper, the *Frankfurter Allgemeine Zeitung*, the Echelon spy system provided both US and Israeli intelligence services warning of the impending terrorist attacks at least three months before the fact. The newspaper reported that Echelon, with its 120 satellites, has been used extensively by Israeli intelligence to monitor Arab terrorist groups.

Largely unreported in the American media was a story that Osama bin Laden himself was overheard telling his stepmother on September 9, 2001, "In two days you're going to hear big news and you're not going to hear from me for a while." This telephone interception, publicly attributed to a "foreign intelligence service," undoubtedly was the product of Echelon. Yet apparently no one in America's defense establishment was alerted to bin Laden's "big news."

The CIA also had another high-tech weapon in their arsenal for use against terrorists. The "Predator," an unmanned surveillance aircraft system consisting of four aircraft, a ground control station (GCS), a primary satellite link communication suite and 55 people. Predator drones had been used under the Clinton administration to track the movements of Osama bin Laden. There had even been talk of using the craft to unleash Hellfire missiles on the al Qaeda leader.

Following the attacks of 9/11, such talk turned into action. An armed Predator was used to attack a convoy of sport utility vehicles in Afghanistan thought to be carrying al Qaeda leaders on February 7, 2002. On November 3, 2002, the CIA used a Hellfire missile fired from a Predator to attack a car in Yemen, killing Qaed Senyan al-Harthi, an al Qaeda leader thought to be responsible for the USS Cole bombing. Reportedly, this was the first direct US strike in the War on Terrorism outside Afghanistan.

About a year later, an RQ-1 Predator was used to attack a remote village in the southern Ghazni Province of Afghanistan thought to be the hideout of Taliban supporters. Nine children and a 25-year-old man were killed in the strike, which failed to kill the intended target. Afghanistan's president Hamid Karzai stated that he was "profoundly shocked" by the CIA attack and demanded closer coordination with Afghan authorities on all future military strikes.

By 2005, the CIA's use of unmanned Predators was becoming more effective. Haitham al-Yemeni, an al Qaeda explosives expert from Yemen, was killed in a village in northwest Pakistan by a Predator again firing a Hellfire missile. On December 3, 2005, a Predator reportedly killed ranking al Qaeda chief Abu Hamza Rabia while sleeping in Haisori, Pakistan. Four others were also killed. On January 13, 2006, several

Predators rained missiles on the Pakistani village of Damadola thought to contain al Qaeda's second-in-command Ayman al-Zawahiri. The CIA drone planes reportedly fired 10 missiles killing 18 civilians, including five women and five children.

There is enticing evidence that ties Osama bin Laden directly to the CIA back at the time the agency was funding and training fighters against the Soviets in Afghanistan. While it has been widely acknowledged that the CIA helped found and fund the al Qaeda network during the Soviet invasion of Afghanistan, the agency steadfastly denied any direct dealings with bin Laden. Despite these denials, there is considerable evidence of prior CIA and Bush family involvement with the bin Laden family going back several decades as will be described later. Many researchers believe the CIA groomed Osama bin Laden for years in preparation for some future need.

For example, one Internet source claimed that bin Laden, under the name Tim Osman, actually was brought to the United States in the late spring of 1986 for a meeting with government agents at the Hilton Hotel in Sherman Oaks, California. Former FBI senior special agent Ted L. Gunderson confirmed this meeting and said he was one of the attendees.

Gunderson said he was contacted by a "top figure" in the Reagan administration and asked to meet with Afghan insurgents to "see what we might do to help them." The four men at the hotel meeting, according to Gunderson, were himself, a quiet Tim Osman (bin Laden), computer expert Michael Riconosciuto, a CIA scientific "asset" with connections in the arms business, and a man identified as Ralph Olberg, who was purchasing weapons on behalf of the Afghan Mujahideen.

Gunderson said conversation during the hour-and-a-half meeting was mostly between Olberg and Riconosciuto while Osman/bin Laden "sat silent in a corner of the room." He added that he was unaware of what, if any, deal was sealed during the meeting but that he is "certain in my own mind" that arrangements were made to provide arms for bin Laden and the Arab fighters. Gunderson's guess has been proven true as it is a historic fact that the CIA supplied both arms and training for bin Laden's fighters in Afghanistan. It should be noted, however, that Gunderson's credibility is questionable.

According to a former staffer of Republican senator David Durenberger, Olberg was a man often seen in the senator's office during the Reagan years talking about the plight of the Afghan people.

Riconosciuto, also tight with Republican bigwigs, had been involved in the development of the PROMIS software initially planned for use against criminals and terrorists. But this promising software soon turned into a scandal when its creator charged that US Government officials, including then-Attorney General Bill Casey, had stolen the software and used it to create a "back door" into computers in both foreign governments and domestic corporations. It was also alleged that the stolen software was used for insider trading including that which preceded the 9/11 attacks as described in the next section. Osama bin Laden is suspected of using the PROMIS software to elude captors and to spy on his enemies.

But by the mid-1990s, the Soviets were out of Afghanistan, the Saudis were our oil friends and, with the exception of certain counterterrorism units, little notice was taken of Osama bin Laden. The CIA, like their brethren in the FBI, apparently became somewhat complacent at the lower levels thanks to the near constant stream of tips, warnings, and information. Workers not actively involved in counterterrorism took a cue from their superiors and never got too serious about terrorism.

And it wasn't as if prior warnings had all proven false. Almost a year before the deadly 1998 bombings of the US embassies in Kenya and Tanzania, an al Qaeda member had warned CIA officials of the coming attacks. The informant's information was dismissed as unreliable and nothing was done.

Though admittedly vague, there was even a warning in a September 1999 National Intelligence Council (NIC) report, which foresaw events similar to the 9/11 attacks. This NIC report, entitled "Sociology and Psychology of Terrorism: Who Becomes a Terrorist and Why?" was prepared by about a dozen senior intelligence officers. The NIC was attached to the CIA.

"Suicide bomber(s) belonging to al Qaeda's Martyrdom Battalion could crash land an aircraft packed with high explosives (C-4 and semtex) into the Pentagon, the headquarters of the Central Intelligence Agency (CIA) or the White House," stated the report, which was issued exactly two years before 9/11.

"This information was out there," noted Robert L. Worden, chief of the Federal Research Division, which prepared the report from open sources, "certainly to those who study the in-depth subject of terrorism and al Qaeda."

In January 2000, Malaysian security agents conducted surveillance of al Qaeda operatives meeting in Kuala Lumpur at the behest of the CIA. One of the operatives was Khalid al-Midhar. It was determined that al-Midhar had a multiple-entry visa to the United States.

CIA agents also found that al-Midhar was traveling with a Saudi, Nawaf al-Hazmi, who had previously entered the United States. Neither man was placed on the State Department "watch list" until August 23, 2001, far too late to prevent their participation in the 9/11 attacks.

Another example of CIA incompetence, if that's what it was, can be found in the case of Khalid Sheikh Mohammed, who, since the capture of Abu Zubaydah in Pakistan in the spring of 2002, was considered the highest-ranking member of the al Qaeda network still at large, as well as a primary planner of the 9/11 attacks.

Mohammed was so highly placed in bin Laden's organization that the joint congressional committee looking into intelligence failures in the fall of 2002 took special notice of him. But they were so stymied by restrictions on classified material that they could only refer to Mohammed as a "key al Qaeda leader," even though the man was identified as a terrorist chief as far back as 1995.

The joint committee criticized the CIA's handling of Mohammed's case, stating, "there was little analytic focus given to him and coordination amongst intelligence agencies was irregular at best." One US intelligence official disputed this charge but told a *New York Times* reporter, "We had identified him as a major al Qaeda operative before September 11."

Such mishandling continued after 9/11 when it was reported that Mohammed was captured on March 1, 2003, following a nighttime shootout in Rawalpindi, Pakistan. US officials expressed jubilation over the arrest but their celebration faded swiftly as questions arose. Witnesses did not agree with the official account and foreign media speculated that Mohammed may have been misidentified, killed at an earlier date, or might even still be on the loose. Oddly, despite these doubts, Khalid Sheikh Mohammed—supposedly now in US custody and a key informant to the US government—is cited more frequently than any other insider as a crucial source for the narrative of *The 9/11 Commission Report.* In fact, by author Griffin's count, Khalid Shaikh Mohammed is cited 272 times in the report, despite the fact that no corroborating evidence has ever been provided as to the fact of his capture, or even the veracity of his testimony to the government.

Author Mike Ruppert even went so far as to name Khalid Sheikh Mohammed as one of the top-level al Qaeda chieftains who may have actually been double agents—trained, funded and continuing to work for the CIA. "[Khalid Sheikh Mohammed and others] worked to further an agenda originating out of Washington, strongly influenced by Tel Aviv, rather than out of some ill-defined Muslim hatred of the US," Ruppert wrote.

Mohamed Atta, the accused chief hijacker, was also named by Ruppert as a double agent secretly working for US intelligence. Atta reportedly was under surveillance by US military intelligence agents who had identified him as an al Qaeda ringleader more than a year prior to his visit to the United States for flying lessons.

This astounding fact, only made public in mid-2005, came from a highly classified anti-terrorism program named "Able Danger" formed under the US Special Operations Command (SOCOM) in October 2004. The Able Danger team specifically targeted al Qaeda for investigation. Prior to the 9/11 attacks the Able Danger team identified Mohamed Atta and three other named 9/11 hijackers as possible members of an al Qaeda cell.

This revelation appeared to contradict government claims that no one in US intelligence had identified Atta as a terrorist before 9/11, although it is unclear if senior government officials were given information regarding Atta in either the Clinton or early Bush administrations.

What is clear is that this case of forewarning was presented to the 9/11 Commission who chose not to mention it in their report. It is also noteworthy that in an unprecedented action, Gen. Pete Schoomaker, one of the officers in charge of Able Danger, was brought out of retirement and made Army chief of staff in 2003.

Upset over claims by 9/11 Commission members that they had not been given critical information concerning Able Danger and its capabilities, Rep. Curt Weldon (R-PA) in the summer of 2005 wrote to the former chairman and vice-chairman of the 9/11 Commission reminding them that commission staffers had received two briefings on Able Danger, once in October, 2003, and another in July, 2004. "The impetus for this letter is my extreme disappointment in the recent, and false, claim of the 9/11 commission staff that the commission was never given access to any information on Able Danger," wrote Weldon. "The 9/11 commission staff received not one but two briefings on Able Danger from former team members, yet did not pursue the matter."

Commission Vice-Chairman Lee Hamilton said staff workers indicated that they could not recall being briefed on Able Danger and that no mention of the program was included in their report because the commission had no "information that the United States government had under surveillance or had any knowledge of Mohamed Atta prior to the attacks."

"[Able Danger] Team members believed that the Atta cell in Brooklyn should be subjected to closer scrutiny, but somewhere along the food chain of administration bureaucrats and lawyers, a decision was made in late 2000 against passing the information to the FBI," Weldon stated in his letter to the commission. If the Able Danger intelligence on Atta and his al Qaeda ties was available in 2000, it would be critical to determine who then blocked this information from going to the FBI. But, as usual, there was no investigative follow-up to this information, so damning to official denials of foreknowledge, and which seemed to point to the possibility that Atta was being protected by US intelligence.

US surveillance of Atta was even reported in European publications long before the Able Danger issue arose. As early as 2001, the German magazine *Focus* reported that US agents, referred to as FBI in some accounts and CIA in others, monitored Atta from January to May 2000 after he was seen buying large quantities of chemicals thought to be used for making bombs. According to the article, the US agents never informed German authorities of Atta's presence or of any suspicions about him.

One of the most outrageous accounts of CIA pre-9/11 activity actually involved Osama bin Laden. One month after the attacks, the French daily *Le Figaro* reported that bin Laden had been treated at an American hospital in the Arab emirate of Dubai in July 2001, and while there was visited by a local CIA agent. According to this report, bin Laden was flown from the Quetta airport in Pakistan to Dubai, where he was admitted to the American hospital located between the Al-Garhoud and Al-Maktoum bridges. He was taken to the urology department for treatment of a kidney infection. The article stated that bin Laden had had mobile kidney dialysis equipment shipped to his hideaway in Pakistan as far back as early 2000.

Furthermore, it went on to say that during his stay at the hospital, between July 4 and 14, bin Laden received visits from family members and prominent Saudis and Emiratis. "During the hospital stay, the local CIA agent, known to many in Dubai, was seen taking the main elevator of the hospital to go to bin Laden's hospital room," stated the *Le Figaro* article, adding, "A few days later, the CIA man bragged to a few friends about having visited bin Laden. Authorized sources say that on July 15th, the day after bin Laden returned to Quetta, the CIA agent was called back to headquarters."

Bin Laden, with both a price on his head and eligible for execution under a last-minute order from outgoing president Bill Clinton, nevertheless was allowed to fly without hindrance from Dubai by private jet on July 14.

The article also reported that in late August, customs agents in Dubai notified both American and French authorities of the arrest of Djamel Beghal. Under interrogation, Beghal said he had been ordered to bomb the US embassy in Paris by al Qaeda leader Abu Zubaydah in Afghanistan. "According to Arab diplomatic sources as well as French intelligence, very specific information was transmitted to the CIA with respect to terrorist attacks against American interests around the world, including US soil," stated the French piece. While this story made the rounds in the European media, nothing but a few scattered Internet reports circulated in the United States. In Europe, CIA officials denied the story.

It is either true or false. If it is false, the American public needs to know this, so that such untruths can be stopped and not distract from the "War on Terrorism." If it is true, then the American people need to know that their own CIA let the world's most wanted man walk away unmolested two months prior to the deadly 9/11 attacks. Yet no major American media organization apparently could spare one good reporter to travel to Dubai to check with the hospital staff and others to confirm the story.

The story of the CIA and bin Laden in Dubai is reinforced by a story in the December 23, 2001, edition of the *Washington Post*, which reported that the CIA had recruited a team of Afghan agents to track bin Laden's movements in their country beginning in early 1998. This effort continued right up until September 11, 2001. According to the paper, these agents sent the CIA daily reports on bin Laden's whereabouts but agency officials often dismissed the information because it sometimes conflicted with other intelligence information.

CIA foreknowledge was also obliquely admitted in April 2002 by its own deputy director, James L. Pavitt. In a speech to the Duke University Law School Conference, Pavitt was simultaneously trying to excuse his agency's failure to prevent 9/11 while touting its efficiency.

"We had very, very good intelligence of the general structure and strategies of the al Qaeda terrorist organization. We knew and we warned that al Qaeda was planning a major strike. There is no question about that," Pavitt told his audience. His speech later was posted on the CIA's website.

Yet Pavitt tried to echo the administration's claim that there was not enough specific intelligence to prevent the 9/11 attacks. He added that within days of the attacks CIA operatives were "on the ground" operating in Afghanistan. "None of this came easy," he explained. "You cannot learn Pashtun overnight and you can't truly understand the complexities of tribalism, regionalism and personalism in Afghanistan by reading the newspaper or a learned book. My people learned about this by years of study and years of practice often in difficult, hostile and, yes indeed, on the ground in Afghanistan itself.

"If you hear somebody say, and I have, the CIA abandoned Afghanistan after the Soviets left and that we never paid any attention to that place until September 11th, I would implore you to ask those people how we were able to accomplish all we did since the Soviets departed. How we knew who to approach on the ground, which operations, which warlord to support, what information to collect. Quite simply, we were there well before the 11th of September."

In early 2005, the results of an internal CIA investigation were made

MISSED OPPORTUNITIES AT THE CIA

public. In a report by CIA Inspector General (IG) John Helgerson, former Agency officials, particularly former intelligence chief George Tenet and former deputy director of operations James L. Pavitt, were criticized for the failure to foresee the 9/11 attacks. Both Tenet and Pavitt had resigned from the CIA in the summer of 2004. The IG's report was requested by Congress in December, 2002, when it asked "whether and to what extent personnel at all levels should be held accountable" for failure to prevent or stop the attacks. Oddly, Tenet had recently been awarded the Presidential Medal of Freedom by President Bush in a special ceremony at the White House on December 14, 2004.

In this connection it is worth remembering that senior government officials had received this report on Osama bin Laden in July, 2001, also quoted earlier: "Based on a review of all-source reporting over the last five months, we believe that [bin Laden] will launch a significant terrorist attack against US and/or Israeli interests in the coming weeks. The attack will be spectacular and designed to inflict mass casualties against US facilities or interests. Attack preparations have been made. Attack will occur with little or no warning."

Even President Bush was fully briefed during this time frame. On July 5, 2001, President Bush received a briefing at his Crawford, Texas, ranch that mentioned the possibility of an airline hijacking as a domestic threat. This information was not made public until nearly nine months after the attacks.

But the most startling revelation of Bush's foreknowledge regarding the attacks did not come until 2004. For nearly two years the Bush administration had attempted to block public access to some of President Bush's Presidential Daily Brief reports (PDB). After much legal wrangling, the 9/11 Commission finally obtained these reports in 2004. One in particular, the PDB for August 6, 2001, makes it clear why someone did not want this report made public. The threat, as detailed in this briefing report, was both clear and imminent.

The PDB headline read "Bin Laden Determined To Strike in US". Items detailed in the report, which will be examined later, included the desire of bin Laden to strike Washington; that al Qaeda had support members including US citizens training for attacks; and that bin Laden had wanted to hijack US aircraft in 1998.

The PDB report added that "FBI information since that time [1998] indicates patterns of suspicious activity in this country consistent with preparations for hijackings or other types of attacks, including recent surveillance of federal buildings in New York."

Yet, despite these warnings, when four jetliners went off course on the morning of September 11, there was little or no immediate reaction.

Thomas H. Kean, chairman of the 9/11 Commission, admitted to the possibility that the attacks could have been prevented but saw no design in the voluminous evidence of foreknowledge.

"My feeling is a whole number of circumstances, had they been different, might have prevented 9/11," Kean said during a TV network interview. "They involve everything from how people got into the country to failures in the intelligence system."

This picture of missed opportunities to stop the 9/11 attacks was darkened further in early 2005 when the Bush administration released a declassified 120-page report to the National Archives detailing how the FAA had received 52 intelligence reports between April and September, 2001, warning of impending attacks. This report, blocked by the Bush administration until more than five months after the release of *The 9/11 Commission Report*, mentioned both bin Laden and al Qaeda by name and the possibility of hijacked aircraft being used as weapons.

Major airports were warned in the spring of 2001 of the possibility that "the intent of the hijacker [may not be] to exchange hostages for prisoners, but to commit suicide in a spectacular explosion…"

The report, only declassified in late January 2005, still contained "heavy redactions" in some areas. It provided more heat in the struggle between the administration and the FAA. The FAA came under attack in the 9/11 Commission's final report for reported failures on September 11, 2001. The 2005 report stated that FAA officials were "lulled into a false sense of security," although it did note that then FAA Administrator Jane F. Garvey told 9/11 commissioners "that she was aware of the heightened threat during the summer of 2001" but that other senior aviation officials, airline officials and veteran pilots were not.

The 2005 report quoted extensively from FAA circulars distributed to some airports although many of these references were blacked out.

Despite the FAA circulars and a barrage of information on the Internet and in the foreign press, the corporate mass media failed to respond until mid-2002, when complaints from CIA and FBI agents and certain members of Congress became too loud to ignore. Even then, they danced around the subject of all the missed clues and cues.

"Because Bush has long insisted he had no inkling of the attacks, the disclosures [in 2002] touched off a media stampede in a capital long deprived of scandal. The fact that the nation's popular war president might have been warned a little over a month before September 11—and that the supposedly straight-talking Bushies hadn't told anyone about it—opened up a serious credibility gap for the first time in the war on terror," wrote *Newsweek* writers Michael Hirsh and Michael Isikoff.

Inflated budgets, further centralization of intelligence functions, and adding more intelligence and law enforcement manpower will add nothing to the search for true national security until the American people demand an honest accounting concerning how our government behaved before and during the 9/11 attacks. The record clearly shows that there was a great deal of foreknowledge of what was to come and even covert contact with the alleged hijackers, yet very little commitment at the highest level to stopping the attacks—in fact, there appeared to be a willingness to allow them to happen.

SELLING STOCKS SHORT INDICATES FOREKNOWLEDGE

Studying recent financial history, one gets the distinct idea that when an event is planned by elite insiders that will dramatically affect the stock market, some greedy individuals with inside connections cannot resist the temptation to profit from others' tragedy.

In 1963, in the wake of the assassination of President John F. Kennedy, the New York Stock Exchange recorded a record $21 billion advance, making for the largest single-day rise in the history of the market. It was estimated that the short selling of stock earned unidentified speculators more than $500 million.

Similar suspicious stock trades were reported following the 9/11 attacks. These activities, which implied foreknowledge of the attacks, were loudly trumpeted in the mass media at the time. However, within weeks, this incredible story of high-level profiteering based on the short selling of certain stocks dropped off the corporate mass media's radar screen never to be heard from again.

The evidence of widespread short selling of airline stocks and other forms of insider trading just prior to September 11, 2001 is compelling. Just as there is growing evidence that many insiders had foreknowledge of these attacks, there are clear indications that some used this prior knowledge—not only to profit directly from the deaths of thousands of people—but to do so with the assurance that they would not be caught in such evil machinations. They would also have to have been in a position to know that the attacks would succeed.

Elementary logic also indicated that direct involvement of al Qaeda terrorists in such insider trading was highly unlikely. The idea that Osama bin Laden or al Qaeda leaders would telegraph their intentions through easily tracked stock trades before their attack is implausible, to put it mildly.

Selling stocks short involves having your broker sell shares you don't yet own at a set price to a given buyer, while betting—or perhaps knowing—you can actually acquire them later at a lower price and supply them to the buyer at the set price within a prescribed short time. If you "bet" right, the difference in price is your profit. This procedure is risky and you can lose at this game, but you can also win big, especially if you have foreknowledge of an event which will impact the market. Historically, if short selling precedes a traumatic event, it is considered to be an indication of foreknowledge.

Although strictly denied by the US government, it is widely known that the CIA uses the PROMIS computer software to routinely monitor stock trades—in real time—as a possible warning sign of a terrorist attack or suspicious economic behavior. We can safely infer that the CIA could have known in virtual real time, from such trading data alone, that the 9/11 attack was imminent and that it would involve two specific airlines. It also follows that they should also have been able to pinpoint the inside traders through the electronic trail.

It was initially reported by the Israeli Herzliya International Policy Institute for Counterterrorism, a think tank involving former Israeli intel-

SELLING STOCKS SHORT INDICATES FOREKNOWLEDGE

ligence officers, that insiders made nearly $16 million profit by short-selling shares in American and United Airlines, the two airlines that suffered the hijackings, as well as the investment firm of Morgan Stanley, which occupied twenty-two floors of the WTC.

According to many other sources, the scandal was much greater even than this. Phil Erlanger, the founder of a Florida firm that tracks short selling and options trading, estimated that traders made off with billions rather than millions of dollars in profit by short selling stocks they knew would tumble in the aftermath of the WTC and Pentagon attacks.

Andreas von Bülow, a former member of the German Parliament and ranking member of the German secret service, estimated profits made by insider traders at $15 billion. CBS offered a far more conservative figure when it reported on Sept 26, 2001, that, "at least seven countries are dissecting suspicious trades that may have netted more than $100 million in profits."

A week after the September 11 attacks, the London *Times* reported that the CIA had asked regulators for the Financial Services Authority in London to investigate the suspicious sales of millions of shares of stock just prior to the terrorist acts. It was hoped that the business paper trail might lead to the terrorists. The *Times* said market regulators in Germany, Japan, and the United States all had received information concerning the short selling of insurance, airlines, and investment banking stocks, all of which fell sharply in the wake of the attacks.

City of London broker and analyst Richard Crossley noted that certain parties had sold shares in unusually large quantities beginning three weeks before the assault on the WTC and Pentagon. Crossley stated that on the Friday preceding the attacks, more than 10 million shares in the US investment bank Merrill Lynch were sold, compared with 4 million on a normal trading day. "What is more awful than he should aim a stiletto blow at the heart of Western financial markets?" he added. "But to profit from it. Words fail me."

Stock market regulators in Germany also reported suspicious short selling just prior to September 11.

In the United States, there was an unusually high volume of five-year US Treasury note purchases made just prior to 9/11. *The Wall Street Journal* on October 2, 2001, noted, "Five-year Treasury notes are among the best investments in the event of a world crisis, especially one that hits the US."

"This could very well be insider trading at the worst, most horrific, most evil use you've ever seen in your entire life, or this would be one of the most extraordinary coincidences in the history of mankind, if it was a coincidence," said *Bloomberg Business News* writer Dylan Ratigan.

What are the specifics? Just prior to the 9/11 attacks, there were an unusually high number of "put" options purchased for the stocks of AMR Corp. and UAL Corp., the parent firms of American and United Airlines. A put option gives the bearer the right to sell at a specified price before a certain date. Just like short selling, placing a put option is betting that the stock will fall in price.

According to pioneer 9/11 researcher and former LA police detective Michael Ruppert, between September 6 and 7, 2001, the Chicago Board of Options Exchange reported 4,744 put options on UAL but only 396 call options. On September 10, there were 4,516 put options placed on American Airlines compared to only 748 calls. (Calls reflect the belief that the stock will increase in worth.) American's 6,000 percent jump in put options on the day before the attacks was not matched by any other airlines.

"No similar trading in any other airlines occurred on the Chicago Exchange in the days immediately preceding Black Tuesday," Ruppert said in an October 2001 interview. "That means that someone had advance knowledge that only the stocks of these two airlines would be adversely impacted. Had it just been an industry-wide slump, then you would have seen the same kind of activity on every airline, not just these two."

There were other questionable stock trades made just prior to 9/11. According to Ruppert, Morgan Stanley Dean Witter & Co., which occupied twenty-two floors of the WTC, witnessed the purchase of 2,157 put options during the three trading days before the 9/11 attacks as compared to 27 per day prior to September 6. Merrill Lynch & Co., which also had offices on twenty-two floors of the WTC, had 12,215 one-month put options bought during four trading days prior to 9/11 compared to the normal 252 contracts per day.

In addition, Ruppert reported that suspicious trades indicating possible 9/11 foreknowledge were reported in 13 countries around the world, and that official investigations had been announced in eight of those countries.

Alex Popovic, vice president of the Investment Dealers Association of Canada, in early October 2001 confirmed that the US Securities and Exchange Commission had provided a list of thirty-eight companies for scrutiny whose shares had been traded suspiciously but said their review need not be limited to those firms listed. "One shouldn't be wearing blinders when looking at that sort of thing," Popovic told the Associated Press.

Earlier, this same commitment to an opened-ended investigation was voiced by SEC chairman Harvey Pitt, who stated his agency's "No. 1 priority" was to pursue the possible trading by people associated with the terrorists.

Interestingly enough, one of the thirty-eight companies was Vornado Realty Trust, a New Jersey-based firm that earlier in 2001 lost a bid to lease the World Trade Center complex from its owner, the Port Authority of New York, to real estate developer Larry A. Silverstein. By early 2003, Silverstein was still in court fighting insurers over whether or not the two planes that struck the WTC constituted one or two separate attacks. Leaseholder Silverstein argued that there were two strikes, which entitled him to a $7.1 billion total payment, $3.55 billion for each attack.

However, by the end of 2001, the story of profiting on terrorism had vanished. Apparently none of the suspicious transactions could be traced to bin Laden, so this news item quietly dropped from sight—or, perhaps more accurately—was quietly removed from sight, despite the official investigations that were ongoing behind the scenes by the SEC, the FBI, and foreign securities regulators, as was later acknowledged in *The 9/11 Commission Report*.

But, if the suspicious trading could not be linked to bin Laden, who was at the end of the investigative trail?

Many people wondered if it tracked back to American firms or intelligence agencies. This appears to be the case.

According to the *San Francisco Chronicle*, "[A] source familiar with the United trades identified Deutsche Bank Alex. Brown, the American investment banking arm of German giant Deutsche Bank, as the investment bank used to purchase at least some of these options."

Mike Ruppert said that both the International Policy Institute for Counter Terrorism and European investigators had tracked the UAL put options to Deutsche Bank Alex. Brown, a firm formed by the joining of the German central bank with Alex. Brown, the United States' oldest investment banking firm.

Until 1998, the chairman of Alex. Brown was A.B. "Buzzy" Krongard, who on March 26, 2001, was appointed executive director of the CIA. Beginning in 1998, he was counselor to CIA director George Tenet.

Krongard is a man with long-standing and close ties to the financial world. Moving up through the ranks of Alex. Brown, Krongard was elected chief executive officer in 1991 and then chairman of the board in 1994. With the merging of Alex. Brown and Bankers Trust Corp. in 1997, Krongard served as vice chairman of the board until joining the CIA. Bankers Trust was acquired by Deutsche Bank in 1999, becoming the single largest bank in Europe.

Krongard also served as chairman of the Securities Industry Association. A native of Baltimore, he received degrees from Princeton University and the University of Maryland School of Law and served as an infantry officer in the Marine Corps.

"Understanding the interrelationships between CIA and the banking and brokerage world is critical to grasping the already frightening implications of [these] revelations," commented Ruppert.

Krongard indeed was just the latest of many prominent Americans connected to both the CIA and Wall Street power. These include Clark Clifford (who was a key player in gaining legitimacy for BCCI, a bank which collapsed in scandal), John Foster Dulles and Allen Dulles (Allen oversaw the failed Bay of Pigs invasion and sat on the Warren Commission, and both Dulles brothers were involved with the Bush-Nazi connection detailed later), William Casey (who moved to the agency after a stint as chairman of the Securities and Exchange Commission), David Doherty (former CIA general counsel, now vice president of the New York Stock Exchange), former president George Herbert Walker Bush (now a paid consultant to the international Carlyle Group, which lists among its clients the bin Ladens), John M. Deutch and Nora Slatkin (Deutch, a former CIA director, and his former executive director Slatkin are both now connected to Citibank and Citigroup) and Hank Greenberg (once nominated as CIA director, then chairman of AIG Insurance representing the third largest pool of investment capital in the world. He is no longer with AIG and is embroiled in a bitter legal battle over the circumstances of his dismissal).

As detailed in *Rule by Secrecy*, the CIA historically has been top heavy with members of the Wall Street elite who desire to advance their globalist agenda. It also operates a number of front companies which themselves deal in stocks and bonds.

Again it should be noted that the CIA's PROMIS computer software that is used to track real-time trades in world stock markets should have alerted the Wall Street/CIA elites to all this unusual stock trading and perhaps even of the pending 9/11 attacks.

The PROMIS software had been developed by a computer program designer named Bill Hamilton, who took his work to the federal government only to have the sophisticated software stolen by President Ronald Reagan's attorney general, Ed Meese. This software, which seemed a promising weapon in tracking criminals and illegal money, was turned into an Orwellian program that integrates databases worldwide, giving its possessor nearly unlimited access to all computer records.

"One of the primary functions of the Central Intelligence Agency, by virtue of its long and very close history of relationships with Wall Street, has been a mandate to track and monitor all financial markets worldwide—and to look for anomalous trades, indicative of either economic warfare, or insider currency trading, or speculation—which might affect the US Treasury, or, as in the case of the September 11 attacks, to look for trades that indicated foreknowledge of attacks like we saw," Ruppert told *OnLine Journal* on October 12, 2001. "I am absolutely convinced that the Central Intelligence Agency had complete and perfect foreknowledge of the attacks, down to the date, time, place and location," he concluded.

Author Don Radlauer, who specializes in stock options and derivatives, noted the suspicious stock trading and stated, "Obviously, anyone who had detailed knowledge of the attacks before they happened was, at the very least, an accessory to their planning; and the overwhelming probability is that the trades could have been made only by the same people who masterminded the attacks themselves."

Now, just who might that be?

The US Government itself was holding the majority of the international and domestic "short" positions, according to commodity trading advisor Walter Burien, a former tenant of the World Trade Center. According to Burien, government money managers are the primary players within the trillion-dollar international derivative market. "A derivative gives the ability for selling the market 'short' on paper even if you do not own the stock, commodity, currency, bonds, etc.," explained Burien. "The government investment managers over the last thirty years have become very familiar with using this tactic to reap hundreds of billions of dollars each year.

"The government—which controls the economic reports, media coverage and wealth—is in a position to manipulate the above and create an environment to secure substantial revenue while everyone else is lying on the shoulder of the road bleeding to death. For three months prior and going into 9/11, the government investment funds had increased their short positions to the largest diversified short positions ever held by them," noted Burien.

As documented previously, foreknowledge of 9/11 was widely distributed. It is not hard to image that this knowledge migrated to highly placed investors throughout the world who felt safe enough to capitalize on this insider information for a quick profit.

The suspicious stock market trading indicating foreknowledge of the 9/11 attacks only added to the ever-growing belief that people in high positions knew what was coming in September 2001.

Speaking of all the warnings that poured into government agencies, Jerry Bremer, a former State Department terrorism expert, said, "We all predicted this. We had strategic warning. This is not something the analysts missed."

The evidence of foreknowledge contained within the stock issue and a desire to cover it up may explain the cursory glance given this subject by the 9/11 Commission, along with its rather questionable logic.

Commission authors dismissed the entire issue of insider trading in a buried footnote, stating, "Some unusual trading did in fact occur, but each such trade proved to have an innocuous explanation." In making this final conclusion, it refers to the "enormous resources" expended on the investigation of the issue by the FBI and the CIA and other agencies both domestic and foreign, but does not provide the reader any means to access to these references in order to independently check on the Commission's conclusions.

Buried in the same footnote, the Commission did manage to trace most of the United Airlines "puts" to one institutional US investor, but dismissed this case simply because this unnamed trader "had no conceivable ties to al Qaeda..."

WHAT ABOUT ISRAELI FOREKNOWLEDGE?

Since the September 11, 2001, attacks, many commentators have noted that the chief beneficiaries of the terrorism were the Bush administration, the United Kingdom, and Israel. All at once, the tragedy spurred the public to rally around President Bush, offering him welcome relief from bad economic news and his own sagging popularity, while the Israel government suddenly found a new pretext for unleashing its forces against the Palestinians. Meanwhile, British Prime Minister Tony Blair was able to quickly discover common ground with Bush for aggressive actions in the Middle East.

At a deeper level, the dominant "neo-conservative" faction in the White House and the Pentagon now had a premise for two of its most cherished projects: a pre-emptive military attack on Iraq as part of a more expansionist US foreign policy, and increased American support for Israel's strategic Middle Eastern objectives.

In concert with that agenda, was there a covert role of Israeli intelligence in the attacks? There were many indications of Israeli foreknowledge of the attacks, and many instances establishing Israel's ability to penetrate deep inside both the al Qaeda network and even its own staunchest ally, the United States.

A major German newspaper, the *Frankfurter Allgemeine Zeitung*, reported on September 13, 2001, that German intelligence sources had stated that both the American and Israeli governments received warnings of the attacks via the Echelon monitoring network. The article said information concerning a plan to hijack commercial airliners to use as weapons against the West was received at least three months prior to the attacks.

Several accounts regarding the number of Israelis killed on 9/11 were disregarded by the corporate mass media as reflections of anti-Semitic bias. But, legitimate questions remain.

On September 12, 2001, a *Jerusalem Post* headline read "Thousands of Israelis Missing near WTC, Pentagon." The accompanying story stated, "The Foreign Ministry in Jerusalem has so far received the names of 4,000 Israelis believed to have been in the areas of the World Trade Center and the Pentagon at the time of the attacks. The list is made up of people who have not yet made contact with friends or family."

It should be noted that this 4,000 figure originated not with US news media or Arabic sources but in Israel. The Arab media, however, was quick to seize on it.

A week later, a Beirut television station reported that 4,000 Israeli employees of the WTC were absent the day of the attack, suggesting foreknowledge of the attacks. This information spread across the Internet but was quickly branded a hoax.

On September 19, the *Washington Post* reported about 113 Israelis were missing at the WTC, and the next day, President Bush noted more than 130 Israelis were victims.

Finally, on September 22, the *New York Times* stated that amazingly only one Israeli was killed when the WTC towers collapsed. "There were, in fact, only three Israelis who had been confirmed as dead: two on the planes and another who had been visiting the towers on business and who was identified and buried," reported the *Times*.

Undoubtedly, WTC victims included many Jews but given the large number of Israelis believed to be working in the towers, this minimal number of dead—along with other factors—would seem to indicate the possibility of Israeli foreknowledge.

There was also a little-noticed story regarding the New York instant messaging firm, Odigo. Officials of Odigo confirmed soon after the attacks that two of their employees in Israel received text messages warning of the attacks two hours before planes crashed into the WTC.

Odigo's vice president of sales and marketing, Alex Diamandis, said employees in the company's research and development and international sales office in Israel received the warnings from another Odigo user un-

WHAT ABOUT ISRAELI FOREKNOWLEDGE?

known to them. They declined to state exactly what was in the messages or who sent them, saying the FBI was looking into the matter.

Micha Macover, Odigo's CEO, later said that while the company usually zealously protects the privacy of registered users, in this case it provided the FBI with the originating Internet Protocol (IP) address of the message so the bureau could track down the Internet Service Provider and the originator of the message. There was no further word from the FBI.

Diamandis explained that Odigo offers a "People Finder" program that allows users to seek out and contact others based on common interests. He said it was possible that other Odigo members got the warnings but that the company had not heard from other recipients.

Another small item that raised eyebrows concerned a broken lease at the World Trade Center just days before the 9/11 attacks by a company with close ties to Israel.

The *American Free Press* reported that Zim American Israeli Shipping Co. broke its lease on two floors of the WTC's North Tower when it vacated the rented offices in early September 2001. The company's lease was good until the end of the year and the early pullout cost the company a reported $50,000.

The company is owned by Zim Israel Navigation Co., one of the world's largest container shipping firms. It is jointly owned by the state of Israel and Israel Corp.

Inquiries on the early withdrawal by Zim were routed to the WTC lease owner Silverstein Properties, which in turn passed questions to its public relations firm, Howard J. Rubenstein, which also represents the nation of Israel.

A spokesman for Rubenstein said they had no information on the lease issue.

But such stories raise the question: Would a staunch friend of the United States like Israel conduct activities detrimental to its ally?

Two academic observers of Middle Eastern politics, Professors John Mearsheimer of the University of Chicago and Stephen Walt of the John F. Kennedy School of Government at Harvard University, sought to answer this question in a controversial 83-page study entitled, "The Israel Lobby and US Foreign Policy." First published in digest form in the

London Review of Books on March 10, 2006 and originally published in full as a working paper of the John F. Kennedy School of Government at Harvard University, the paper quickly prompted a raging controversy between pro and anti-Zionists.

"The US national interest should be the primary object of American foreign policy," the pair wrote. "For the past several decades, however, and especially since the Six Day War in 1967, the centerpiece of US Middle East policy has been its relationship with Israel. The combination of unwavering US support for Israel and the related effort to spread democracy throughout the region has inflamed Arab and Islamic opinion and jeopardized US security.

"This situation has no equal in American political history. Why has the United States been willing to set aside its own security in order to advance the interests of another state? One might assume that the bond between the two countries is based on shared strategic interests or compelling moral imperatives...However, neither of those explanations can account for the remarkable level of material and diplomatic support that the United States provides to Israel."

The true explanation, say the professors, is that a pro-Israel lobby in the US has exercised pervasive influence in Washington and in the US through its intimidation of the press, and by the use of powerful think tanks and influential positions in academia. Some members of the neo-con faction even carry duel citizenship with Israel.

The Israeli lobby keeps press scrutiny away from Israeli activities and this lack of attention may well serve as a cover for Israeli intelligence activities that may not be in our best interests, asserted Mearsheimer and Walt.

This allegation found support by studying the number of shocking instances of US penetration by agents of the Israeli Mossad in the wake of the 9/11 attacks.

To begin with, it might be remembered that on the day of the attacks, five Israelis were arrested for "puzzling behavior," namely shouting and dancing just after shooting video of the destruction of the World Trade Center from the roof of the New Jersey building where they worked.

The five, identified as Oded Ellner, Omer Marmari, Yaron Shmuel, and Sivan and Paul Kurzberg, were seen videotaping the WTC attack by

WHAT ABOUT ISRAELI FOREKNOWLEDGE?

neighbors, who interpreted their shouts as jubilation and agreement with the tragedy. Police were notified and later stopped their van bearing the company name Urban Moving Systems. In their van, police found $4,000 in cash and a box cutter. One investigator told the *Bergen Record* on September 12, "There were maps of the city in the car with certain places highlighted. It looked like they're hooked in on this. It looked like they knew what was going to happen." ABC News quoted one of the Israelis as saying, "Our purpose was to document the event."

After the names of two of the five turned up on a CIA-FBI database of foreign intelligence nationals, Marc Perelman of *Forward* reported that the FBI launched a Foreign Counterintelligence Investigation (FCI), which is undertaken quietly at the highest levels of the bureau. One of the men's attorneys, Steven Gordon, confirmed that "counterintelligence officials from the FBI" were involved in the case.

Dominick Suter, owner of the Weehawken, New Jersey, moving company, was questioned by the FBI agents, who took documents and computer hard drives but allowed Suter to go free. A few days later, Suter left the US for Israel.

In late November, the five were quietly released and sent back to Israel, where they charged that American authorities tortured them by keeping them unclothed in solitary confinement, beating them, and depriving them of food.

Irit Stoffer, a spokesperson for the Israeli Foreign Ministry, denied the men were spies and said they were deported for "only visa violations."

Chip Berlet, a senior analyst for Political Research Associates in Boston, explained, "[There] is a backdoor agreement between allies that says that if one of your spies gets caught and didn't do too much harm, he goes home. It goes on all the time. The official reason is always a visa violation."

But was there no real harm done? This case seemed to be just another odd anomaly in the cascading news of the attacks and the subsequent bombing of Afghanistan.

But it turned out to be only the barest tip of an iceberg that was to become public in mid-2002. The story began to surface in early 2002 when a secret report by the Drug Enforcement Agency (DEA) was leaked to the European media. The report stated that most distribution of the drug

Ecstasy was "controlled by organized crime figures in Western Europe, Russia and Israel." According to several reports, a DEA investigation into the Ecstasy supply uncovered a number of Israeli citizens operating in the United States.

"The report shows the clandestine network was engaged in several intelligence operations. It was a long-term project," said Guillaume Dasquie, editor of *Intelligence Online*, which broke the story in March 2002. The French website threatened to publish the entire DEA report if US and Israeli officials continued to deny its existence. The report mentioned investigations of the spy network in Florida, Texas, and California, with many of its participants posing as art students.

Beginning in early 2002, Fox News reporter Carl Cameron began to break the story that the US government was holding more than one hundred Israeli citizens with direct links to foreign military, criminal, and intelligence organizations. A bureau spokesperson would not talk about the case but did not deny it either. He referred reporters to the FBI's National Security Division.

Cameron too said he was hampered in trying to obtain information. "It's very explosive information, obviously, and there's a great deal of evidence that they say they have collected."

Cameron added that the biggest question that investigators shared with him was "How could they [the Israelis] not have known?"

By summer 2002, the estimated number of Israeli nationals being held had climbed to nearly two hundred, yet still the story went largely unreported by America's corporate mass media. One can only imagine what the newspaper headlines and TV crawl tags would look like if a gigantic Iraqi spy ring had been uncovered.

Reportedly, several of the Israelis lived in close proximity to some of the 9/11 terrorists, increasing the speculation that Israel knew more about the attacks than officially admitted. More than one-third of 120 deported Israelis lived in Florida, home to at least 10 of the 19 identified hijackers. At least 5 lived in Hollywood, Florida, home to Mohamed Atta and three other hijackers. Two others lived near Delray Beach, where other hijackers temporarily stayed. Six of the Israelis used cell phones purchased by a former Israeli vice consul in the United States, reported *Le Monde*.

WHAT ABOUT ISRAELI FOREKNOWLEDGE?

Furthermore, several of the persons involved in this "art student scandal" were observed taking pictures and reconnoitering US military bases and the homes of government officials.

In March 2001, the National Counterintelligence Center (NCIC) issued a warning that "in the past six weeks, employees in federal office buildings have reported suspicious activities concerning individuals representing themselves as foreign students selling artwork."

Paul Rodriguez with *Insight* magazine reported, "Besides federal law enforcement incidents, DEA's I[nternal] S[ecurity] unit found that several military bases also had experienced unauthorized entries by some of the students including two bases from which Stealth aircraft and other super secret military units operate. Unauthorized photographing of military sites and civilian industrial complexes, such as petroleum storage facilities, also was reported to the DEA, the documents show and interviews confirm."

Many of these young men and women had known connections to Israeli military, intelligence, or even criminal organizations. Some even worked in electronic signal intercept units in the Israeli army.

Most claimed to be art students from Israel's Bezalel Academy or the University of Jerusalem. The Jerusalem university does not exist, and officials with Bezalel Academy said no names of the "art students" turned up in the school's data bank.

According to the prestigious French newspaper *Le Monde*, student art sales were merely a cover for a vast Israeli spy ring whose primary purpose was to track al Qaeda in the United States without informing American authorities. The paper said this was the biggest Israeli spy case in the United States since 1984, when naval intelligence officer Jonathan Pollard, an American Jew, was caught giving military secrets to Israel.

The German newspaper *Die Zeit* reported in late 2002 that the CIA was given a detailed report on the actions of terrorists within the United States by the Mossad but failed to act on the information. According to BBC News, "The paper has uncovered details of a major Israeli spy ring involving some 120 agents for the intelligence service Mossad operation across America and some masquerading as art students. The ring was reportedly hard on the heels of at least four members of the hijack gang, including its leader Mohamed Atta. But the Israeli agents were detected by their American counterparts and thrown out of the country. The US authorities said then that they were students whose visas had expired."

The paper also said that if the CIA had notified German authorities that Ramzi bin al-Shibh, a key logistician for the attacks, had attended the meeting of al Qaeda members in Malaysia more than eighteen months prior to 9/11, the Germans could have prevented him from entering Germany and making contact with the Hamburg cell that planned the 9/11 atrocities.

Central to this tale of spies infiltrating the United States is the fact that the people taken by the FBI in connection with the spy ring included employees of two Israeli-owned high-tech companies that currently perform nearly all official wiretaps in the United States.

Such wiretaps are authorized by the Communications Assistance for Law Enforcement Act (CALEA). Actually wiretap is a misnomer, because today's communications systems may be accessed by electronic signals rather than physical "taps," but the end result is the same—eavesdropping.

Two firms that handle most of this wiretapping are Amdocs, Ltd. and Comverse Infosys, both identified by Fox News as Israeli telecommunications companies. Amdocs reportedly keeps records of virtually every call made in the United States, although not the content of the calls. Comverse provided custom computers and software that allowed US investigators to intercept, record, store and receive data from the US phone system.

According to NewsMax.com reporter Charles R. Smith, "The spy ring enabled criminals to use reverse wiretaps against US intelligence and law enforcement operations. The [spy ring's] illegal monitoring may have resulted in the deaths of several informants and reportedly spoiled planned anti-drug raids on crime syndicates."

Officials at both Amdocs and Comverse denied any knowledge of the Israeli spy ring. Comverse spokesman Paul Baker stated, "In full compliance with the US Department of Defense regulations, this subsidiary's operations are completely segregated from all other Comverse businesses and are insulated from any foreign influence."

The official response to the allegations of widespread spying and even foreknowledge of the 9/11 attacks has prompted overly strenuous denials from US officials and even attacks in the major media.

Daniel Pipes in an article for *Jewish World Review*, which was then published as an op-ed piece in the *New York Post*, decried the spy ring story as "conspiracy theories" based on a "crazy-quilt of unsourced allegations, drive-by innuendoes, and incoherent obscurities, but no hard facts." Pipes, director of the Middle East Forum and the author of *Conspiracy: How the Paranoid Style Flourishes and Where It Comes From*, is trotted out from time to time to dispel what he considers conspiracy theories. But Pipes himself holds some extreme political views for a Middle Eastern scholar. The only road to peace in Israel, he told a recent Zionist conference in Washington, D.C., is "an Israeli victory and a Palestinian defeat."

If the major news media are cowed about negative reporting on Israel, US government officials may be worse. *Insight* magazine reporter Paul Rodriguez said one Justice Department official told him, "We think there is something quite sinister here but are unable at this time to put our finger on it." Another official flatly stated, "The higher ups don't want to deal with this and neither does the FBI because it involves Israel." Fox News reported that, "investigators within the DEA, INS and FBI have all told Fox that to pursue or even suggest Israel is spying through Comverse is considered career suicide."

Critics have voiced opposition to the wiretapping system. "From the beginning, both the political right and left warned Congress and the FBI that they were making a huge mistake by implementing CALEA, that it would jeopardize the security of private communications, whether it's between a mother and her son or between government officials," said Lisa Dean, vice president for technology policy at the Free Congress Foundation. The foundation's Brad Jansen added, "The CALEA form of massive surveillance is a poor substitute for real law enforcement and intelligence work. Massive wiretapping does not equal security. Instead, we have elected to jeopardize our national security in exchange for poor law enforcement. The current mentality of law enforcement is what failed to protect the US from 9/11. CALEA wiretaps will not protect us from terror attacks in the future. The system does not provide better intelligence information. It actually leads to less security and more crime. We get the worst of both worlds."

Some observers of today's geopolitical scene, including the authors of the aforementioned study entitled "The Israel Lobby and US Foreign Policy," Professors Mearsheimer of the University of Chicago and Walt of the John F. Kennedy School of Government at Harvard University, believe that the 9/11 attacks provided a pretext to implement a plan to strengthen Israel, as articulated in a 1996 paper by an Israeli think tank that was influential in the Clinton administration.

The leader of the study group that produced this paper was Richard Perle. In 2002, Perle was chairman of Bush's Defense Policy Board, which reported to Deputy Defense Secretary Paul Wolfowitz. Perle is a ranking member of the Council on Foreign Relations and a key advocate of "neo-conservative" foreign policy.

Perle's 1996 paper, entitled "A Clean Break: A New Strategy for Securing the Realm," was prepared for the Institute for Advanced Strategic and Political Studies (IASPS), a Jerusalem-based think tank with an affiliated office in Washington. The institute issues policy studies and trains Israeli graduates in economic and strategic studies, helping them become research aides in the Israeli Parliament (Knesset) and the US Congress.

The "Clean Break" paper, prepared by IASPS consultants—two of whom were also members of the CFR, stated in 1996 that Israel had an opportunity to make a "clean break" with past policies and formulate "a new strategy to seize the initiative." The paper urged Israeli leaders to "work closely with Turkey and Jordan to contain, destabilize, and roll back some of its most dangerous threats. This implies a clean break from the slogan 'comprehensive peace' to a traditional concept of strategy based on balance of power." This would mean, as the paper goes on to explain, that "Israel can shape its strategic environment, in cooperation with Turkey and Jordan, by weakening, containing, and even rolling back Syria. This effort can focus on removing Saddam Hussein from power in Iraq—an important Israeli strategic objective in its own right—as a means of foiling Syria's regional ambitions."

Perle's paper also calls for changing "the nature of [Israel's] relations with the Palestinians, including the right of hot pursuit for self-defense into all Palestinian areas and nurturing alternatives to Arafat's exclusive grip on Palestinian society."

On February 19, 1998, Richard Perle and former Congressman Stephen Solarz released an Open Letter to the President, demanding a full-scale US-led drive for "regime change" in Baghdad. Among the signers of the original Perle-Solarz letter were the following current or recent Bush administration officials: Elliot Abrams (National Security Council), Richard Armitage (State Department), John Bolton (State Department), Doug Feith (Defense Department), Fred Ikle (Defense Policy Board), Zalmay Khalilzad (White House), Peter Rodman (Defense Department), Donald Rumsfeld (Secretary of Defense), Paul Wolfowitz (Defense Department), David Wurmser (State Department), and Dov Zakheim (Defense Department).

Considering that seven of the eleven men listed above are members of the Council on Foreign Relations, this plan could also be viewed as advancing the policy of that globalist organization as well. Once the Bush II administration had brought these men back in power, these neo-conservatives—along with the Israeli government and the US Israeli lobby—were able to see their favored policies acted upon, virtually without restraint.

Shortly after the invasion of Iraq began in late March 2003, Perle resigned as chairman of the Bush administration's Defense Policy Board amid charges of conflict of interest. The *New Yorker* magazine's investigative writer Seymour Hersh reported that Perle had met in France with a Saudi arms dealer while soliciting investments for Trireme Partners, a firm he helped create and that planned to profit from homeland security activities. Perle threatened to sue Hersh and called him "the closest thing American journalism has to a terrorist" shortly before resigning.

According to Mearsheimer and Walt's study, the ongoing drive to induce President Bush to launch a war against Iraq was virtually foisted upon the President by the Israeli lobby, after years of efforts to implement the precepts of the "Clean Break" paper. The events of 9/11 finally gave them the premise they needed for aggressively pursuing their objective.

And there are other intriguing sources filling in this picture. General Hameed Gul, former director general of the Pakistani intelligence services, or ISI, who worked closely with the CIA during the years of fighting against the Soviets in Afghanistan, made the incredible statement during an interview with UPI news service that it was his belief that the Israeli Mossad orchestrated the 9/11 attacks with the support of its own assets already within the United States.

While obviously anti-Israel, Gul nevertheless was in an insider's position. His views should be considered when he explained how there was little or no response from security forces on the morning of 9/11. "This was clearly an inside job," Gul said.

Gul went on to explain that Israel had grown to detest both President Bush and his father because they are considered "too close to oil interests and the [Arab] Gulf countries."

"Bush conveniently overlooks—or is not told—the fact that Islamic fundamentalists got their big boost in the modern age as CIA assets in the covert campaign to force the Soviets out of Afghanistan. All summer long [2001] we heard about America's shrinking surplus and that the Pentagon would not have sufficient funds to modernize for the 21st century. And now, all of a sudden, the Pentagon can get what it wants without any Democratic Party opposition. How very convenient.

"Even [America's] cherished civil liberties can now be abridged with impunity to protect the expansion of the hegemony of transnational capitalism. There is now a new excuse to crush anti-globalization protests. And now the Israelis have given the US the pretext for further expansion into an area that will be critical in the next 25 years—the Caspian basin," Gul stated.

Later examined is the tight relationship between the Pakistani ISI and our CIA, which may include evidence of cooperative ties between the two agencies in providing covert funding to lead hijacker Mohamed Atta. Thus, by blaming Israel, Gul might well be attempting to deflect attention from the involvement of the ISI on behalf of the terror plot.

But lest one think that Gul had his own agenda for making such statements, similar ideas about Israel's role were expressed by two former German intelligence chiefs. Eckhardt Werthebach, former president of Germany's domestic intelligence service, *Verfassungsschutz*, and Andreas von Bülow, Germany's former defense minister who also served on a parliamentary commission with oversight over Germany's secret service, both said the 9/11 attacks gave every evidence of being a state-sponsored event. Recall that US Attorney General Ashcroft soon after 9/11 announced that at least three of the hijackers were traced to a terrorist cell that had operated out of Hamburg, Germany, since at least 1999.

WHAT ABOUT ISRAELI FOREKNOWLEDGE?

Werthebach said a sophisticated operation such as displayed on 9/11 would require a state intelligence service behind it, totally unlike the "loose group" of terrorists reportedly led by Mohamed Atta.

Von Bülow said the 9/11 planners used mercenaries or "guns for hire," such as Palestinian terrorist leader Abu Nidal, whom von Bülow described as an "instrument of the Mossad." Such people as Nidal and other Arab mercenaries are the "working level," according to von Bülow, pointing out the problems with such low-level agents.

He said they were "like assailants who, in their preparations, leave tracks behind them like a herd of stampeding elephants. They made payments with credit cards with their own names; they reported to their flight instructors with their own names. They left behind rented cars with flight manuals in Arabic for jumbo jets. They took with them, on their suicide trip, bills and farewell letters, which fall into the hands of the FBI, because they were stored in the wrong place and wrongly addressed. Clues were left behind like in a child's game of hide-and-seek, which were to be followed!"

He said such an operation is carefully conducted with an eye toward deception that is widely propagated in the mainstream media, creating an accepted version of events.

"Journalists don't even raise the simplest questions," he added. "Those who differ are labeled as crazy."

Von Bülow specified Israel as the most likely sponsor and said that the attacks were designed to turn public opinion against Arabs while boosting military and security spending.

Interestingly enough, the day before the 9/11 attacks, the *Washington Times* ran a story, quoting members of the US Army's School of Advanced Military Studies (SAMS). Speaking about the capability of Israel, the paper noted, "Of the Mossad, the Israeli intelligence service, the SAMS officers say: 'Wildcard. Ruthless and cunning. Has capability to target US forces and make it look like a Palestinian/Arab act.'"

While bearing in mind these remarkable and controversial statements and allegations, it must be remembered that—in the convoluted world of international covert operations—almost nothing is as it seems. The whole spectrum of Middle East politics is so full of agents, spies, counterspies, dupes, mercenaries and provocateurs that one needs an almost impossible degree of sophistication to be able to tell the players apart.

9/11 researchers have presented evidence of significant collusion by elements of the Pakistani government in the events of 9/11 and it is widely believed that Pakistani Intelligence is controlled by the CIA.

This story was first broken by Michel Chossudovsky, a professor of economics at the University of Ottawa and author of *War and Globalisation: The Truth Behind 9/11*. He also serves as director of the Center for Research on Globalization which hosts globalresearch.ca, an important background source for 9/11 researchers.

In a little-noticed mainstream television news story cited by Chossudovsky, it was revealed that the FBI had told ABC News in late September 2001 that the 9/11 "ring leader," Mohamed Atta, had been financed by unnamed sources in Pakistan: The FBI had tracked more than $100,000 that had been wired from banks in Pakistan into accounts held by Atta in two Florida banks.

A short time later, according to Chossudovsky, "these findings of the FBI were confirmed by *Agence France Presse* (AFP) and the *Times of India*, which quoted an official Indian intelligence report dispatched to Washington. According to these two reports, the money used to finance the 9/11 attacks had allegedly been 'wired to WTC hijacker Mohamed Atta from Pakistan, by Ahmad Umar Sheikh, at the insistence of [ISI Chief] General Mahmoud [Ahmad].' And, according to the AFP [quoting the intelligence source]: 'The evidence we have supplied to the US is of a much wider range and depth than just one piece of paper linking a rogue general to some misplaced act of terrorism.'"

As if this were not enough, Chossudovsky discovered that none other than General Mahmoud Ahmad himself, the successor of Hameed Gul and the alleged "money-man behind 9/11," was in the US when the attacks occurred. The ISI chief arrived on September 4, 2001, one week before 9/11, on what was described as routine consultations with his US counterparts, including meetings at the Pentagon, the National Security Council, and with CIA Director George Tenet. And on the morning of September 11, Pakistan's chief spy was at a breakfast meeting on Capitol Hill hosted by Senator Bob Graham and Representative Porter Goss, the then chairmen of the Senate and House Intelligence committees. Goss would later serve as Director of the CIA from 2004-2006.

WHAT ABOUT ISRAELI FOREKNOWLEDGE?

As to which foreign government entity may be behind the events of 9/11 and in collusion with a rogue faction in the US—the Saudis, the Israeli Mossad, the Pakistani ISI, or some combination—it can only be said at this point that current evidence points to the likelihood that 9/11 marks the convergence of overlapping and surreptitious agendas of several hidden parties, both international and domestic. Further research will be needed to connect the many dots on the global landscape that have been revealed thus far.

WERE THE HIJACKED PLANES REMOTELY CONTROLLED?

On October 7, 2001, the first operational deployment of "Global Hawk" spearheaded the American air and missile strikes on Afghanistan.

Global Hawk is the name of the latest version of a high-altitude, long-endurance unmanned air vehicle (UAV); in other words, an unarmed pilotless drone plane that can take off, conduct missions such as photographing battlefields and land by remote electronic control. Armed versions are in the works. The jet aircraft, equivalent in wing size to a Boeing 737 commercial airliner, has a publicly announced range of 14,000 nautical miles (about halfway around the world) and can fly at altitudes of 65,000 feet for about forty hours.

"Working alongside other UAV reconnaissance assets, at least one Global Hawk was used to provide reconnaissance prior to the [Afghanistan] strikes and for successive post-strike battle damage assessment," reported *Jane's Aerospace* on October 8, 2001.

This Buck Rogers equipment had been developed in the 1970s and, by several credible accounts, was operational in the 1980s. By the spring of 2001, this unmanned drone, designated the RQ-4A Global Hawk UAV, was capable of flying a mission to Australia.

"On 23 April 2001," according to Australia's Defence Science and Technology Organisation (DSTO), "Global Hawk flew non-stop from Edwards Air Force Base, California, to Edinburgh Air Force Base, South Australia, where it was based for nearly two months undergoing a series of demonstration flights. Global Hawk returned to the US on 7 June 2001."

Dr. Brendan Nelson, Australia's parliamentary secretary to the minister of defense, said Global Hawk made aviation history when it became the first unmanned aircraft to fly nonstop across the Pacific Ocean in twenty-three hours and twenty minutes. The previous record had stood for twenty-six years.

During its six weeks of demonstrations in Australia, Global Hawk undertook eleven missions with crews from both the US Air Force and the Royal Australian Air Force. It was the first time the United States had operated Global Hawk with another nation.

According to the Defense Advanced Research Projects Agency (DARPA), a newly designed Global Hawk aircraft was first flown at Edwards AFB on February 28, 1998. A Defense Department news release said, "The entire mission, including take-off and landing, was performed autonomously by the aircraft based on its mission plan." The craft's ground controllers monitored the status of the flight.

The Global Hawk program is managed by DARPA for the Defense Airborne Reconnaissance Office. The primary contractor is Teledyne Ryan Aeronautical and the principal suppliers are Raytheon Systems, Allison Engine Co., Boeing North American, and L3 Com.

So what does this unmanned flight system have to do with September 11?

Former German defense minister Andreas von Bülow, in a January 13, 2002, interview with the newspaper *Tagesspiegel*, in speaking about the 9/11 attacks, noted, "There is also the theory of one British flight engineer [and] according to this, the steering of the planes was perhaps taken out of the pilots' hands from outside. The Americans had developed a method in the 1970s whereby they could rescue hijacked planes by intervening into the computer piloting [the electronic flight system]. This theory says this technique was abused in this case." Von Bülow could well have knowledge of this technology as several researchers and websites have stated that Lufthansa, Germany's national airline, was aware of the possibility of electronic capture and had quietly stripped the flight control systems out of American-built jetliners in the early 1990s.

The British flight engineer Von Bülow mentioned is Joe Vialls, a journalist, author, private investigator, and a former member of the Society of Licenced Aeronautical Engineers and Technologists based in London. In an article published on several websites, Vialls claimed, "[T]wo American multinationals collaborated with the Defense Advanced Research Projects Agency (DARPA) on a project designed to facilitate the remote recovery of hijacked American aircraft. Brilliant both in concept and operation, 'Home Run' [Vialls' designation, not its real code name] allowed specialist ground controllers to listen in to cockpit conversations on the target aircraft, then take absolute control of its computerized flight control system by remote means.

"From that point onwards, regardless of the wishes of the hijackers or flight deck crew, the hijacked aircraft could be recovered and landed automatically at an airport of choice, with no more difficulty than flying a radio-controlled model airplane. The engineers had no idea that almost thirty years after its initial design, Home Run's top-secret computer codes would be broken [or passed to unauthorized personnel] and the system used to facilitate direct ground control of four aircraft used in the high-profile attacks in New York and Washington on 11th September, 2001."

Even when news of Global Hawk and its remote-controlled capability was first released, there was speculation that UAV technology might be used to thwart airline hijackings. Once a hijacking took place, the Global Hawk flight technology would be triggered and the electronically captured plane flown to a landing at a safe location regardless of the actions of the flight crew or the hijackers.

The seemingly outlandish suggestion that remote-controlled planes were crashed into American targets is backed by several intriguing facts, beginning with a little-noticed item in the September 28, 2001, edition of the *New York Times* in which President Bush announced his plans to protect air passengers. Along with the usual proposals, such as strengthening cockpit doors and transponders that cannot be turned off, he mentioned "new technology, probably far in the future, allowing air traffic controllers to land distressed planes by remote control." Apparently, Bush was familiar with the Global Hawk technology but chose to present it as technology not yet available. Yet earlier that year, a former chief of British Airways suggested that such technology could be used to commandeer an aircraft from the ground and control it remotely in the event of a hijacking.

After the 2001 attacks, many websites speculated that perhaps Global Hawk's first true operational use might have been conducted on September 11. After all, as all experienced aviation and military persons well know, if a technology such as Global Hawk is publicly revealed, it most probably has been in secret use for many years.

According to aviation insiders, while it may indeed be years before air traffic controllers can take control of flying airliners, such technology already exists in certain modern jumbo jets equipped with electronic flight control systems, such as the Boeing 757 and 767, both of which were involved in the 9/11 attacks.

This assertion seemed to be confirmed by a technical and operational analysis white paper published shortly after the 9/11 attacks by two Arizona technology companies, KinetX, Inc. of Tempe and Cogitek Corp. of Chandler.

These firms were trying to market their version of Global Hawk as an antihijacker system. "The National Flight Emergency Response System (NFERS) was developed to prevent the terrorist incident of 9/11 from ever happening again," stated the companies' white paper. "This system will protect passenger and cargo aircraft from being used as terrorist weapons. NFERS is essentially the integration of *existing technology* [emphasis added] for the purpose of transferring cockpit operations to a secure ground station in case of an emergency. It is important to note that the essential technology exists now."

The two Arizona companies reported that they could have a prototype system ready for use in twelve months. If independent firms could manage a prototype that soon, it is clear that the government most probably has the same technology operational.

Under such a system, a computer command ground station could electronically capture a plane equipped with such technology and direct it wherever the controllers wished it to go. Some experts contended that flying electronic command centers—Airborne Warning and Control System (AWACS) aircraft—can perform the same function as a ground station.

Other news items that reinforce the idea that electronically captured planes were used on 9/11 include the tape of Osama bin Laden made public by the CIA in late 2001, in which he revealed that some, if not all,

WERE THE HIJACKED PLANES REMOTELY CONTROLLED?

of the hijackers did not realize they were on a suicide mission. This could explain the Boston reports that the hijackers spent their last night drinking heavily and looking for hookers.

Speaking about Flight 77, which reportedly struck the Pentagon, the *Washington Post* noted, "Aviation sources said that the plane was flown with extraordinary skill, making it highly likely that a trained pilot was at the helm, possibly one of the hijackers. Someone even knew how to turn off the transponder, a move that is considerably less than obvious."

This same story noted, "But just as the plane seemed to be on a suicide mission into the White House, the unidentified pilot executed a pivot so tight that it reminded observers of a fighter jet maneuver. The plane circled 270 degrees from the right to approach the Pentagon from the west, whereupon Flight 77 fell below radar level, vanishing from the controller's screens, the sources said."

As previously noted and as detailed in the Appendix, it is quite possible that the plane executing this amazing maneuver was not Flight 77, but actually a fighter jet ordered to buzz the Pentagon moments after the building was rocked by an explosion.

However, at least one Internet source said this was proof that the plane had been electronically captured because software with built-in safety programs would not have allowed such a maneuver. But the software could have been overridden if the craft was taken over electronically as the outside capture would have negated the airliner's safety software.

A news story has already been cited about the suspected pilot of Flight 77, Hani Hanjour, who reportedly had flown so poorly in a flight test just weeks before 9/11 that he was rejected for a small plane rental at a suburban airport. Another news article also pointed out that Hanjour had trained for a few months in Scottsdale, Arizona, but did not finish the course "because instructors felt he was not capable."

Mohamed Atta and Marwan-al-Shehhi, two other hijackers suspected of flying planes, also were reported to be mediocre-to-poor pilots. One flight instructor said neither man was able to pass a Stage 1 rating test.

In addition, suspected hijackers Nawaf al-Hazmi and Khalid al-Midhar both were sent packing from Sorbi's Flying Club in San Diego. "Their English was horrible and their mechanical skills were even worse," commented one flight instructor. "It was like they had hardly even ever driven a car."

Could a capture by Global Hawk and NFERS technology explain why none of the recordings from either air traffic controllers or the cockpit recorders have been made available to the public? Some reports claimed the tapes were blank. It could also explain how the transponders in all four captured aircraft were switched off nearly simultaneously, a most unlikely event if the planes were truly taken by different persons at different times.

According to some, an electronic capture of the flight control systems would have prevented any normal recordings. Others argue that the recordings were sequestered to prevent the public from hearing how the crews were unable to control their planes.

Investigator Vialls offered this explanation of why the cockpit voice recorder did not send a warning of the hijacking via their transponders. "Technically, a transponder is a combined radio transmitter and receiver which operates automatically, in this case relaying data between the four aircraft and air traffic control on the ground. The signals sent provide a unique 'identity' for each aircraft, essential in crowded airspace to avoid mid-air collisions, and equally essential for Home Run controllers trying to lock onto the correct aircraft.

"Once it has located the correct aircraft, Home Run 'piggy backs' a data transmission onto the transponder channel and takes direct control from the ground. This explains why none of the aircraft sent a special 'I have been hijacked' transponder code. This was the first hard proof that the target aircraft had been hijacked electronically from the ground."

To explain the reported cell phone calls from passengers on the flights, Vialls stated his belief that many of the calls were concocted after the fact. "There are no records of any such calls," he said. "We had the media's invisible 'contact' at an airline who 'said' a hostess called to report a hijacking and we had a priest who 'said' he received a call from a man asking him in turn to call his wife and tell her he loved her."

Lending support to Vialls' allegations was a news release in July, 2004, detailing a joint effort between the San Diego-based electronics firm Qualcomm and American Airlines to development a practical method for allowing airline passengers to make a cell phone call at altitude in mid-flight. Cell phones long have been banned from use in flight as a precaution against interference with flight and navigation systems.

New technology was announced in 2004 using a satellite system and a "Pico cell," which acted as a cellular tower, to allow airline passengers to make an in-flight cell phone call. "Before this new 'Pico cell,' it was nigh on impossible to make a call from a passenger aircraft in flight. Connections were impossible at altitudes over 8,000 feet or speeds in excess of 230 mph," noted Alan Cabal of the *New York Press*.

As the idea that cell phones could not have been successfully used on September 11 gained credence, the official story that passengers Barbara Olson and others had used cell phones changed. It was argued that Olson and others, such as Edward Felt, actually had used the airline $10-a-minute back-of-seat Airfones. This explanation crumbled because Olson and Felt reportedly called from inside locked lavatories, which carry no Airfones.

One apparently legitimate account of a call from one of the doomed airplanes involved Jeremy Glick, an Internet company salesman. Left unguarded with the rest of the passengers in the rear of Flight 93, Glick called his family using an Airfone, not his cell phone. "These three Iranian guys took over the plane," Glick told his wife, Lyz. "They put on these red headbands. They said they had a bomb. I mean, they looked Iranian....A passenger said they're crashing planes into the World Trade Center, is that true?" Told that the World Trade Center buildings were on fire and that the Pentagon had just been struck, Glick cursed and said, "Okay, I'm going to take a vote. There's three other guys as big as me and we're thinking of attacking the guy with the bomb."

Researcher Vialls said one big reason why electronic capture of jetliners cannot be admitted is the billions of dollars required to replace the flight control systems, an expense the already hard-pressed airlines cannot afford.

"The most innovative antihijacking tool in the American arsenal has now become the biggest known threat to American national security," he lamented.

Vialls' thoughts were echoed by Donn de Grand Pre, a retired US Army colonel and author of *Barbarians Inside the Gates*. Shortly after the 9/11 attacks, Grand Pre, along with several commercial and military pilots, participated in a marathon discussion of the events. He acknowledged that the USA, Russia, China, and Israel all possess AWACS aircraft that "have the capability to utilize electromagnetic pulsing [EMP] to knock out onboard flight controls and communications of targeted aircraft, and then, fly them by remote control.

"The 9/11 activity and horrific destruction of US property and lives was intentionally meant to trigger a psychological and patriotic reaction on the part of the US citizens, which is paving the way for 'combined UN activity' (using the fig leaf of NATO) for striking key targets in both the Middle East/South Asia and the Balkans.

"The goal continues to be the ultimate destruction of all national sovereignty and establishment of a global government," he said.

WHAT REALLY HAPPENED TO FLIGHT 93?

It is indeed difficult for many people to believe that four jetliners with crews trained in detecting and deflecting a hijacking attempt could all be taken at the same time by a handful of men armed only with knives [some reports said plastic knives] and "box cutters" and then flown with great precision into targets while evading the defenses of the American military on its home turf—and to do all this with rudimentary flying skills at best. It is more believable to think that the four craft were captured by electronic technology such as that used on Global Hawk.

After learning of the WTC and Pentagon attacks and the news that a fourth jetliner was in the air and that fighter jets had been scrambled, many people's first thought upon learning of the Flight 93 crash was that it had been shot down.

The government quickly denied this and, instead, built up the legend of the courageous passengers deciding to attack their captors. This, of course, provided a foundation for the story that the jet crashed during a ferocious battle on board. It would appear, however, that this story was constructed to give the American people an inspiring drama of struggle around which rally during the grim aftermath of the attacks.

Sadly, the facts concerning Flight 93's demise don't fit this media-created image of grassroots heroism.

For example, the last cell phone call received from the doomed flight came from an unidentified male passenger who called the 911 emergency number about eight minutes before the plane crashed. Operator Glen Cramer told the Associated Press on September 11 that the man said he had locked himself in a toilet. "We're being hijacked! We're being hijacked!" the man screamed into his phone.

"We confirmed that with him several times," said Cramer, "and we asked him to repeat what he had said. He was very distraught. He said he believed the plane was going down. He did hear some sort of an explosion and saw white smoke coming from the wing, but he didn't know where. And then we lost contact with him."

The FBI confiscated Cramer's tape and ordered him not to discuss the matter further. No explanation of this cell phone conversation has been offered.

Supporting the original theory of a shoot-down was a statement by top government officials that President Bush had authorized the use of military force early on the morning of September 11.

Speaking on NBC's *Meet the Press* less than a week after the attacks, Vice President Cheney said Bush "made the decision that if the plane [Flight 77, which reportedly struck the Pentagon] would not divert, if they wouldn't pay any attention to instructions to move away from the city, as a last resort, our pilots were authorized to take them out."

Deputy Defense Secretary Paul Wolfowitz acknowledged that the military was closing in on Flight 93. "We responded awfully quickly, I might say, on Tuesday," he said in a PBS interview. "And in fact, we were already tracking in on that plane that crashed in Pennsylvania. I think it was the heroism of the passengers on board that brought it down, but the air force was in a position to do so if we had had to."

General Richard Myers, chairman of the Joint Chiefs of Staff, also confirmed that fighters approached Flight 93, but denied that they fired on the craft.

Adding to this confusion was the small furor created in late 2004 by an off-the-cuff remark from Donald Rumsfeld during a surprise Christmas Eve visit to troops in Iraq. Recalling past terrorist events, Rumsfeld included, "...the people who did the bombing in Spain or the people who attacked the United States in New York, shot down the plane over Pennsylvania and attacked the Pentagon..."

The Pentagon later said this was simply a misstatement, not some sort of Freudian slip of the tongue.

Many ground witnesses reported sighting a small aircraft—some described it as a military jet—circling the area before and after Flight 93 crashed. Later, the FBI explained that it was a business jet that had been requested by authorities to descend and provide the location of the crash.

The FBI's explanation is wanting for a number of reasons. First of all, by the time of the crash of Flight 93—at 10:06 am and not 10:03 am (according to this book's independent timeline)—all air traffic nationwide had been grounded for about a half hour. In addition, the plume of smoke from the wreckage, plus numerous calls to 911, would have provided a sufficient location bearing. Furthermore, FBI has failed to provide any information concerning this aircraft or its passengers, none of whom has come forward to give their account.

One craft that was in the area was a single-engine Piper piloted by Bill Wright. Wright said he was within sight of Flight 93, in fact so close he could see its United markings. He said he suddenly received orders to get away from the airliner and land immediately. "That's one of the first things that went through my mind when they told us to get as far away from it as fast as we could, that either they were expecting it to blow up or they were going to shoot it down," Wright told newsmen.

There is also a serious factual question concerning the wreckage. According to the official story, Flight 93 barreled into the ground at close to five hundred miles per hour. Yet, wreckage was strewn for up to eight miles, including paper mail, personal belongings and even magazines and newspapers the plane was carrying. One engine, which weighs in excess of one thousand pounds, was found more than two thousand yards from the crash scene, indicating it came loose prior to ground impact.

Wally Miller was the local coroner at the time of the crash and was required by law to establish the cause of death of the victims. "I put down 'murdered' for the 40 passengers and crew, 'suicide' for the four terrorists," Miller told a reporter, adding significantly that he could not prove what actually happened.

Subsequent actions by government authorities did little to dissuade conspiracy theorists. For example, the FBI didn't make public the flight data recordings until April 18, 2002, and then only played edited excerpts to the victims' family members, who were ordered not to discuss what they heard. It was played once again in closed chambers for the jury at the Zacarias Moussaoui trial on April 12, 2006. A transcript that included English translations of Arabic statements that were alleged to have been made by the hijackers was made available to the public at that time. However, this translation could not be compared to the recording itself.

Bureau agents also muzzled Cleveland air traffic controllers involved in the last moments of the flight, ordering them not to speak about what they saw on their radar screens.

Amidst near-hysterical cries of national security, the public was once again asked to blindly accept official pronouncements backed by little, no, or even contradictory evidence. With all hard evidence locked away by the government, speculation has run rampant on the true cause of Flight 93's demise. Countering the official story of the crash occurring during a heroic battle with the hijackers are other equally credible theories.

The most prevalent theory is that a US fighter downed the craft with missile and/or cannon fire, a suspicion supported by all the available evidence.

Furthermore, the shoot-down theory takes on great strength when one analyzes the obvious distortions of known facts about Flight 93 in *The 9/11 Commission Report*, which appear to be an attempt to cover-up the truth about the real fate of that flight. We've noted earlier that the report falsely claims that the military was not even notified that Flight 93 had been hijacked until after it had crashed at 10:06 am. But even the aforementioned statements attributed to Cheney and Wolfowitz themselves flatly contradict that assertion, with Wolfowitz saying for example that "the air force was in a position" to shoot the plane down if need be. The Commission's assertion also conflicts with statements of Norman Mineta, Richard Clarke and Barbara Honegger as well. Furthermore, numerous reports in the *New York Times*, the *Washington Post*, and other major newspapers made it clear a few days after 9/11 that the final shoot-down order had been issued at least by 9:56 am, in time to engage Flight 93 before it was supposedly brought down by the on-board struggle. Author David Ray Griffin convincingly shows that, while offering no supporting evidence for its revisionist position, the 9/11 Commission ignores the well-established fact that the shoot-down order had been issued earlier and simply asserts that this order was not given until 10:25 am. It is not hard to see that this falsehood was promulgated in a "desperate attempt," as Griffin puts it, to rule out the possibility that an American president could actually shoot down a civilian plane.

In this connection, a variety of theorists have suggested that the shoot-down was implemented and then covered up when it was realized that—if the plane had been successfully taken over and landed by the passengers—the real truth about the plot might have been more easily extracted through interviews with the surviving hijackers. Others have even suggested that Flight 93 was headed toward WTC Building 7, with the mission of obliterating the evidence of the plot contained in its OEM center. Its failure to arrive necessitated the "plan B" demolition of Building 7 later in the day.

Yet another plausible theory holds that, since one air traffic controller tape available on the Internet speaks of a bomb on board and considering the Airfone call from Jeremy Glick, one of the hijackers may have detonated such a device in the air.

A more fanciful theory, though not backed by solid science, was offered by researchers citing Harvard academic Elaine Scarry. In a series of articles and books, Scarry postulated that some recent airline crashes were caused by high-tech military "electronic warfare" weaponry akin to Global Hawk technology and capable of disrupting an aircraft's control system, the FBI did confirm that a C-130 military plane was within twenty-five miles of Flight 93, and since 1995 the air force has installed "electronic suites" in twenty-eight of its C-130 aircraft.

This Scarry scenario leads to yet another theory positing that the plane's passengers were successful in their attempt to regain control of the craft but then found they could not control the plane due to electronic seizure.

Under the theory that all the aircraft were captured and flown remotely using Global Hawk technology, the masterminds behind such a scheme could not possibly allow Flight 93 to land safely and give away the game. Since both the shoot-down orders and the fighters were in place, it would be simply a matter of giving the go-ahead and then sweeping it all under the rug of "national security."

But regardless of what truly happened to Flight 93 and why, or the issue of how the hijacked planes were controlled, it is clear that many unanswered questions remain about the fate of the four airliners involved in the 9/11 attacks.

REMOTE VIEWERS LOOK AT 9/11

For several decades, the US intelligence community and the Army secretly developed and utilized a technique called "remote viewing" as a means of obtaining critical national security data on the activities of our enemies.

Thus it is not farfetched to use this tool in an effort to look at 9/11 from an entirely different point of view. Several experienced remote viewers were commissioned by this author to make a remote viewing study of the people and circumstances surrounding the 9/11 attacks.

One of the viewers who agreed to participate in this study was Lyn Buchanan, formerly the trainer of the US Army's then-Top Secret *GRILL FLAME* and *STARGATE* remote viewing programs. This technique for viewing persons, places and things by means other than the normal five senses has been known in the past as clairvoyance. The term "remote viewing" was substituted to avoid the ongoing arguments over psychic phenomena and is used to describe the controlled use of psychic abilities.

Remote viewing was extensively studied in the 1960s, '70s, and '80s first by the CIA, then by the US Army, Defense Intelligence Agency and National Security Agency. Many believe this approach to be a valid means for getting at the truth as this once-secret program was funded through six administrations, both Republican and Democrat, for more than a quarter of a century.

The use of this faculty of the mind has been pervasive in all of the world's religions, from the Bible to the Koran to Oriental mysticism. Most spiritual traditions contain a wealth of stories involving prophecy, visions, shamanic "journeying," and spiritual instruction. And all seem to involve visual input.

The Biblical book of Isaiah, for example, opens with the statement, "These are the messages that came to Isaiah, son of Amoz, in the visions he saw during the reigns of King Uzziah, King Jotham, King Ahaz and King Hezakiah—all kings of Judah."

Biblical prophecy was not limited to men. In the Old Testament book of Judges, we find that a "prophetess" named Deborah provided the Israelite leader Barak with information about the military disposition of Sisera, the commander of the forces of Jabin, the King of Canaan. Sisera's forces were routed and thus Deborah, using psychic intelligence, played a pivotal role in the conquest of the Promised Land. She might rightly be called the world's first military remote viewer.

Even in the New Testament, prophesy and visions played an important role as the messianic plan unfolded. St. Paul offered some advice on remote viewing that modern people might well take to heart. "Do not scoff at those who prophesy, but test everything that is said to be sure if it is true, and if it is, then accept it," he wrote to church members in Thessalonica.

Throughout the ages, men and women have practiced "spiritualism," to include versions of remote viewing but it was never accepted by the mainstream public because modern science, while able to demonstrate that some phenomenon was occurring in laboratory experiments, could never quite get a handle on the how and why of it.

But after reports leaked out from behind the Iron Curtain in the early 1970s that Soviet Russia and its Eastern European allies were experimenting with psychics, the American intelligence establishment felt the need to join in the pursuit of psychic spies. Beginning in 1972, the CIA began funding scientific studies into psychic phenomena at California's Stanford Research Institute (SRI). According to former investigator Jack Anderson and author Ron McRae, it was "the most severely monitored scientific experiment in history." And it got results. By 1976, the remote viewing program had left the CIA and by 1977 was under the US Army's newly-formed Intelligence and Security Command (INSCOM). Soon a full-time operational unit, code named GRILL FLAME, was underway and producing remarkable results from about a dozen remote viewers. In 1985, the unit was placed within the secretive Defense Intelligence Agency (DIA).

Some people have argued that the use of psychic spies by both sides may have ended the Cold War, which was based primarily on secrecy. Once this secrecy was penetrated by remote viewers, the impasse between the USA and Russia fell apart. In 1995, the story of remote viewing broke in the *Washington Post* and the *New York Times* after the CIA issued a press release acknowledging the psychic program. The story never really reached the American heartland and many people are still unaware of this most significant issue.

According to several sources, remote viewing continues to be used within both the military and intelligence communities. Most recently, according to some sources, military-trained remote viewers have been used in the search for Osama bin Laden. Viewers were also used to help identify and locate the sniper around Washington in October 2002, according to several news reports.

In this specially commissioned study, eleven remote viewers with extensive track records took a psychic look at the events of September 11, 2001. Several of the viewers involved asked not to be identified. Among those who agreed to be identified were Lyn Buchanan, who now heads up Problems Solutions Innovations of Alamogordo, NM, and Gail Ferguson, author of *Cracking the Intuition Code*.

These eleven viewers gave yes-or-no answers to questions. The answers below reflect the majority of the viewers' responses:

1. Did President George Bush have foreknowledge of the 9/11 attacks? *No.*
2. Did George Bush, Sr. have foreknowledge of the 9/11 attacks? *Yes.*
3. Did Dick Cheney have foreknowledge of the 9/11 attacks? *Yes.*
4. Did the Israeli Mossad have foreknowledge of the 9/11 attacks? *Possibly.*
5. Did Osama bin Laden have foreknowledge of the 9/11 attacks? *Yes.*
6. Were the planes that crashed into the WTC controlled from the planes' cockpits? *No.*
7. Was the collapse of the WTC towers caused only by the planes striking the buildings? *Equally divided.*

8. Was any US intelligence agency involved in the 9/11 attacks? *Yes.*

9. Were any members of The Trilateral Commission, Council on Foreign Relations or Bilderberger group responsible of the 9/11 attacks? *Yes.*

10. Was United Airlines Flight 93 shot down? *Yes.*

Since the answers to most of these questions would seem provocative to many people, it should be pointed out that remote viewing, despite extensive and careful laboratory experiments, is more of an art than a science. It also should be noted that none of the remote viewers knew the questions before their session.

They were simply given a 10-digit set of numbers that represented each question. It was discovered in the research of remote viewing that these numbers somehow directed the viewer's mental attention to the object of the query on a subconscious level. The viewer picked up the question of the tasker.

For example, the question concerning President Bush was "48965-74123." Those numerals were the extent of information given to the viewers, yet there was a certain consistency in their answers with the exception of one question that was nearly a tie. Some of the answers were obvious. For example, the question of whether or not the WTC planes were controlled from the cockpits of the craft resulted in seven "no's," only three "yes's" and one "no answer." "No answer" responses resulted from either no data returned or no answer given due to an inconclusive session.

Other answers were much closer. The question concerning the involvement of the Israeli Mossad prompted an almost even split, with six "yes's" compared to five "no's." The question regarding President Bush's foreknowledge yielded seven "no's" to four "yes's" while the same question regarding his father resulted in the opposite, seven "yes's" to three "no's" with one "no answer."

Another near tie was the question that asked if the planes alone were responsible for the collapse of the WTC towers. This query brought five "yes" responses to four "no's" with two "no answer's." The question regarding the involvement of secret society members also was a near tie, with five answering "yes," four "no" and two "no answer."

While this one small remote viewing study cannot be taken by anyone as ground truth, based on the remarkable track record of the US government's operational use of this mental technology, it certainly should be the cause for sober reflection and further investigation.

If even half of the information outlined in this remote viewing section as well as the preceding sections is proven in error, the balance remains a damning indictment of official malfeasance. It's much worse than what *Newsweek* termed "a whole summer of missed clues."

The totality of the information available today can only lead to two inescapable conclusions: either the highest leadership of the United States is composed of imbeciles and incompetent blunderers or they are criminally negligent accessories to the crimes, if not worse.

Researchers who believe the latter thesis will want to test their evidence and arguments against the chief bulwark of the official "incompetence" theory, *The 9/11 Commission Report*, the product of the only major investigation of the 9/11 attacks, as well as the long-awaited Commission that produced it.

THE OFFICIAL 9/11 INQUIRY: ANOTHER WARREN COMMISSION?

The National Commission on Terrorist Attacks upon the United States, popularly known as the 9/11 Commission, released its final report to the public in mid-summer 2004, nearly three full years after the horrifying attacks of September 11, 2001.

The voluminous 567-page report answered virtually none of the vital questions that have been raised by independent researchers and the 9/11 families.

It also quickly became clear that when it came to the two prominent views of history—conspiracy or accidental—the commissioners were solid supporters of both schools. According to them, the attacks of 9/11 resulted from a malignant conspiracy of freedom-hating Muslim fanatics who successfully carried out a complex terrorist plot for less than $1 million. However, they were aided and abetted by a systematic series of miscues, mistakes and malfeasance on the part of a variety of US government officials and agencies that lacked "imagination" due to hardened Cold War mindsets. Yet, to date, not one single government employee has been fired, re-assigned or even disciplined due to the failures of that day.

Immediately, many commentators likened the report to that of the infamous Warren Commission Report issued less than one year after the assassination of President John F. Kennedy. And the similarities are indeed striking.

Like the Warren Report before it, *The 9/11 Commission Report* has no index, making it difficult for any serious researcher to move through it and connect both personages and events. And like that earlier report, this latest government account has met unqualified acceptance by the corporate-controlled mass media as well as those members of the public who blindly accept the views presented on television and the major print publications. As occurred with the Warren Report, will it also take 40 years for the general public to learn of the many revelations that undo the official 9/11 account?

As with the Warren Report, this latest document inundates the readers with pages of superfluous and tedious historical and operational data on government agencies and policies. Yet, it fails to adequately address some of the more serious issues raised in this book and elsewhere.

Numerous factual distortions have already been pointed out, but there are just as many large omissions. For example, the report fails to even mention "Operation Northwoods," the early 1960s plan approved by the Joint Chiefs of Staff to encourage public support for another attack upon Castro's Cuba by setting off bombs in American cities and hijacking planes and ships in a manner designed to incriminate Castro. Nor is there any mention of the Project for a New American Century, a neo-conservative think tank filled with current Bush Administration officials that laid out a plan to invade Afghanistan and Iraq long before the events of 9/11.

The Warren Report rested on the shaky premise of Arlen Specter's single bullet theory—the idea that one rifle slug passed through both President Kennedy and Texas Governor John Connally—causing seven separate wounds to both men including hitting at least two bones—yet emerged to be found unscathed at the hospital. Similarly, the 9/11 Commission's verdict that 9/11 was simply the result of miscues, miscommunication and a system badly in need of centralization is based on the equally implausible premise that at least 19 fanatical Arab Muslims—some with expired visas or questionable passports and some on security watch lists—traveled to various countries where plans were hatched, came in and out of the USA and trained at US flight schools directly under the nose of US authorities without arousing any notice or suspicion, but were then easily identified to a man within hours of the attacks.

Likewise, the 9/11 Commission failed to report the historic fact that Osama bin Laden's al Qaeda network grew directly out of the force of Islamic fundamentalists recruited to fight the Soviets in Afghanistan under the auspices of the CIA. It even omits mention of the fact that Osama himself had received aid and training from US military and intelligence assets.

Even if there was no intent to cover up the truth, the Commission was not funded at a level sufficient to do its work. Incredibly, more than three times as much money was spent on George W. Bush's 2005 inauguration than was originally allocated to investigate the attacks on September 11, 2001. While a total of $112.6 million was spent to investigate the 2003 space shuttle *Columbia* disaster and $50 million was once spent to look into Las Vegas gambling casinos, the 9/11 tragedy received a mere $13 million to probe the greatest attack on America since 1812. The Presidential Inaugural Committee estimated Bush's 2005 inauguration events cost about $40 million, with the federal government and District of Columbia bearing an additional $20 million as the cost of providing security.

From the outset, President Bush made clear that he wanted no independent investigation into the attacks. Bowing to the entreaties of 9/11 families, the Bush administration initially promised only $3 million to investigate 9/11; it later relented after additional public pressure and released another $10 million. Previously it was noted that even the inadequate first official inquiry into 9/11—the Joint Intelligence Congressional Inquiry in 2002 which probed activities of the intelligence community in connection with the attacks—also was resisted by the Bush administration.

With many of the 9/11 families embittered by the omissions and limitations of the Congressional inquiry, these bereaved Americans found themselves back in Washington lobbying for a truly independent commission, while submitting a lengthy list of unanswered questions.

President Bush staunchly resisted further efforts to investigate the 9/11 attacks until November 2002, when, under intense pressure from victims' families and the public alike, he signed into law a bill creating the National Commission on Terrorist Attacks Upon the United States— usually referred to as simply the 9/11 Commission. The new Commission, whose charter was to conduct an independent and nonpartisan investigation, was intended to pick up where the congressional inquiry left off. It held its first hearings in late March 2003.

Curiously, as if historical amnesia had settled over it, the Commission's final report never mentioned the delays and the obstructions perpetrated by the Bush administration, including numerous instances of administration stonewalling during the entire life of the Commission.

In an incident filled with incredible irony, Bush's first choice to head the 9/11 Commission was Henry Kissinger, a prominent secret society member and perhaps the man most responsible for producing the past thirty years of United States foreign policy. It is this deeply flawed foreign policy, mostly thinly disguised neocolonialism and nation looting, that has resulted in worldwide antipathy for America's role in the world in recent years. Many observers believe that events like 9/11 represent "blowback" for such neo-imperial policies.

Though considered a prominent statesman, there is a darker side to Kissinger, as evidenced by several warrants outstanding in two European countries for war crimes and complicity in murder. In May 2001, for example, during a stay at the Ritz Hotel in Paris, he was visited by the criminal brigade of the French police, and served with a summons. Kissinger made a hasty exit, never to return to France.

Christopher Hitchens, a regular contributor to *Vanity Fair* and author of several noted books, including *The Trial of Henry Kissinger*, presents a wealth of documentation showing that Kissinger was the responsible party behind a number of acts that can be considered war crimes, including atrocities during the war in Indochina—notably in Vietnam and Cambodia—and planned assassinations in Santiago, Nicosia, and Washington, D.C., and even genocide in East Timor. For example, in 1970,

Kissinger ordered the removal of Chilean army commander in chief Rene Schneider. Schneider was a supporter of Chile's constitution who opposed what later became a right-wing coup against Socialist President Salvadore Allende, and was murdered in 1970 by right-wing plotters within the Chilean military. Former US ambassador to Chile Edward Korry confirmed Kissinger's direct role in these events. Strong evidence ties Kissinger to the actual CIA-sponsored coup itself on September 11, 1973, which resulted in the deaths of Allende and thousands of his left-wing supporters, and the imposition of a military dictatorship in that country for almost two decades.

Following a public outcry over Bush's choice to head the 9/11 Commission, Kissinger quickly withdrew, claiming he did not want to make known the client list of Kissinger Associates. It was known in Washington that Kissinger's firm was receiving consulting fees from corporations with large investments in Saudi Arabia, and from the oil giant Unocal, whose desire to build a pipeline through Afghanistan is discussed later in this book. Kissinger also has long been a prominent member of secretive societies such as the Council on Foreign Relations and the Bilderbergers.

Bush continued to look to the secret societies for appointments, finally settling on former New Jersey Governor Thomas H. Kean and former Indiana Representative Lee Hamilton to chair the commission. Both Kean and Hamilton are members of the secretive Council on Foreign Relations as were Allen Dulles and John J. McCloy of Warren Commission fame. Conflicts of interests abound with both men.

Kean's connections to the oil industry go deep. He was an official of Amerada Hess, one of the giant oil companies involved in planning the oil pipeline through Afghanistan. One Hess oil project involves a partnership with Saudi oil executive Khalid bin Mahfouz, whose name has been linked to President George W. Bush in both Texas oil deals and the BCCI banking scandal. Kean also has had exceptional input into our nation's security reformation through his co-chairmanship of this Homeland Security project.

From the Bush administration's point of view, Hamilton was ideal for the job of vice chair. Former Congressman Hamilton chaired a House committee looking into the October Surprise, a reported plan in which

Reagan-Bush campaign officials made a deal with Iranian authorities not to release US hostages held in Tehran so as to insure the election of Ronald Reagan in 1980. But Hamilton could find no wrongdoing despite testimony from the pilot who claimed to have flown both CIA Director William Casey and Vice-President-Elect George H. W. Bush to Paris for talks with the Iranians and the fact that the hostages were released within hours of Ronald Reagan being sworn in as president on January 20, 1981. As co-chair of the House Select Committee investigating the Iran-Contra Affair, Hamilton again could find no wrongdoing in the Reagan administration's decision to secretly and illegally sell arms to Iran, as part of a national scandal that included the administration's usurpation of Congress by secretly using profits from such illegal arms sales to covertly fund a civil war in Nicaragua—plus the systematic cover-up by the Reagan Administration that followed these events. Hamilton told PBS's *Frontline* in the late 1980s he felt it would not have been "good for the country" to put the public through the impeachment process. Hamilton likewise turned his head from the massive documentation concerning drug smuggling by the CIA to fund the Iran-Contra operations. In the late 1990s, a CIA inspector general's report confirmed direct CIA involvement in the importation of cocaine.

It should be recalled that many of the names involved in the Iran-Contra Affair, described by journalist Bill Moyers as an attempted *coup d'etat*, are currently members of the Bush Administration, including John Poindexter who was convicted of lying to Congress and by extension the American public.

Hamilton is a member of the Homeland Security Advisory Council and also on the board of the National Endowment for Democracy, a Congressionally supported non-profit organization notorious for funneling money in support of candidates for office in foreign countries who support the rights of US corporations to invest in those countries.

Other commission members also were former senior government officials and Washington insiders, such as Fred Fielding, former White House counsel to Nixon; Jamie Gorelick, deputy attorney general under Clinton; and John Lehman, Reagan's secretary of the navy.

Gorelick, yet another CFR member on the 9/11 Commission as well as a sitting board member of the oil drilling giant Schlumberger, also co-chaired the Intelligence Community Law Enforcement Policy Board along with CIA Director George Tenet at the time that Philippine authorities were reporting "Project Bojinka," a terrorist plot to hijack commercial airliners and fly them into prominent structures. The Pentagon and the World Trade Center towers were specifically named. Gorelick was one of only two 9/11 commissioners allowed access to Bush Administration classified materials.

Without belaboring the point, it becomes clear that the 9/11 Commission was loaded with persons who most probably should have been called as witnesses rather than sitting in judgment.

As with the Warren Commission, the 9/11 Commission's final report is notable not so much for what it says but for what it does not say. Presenting time lines that contradict sworn testimony, the report nevertheless offers to the unwary a compelling and detailed narrative of the hijacking horrors of that morning.

Yet even the accommodating Commission soon found itself stymied by the Bush administration, which continued to drag its feet in supplying White House key internal documents and intelligence briefings to the Commission, in addition to various forms of procedural delay.

The stonewalling reached its highest point when Bush himself was asked to testify. After a long period of declining its invitations, in February 2004 the president finally agreed to meet with the Commission. This meeting took place on April 29, but not until White House counsel had negotiated restrictive terms: Vice President Cheney had to be present also, the two men were not to testify under oath, and the meeting had to take place in the Oval Office. In addition, no recording was to be made of the session, nor was a stenographer permitted to be in the room. Bush and Cheney also declined to permit notes of the three-hour session to be shared with the 9/11 families.

Through the spring of 2004, commissioners continued to complain that their work was delayed repeatedly because of disputes with the administration over access to documents and other witnesses.

"It's obvious that the White House wants to run out the clock here…" commented former Senator Max Cleland, a Democrat who was widely regarded to be the Commission's most vociferous and outspoken critic of the Bush administration. Such activity by Cleland came to a halt almost halfway through the Commission's work when he resigned to accept a position on the board of directors of the Export-Import Bank of the United States after being nominated by President Bush on November 21, 2003. Many observers saw Cleland's new job as nothing less than a blatant buy-off by the Bush administration.

The Commission's executive director was Philip Zelikow. Hardly "independent" or "nonpartisan," Zelikow was, for starters, a Republican and a member of President Bush's own Foreign Intelligence Advisory Board. He had previously served as a national security adviser in the Ford and Bush I administrations, and was director of the Aspen Strategy Group, a policy program of the Aspen Institute, considered by many as a key globalist think-tank. Zelikow, along with national security advisor Condoleezza Rice, both prominent members of the Council on Foreign Relations, co-authored a book entitled *Germany Unified and Europe Transformed*. In yet another example of blatant conflict of interest, Zelikow was also a member of the Bush-Cheney transition team, which helped form the current National Security Council, which oversees national security policy.

Zelikow was widely considered by many as Bush's "gatekeeper" on the 9/11 Commission. Zelikow tightly controlled the scope and reach of the investigation. As executive director, he guided the staff, which did virtually all the work of the Commission, and decided which topics were to be investigated and which witnesses would be interviewed.

In concluding his comprehensive study of the Commission's report, Professor David Ray Griffin declared that, given the direct ties of Zelikow to the White House and his ability to shape the investigation, his presence as the executive director was the equivalent of its work being "conducted by Condoleezza Rice, Dick Cheney, or George Bush."

Zelikow was, without a doubt, a White House insider with longstanding connections to foreign policy decisions. Recently, Griffin revealed his discovery that Zelikow was the principal author of the administration's *National Security Strategy* statement of 2002, in which the controversial new neo-conservative doctrine of preemptive warfare was first articulated and adopted as a foundation of US foreign policy.

This document was to provide crucial doctrinal support for the preemptive wars in Afghanistan and Iraq soon to follow. "We can understand, therefore," says Griffin, "why the Commission, under Zelikow's leadership, would have ignored all evidence that would point to the truth: that 9/11 was a false flag operation intended to authorize the doctrines and funds needed for a new level of imperial mobilization."

It is quite apparent that the Commission that probed the events of 9/11 was as compromised and controlled as the Warren Commission of 1964, which declined to ask any hardball questions of the new president or his staff.

The hardball, according to some, was instead reserved for 9/11 witnesses. New York firefighter Louie Cacchioli appeared before Commission staffers in 2004 but quickly left. "I felt like I was being put on trial in a court room," said Cacchioli, "They were trying to twist my words and make the story fit only what they wanted to hear. All I wanted to do was tell the truth and when they wouldn't let me do that, I walked out."

"I met with the 9/11 Commission behind closed doors and they essentially discounted everything I said regarding the use of explosives to bring down the north tower," said William Rodriguez, who previously had been invited to the White House for his heroism on 9/11.

In fact, neither the names of Cacchioli, Rodriguez nor the names of any other witness who reported multiple explosions at the World Trade Center can be found in the 567-page *9/11 Commission Report.*

Another wrinkle in the progress of the 9/11 Commission came about due to the actual interpretation of its charter by the commissioners. This interpretation was voiced by Vice Chairman Hamilton who explained, "The focus of the Commission will be on the future. We're not interested in trying to assess blame; we do not consider that part of the commission's responsibility."

So, it was now openly acknowledged that the Commission would not hold key officials accountable for their actions; instead, it would focus on ways to prevent a recurrence in the future. And indeed, the Commission has lived up to this charter. This was especially revealed in its forgiving and friendly treatment of government officials offering conflicting testimony under oath.

For starters, the Commission's account of its interview with President Bush, with Dick Cheney present—though not under oath—was marked by the extremity of its deferential treatment of the president. In fact, according to one exhaustive review that appeared in *Harper's Magazine*, the commissioners permitted the president to lie repeatedly about crucial questions of fact, without challenge—according to the Commission's own account of these facts.

This time on national television and for all to see, Attorney General John Ashcroft's appearance before the Commission provided one of the best examples of the kid-glove treatment afforded to high administration officials who should have been directly in the line of fire for the greatest crime ever committed on American soil.

According to the mainstream Democratic think tank, the Center for American Progress, Ashcroft's testimony was a "deceptive, disingenuous, and dishonest account of his record prior to 9/11 and a Pollyanna-type view of his actions following the attack. Worse, the commissioners largely accepted Ashcroft's testimony at face value and passed on opportunities to aggressively question the attorney general on inconsistencies and inaccuracies in his statements.

The acting FBI director for the three months before 9/11, Thomas Pickard, had just testified to the Commission that Ashcroft had waved off an update on the terrorist threat, telling Pickard that he didn't want to hear about the subject anymore.

It fell to former Illinois Governor Jim Thompson—usually the fiercest Republican defender on the commission—to ask the only critical question about this statement. When asked by Thompson about Pickard's claim, Ashcroft replied, "I never said I didn't want to hear about counterterrorism."

But the exchange ended there, with no follow-up question. Obviously, either Ashcroft or Pickard was lying—but the commissioners didn't seem to notice this obvious contradiction. Later in his testimony, Ashcroft insisted that he had added more money to the Justice Department's budget for counterterrorism than for any other function. But according to *Slate* magazine, this claim is patently untrue. "It has been disputed by the commission's staff, several previous witnesses, and public budget documents. Yet none of the commissioners called him on it." As indicated earlier, the fact is that in August 2001, Attorney General Ashcroft, had turned down a bureau request for $50 million to beef up its counterterrorism efforts.

Even commissioner Richard Ben-Veniste, the Democratic former Watergate prosecutor, went easy on the attorney general. He asked why Ashcroft's top five priorities listed in a policy document of May 10, 2001, did not include fighting terrorism. Ashcroft answered that at the May 9 hearings before the Senate Appropriations Committee he had cited terrorism as his No. 1 priority. Ben-Veniste let Ashcroft go unchallenged, even though the Commission staff report released just prior to Ashcroft's testimony revealed that a May 10, 2001, budget guidance paper he released made no mention of counterterrorism.

Many had predicted before the Ashcroft appearances that the attorney general was so vulnerable on the issue of 9/11 that he might have to be sacrificed as an administration fall guy. But Ashcroft was left unscathed by the Commission.

Perhaps the chief embarrassment to the Bush administration during this period of testimony before the Commission was the revelations of Richard A. Clarke, the Reagan appointee who was the government's top counterterrorism expert under President Clinton and President George W. Bush. On the CBS television program *60 Minutes*, and in dramatic testimony before the 9/11 Commission that electrified the country, Clarke charged that the Bush administration "failed to act prior to September 11 on the threat from al Qaeda despite repeated warnings." Clarke alleged that the Bush administration received repeated warnings that an al Qaeda attack was imminent, yet it under-funded and subordinated counterterrorism in the months leading up to 9/11—and even after.

Among the casualties of this downgrade was "a highly classified program to monitor al Qaeda suspects in the United States," which the White House suspended in the months leading up to 9/11, according to Clarke. Clarke went on to claim that the president was improperly attempting to "harvest a political windfall" from 9/11, charging that the administration began making plans to attack Iraq on 9/11—despite evidence that the terror attack had been engineered by al Qaeda.

Clarke's latter assertion was consistent with earlier reports. CBS News had reported on September 4, 2002, that five hours after the 9/11 attacks, "Defense Secretary Donald Rumsfeld was telling his aides to come up with plans for striking Iraq—even though there was no evidence linking Saddam Hussein to the attacks." Similarly, then Secretary of Treasury

Paul O'Neill said the administration "was planning to invade Iraq long before the September 11 attacks and used questionable intelligence to justify the war."

Noted earlier in this book is the fact that the Commission's official timeline grossly contradicts Clarke's own hands-on, eyewitness account of the government's response to the events of the morning of the attacks, despite the preponderance of evidence for Clarke's version.

National Security Adviser Condoleezza Rice emerged as the administration's point person in its efforts to refute Clarke's accusations. In an opinion piece in the *Washington Post* on March 22, Rice wrote: "Despite what some have suggested, we received no intelligence that terrorists were preparing to attack the homeland using airplanes as missiles, though some analysts speculated that terrorists might hijack planes to try and free US-held terrorists." This claim was restated on numerous TV talk shows, and Rice elaborated on these assertions in her reluctant testimony before the 9/11 Commission; the National Security Adviser of the United States had agreed to testify under oath about the greatest security breach in modern history only after extreme public pressure.

To its credit, pressure from the Commission in connection with the testimony of Rice forced the rather embarrassing release of the President's Daily Briefing (PDB) for August 6, 2001 a document that clearly outlined al Qaeda plans to strike within the United States. The PDB was declassified on Saturday, April 10, 2004. Below is the entire text of the intelligence briefing that was released by the White House. Most remarkable are the chilling revelations in its final two paragraphs.

Bin Ladin Determined To Strike in US

Clandestine, foreign government, and media reports indicate bin Ladin since 1997 has wanted to conduct terrorist attacks in the US. Bin Ladin implied in US television interviews in 1997 and 1998 that his followers would follow the example of World Trade Center bomber Ramzi Yousef and "bring the fighting to America."

After US missile strikes on his base in Afghanistan in 1998, Bin Ladin told followers he wanted to retaliate in Washington, according to a...(redacted portion)...service. An Egyptian Islamic

Jihad (EIJ) operative told an...(redacted portion)...service at the same time that Bin Ladin was planning to exploit the operative's access to the US to mount a terrorist strike.

The millennium plotting in Canada in 1999 may have been part of Bin Ladin's first serious attempt to implement a terrorist strike in the US.

Convicted plotter Ahmed Ressam has told the FBI that he conceived the idea to attack Los Angeles International Airport himself, but that Bin Ladin lieutenant Abu Zubaydah encouraged him and helped facilitate the operation. Ressam also said that in 1998 Abu Zubaydah was planning his own US attack.

Ressam says Bin Ladin was aware of the Los Angeles operation. Although Bin Ladin has not succeeded, his attacks against the US Embassies in Kenya and Tanzania in 1998 demonstrate that he prepares operations years in advance and is not deterred by setbacks. Bin Ladin associates surveilled our Embassies in Nairobi and Dar es Salaam as early as 1993, and some members of the Nairobi cell planning the bombings were arrested and deported in 1997.

Al Qaeida members—including some who are US citizens—have resided in or traveled to the US for years, and the group apparently maintains a support structure that could aid attacks. Two al-Qa'ida members found guilty in the conspiracy to bomb our Embassies in East Africa were US citizens, and a senior EIJ member lived in California in the mid-1990s.

A clandestine source said in 1998 that a Bin Ladin cell in New York was recruiting Muslim-American youth for attacks.

We have not been able to corroborate some of the more sensational threat reporting, such as that from a...(redacted portion)...service in 1998 saying that Bin Ladin wanted to hijack a US aircraft to gain the release of "Blind Shaykh" Umar Abd al-Rahman and other US-held extremists.

Nevertheless, FBI information since that time indicates patterns of suspicious activity in this country consistent with preparations for hijackings or other types of attacks, including recent surveillance of federal buildings in New York.

The FBI is conducting approximately 70 full field investiga-
tions throughout the US that it considers Bin Ladin-related. CIA
and the FBI are investigating a call to our Embassy in the UAE in
May saying that a group of Bin Ladin supporters was in the US
planning attacks with explosives.

A few days after her testimony, a damning response to Rice swiftly came from a major new whistleblower, reviewed in an earlier section. In public statements intended to directly contradict Condoleezza Rice's testimony before the Commission, Sibel Edmonds revealed that she had previously provided information to the panel investigating the September 11 attacks, which she believes proved that senior officials knew of al Qaeda's plans to attack the US with aircraft months before the strikes happened. In three hours during a closed session with the Commission, she reiterated that information was circulating within the FBI in the spring and summer of 2001 that strongly suggested that an attack using aircraft was just months away and the terrorists were in place.

True to form, the Bush administration immediately sought to silence Edmonds, obtaining a gag order from a court as earlier noted. On March 24, 2004, in front of about fifty reporters and a dozen news cameras, Edmonds said "Attorney General John Ashcroft told me 'he was invoking State Secret Privilege and National Security' when I told the FBI I wanted to go public with what I had translated from the pre-9/11 intercepts."

In an effort to place a popular stamp of approval on the shoddy 9/11 Commission work, *Popular Mechanics* in March, 2005, published an issue largely devoted to an article entitled "9/11—Debunking the Myths." The magazine's cover uses the word "lies" instead of "myths" and stated: "Conspiracy Theories Can't Stand Up To The Hard Facts."

But did we get the hard facts? Not according to many 9/11 researchers who studiously combed through the popular magazine's report.

The "senior researcher" for this piece was Benjamin Chertoff. When contacted by reporter Christopher Bollyn and asked if he was any relation to Homeland Security chief Michael Chertoff, Benjamin replied, "I don't know."

Yet, when Bollyn contacted Benjamin Chertoff's mother and ask the same question, she promptly replied, "Yes, of course, he is a cousin." This is just one small example of the deceit which riddles the entire 9/11 case.

"This means that Hearst [Corporation] paid Benjamin Chertoff to write an article supporting the seriously flawed explanation that is based on a practically non-existent investigation of the terror event that directly led to the creation of the massive national security department his 'cousin' now heads," Bollyn noted dryly.

Longtime conspiracy writer Joel Skousen said the authors of articles attempting to debunk 9/11 theories use four primary tactics:

- They refuse to mention, much less attempt to disprove, the most irrefutable and damaging evidence.
- They take great delight in debunking only those conspiracy theories that are the weakest or that are planted by other government sympathizers to try and discredit the more credible conspiracy facts.
- They select only those "experts" who agree with the official conclusions.
- The snicker at or mock anyone who suggests that the government might engage in criminal behavior or would cover up crimes in collusion with judges, investigators, prosecutors, media heads and hand-picked commissions.

Skousen noted that these tactics were used extensively in the *Popular Mechanics* story. "In the March, 2005, PM magazine singled out 16 issues or claims of the 9/11 skeptics that point to government collusion and systematically attempted to debunk each one," he wrote. "Of the 16, most missed the mark and almost half were 'straw men' arguments—either ridiculous arguments that few conspiracists believed or restatements of arguments that were highly distorted so as to make them look weaker than they really were. PM took a lot of pot shots at conspiracy buffs, saying that those "who peddle fantasies that this country encouraged, permitted or actually carried out the attacks are libeling the truth—disgracing the memories of the thousands who died that day.'"

Serious researchers were just as quick to attack the work of the official 9/11 Commission.

Nafeez Mosaddeq Ahmed is executive director of the Institute for Policy Research & Development in Brighton, England, and author of the award-winning book *The War on Freedom: How & Why America was Attacked:*

September 11, 2001. After a detailed study of the 9/11 Commission's work, he concluded, "...the National Commission on Terror Attacks Upon the United States has failed dismally to investigate the 9/11 terror attacks in an appropriately credible and critical manner. Huge amounts of relevant historical and contemporary data have been ignored; irrelevant data and narratives have been used to construct an inaccurate chronology of 9/11 and its historical context; the embarrassing and damaging implications of ample evidence, including testimony presented to the Commission, have been overlooked; blatantly dishonest testimony contradicting well-documented facts has been uncritically accepted."

After closely studying the final *9/11 Commission Report*, author David Ray Griffin concluded that far from refuting the evidence of government complicity in the attacks, the Commission "simply ignored most of it and distorted the rest." He added, "I suggested that the Commission's attempt to defend the US military in particular against [public] suspicion is at best seriously flawed, at worst a set of audacious lies." Throughout the text of his scholarly study, Griffin repeatedly points out that the Commission took great pains to give an account of only those facts that were consistent with the Bush administration's official story.

In a later essay entitled *"The 9/11 Commission Report*: A 571-Page Lie,"* Griffin analyzed the pattern of lying in the report's pages, and provided a long list of 115 omissions and distortions that could be justifiably be portrayed as lies.

For reasons of space, these few items should suffice to demonstrate the omissions of the 9/11 Commission:

1. No mention of that fact that several credible sources stated that at least six of the alleged hijackers are still alive—including Waleed al-Shehri, accused of stabbing a flight attendant on Flight 11 before it crashed into the WTC North Tower.

2. The omission of reports concerning Mohamed Atta's fondness for alcohol, pork, and lap dances at odds with the Commission's claim that he had become a religious fanatic.

3. No mention of the role of Pakistani Intelligence (ISI), a pivotal element with reported ties to both the 9/11 hijackers and the CIA.

THE OFFICIAL 9/11 INQUIRY: ANOTHER WARREN COMMISSION?

4. No reporting on the blocking of meaningful terrorist investigations by the FBI during both the Clinton and Bush administrations.

5. The total lack of reporting on the 200 Israelis expelled from the US in 2002 as part of a massive spy ring, including five arrested after filming the destruction of the WTC from a New Jersey rooftop.

6. No mention of that fact that the CIA created al Qaeda in the 1980s when former CIA Director and then Vice President George Bush, Sr., controlled the government following the shooting of President Reagan.

7. Not one word about the close business and social ties between the Bush family and the bin Ladens nor of the fact that about 140 Saudis, including about 40 bin Laden family members, were allowed to congregate by air during the "no fly" period beginning the morning of 9/11.

8. The obfuscation of the evidence that Hani Hanjour was too poor a pilot to have flown an airliner into the Pentagon.

9. The omission of the fact that the publicly released flight manifests contain no Arab names.

10. No explanation of how, within hours of the attacks, FBI agents turned up in hotels, restaurants and flight schools used by the hijackers, and knew where to look.

11. The omission of the fact that fire has never, before or after 9/11, caused steel-frame buildings to collapse.

12. No mention of how it was possible that the South Tower collapsed first even though it had been burning a much shorter time the North Tower and also had less fire.

13. Omission of the fact that WTC7—which was not hit by an airplane and which had only small, localized fires—also collapsed, an occurrence that FEMA admitted it could not explain.

14. The omission of the fact that the collapse of the Twin Towers—like that of Building 7—demonstrated at least 10 features suggestive of controlled demolition.

15. No explanation for the claim that the core of the Twin Tow-

ers was "a hollow steel shaft," even though even a cursory examination of the WTC plans showed 47 massive steel columns constituting the core of each tower which should have prevented the "pancake theory" of the collapses.

16. The omission of WTC lease-holder Larry Silverstein's statement that he and the fire department commander decided to "pull" Building 7.

17. No mention of the fact that the steel from "ground zero" was quickly removed from the crime scene and shipped overseas before it could be analyzed for evidence of explosives.

18. Omission of Mayor Giuliani's statement that he had evacuated his temporary command center because he had received word that the World Trade Center towers were about to collapse.

19. No presentation of the fact that President Bush's brother Marvin and his cousin Wirt Walker III were both principals in the company in charge of security for the WTC.

20. Omission of the fact that there have been no photos released of the reconstructed debris of Flight 77 although this has been standard procedure in past airline disasters.

21. No discussion on how the damage done to the Pentagon was inconsistent with the impact of a Boeing 757 going several hundred miles per hour.

22. Omission of the fact that photos of the Pentagon's west wing's facade prior to its collapse 30 minutes after the strike revealed a hole too small to accommodate a Boeing 757.

23. No mention of all the various testimony that has been used to cast doubt on whether remains of a Boeing 757 were visible either inside or outside the Pentagon.

24. The omission of any discussion of whether the Pentagon had an anti-missile defense system that would have brought down a commercial airliner— even though the Commission suggested that the al Qaeda terrorists did not attack a nuclear power plant because they assumed that it would be thus defended.

25. Absolutely no mention of fatal anthrax attacks in the days

following 9/11, which involved weapons-grade pathogens obtainable only through the US military and were directed against leading Democrats who might have balked at the anti-terrorist measures within the PATRIOT Act.

26. Only one small footnote mentioned the "Vigilant Guardian" war games exercises which many feel were responsible for the confusion within the FAA and NORAD on 9/11.

It has been noted here that the 9/11 Commission unilaterally altered the time frame of 9/11 events, ignoring or brushing aside contradicting evidence presented under oath.

Such manipulation may have even reached into some US agencies. Democratic Senator Mark Dayton of Minnesota noted such inconsistencies during the first congressional hearing on the 9/11 Commission's report. He angrily accused, "NORAD lied to the American people, they lied to Congress and they lied to your commission." "We can set up all the organizations we want, but they won't be worth an Enron [the failed energy corporation] pension if the people responsible lie to us."

Considering the secret societies' goal of concentrating power through "globalization," it was no surprise that the commission's report called for a number of sweeping changes in government structure and policies—all without exception aimed at gathering more power to a centralized authority armed with vastly increased budgets.

Their call for revamping the intelligence community reflected further inconsistency. After detailing the problems the Director of Central Intelligence (DCI) has in coordinating various government agencies, the Commission commented, "No one person can do all these things." Their solution? Place all such intelligence operations under the control of one person, a new cabinet-level "National Intelligence Director."

The final 9/11 report is chock full of inconsequential and distracting details and backgrounding, filled with gaps and inconsistencies and, over all, merely a clarion call for a more centralized federal government presented as our best protector against further terrorism.

As in the Kennedy assassination, it is apparent that the federal government cannot be trusted to police itself. And as before, uncovering answers to the many 9/11 mysteries will be left to a grassroots army of private researchers.

After noting the distortions and the myriad omissions of the 9/11 Commission, Griffin concluded, "far from lessening my suspicions about official complicity, [the Commission's report] has served to confirm them. Why would the minds in charge of this final report engage in such deception if they were not trying to cover up very high crimes?"

Why indeed? But what crimes or agenda would high-level officials in the US government desire to cover up? To learn the answer to this question, attention should be directed to the Middle East.

PART II – WAR FOR OIL AND DRUGS

"We haven't heard from [Osama bin Laden]
in a long time.

I truly am not that concerned about him."

—President George W. Bush,
in a news conference on March 13, 2002

Oil and drugs are among the most profitable commodities in the world, coming in close behind the top moneymaker—armaments.

Therefore, it should be no surprise that foreign policy, political maneuvering and open warfare have resulted from the struggle to control oil and drugs. This struggle can be clearly seen in the US military action in Afghanistan.

Its genesis began on the high plateau of Iran, which curves along the southern shore of the Caspian Sea. In ancient times, this area was known as Persia and was the spawning ground of several great civilizations. It was also the home of the "eternal pillars of fire" worshiped by the followers of Zoroaster, a sixth-century B.C.E. sage who added monotheism to an even older Aryan creed. Today, most believe that the pillars of fire were flaming petroleum gas escaping through holes in the local limestone. Marco Polo wrote of springs in the area that produced water that was undrinkable but burned well and removed mange from camels. It was not until the modern era that man found a practical use for liquid petroleum—fuel for transportation and the machines of war.

In 1873, Robert and Ludwig Nobel, sons of the famed inventor of dynamite, Alfred Nobel, came to the Baku area on the western shore of the Caspian Sea and soon were supplying half of the world's petroleum supply. The Swedish Nobel brothers were soon in competition with the French branch of the powerful Rothschild banking family. At the same time, John D. Rockefeller's Standard Oil was becoming a major force in the burgeoning oil industry and also coveted the Caspian Sea oil. With the help of their respective governments, these powerful families competed for control over the Caspian Sea oil for decades. This struggle has been called "the Great Game."

Today, with the claim that the world is rapidly running out of oil, public attention has been focused on the issue of "Peak Oil." But the quest for oil is nothing new.

Petroleum has been behind all recent wars, beginning in the early 1940s, when a mostly rural and isolationist America was suddenly thrown into a world war as a reaction to the Japanese attack on Pearl Harbor. Americans mourned the loss of some three thousand soldiers and civilians in Hawaii and, in righteous indignation, allowed their country to be turned into a giant military camp. The federal government, which had consolidated so much power unto itself under the Depression-busting policies of President Franklin Delano Roosevelt, would now grow even stronger and more centralized under the aegis of "national security." It all seemed quite natural and necessary at the time.

But serious students of history now know that even that "good war" was the result of machinations by a handful of wealthy and powerful men. By closing off Japan's oil supplies in the summer of 1941, Roosevelt, closely connected to Wall Street power, ensured an eventual attack on the United States. It has now been well established that Roosevelt and a few close advisers knew full well that Pearl Harbor would be attacked on December 7, 1941, but chose to allow it to happen to further their agenda for dragging the isolationist American population into war.

In an odd addendum, the 9/11 attacks apparently blocked an effort to bring the truth concerning foreknowledge of the Pearl Harbor attack to the American public.

Ever since the war, efforts have been mounted to exonerate the two military commanders who were initially blamed as being unprepared for the attack on Pearl Harbor. The latest attempt, aided by Delaware Representative Michael Castle, was stopped when White House Chief of Staff Andrew Card refused to pass along a plea for exoneration to President Bush despite the admission that Rear Admiral Husband Kimmel and Major General Walter Short "were, without question, honorable and patriotic Americans who served our country with bravery and dedication." Furthermore, *White House Weekly*, in reporting this effort, declared, "Subsequent investigations by those inside and outside the military proved that Washington knew the Japanese were on the move but never told Hawaii."

According to reporter James P. Tucker, Jr. the rationale for not forwarding the plea from the officers' families to Bush was that the White House considered the issue too explosive in light of the questions being raised regarding the Bush administration's foreknowledge of the 9/11 attacks.

During World War II, Hitler's Army Group South rampaged through the Ukraine in Russia and moved inexorably toward Baku and the rich Caucasian oil fields. With these oil reserves in hand, Hitler planned to turn south and capture the oil of the Middle East in a combined operation with Field Marshal Erwin Rommel's famed Afrika Korps' assault from North Africa. This scheme was thwarted by Rommel's defeat at El Alamein and the eventual destruction of the German Sixth Army at Stalingrad.

The Vietnam War was about the oil and mineral wealth of Southeast Asia and was prosecuted by men who had been close to Roosevelt and the secretive Council on Foreign Relations (CFR). CFR position papers had long voiced a desire for the United States to gain control over Indochina's oil, magnesium and rubber assets. There also has been incessant speculation that drugs played a major role in US activities in the region, as some have argued that the war was a cover for allow covert protection for the "Golden Triangle" of opium production and to insure the clandestine importation of drugs to the United States.

In order to move into position in Southeast Asia, a provocation was again created. In August 1964, President Lyndon Johnson whipped Congress into a frenzy claiming that North Vietnamese gunboats had attacked the US Sixth Fleet in the Gulf of Tonkin off the coast of Vietnam. "Our boys are floating in the water," he cried. Congress responded by passing the Gulf of Tonkin Resolution, which bypassed the Constitution and gave Johnson the power to wage war to stop attacks on Americans. Soon after this, ground combat troops augmented American military advisers there. It was the beginning of the real shooting in the Vietnam War.

But the attack was all a lie. No evidence has ever been brought forward that such an attack ever took place. In fact, editors for *US News & World Report* (July 23, 1984) called it "The 'Phantom Battle' That Led to War."

While America was waging war against North Vietnam, which we were told was merely a puppet of communist Russia and China, Johnson was encouraged by his CFR advisers to grant the Soviet Union loans at higher levels than offered during World War II, when they were our ally. US-backed loans provided Russia with funds to build facilities that turned out war materials that were then sent to North Vietnam for use against American troops. This support for the opposing sides was a prime example of the duplicity of the financiers behind our modern wars.

Everyone understood that the Persian Gulf War of 1991, as with most Middle-East conflicts, was a war for oil that ended with its cause celebre, Saddam Hussein, the "new Hitler," still in power. This conflict also began with a fabricated provocation.

The well-publicized testimony of a young girl named Nayirah telling Congress how babies were dumped onto the floor from their incubators in a Kuwaiti hospital stirred angry support for war with Iraq. Months later, it was learned that "Nayirah" was actually the daughter of Kuwait's ambassador to the United States and that she had not actually seen the reported atrocities.

It was also learned that the American public relations firm of Hill & Knowlton had been paid $10.7 million by the Kuwaiti government to orchestrate a campaign to win American support for the war. Hill & Knowlton president Craig Fuller had been then-President George Bush's chief of staff when the senior Bush served as vice president under Ronald Reagan.

Interestingly, no one in Congress or the US news media bothered to substantiate the atrocity story. Similar unsubstantiated stories were presented to the UN a few weeks later by "witnesses," who were never placed under oath and were also coached by Hill & Knowlton.

Fabricated atrocity stories, stock purchases, oil and grain deals, arms sales, loans and guarantees, the weakening of the Arabs to benefit Israel, the movement toward a global army and government controlled by a global elite created a mind-numbing entanglement during this struggle. "It is doubtful whether the 'real' reasons why the United States went to war in the Persian Gulf will ever emerge," wrote authors Jonathan Vankin and John Whalen. "Unlike in Vietnam, where the ambiguous outcome elicited natural suspicions, in the Gulf the decisiveness of victory has buried the reality deeper than any Iraqi or American soldier who went to a sandy grave."

But at least one American leader understood the futility of attempting to occupy Iraq to further objectives of the West. In a 1998 book entitled *A World Transformed*, former President George H. W. Bush explained his decision to call a halt to the Gulf War.

"Trying to eliminate Saddam, extending the ground war into the occupation of Iraq, would have violated our guideline about not changing objectives in midstream, engaging in 'mission creep,' and would have incurred incalculable human and political costs. Apprehending him was probably impossible...We would have been forced to occupy Baghdad and, in effect, rule Iraq. The coalition would instantly have collapsed, the Arabs deserting it in anger and other allies pulling out as well. Under the circumstances, there was no visible 'exit strategy' we could see, violating another of our principles. Furthermore, we had been self-consciously trying to set a pattern for handling aggression in the post-Cold War world. Going in and occupying Iraq, thus unilaterally exceeding the United Nations' mandate, would have destroyed the precedent of international response to aggression that we hoped to establish. Had we gone the invasion route, the United States could conceivably still be an occupying power in a bitterly hostile land. It [the Gulf War] would have been a dramatically different—and perhaps barren—outcome."

Apparently, Bush's reasoned argument against the occupation of Iraq was lost on his son.

THE CENTRAL ASIAN GAS PIPELINE

Oil also came to drive the politics of Central Asia when, in the late 1970s, the Soviet Union discovered further untapped oil in the southern republic of Chechnya. This discovery, along with the oil deposits throughout the Caspian Sea region, upped the ante for the lands north of Persian Gulf nations. The region was ripe for exploitation but control over Afghanistan was needed to ensure the safety of a pipeline to bring the oil to world markets.

With the withdrawal of the Soviets from Afghanistan in 1989, international bankers and oilmen gained a foothold in cash-strapped Russia and the estimated $3 trillion in Caspian Sea oil was once again attracting serious attention. In 1997, six international companies and the government of Turkmenistan formed Central Asian Gas Pipeline, Ltd. (Cent-Gas) to build a 790-mile-long pipeline to link Turkmenistan's natural gas reserves with Pakistan and perhaps on to the New Delhi area of India.

Leading this consortium was America's Unocal Corporation, whose president, John F. Imle, Jr., said the project would be "the foundation for a new commerce corridor for the region often referred to as the Silk Road for the 21st Century."

Also involved were these companies: Delta Oil Company Limited of Saudi Arabia, Indonesia Petroleum Ltd. of Japan, ITOCHU Oil Exploration Co. Ltd. of Japan, Hyundai Engineering & Construction Co., Ltd. of Korea, and the Crescent Group of Pakistan. RAO Gazprom of Russia also was interested in joining the consortium.

But problems developed with the fundamentalist Muslim government in Afghanistan, not the least of which was the Taliban government's treatment of women, which prompted feminist-led demonstrations in America against firms seeking to do business there. Additionally, the Taliban regime was creating chaotic conditions by pitting the various Islamic sects against each other in order to maintain control. In early December 1998, Unocal withdrew from the pipeline consortium, citing the hazardous political situation, and the project languished.

Some event, some provocation, was required to propel the normally disinterested American public into supporting some sort of action in Afghanistan.

Many people have noticed that in President Bush's declaration of war on terrorism, he never mentioned terrorists in Northern Ireland or the Palestinian suicide bombers. Attention was only focused on Afghanistan, the one nation necessary to complete the lucrative pipeline and the leading supplier of opium. It should also be noted that Vice President Dick Cheney had been heavily involved in the oil industry. He headed the giant oil industry service company Halliburton and is generally thought to wield more power than the president. Halliburton had a major stake in the central Asian pipeline project as it would gain lucrative service contracts.

Despite Unocal's public announcement that it was withdrawing from the CentGas project, industry insiders said the firm never completely abandoned hopes for the project. The Texas-based Unocal never actually dropped plans for a trans-Afghanistan oil pipeline, which it considered a separate venture, and even held discussions on worker safety with the Taliban regime in March 2000.

With the shooting all but ended in Afghanistan by mid-2002, the gas pipeline project was back on a front burner. *BBC News* reported on May 13 of that year that interim leader Hamid Karzai was to hold talks with Pakistan and Turkmenistan officials to revive the $2 billion pipeline. Karzai, according to European news reports, formerly worked for Unocal, as did US envoy John J. Maresca. "The work on the project will start after an agreement is expected to be struck at the coming summit," said Mohammad Alim Razim, minister for Mines and Industries.

Mr. Razim stated Unocal was the "lead company" among those that would build the pipeline. He added that the pipeline is expected to be built with funds from donor countries earmarked for the reconstruction of Afghanistan.

A mere nine days after the new interim government of Hamid Karzai took power in Afghanistan, President Bush appointed National Security Council official Zalmay Khalilzad his special envoy. Unsurprisingly, Khalilzad, an American born in Afghanistan, had been employed by the oil giant Unocal. He also had taught political science at Columbia where he worked with former national security adviser Zbigniew Brzezinski, a co-founder of the Trilateral Commission. Khalilzad had been a longtime supporter of the Taliban.

THE CENTRAL ASIAN GAS PIPELINE

Khalilzad was also a member of the Project for the New American Century (PNAC), the neo-con think tank which in a 2000 paper declared that it would require a "catastrophic and catalyzing event—like a new Pearl Harbor" to gain the support of the American public for their Middle East agenda.

When George W. Bush was appointed president, Khalilzad was selected by Cheney to head the Bush transition team in the area of defense. In the spring of 2002, he was named by Bush as the chief National Security Council official working under National Security Adviser Condoleezza Rice, dealing with issues pertaining to the Persian Gulf and Central Asia. According to BBC reporter Mike Fox, Khalilzad "played an important part in developing the defense strategy of the Bush administration, both before and after the September the eleventh attacks."

The need for more and more petroleum even impacted on America's security in other odd ways. Former FBI counterterrorism chief John O'Neill said in an interview with French authors Jean Charles Brisard and Guillaume Dasquie, "(T)he main obstacles to investigate Islamic terrorism were US oil corporate interests and the role played by Saudi Arabia in it." Early in 2002, the former oil minister of Saudi Arabia, Ahmad Zaki al-Yamani, put it bluntly when he stated, "[The] US has a strategic objective, which is to control the oil of the Caspian Sea and [thereby] to end dependence on the oil of the [Persian] Gulf."

Of course, to challenge the oil and gas monopoly is to challenge the inner core leadership of Wall Street, the Council on Foreign Relations and other powerful interests, who have owned or controlled the federal government since before World War II. Until the American people gather the will to wean politicians off the oil spigot, this nation will continue to pursue a petroleum-based energy policy.

AFGHAN ATTACK WAS PLANNED LONG AGO

With $3 trillion in Caspian Sea oil as the prize, it can be demonstrated now that military action against Afghanistan has been in the works long before the September 11 attacks.

Shortly after Bush was selected for the presidency in late 2000, S.

Frederick Starr, head of the Central Asia Institute at Johns Hopkins University, stated in the *Washington Post*, "The US has quietly begun to align itself with those in the Russian government calling for military action against Afghanistan and has toyed with the idea of a new raid to wipe out bin Laden."

Others in that area were gearing up for an armed attempt to oust the Taliban.

Officials in India said their nation and Iran would only play the role of "facilitator" while the US and Russia would combat the Taliban from the front with the help of two Central Asian countries, Tajikistan and Uzbekistan, to push the Taliban lines back to the 1998 position.

Thus began the build up of American-led military operations against Afghanistan as reported by the Indian News Agency on June 26, 2001, more than two months prior to the attacks on the World Trade Center and the Pentagon.

As reported by BBC's George Arney, former Pakistani foreign secretary Niaz Naik was alerted by American officials in mid-July that military action against Afghanistan would be launched by mid-October. At a UN-sponsored meeting in Berlin concerning Afghanistan, Naik was informed that unless bin Laden was handed over, America would take military action either to kill or capture both him and Taliban leader Mullah Omar as the initial step in installing a new government there.

In other words, contrary to the words of America's leadership, who proclaimed that "everything has changed" because of the 9/11 attacks, US foreign policy stayed right on track, right down to the October date given out in the summer for military action in Afghanistan.

This was confirmed in early 2004 in a preliminary report by the 9/11 Commission. The report said the decision to overthrow the Taliban government of Afghanistan was made by senior Bush administration officials the day before the September 11, 2001, attacks. The panel stated that despite diplomatic efforts of both the Clinton and early Bush administrations coupled with a pledge to Saudi Arabia, the Taliban still had not made any effort to expel Osama bin Laden by September, 2001. No mention was made of the oil/gas pipeline deals.

However, it should be noted that American intervention in Afghanistan had actually begun years ago, even prior to the Soviet occupation.

AFGHAN ATTACK WAS PLANNED LONG AGO

In a 1998 interview with former national security adviser Zbigniew Brzezinski in the French publication *Le Nouvel Observateur,* he admitted that American activities in Afghanistan actually began six months prior to the 1979 Soviet invasion.

Brzezinski, Jimmy Carter's national security adviser, said the Carter administration began secretly funding anti-Soviet rebels in July 1979 with the full knowledge such action might provoke a Soviet invasion. Soviet leaders at the time argued the invasion was necessary to thwart American aggression in Afghanistan.

Brzezinski told French interviewers, "According to the official version of history, CIA aid to the Mujahideen began during 1980, that is to say, after the Soviet army invaded Afghanistan, 24 December, 1979. But the reality, secretly guarded until now, is completely otherwise. Indeed, it was July 3, 1979, that President Carter signed the first directive for secret aid to the opponents of the pro-Soviet regime in Kabul."

Based upon this admission, it would appear that the Soviets were speaking the truth when they told the world they were forced to move Russian troops into that nation to prevent a secret American takeover.

Brzezinski expressed no regret at this secret provocation, stating, "That secret operation was an excellent idea. It brought about the demoralization and finally the breakup of the Soviet empire." It also led to the creation of the Taliban regime as well as empowering Osama bin Laden.

But after almost ten years of brutal, no-quarter fighting against Afghans and Arab mercenaries backed by the United States, including Osama bin Laden, the Soviets were forced to withdraw. The economic stress of this Russo-Afghan War was enough to help topple communism in the early 1990s and Brzezinski was happy enough to take full credit for this even though it resulted in introducing militant Muslim theology into that volatile region.

Asked if he regretted such activities, Brzezinski replied, "What is most important to the history of the world? The Taliban or the collapse of the Soviet Empire? Some stirred up Moslems or the liberation of Central Europe and the end of the cold war?"

It is pertinent to note three things about the Brzezinski interview: one is that he is a leading luminary of the Council on Foreign Relations as well as a founder and today a member of the Trilateral Commission's executive committee; second, that with the apparent exception of a copy in the Library of Congress, his interview was not included in a truncated version of the article circulated in the United States; and third, no one in 1979 could have foreseen the collapse of communism, with or without the Afghan incursion.

In a 1997 Council on Foreign Relations study entitled *The Grand Chessboard: American Primacy and its Geostatic Imperatives*, Brzezinski clearly showed why he and his fellow CFR members believed it necessary for the United States to maintain a military presence in the Near East. "[A]s America becomes an increasingly multicultural society, it may find it more difficult to fashion a consensus on foreign policy issues," he wrote, "except in the circumstance of a truly massive and widely perceived direct external threat." He was explicit that such a threat would need to be on the order of the one that involved America in the last world war. "The attitude of the American public toward the external projection of American power has been much more ambivalent. The public supported America's engagement in World War II largely because of the shock effect of the Japanese attack on Pearl Harbor," Brzezinski wrote.

Shortly after 9/11, the *Guardian*, a British newspaper, conducted its own investigation and concluded that both Osama bin Laden and the Taliban received threats of possible American military attacks on them two months before 9/11. According to "senior diplomatic sources," the threats were passed along by the Pakistani government.

The newspaper elaborated on BBC reporter Arney's report of the pre-attack warnings by stating that the warning to the Taliban originated at a four-day meeting of senior Americans, Russians, Iranians and Pakistanis at a hotel in Berlin in mid-July 2001. The conference, the third in a series dubbed "brainstorming on Afghanistan," was part of a classic diplomatic device known as "track two," a method whereby governments can pass messages to each other. "The Americans indicated to us that in case the Taliban does not behave and in case Pakistan also doesn't help us to influence the Taliban, then the United States would be left with no option but to take an overt action against Afghanistan," said Niaz Naik, former foreign minister of Pakistan, who attended the Berlin meeting.

Many Internet sources have quoted from an interview with French authors Jean Charles Brisard and Guillaume Dasquie who told of US rep-

AFGHAN ATTACK WAS PLANNED LONG AGO

resentatives threatening, "Either you accept our offer of a carpet of gold, or we bury you under a carpet of bombs." However, no other source, including Naik, has confirmed this quote.

But the implication of the talks was much the same. Naik did say he was told that unless bin Laden was handed over quickly, America would take military action to kill or capture, not only bin Laden, but also Taliban leader Mullah Omar. He added that he was informed that the broader objective was to end the Taliban regime and install a transitional government in Afghanistan, presumably one less intransigent on the oil pipeline negotiations.

The former Pakistani diplomat was further informed that if such military action were to commence, it would happen before the first snows in Afghanistan, no later than the middle of October. Naik's prophetic words were reported on September 18, 2001, almost three weeks before the start of the US bombing campaign.

According to the *Guardian* article, the American representatives at the Berlin meeting were Tom Simons, a former US ambassador to Pakistan, Karl "Rick" Inderfurth, a former assistant secretary of state for South Asian affairs, and Lee Coldren, who headed the office of Pakistan, Afghan and Bangladesh affairs in the State Department until 1997.

Naik was quoted as saying that he specifically asked Simons why such an attack would be more successful than President Clinton's missile strikes against Afghanistan in 1998. That attack killed twenty persons but missed bin Laden.

"He said this time they were very sure. They had all the intelligence and would not miss him this time. It would be aerial action, maybe helicopter gunships," Naik said, adding, "What the Americans indicated to us was perhaps based on official instructions. They were very senior people. Even in 'track two' people are very careful about what they say and don't say."

No representative from the Taliban was present but Naik, representing one of only three governments that recognized the Taliban, said he passed the warning along to the Afghan authorities.

Coldren told the British paper, "I think there was some discussion of the fact that the United States was so disgusted with the Taliban that they might be considering some military action." But he added that it was not an agenda item at the meeting.

According to the article, Nikolai Kozyrev, Moscow's former special envoy on Afghanistan and one of the Russians in Berlin, would not confirm the contents of the US conversations, but said: "Maybe they had some discussions in the corridor. I don't exclude such a possibility."

Naik's recollection is that "we had the impression Russians were trying to tell the Americans that the threat of the use of force is sometimes more effective than force itself."

Simons denied having said anything about detailed operations and Inderfurth told the *Guardian*, "There was no suggestion for military force to be used. What we discussed was the need for a comprehensive political settlement to bring an end to the war in Afghanistan that has been going on for two decades and has been doing so much damage."

Told the American participants were denying the pre-attack warnings, Mr. Naik was quoted as saying, "I'm a little surprised but maybe they feel they shouldn't have told us anything in advance now we have had these tragic events."

Perhaps the reason that no one in the American delegation wanted to admit the pre-attack threats was given by the *Guardian* writers who speculated, "The Taliban refused to comply but the serious nature of what they were told raises the possibility that bin Laden, far from launching the attacks on the World Trade Center in New York and the Pentagon out of the blue ten days ago, was launching a pre-emptive strike in response to what he saw as US threats."

A pre-emptive strike? Could Osama bin Laden have been acting in self-defense? No one has mentioned that in the major corporate media.

The destruction of the Taliban actually was the object of several diplomatic discussions months before the events of 9/11, including a May 2001 meeting between the State Department and officials from Iran, Germany and Italy. The talks centered around replacing the Taliban with a "broad-based government." This same topic was raised at the Group of Eight (G-8) talks in Genoa, Italy, in July 2001.

Many people have questioned why we bombed Afghanistan when apparently none of the listed hijackers was an Afghan, but instead all but four were Arabs from Saudi Arabia. Since Iraq was implicated in the 1993 WTC attack, why did we not bomb that "rogue" nation in 2001? Bet-

AFGHAN ATTACK WAS PLANNED LONG AGO

ter yet, since Attorney General John Ashcroft announced soon after 9/11 that the "masterminds" of the attacks were operating out of Hamburg, Germany, why not bomb Germany, an activity with which America has had considerable experience in the past?

Such questions grew as American troops moved into Afghanistan, especially when it was found that the oil reserves might not be as productive as first believed.

Sources in the oil industry have reported that with the American military incursion into Afghanistan came the troubling news that the country might prove to be a dry hole. Once old seismic data was compared with actual drilling, it was learned that the Caspian Sea oil was concentrated in small pools rather than in large deep reserves. Another source of plentiful oil was needed.

That source may have become known to the public in late 2002, when the Bush administration appeared hell-bent on attacking Iraq despite howls of protest from other Middle East nations, many Americans and other NATO countries.

Despite the questions over Afghanistan's oil supply, American military action there was swift and deadly effective and not always aimed at strictly military targets.

Only three days after the US bombing began in early 2003, American firepower appeared to violate international conventions. In Afghanistan's capital, Radio Kabul was knocked off the air by US bombs, silencing the voice of the Taliban. Farhad Azad of Afghanmagazine.com reported that the station's stored musical library was lost. "The Taliban made music illegal, but it was US bombs that physically destroyed the hidden archive," he said. But more suspiciously, a month later the Kabul offices of satellite television station Al-Jazeera, which sat in the middle of a residential neighborhood, were struck by two five hundred-pound bombs.

Colonel Brian Hoey, a spokesman for the US Central Command, confirmed that the United States had bombed the building but stated, "[T]he indications we had was that this was not an Al-Jazeera office."

Al-Jazeera had already come under figurative fire from US authorities for broadcasting interviews with Osama bin Laden. The station also had aired interviews with Donald Rumsfeld and National Security Adviser Condoleezza Rice.

The military action against a civilian TV station "could prove to be a public relations fiasco for the US government," noted the *Washington Post* at the time. But this could only occur if the American people were told about it. In fact, little or no reporting on this incident reached the public.

The evidence that operations against Afghanistan were planned long before the 9/11 attacks prompted author Gore Vidal to remark, "With that background, it now becomes explicable why the first thing Bush did after we were hit was to get Senator Daschle and beg him not to hold an investigation of the sort any normal country would have done. When Pearl Harbor was struck, within twenty minutes the Senate and the House had a joint committee ready. Roosevelt beat them to it, because he knew why we had been hit, so he set up his own committee. But none of this was to come out and it hasn't come out."

Since it is now plain that military operations against Afghanistan were in the planning stages months before 9/11, the question must be asked why there was no buildup of propaganda in the American media. Before every military action, the reasons and rationales must be placed before the public to accustom them to the idea and gain their support. Yet, while both diplomatic and military preparations were being made for war against Afghanistan, the American public remained ignorant and contented. Some researchers contend this is an indication that national leaders knew such a propaganda campaign would be unnecessary because a surprise attack would do the job.

WAG THE DOG IN IRAQ?

Just such a propaganda campaign was in progress prior to the invasion of Iraq in March 2003, President Bush told Americans that Saddam Hussein was preparing weapons of mass destruction that demanded a preemptive strike.

There was little mention of other nations who also have weapons of mass destruction, such as India, Pakistan, France, Israel, Russia and China. At the time, India and Pakistan seem frighteningly determined to use theirs. Nor was there any mention of traditional terrorist groups like the Irish Republican Army, the Shining Path, Hamas, Islamic Jihad or others.

In fact, it was later announced that the Bush administration had been informed as early as October 3, 2002, that North Korea, a military power more than twice the size of Iraq, had developed nuclear capability as well as even "more powerful" chemical or biological weapons. Yet no mention of this "Axis of Evil" nation was made during the remainder of the month when Bush sought and won a congressional resolution approving an attack on Iraq. Democrats, especially in the Senate, fumed because Bush officials kept them in the dark about North Korea's plans just as they were deliberating the Iraqi resolution. Ordinary Americans snickered that, of course, North Korea has no oil to covet.

Also missing amongst the press coverage of North Korean's nuclear development plans was the fact that the funds needed to produce weapons-grade plutonium in their nuclear reactors came from US taxpayers, approved by President Bush in the spring of 2002.

In early April, Bush released about $94 million to North Korea as part of the 1994 Agreed Framework agreement to replace older nuclear reactors despite suspicions that their nuclear project was being used to produce weapons (North Korea had refused to allow UN inspections). According to *BBC News*, Bush argued that his decision was "vital to the national security interests of the United States." About that same time, Bush argued that it was equally vital to attack Iraq.

Prominently missing from the crescendo of corporate mass media pieces on the need to move into Iraq were the names and arguments of many prominent persons who counseled caution. Eighteen former high-ranking US military leaders, intelligence analysts, diplomats and academics in early 2002 sent President Bush a letter urging him to "resist military actions against Iraq and focus on capturing the terrorists responsible for the September 11 attacks."

Among those who signed the letter were retired navy admiral Eugene Carroll, former CIA national intelligence officer William Christison, former chief of mission to Iraq Ed Peck, former ambassador to Saudi Arabia James Atkins, and former senator George McGovern.

The story of this letter was featured in China's official news agency Xinhau but received little attention at home.

Democratic Senator Robert Byrd of West Virginia claimed Bush's effort to start a war with Iraq was nothing more than a conscious effort to distract public attention from domestic problems. "This administration, all of a sudden, wants to go to war with Iraq," Byrd said. "The polls are dropping, the domestic situation has problems. All of a sudden we have this war talk, war fervor, the bugles of war, drums of war, clouds of war. Don't tell me that things suddenly went wrong." Byrd said his allegiance to the Constitution prevented him from voting for Bush's war resolution. "But I am finding that the Constitution is irrelevant to people of this administration."

It was soon discovered that the decision for war against Iraq had come just hours following the 9/11 attacks, at a time when there was no evidence indicating Iraqi involvement. According to CBS Correspondent David Martin, notes taken by aides just five hours after the attacks show Secretary of Defense Rumsfeld ordered up plans for a strike against Iraq. According to notes made at the time, Rumsfeld ordered, "Go massive; sweep it all up; destroy it all. Things related and not, it doesn't matter."

By mid-2002, the push for war against Iraq was increasing within the Bush administration despite lack of any real proof that Saddam represented a threat to the United States. In fact, much of the proof that was presented later proved dubious.

For example, on September 7, 2002, President Bush was trying to summon support for an attack on Iraq. In a news conference with British Prime Minister Tony Blair, Bush announced, "I would remind you that when the inspectors first went into Iraq and were denied access, a report came out of the IAEA [International Atomic Energy Agency] that they were six months away from developing a weapon; I don't know what more evidence we need."

However, Mark Gwozdecky, chief spokesman for the IAEA, stated days later, "There's never been a report like that issued from this agency. We have never put a time frame on how long it might take Iraq to construct a nuclear weapon." Bush and Blair also cited an IAEA report claiming satellite photography had revealed that the Iraqis were starting construction at several nuclear-related sites. Again, the IAEA, the agency charged with assessing Iraq's nuclear capability for the UN, denied any such report.

When asked about the contradictions Bush White House Deputy Press secretary Scott McClellan said, "He's [Bush] referring to 1991 there. In

'91, there was a report saying that after the war they found out they were about six months away."

1991? More than six months had passed between 1991 and late 2002.

Gwozdecky, speaking from IAEA headquarters in Vienna, said there was no such report issued in 1991 either. In fact, in an October 1998 report to the UN secretary-general, IAEA director-general Mohamed El-baradei stated, "There are no indications that there remain in Iraq any physical capability for the production of weapon-usable nuclear material of any practical significance."

Gwozdecky told one reporter, "There is no evidence in our view that can be substantiated on Iraq's nuclear weapons program. If anybody tells you they know the nuclear situation in Iraq right now, in the absence of four years of inspections, I would say they're misleading you because there isn't solid evidence out there."

The chief UN weapons inspector Hans Blix confirmed in April 2003 that plans to attack Iraq were longstanding and had little to do with weapons of mass destruction. "There is evidence that this war was planned well in advance," Blix stated in an interview with the Spanish daily *El Pais*. Blix said that despite assurances from President Bush in late 2002 that he supported the UN's efforts to determine if Iraq had any biological, chemical or nuclear weapons, "I now believe that finding weapons of mass destruction has been relegated, I would say, to fourth place...Today, the main aim is to change the dictatorial regime of Saddam Hussein."

On February 5, 2003, Secretary of State Colin Powell stood before the United Nations and presented a scathing indictment of Iraq's transgressions and called for a coalition to oust the regime of Saddam Hussein. "My colleagues, every statement I make today is backed up by sources, solid sources. These are not assertions. What we're giving you are facts and conclusions based on solid intelligence," Powell told his audience.

It was later learned and widely reported in Europe that Powell's presentation was based on a British government dossier which had plagiarized the work of a California graduate student named Ibrahim al-Marashi. Large portions of al-Marashi's essay had been taken by British intelligence and, in some cases, altered in a manner damaging to Iraq. The essay had been published in September 2002 in a small journal entitled the *Middle East Review of International Affairs*.

If this wasn't problem enough to the hawks pushing for war in Iraq, Powell also produced for the UN a satellite photo of a northern Iraqi installation said to be producing chemical weapons for both Saddam Hussein and the al Qaeda network. Some days later when news reporters actually toured the camp they found nothing but a bunch of dilapidated huts with no indoor plumbing or the electrical capability to produce such weapons.

But the most amazing evidence of official duplicity came with media reports concerning a meeting in the Waldorf Astoria between Powell and British Foreign Secretary Jack Straw just prior to his rousing speech at the UN. Powell complained that the claims coming out of the Pentagon—particularly those made by Deputy Secretary Wolfowitz—could not be substantiated. Faced with the possibility that the evidence for WMD in Iraq might "explode in their faces," Powell reportedly tossed briefing documents into the air and cried, "I'm not reading this. This is bullshit!"

Despite all this, Powell went ahead with his speech and the corporate-controlled mass media did their job of dutifully supporting his assertions.

Even his own staff was apparently taken in by the "evidence" put before them.

US Army Colonel (Retired) Lawrence B. Wilkerson served as the Department of State's chief of staff from August 2002 to January 2005. He also served as special assistant to General Colin Powell when Powell was chairman of the US Joint Chiefs of Staff.

In a February, 2006, interview with PBS host David Brancaccio, Wilkerson said that despite the fact that both the Intelligence Bureau and the State Department concluded there was no active nuclear program in Iraq, "…neither of those dissents in any fashion or form were registered with me [or others]…In fact it was presented in the firmest language possible that the mobile biological labs and the sketches we had drawn of them for the Secretary's presentation were based on the iron clad evidence of multiple sources…

"My participation in that presentation at the UN constitutes the lowest point in my professional life. I participated in a hoax on the American people, the international community and the United Nations Security Council. How do you think that makes me feel?"

WAG THE DOG IN IRAQ?

Host Brancaccio suggested that senior government officials also might not have known the truth. "I have to believe that. Otherwise I have to believe some rather nefarious things about some fairly highly placed people in the intelligence community and perhaps elsewhere," responded Wilkerson.

Unaware of Powell's doubts and concerns, the American public only heard comments such as these from corporate media commentators and pundits: "an accumulation of painstakingly gathered and analyzed evidence," so that "only the most gullible and wishful thinking souls can now deny that Iraq is harboring and hiding weapons of mass destruction," "a massive array of evidence," "a detailed and persuasive case," "a powerful case," "an overwhelming case," "a compelling case," "the strong, credible and persuasive case," "a persuasive, detailed accumulation of information," "a smoking fusillade...a persuasive case for anyone who is still persuadable," "The skeptics asked for proof; they now have it," "Powell's evidence overwhelming," "ironclad...incontrovertible," "succinct and damning...the case is closed," "If there was any doubt that Hussein...needs to be...stripped of his chemical and biological capabilities, Powell put it to rest."

Such problems with the rationales given for war prompted one Democratic Congressman to state that President Bush would lie to provoke war with Iraq.

Jim McDermott of Washington State in an ABC interview pointed out that in fall 2002, the Iraqis had pledged to allow unrestricted inspections within their country. "They should be given a chance," said McDermott, who voted against war with Iraq in 1991, "otherwise we're trying to provoke them into war." Following a visit to Iraq, McDermott said he believed Bush "would mislead the American people" to go to war with Iraq.

Another congressman on the visit to Baghdad, Michigan Democrat David Bonior, said a renewed war with Iraq would bring further suffering to the Iraqi people, especially children suffering from cancers caused by the US use of depleted uranium shells, which he described as "horrific and barbaric."

Apparently lacking the spirit of American freedom of speech, Senate Minority Leader Trent Lott referred to McDermott saying, "He needs to come home and keep his mouth shut."

Even former president Clinton weighed in by urging the Bush administration to finish the job with Osama bin Laden before taking on Iraq. Speaking at a Democratic Party fund-raiser in early September 2002, Clinton undoubtedly spoke for millions of Americans when he said, "Saddam Hussein didn't kill 3,100 people on September 11. Bin Laden did, and as far as we know he's still alive. I also believe we might do more good for American security in the short run at far less cost by beefing up our efforts in Afghanistan, Pakistan and elsewhere to flush out the entire network."

One pivotal Democrat who spoke out against war with Iraq was Minnesota Senator Paul Wellstone, who also was one of the few congressmen calling for an independent investigation of the 9/11 attacks. Wellstone, who according to supporters worked for the benefit of all his constituents including workers, unionists and the needy, in late October 2002 was in a tough political fight against a Republican challenger backed by both GOP money and the Bush White House. Wellstone's seat could have tipped the entire Senate into the Republican camp, giving Bush a majority in Congress.

But the question of whether Wellstone might have won his battle will never be answered. He, his wife and daughter, three staffers and two pilots were killed in a private plane crash on October 25, 2002. It was reminiscent of the many plane crashes that have taken so many members of Congress, especially during the Reagan administration. In fact, even in 2006, disturbing questions were still being raised about the cause of Wellstone's fatal crash.

Texas Representative Ron Paul even noted that his challenge to the constitutionality of a war with Iraq was blocked on live TV and prompted the chairman of one congressional committee to openly declare that the US Constitution is no longer relevant. In a late 2002 newsletter to his constituents, Paul wrote that during hearings on the Iraqi war resolution before the International Relations Committee being televised live by C-SPAN, he tried to bring up the issue that declaring war was a power granted only to Congress by the Constitution, but the ranking minority member called his attempt to add an amendment declaring war "frivolous and mischievous." "The proposed resolution on the use of force mentioned the United Nations twenty-five times. That was considered safe. Not once did it mention the Constitution. I do not look to the UN to find the authority for this sovereign nation to defend herself," stated Paul. "It was almost noon on October 3, the second day of the hearings, when my turn came [after offering his war amendment] I reminded the committee of the words of James Madison, who in 1798 said, 'The Constitution supposes what the history of all governments demonstrates, that the Executive is the branch of power most interested in war and most prone to it. It has accordingly, with studied care, vested the question of war in the legislature.' The Chair[man, Illinois Republican Henry J. Hyde] went on to say that the Constitution has been 'overtaken by events, time' and is 'no longer relevant.' At least it was out in the open. Now surely the display of such disdain for their oath to 'support and defend the Constitution' would light up Capitol Hill switchboards with angry callers!

"Little did I know that no one watching the hearings over C-SPAN not one single person of what statistically is an audience of several million Americans even heard those inflammatory comments. When my staff called C-SPAN to get a copy of the video record to document these outrageous statements, we were told 'technical difficulties' prevented that portion of the proceedings from being recorded and that same portion of the proceedings was also the only part missing on the internal record the House makes of such official hearings. It was as though it never happened."

One Democrat who dared to simply raise questions about the War on Terrorism lost her seat in Congress. Representative Cynthia McKinney represented the 4th District of Georgia, which includes Decatur, just outside Atlanta. This was the district that sent Newt Gingrich to Washington. McKinney had three strikes against her in this Dixie district: she was a woman, black and a Democrat. The forty-seven-year-old former college professor was also quite outspoken.

At a peace rally in Washington on April 20, 2002, Rep. McKinney told the crowd, "despite our differences, we are here today as one community with one thing in common: a desire to see the restoration of the true ideals of America. America—where the fundamental rights to vote, speak and practice religion mean something. But America today is still a far cry from the noble Republic founded upon these words: All men are created equal." She then declared, "Sadly, nor is ours a democratic society. In November 2000, the Republicans stole from America our most precious right of all: the right to free and fair elections.

"Florida Governor Jeb Bush and his secretary of state, Katherine Harris, created a phony list of convicted felons, 57,700 to be exact, to 'scrub' thousands of innocent people from the state's voter rolls. Of the thousands who ultimately lost their vote through this scrub of voters, 80 percent were African-Americans, mostly Democratic Party voters. Had they voted, the course of history would have changed. Instead, however, Harris declared Bush the victor by only 537 votes. [Note that within two months of the 2000 election, according to *US News & World Report*, Harris was inducted into the Council on Foreign Relations.]

"Now President Bush occupies the White House, but with questionable legitimacy. But, however he got there, his Administration is now free to spend one to four billion dollars a month on the wars in Afghanistan and Iraq; free to cut the high deployment overtime pay of our young service men and women fighting in that war; free to propose drilling in the Arctic National Wildlife Reserve National Park; free to stonewall on the Enron and Energy Task Force investigations; free to revoke the rules that keep our drinking water free of arsenic; free to get caught in Venezuela and free to propose laws that deny our citizens sacred freedoms cherished under the Constitution.

"We must dare to remember all of this. We must dare to debate and challenge all of this."

Some time later, McKinney drew the ire of Washington insiders when she dared to suggest that Bush administration officials may have ignored warnings of the terrorist attack to further their political agenda and that they and their cronies were profiting from the War on Terrorism. The war-for-profit argument has much objective data to support it, as will be seen later. McKinney certainly spoke for many when she said that the Bush administration has created a climate in which elected officials must censor themselves or be branded as less than patriotic.

McKinney also suggested that the War on Terrorism has benefited the Washington based Carlyle Group investment firm, which employs a number of former high-ranking government officials, including former president George H. W. Bush.

WAG THE DOG IN IRAQ?

A Carlyle Group spokesman, while not addressing McKinney's facts, nevertheless asked, "Did she say these things while standing on a grassy knoll in Roswell, New Mexico?" It was truly ironic that such dismissive tactics should come at a time when a growing number of persons believe there is compelling evidence that there was a conspiracy to kill President Kennedy, and have a willingness to consider that there may be substance to the claims of a UFO crash near Roswell in 1947.

Typical of the attacks against McKinney to be found in the mainstream corporate media were the remarks of *Orlando Sentinel* columnist Kathleen Parker, who described the congresswoman as "a delusional paranoiac" and called for an investigation of the woman "as passionately as she demands we investigate Bush's 'involvement' in the 9/11 terror attacks." Parker added, "We no longer can afford to tolerate people like McKinney, who should never be taken seriously."

In the face of such mass media diatribes, not to mention that Georgia allows cross-over voting, McKinney was defeated in the 2002 Democratic Primary but rallied by regaining her congressional seat in the 2004 election. She went on to conduct crucial Congressional hearings concerning the possibility of administration complicity in 9/11 in the summer of 2005 and early 2006.

Columnist Parker's attack was echoed throughout the mass media, which called attention to the fact that McKinney had accepted, long before 9/11, campaign contributions from Abdurrahman Alamoudi, founder of the American Muslim Council, and a man who has voiced support for terrorist organizations such as Hamas and Hezbollah.

Naturally, no one in the mainstream media called attention to the fact that the Bush administration blocked a number of investigations into their connections with terrorist groups or that the family has been longtime friends with the Saudi royalty.

For example, about a week after McKinney's primary defeat, President Bush telephoned Saudi crown prince Abdullah and praised "eternal friendship" between the United States and Saudi Arabia. The president then retired to his Crawford, Texas, ranch for some private time with Saudi ambassador Prince Bandar bin Sultan and his family. The visit was styled as a family trip and a casual get-together. No cameras were allowed and neither Bush nor his royal guest would agree to be interviewed.

Also the media failed to mention that, according to British publications, the Republican Party had been receiving sizeable contributions from the Arabic Safa trust, which at the same time was funneling money to terrorist groups.

All of this came about shortly after a Rand Corporation analyst briefed a Pentagon advisory panel, stating, "The Saudis are active at every level of the terror chain, from planners to financiers, from cadre to foot soldier, from ideologist to cheerleader. Saudi Arabia supports our enemies and attacks our allies."

It must be noted that no one disputes the fact that fifteen of the nineteen 9/11 hijackers named by the FBI were Saudis and that six hundred families of 9/11 victims of the attacks filed a trillion-dollar lawsuit against Saudi officials, including members of the royal family, contending complicity in the terror attacks.

It is also interesting to note that some media lose enthusiasm for polling when the outcome deviates from the desired results. For example, in 2002 the *Atlanta Journal-Constitution* placed a poll on its Web site asking, "Are you satisfied the Bush administration had no warning of the September 11 attacks?"

Visitors could vote "Yes," "No, I think officials knew it was coming" or "Not sure." The vote seesawed back and forth for one day. When the final count of 23,145 voters showed 52 percent for "Yes," 46 percent "No" and only 1 percent "Not sure," the poll was suddenly pulled with no real explanation.

Even more odd was the lack of mass media attention given to a Zogby International poll conducted between August 24 and 26, 2004, on the eve of the Republican National Convention.

The poll showed that one half of New York City residents (49.3 percent) and 41 percent of New York state residents believed that some national leaders "knew in advance that attacks were planned on or around September 11, 2001, and that they consciously failed to act."

Despite the political implications of such an accusation, nearly 30 percent of registered Republicans and more than 38% of those who described themselves as "very conservative" supported this proposition.

The Bush administration continued its push for war with Iraq despite such polls and massive, though under-reported, anti-war demonstrations in American cities.

What were considered controversial concerns over the pretext for war against Iraq in 2002 became solidified in May, 2005, with the public release of a "secret" memo in the United Kingdom.

What came to be known as the "Downing Street Memo" was a report written by British National Security Aide Matthew Rycroft of a July, 2002, meeting between British Prime Minister Tony Blair and advisers, including Richard Dearlove, head of the MI6 intelligence service, who had just returned to England from Washington after a briefing on Iraq by Bush administration officials.

The contents of the memo caused a considerable stir in Europe but were largely unreported by the US mass media.

The memo fully supported accusations that Bush—contrary to his public statements—had not taken seriously any course of action but military. Further, it revealed that the intelligence on Weapons of Mass Destruction (WMD) was known to be flimsy and that Bush and Blair had no clear exit strategy. It stated, "...There was a perceptible shift in [the administration's] attitude [toward Iraq]. Military action is now seen as inevitable. Bush wanted to remove Saddam, through military action, justified by the conjunction of terrorism and WMD. But the intelligence and facts were being fixed around the policy. The NSC [National Security Council] had no patience with the UN route and no enthusiasm for publishing material on the Iraqi regime's record. There was little discussion in Washington of the aftermath after military action."

Farther down in the document, it added, "It seemed clear that Bush had made up his mind to take military action, even if the timing was not yet decided. But the case was thin. Saddam was not threatening his neighbors, and his WMD capability was less than that of Libya, North Korea or Iran."

The crucial passage in this memo, of course, was that Bush was "fixing" the intelligence around his policy. Yet, this admission by America's strongest ally did not seem to faze either the US corporate mass media or the ill-informed American public.

Hearst Newspaper columnist Helen Thomas lamented the lack of public response, writing, "I am not surprised at the duplicity. But I am astonished at the acceptance of this deception by voters in the United

States and the United Kingdom. I've seen two US presidents go down the drain—Lyndon B. Johnson on Vietnam and Richard Nixon in the Watergate scandal—because they were no longer believed. But times change—and I guess our values do, too."

Other commentators politicized the implication of the memo by blaming Bush's enemies and by tossing its contents off as unworthy of serious debate. *Christian Science Monitor* columnist Bud Beck wrote, "This is not the Watergate burglary and it is not a fabricated Gulf of Tonkin incident. It is nothing new, just a new version of something that is old—so old it has become all but too boring."

But by 2006, the deceitful ramp-up to the Iraqi invasion gained further confirmation, again from a once-secret British document.

Philippe Sands, a professor of international law at University College in London, made public a memo regarding a January 31, 2003 meeting between Bush and Blair in which Blair gave assurance he was "solidly" behind plans to attack Iraq. This was despite any second UN resolution and before Blair sought advice on the invasion's legality.

In this memo, there was even the mention of the bizarre possibility that Bush was contemplating a provocation to tempt Saddam into firing on United Nations' aircraft. According to the memo, Bush was so concerned about the failure to find any hard evidence against Saddam, he considered "flying U2 reconnaissance aircraft planes with fighter cover over Iraq, painted in UN colors" hoping that "[i]f Saddam fired on them, he would be in breach [of UN resolutions]."

It should be noted that the two British memos have been acknowledged as genuine by the British government, but White House spokesman Scott McClellan, true to form, denied the interpretation of the Downing Street Memo brandished by Bush critics.

Despite such ongoing controversy over the deceptive plan to go to war with Iraq—including peace demonstrations rivaling those during the Vietnam era—a cowed and compliant Congress had long before opted out. In the wake of the wave of fear generated by 9/11, it had voted overwhelmingly in October 2002 to authorize Bush to launch his war whenever he desired. Once again the ugliest side of politics revealed itself: The politicians in Congress knew that if Bush's action in Iraq proved successful, they could share the credit and glory come the next elections; but if it proved to be an unwise decision, they could shift the blame to the president. So, an affirmative vote was much safer than to stand among the courageous few for the sake of honesty and integrity.

The irony of Bush urging war with Iraq because of Saddam Hussein's actions was not lost on commentators in other parts of the world. "There is something almost comical about the prospect of George Bush waging war on another nation because that nation has defied international law," wrote George Monbiot of London's *Guardian*. "Since Bush came to office, the United States government has torn up more international treaties and disregarded more UN conventions than the rest of the world has in twenty years."

As the occupation of Iraq continued with mounting losses a worldwide poll showed most respondents did not believe themselves any safer from terrorism.

In one of the largest polls ever conducted, the British BBC World Service in early 2006 reported that the majority of those polled worldwide believe the war in Iraq has increased rather than diminished the chances of terrorist attacks.

This survey of 41,856 people in 35 countries found about 60 percent of those polled shared this view. Only 12 percent thought the war had reduced the chances of an attack, with 15 percent saying it had no effect either way. In Britain, 77 percent of those questioned thought the terrorist threat had risen since the 2003 invasion.

"Though the Bush administration has framed the intervention in Iraq as a means of fighting terrorism, all around the world most people view it as having increased the likelihood of terrorist attacks." said Steven Kull, director of the Program on International Policy Attitudes at the University of Maryland, which helped conduct the survey between October 2005 and January 2006.

Even more disconcerting were the results of a poll of US troops in Iraq in early 2006. This poll, conducted by Zogby International and Le Moyne College, showed 72 percent of respondents said they should withdraw from Iraq within 12 months. A surprising 29 percent said there should be an immediate pull-out. Only 23 percent said US troops should remain in Iraq "as long as they are needed."

The president of Zogby International, John Zogby, said US commanders in Iraq unofficially approved the poll of 944 respondents, which was conducted before the escalation in violence in February 2006.

Showing that military personnel are not immune to misconceptions, the poll of service personnel indicated 85 percent of the troops agreed that the US mission in Iraq was "to retaliate for Saddam's role in the 9/11 attacks," even though President Bush has publicly acknowledged that Iraq played no role in the attacks. John Zogby described this notion as "bewildering."

The disillusionment of American service personnel was reflected in a CBS News poll conducted in late February 2006, which show less than 30 percent of respondents approved of Bush's handling of the war.

Despite such opinions and the questionable intelligence leading to the US invasion, there were still large profits to be made in Iraq. Vice President Dick Cheney, already under attack for his involvement in profiting from doing business in Iraq despite US sanctions in place since the Gulf War, was pinpointed as one whose business interests profited from the 9/11 attacks.

CHENEY'S DEALINGS IN IRAQ

"**U**nder the guidance of Richard Cheney, a get-the-government-out-of-my-face conservative, Halliburton Company over the past five years [1995 to 2000] has emerged as a corporate welfare hog, benefiting from at least $3.8 billion in federal contracts and taxpayer-insured loans," stated a report by the Washington-based Center for Public Integrity.

And it was Cheney who led the effort to wage war on Iraq and Afghanistan. "But Cheney isn't just selling the policy. He is on the inside making it," noted Kenneth T. Walsh of *US News & World Report*. "In fact, to understand the Bush presidency, it is necessary to understand how central Cheney's role actually is and how his innate conservatism is an anchor for administration policy not just on Iraq but across the board."

In 1991, the elder President Bush awarded Cheney the Presidential Medal of Freedom. Cheney, age sixty-one in 2002, was an important choice for Bush Jr. in the election year of 2000. Cheney had, ironically, promised the nation "light at the end of the tunnel" in Vietnam during his stint with the Nixon administration. He was a crucial part of the defense policy team around Rumsfeld, Wolfowitz, and other up-and-coming neo-conservatives who succeeded in exaggerating the Soviet threat of WMDs during the Ford and Reagan administrations; these efforts led to the greatest peace-time military buildup in American history, and to a nuclear confrontation with USSR in the mid-1980s. Cheney had also staunchly supported such questionable covert operations as the Contra war in Nicaragua and the CIA-led war in Afghanistan during his congressional service under the Reagan administration. And he had overseen the 1989 invasion of Panama, with its egregious loss of civilian life, and the massive destruction of Saddam Hussein's war machine while serving as Secretary of Defense during the Gulf War under the previous Bush administration. He then helped push through onerous trade sanctions against Iraq through the United Nations that impoverished the country.

Following the defeat of Bush Sr. in 1992 Cheney entered the world of corporate business and by 1995 became president and chief executive officer of the Halliburton Company of Dallas. Halliburton is the world's largest oil service firm and, according to *Oil & Gas Journal*, the company ranks twenty-fourth in the top energy corporations in the world, with a market value of $18.2 billion. The company employs about 100,000 people in 120 countries.

Cheney's firm soon began to lay down a record of questionable ethics—and through a subsidiary, gained a lion's share of the $30 billion emergency funds appropriated in 2001 by Congress in the War on Terrorism.

"From building cells for detainees at Guantanamo Bay in Cuba to feeding American troops in Uzbekistan, the Pentagon is increasingly relying on a unit of Halliburton called KBR, sometimes referred to as Kellogg, Brown & Root," reported Jeff Gerth and Don Van Natta Jr. of the *New York Times*. "Although the unit has been building projects all over the world for the federal government for decades, the attacks of September 11 have led to significant additional business. KBR is the exclusive logistics supplier for both the Navy and the Army, providing services like cooking, construction, power generation and fuel transportation. The contract recently won from the Army is for 10 years and has no lid on costs, the only logistical arrangement by the Army without an estimated cost."

As detailed in *Crossfire: The Plot That Killed Kennedy*, George and Herman Brown, who created the construction firm back in the late 1930s, are credited with putting Lyndon B. Johnson in Congress and have benefited from prime government contracts ever since, beginning with a large naval base in Corpus Christi, Texas, and later in South Vietnam. After merging with Halliburton, the company provided logistical support for the Pentagon in Haiti, Somalia, the Balkans and more recently, in Afghanistan and Iraq.

Halliburton officials denied that Cheney played any role in assisting KBR in obtaining government contracts but did admit that the senior vice president responsible for the lucrative KBR contracts, former four-star navy admiral Joe Lopez, was hired in 1999 on the recommendation of Cheney.

There have been a number of other accusations made against Halliburton during Cheney's stint as CEO. According to the Environmental Rights Action (ERA) group, Halliburton ordered Nigerian Mobile Police officers to shoot youthful demonstrators protesting what they perceived as environmental damage caused by Chevron Oil, which had contracted for Halliburton's services. One youth, Gidikumo Sule, was killed, and others claimed to have been beaten. The oil companies countered this charge by claiming the youth was killed during an attempt to rescue officers who had been detained and disarmed by the youths.

It should come as no surprise that environmental groups have long been upset with Halliburton in general and Cheney in particular. Among other actions in his career unfriendly to environmental concerns, Cheney has co-sponsored legislation to open the Arctic Wildlife Refuge in Alaska to oil drilling and supported it while in the White House. He had even voted against the Clean Water Act while serving as a representative from Wyoming. And Halliburton's environmental record was deplorable under Cheney's tenure. Its Duncan, Oklahoma, facility was identified by the Environmental Protection Agency in 1997 as one of the top 20 percent of polluting companies in the nation.

Aspersions have also made about the fact that Halliburton joined Bush's now-defunct Harken Energy in maintaining offshore subsidiaries in the Cayman Islands, the favorite site for tax dodgers, such as Enron, which had 692 subsidiaries of its own there.

Under Cheney's leadership, Halliburton's subsidiaries in tax havens grew from nine in 1995 to forty-four in 1999. This coincided with a drop in Halliburton's federal taxes from $302 million in 1998 to an $85 million tax refund in 1999.

But the deepest criticism of Cheney came from his company's dealings in Iraq and his role in the Enron scandal.

In 1998, the UN passed a resolution permitting Iraq to purchase material to repair and maintain its oil industry, which had become dilapidated following the country's defeat in the Gulf War. Immediately, US companies, including Halliburton, Baker Hughes, Schlumberger, Flowserve, Fisher-Rosemount and others, moved surreptitiously to get a part of this lucrative business.

These firms used European subsidies to front for multimillion-dollar business deals. "It is a wonderful example of how ludicrous sanctions have become," noted Raad Alkadiri, an analyst for Petroleum Finance Company, a Washington consulting firm.

Furthermore, Halliburton brought in substantial business in other markets by hiding behind other business entities. Reporter Carola Hoyos noted, "From September 1998, until it sold its stake last February [2000], Halliburton owned fifty-one percent of Dresser-Rand. It also owned forty-nine percent of Ingersoll-Dresser Pump, until its sale in December 1999. During the time of the joint ventures, Dresser-Rand and Ingersoll-Dresser Pump submitted more than $23.8 million worth of contracts for the sale of oil industry parts and equipment to Iraq. Their combined total amounted to more than any other US company; the vast majority was approved by the sanctions committee."

Cheney also came under fire for Enron-like accounting practices. According to Judicial Watch, which in 2002 filed a lawsuit in Dallas, Texas, against Cheney on behalf of Halliburton shareholders, he artificially boosted the share price of Halliburton stock while he was CEO. The suit charges that Cheney overstated profits by $445 million between 1999 and 2001, resulting in "huge losses" for some investors.

In early 2002, Cheney was considered as the object of an unprecedented lawsuit by the General Accounting Office for his failure to give congressional investigators documents relating to the formulation of energy plans by the energy task force he once headed. Cheney claimed the GAO did not have the authority to demand the information, despite the fact that the Bush administration task force was funded by public money. The task force's energy proposals carried many provisions sought at the time by the energy giant Enron, a major contributor to the Bush/Cheney campaign, but Cheney never disclosed which energy corporations and lobbyists had met with his task force. In early 2003, the GAO, under pressure from Republicans who threatened to cut its budget, quietly dropped the matter. A private lawsuit asking for full disclosure, launched soon thereafter by the Sierra Club and the conservative Judicial Watch, made its way to the US Supreme Court. The Justices upheld Cheney's claim to complete secrecy.

During the 2000 campaign, Cheney told audiences that since leaving government under the original Bush administration, he had been "out in the private sector creating jobs." He did not mention that just after Halliburton absorbed Dresser, Cheney laid off 10,000 workers.

Meanwhile, Halliburton announced in May 2002 that the Securities and Exchange Commission was investigating the company for accounting practices related to how it reported cost overruns on construction projects, but no charges were immediately filed.

Many researchers and more knowledgeable members of the public have questioned the hypocrisy and ethics of Cheney, the man who prosecuted a war against Iraq in the early 1990s, and then oversaw $23.8 million in business to Iraq during a time of UN sanctions against that nation. Next, as Vice President, he led the effort to put an end to the "murderous dictator" that was marked by fear-mongering and deception, and whose firm had now became embroiled in profiting from a second war in that country.

Such talk only gained strength as reports of no-bid contracts and overcharges continued to plague Halliburton.

In early 2003, Bunnatine Greenhouse, the top contracting officer for the Army Corps of Engineers, objected to Halliburton's $7 billion no-bid contract for services in Iraq. She said the Halliburton deal should have been the standard one-year contract and that an official of the company should not have been present during contract discussions.

Halliburton was forced to bid for half the contract and Greenhouse was forced into protection under Whistleblower legislation. In early 2006, she was still fighting Halliburton misconduct while making appearances on CNN and PBS.

Meanwhile, the FBI apparently is still investigating Halliburton after a December, 2003 audit revealed that the company overcharged the government $61 million for fuel in Iraq. Halliburton subsidiary KBR had hired a Kuwaiti firm, Altanmia Commercial Marketing Company, to supply fuel at twice the current price while adding a markup.

Following in the steps of Bunnatine Greenhouse, Mary Robertson, a senior contracting officer at the Army Corps of Engineers, protested that Altanmia's cost estimates were too high. "Since the US government is paying for these services, I will not succumb to the political pressures from the [government of Kuwait] or the US embassy to go against my integrity and pay a higher price for fuel than necessary," she wrote in an internal memo made public by Corpwatch.org.

The internal documents also revealed that due to the Altanmia deal, US taxpayers were paying an average of $2.64 a gallon and as much as $3.06 for fuel. By comparison, the Defense Department's Energy Support Center (ESC) had been doing a similar job supplying fuel at $1.32 a gallon, and SOMO, the local oil company, was doing the same provision for only $0.96 a gallon. The total bill to the taxpayer for 61 million gallons of fuel from Kuwait and about 179 million gallons from Turkey was $383 million, more than $100 million more than local providers would have charged.

In mid-2004, the Pentagon's Defense Contract Audit Agency "strongly" urged the Army to withhold about $60 million a month from Halliburton payments until full documentation was provided for $1.8 billion of charges made by the company.

In late 2004, several sub-contractors working for Halliburton in Iraq filed suit to recover what they said were unpaid bills. One firm, La Nouvelle, filed a lawsuit against Halliburton subsidiary KBR in the US District Court of Eastern Virginia demanding $224 million.

A separate lawsuit charged that KBR refused to pay $20.4 million for food services and other work near the city of Tikrit provided in 2003 by the Kuwait Company for Process Plant Construction & Contracting (KCPC) and the Morris Corporation of Australia for several months after the invasion of Iraq.

Allegations of demands for a $3 million kickback during the original 2003 contract negotiations from individuals associated with KBR first surfaced after KBR fired KCPC and Morris because the two companies had fallen behind schedule.

"They wanted kickbacks of 3 percent to 4 percent, which pushed up the prices because then the subcontractors would add the price of the kickbacks to their costs," an unnamed source told the *Sydney Morning Herald*.

Laszlo Tibold, a former KBR official, told journalist David Phinney that if anyone is to blame for KBR's poor contracting process in Iraq, it is KBR's senior management and planners at the US Defense Department who were woefully unprepared for establishing an immediate presence for occupying the war-torn country.

Tibold said when he first arrived at Anaconda base in Iraq, KBR failed to provide even the most basic of office supplies such as computers, reliable telephones, contract forms or a list of pre-approved contractors to work with.

"Everyone was in pure reactionary mode," he said, adding that KBR's staff at Camp Anaconda began with six employees who were burdened with work "by industry standards" that only a staff of 185 could effectively handle. After a month, KBR's staff at Camp Anaconda was increased to 30, he said, yet was responsible for writing contracts totaling a value in the hundreds of millions of dollars.

"KBR had no clue," he said. "They didn't know what they were getting into."

And there is even more: In mid-2005, even as the Bush administration tried to work up national passion against Iran's nuclear program, Halliburton sources leaked to the press the fact that the scandal-plagued oil services company had sold Iran key components for a nuclear reactor.

Company sources said Halliburton officials worked with Cyrus Nasseri, vice chairman of the board of directors of Oriental Oil Kish, one of Iran's largest private oil companies, on oil development projects. Nasseri has been identified as a key member of Iran's nuclear development program. According to Iranian officials, Nasseri was questioned in mid-2005 regarding his providing Halliburton with Iran's nuclear secrets and accepting as much as a $1 million bribe from the company.

This connection became public in January 2005, when Halliburton announced it had subcontracted an Iranian natural gas drilling project to Halliburton Products and Services, a subsidiary of Dallas-based Halliburton registered in the Cayman Islands.

IRAQIS AND THE MURRAH FEDERAL BUILDING BOMBING

Many researchers consider the April 19, 1995, bombing of the Alfred P. Murrah Federal Building in Oklahoma City to be yet another case of an inside job—one that foreshadows the covert machinations that led to 9/11 six years later. The connection of the Oklahoma bombing to the widening scandal around 9/11 and the Iraq war becomes evident in the account below.

Despite a loud silence in the corporate-controlled mass media, many alternative articles as well as researchers have pointed to the involvement of Iraqis in the event.

So much evidence became available pointing to Iraqi complicity in that terrorist act that in March of 2002, Judicial Watch filed suit against the Republic of Iraq on behalf of seventeen survivors of the bombing. The complaint, filed in the US District Court for the District of Columbia, was brought against Iraq, as a State Department-designated terrorism sponsor, under the provisions of the Antiterrorism and Effective Death Penalty Act of 1996. This suit was still being pursued in 2006 but seemed destined for oblivion following the US invasion of Iraq.

According to court papers, the bombing of the Murrah Federal Building "was not as simple as has been portrayed by the United States Government. The entire plot was, in whole or in part, orchestrated, assisted technically and/or financially and directly aided by agents of the Republic of Iraq." However, researchers looking into recent developments in the investigation are encountering confusion and obstructions in confirming such a connection.

The suit also charges that Iraq knew in advance of the 9/11 attacks and that there was wrongdoing in both the Clinton and Bush administrations.

A portion of the evidence concerning foreknowledge of 9/11 involves an Iraqi newspaper column published on July 21, 2001, in which it stated that Osama bin Laden was thinking "seriously, with the seriousness of the Bedouin of the desert, about the way he will try to bomb the Pentagon after he destroys the White House." The column also mentioned that bin Laden was "insisting very convincingly that he will strike America on the arm that is already hurting," an apparent reference to the 1993 World Trade Center bombing.

Jim Kreindler, one of the lawyers pursuing the suit, said the columnist, Naeem Abd Muhalhal, had advance knowledge of bin Laden's plans and that "Iraqi officials were aware of plans to attack American landmarks." He added, "Further, we have evidence that Iraq provided support for bin Laden and his al Qaeda terror organization for nearly a decade."

This charge was supported by Craig Roberts, a former Oklahoma policeman and National Guard officer, who said, "At the end of the Gulf War, over 5,000 former Iraqi soldiers (mainly consisting of officers) were transported (illegally) to this country by the administration for 'humanitarian purposes' and resettled at taxpayer expense. This created a massive stir in the veterans organizations, who remembered how many American POWs had been abandoned by our government in past wars, but was only publicized in their magazines."

Roberts, a Vietnam veteran and author who participated in the official Oklahoma City investigation of the Murrah Building bombing, said these Iraqi officers had worked with the CIA during the eight-year war between Iraq and Iran. They feared Saddam's wrath after losing the Gulf War. Within this group were many men who joined various Muslim extremist groups, such as Hamas and the Islamic Jihad, after arriving in the US. Some of these soldiers, along with a considerable amount of Semtex and other military explosives, were transported to Fort Sill, Oklahoma.

"This [transfer of Iraqi soldiers] was well publicized. One of the largest groupings of resettled former Iraqi soldiers, coincidentally, became Oklahoma City. This places the Iraqis who were experts in demolition (re: Kuwaiti oil field destruction) only 60 miles from the stored Semtex, cratering charges and other military explosives stored at Fort Sill," stated Craig.

Initial reports from witnesses placed two "Middle Eastern males"

IRAQIS AND THE MURRAH FEDERAL BUILDING BOMBING

wearing blue jumpsuits or jogging suits in the vicinity of the Murrah building at the time of the explosions. The FBI put out "John Doe" sketch bulletins on at least three men, all of whom resembled Middle Eastern males. In fact, one such man, a Jordanian living in Oklahoma City, was arrested at London's Heathrow Airport only to be released shortly thereafter. FBI and media attention then shifted to right-wing extremists. Interestingly, the British media reported that this man had photos of weapons and missiles in his possessions as well as a blue jogging suit.

Yet despite the compelling evidence of Iraqi involvement in what to that time had been the worst bombing in US history, there was no federal-level investigation. Despite the rush to judgment by the federal authorities that only one man, Timothy McVeigh, bombed the Murrah Federal Building, controversy continues today over the facts of the tragedy. Oklahoma City has been added to the list of controversial and never properly investigated American tragedies beginning with the assassinations of President John F. Kennedy, Martin Luther King, Jr., Robert Kennedy, and the killings at Ruby Ridge, Idaho, and Waco, Texas. Sadly, public interest in the Okalahoma City bombing waned following the attacks of 9/11.

Oklahoma State Representative Charles Key in 1997 tried to bring facts concerning the Middle East connection in the Oklahoma City bombing to the public and finally produced a five hundred-page report released in 2001. As far back as 1997, Key and many others had raised questions about McVeigh's contacts prior to the bombing that killed 161 men, women and children.

Many still recall the FBI bulletins issued immediately after the bombing seeking several Middle Eastern men reportedly driving a brown pickup truck. This was in addition to the reports of the alleged Arab men seen in the vicinity of the federal building shortly before the explosions.

As in the case of District Attorney Jim Garrison attempting to question the official verdict of the Kennedy assassination, Key was raked over the coals by the mainstream media and accused of "howling at the moon" by Oklahoma governor Frank Keating, a former FBI agent.

"Why was there such extreme opposition?" Key wrote in a letter to constituents. "I believe the answer is because some in our federal law enforcement agencies (i.e., ATF and FBI) had prior knowledge that certain individuals were planning to bomb the Murrah Federal Building! I believe that because of at least four reasons:

"1. Six different individuals have come forward and reported seeing the bomb squad in the immediate vicinity of the Murrah Building early on the morning of the bombing.

"2. The Oklahoma City Fire Department received a call from the FBI the Friday before the bombing and was told to be on the alert for a possible terrorist attack on a government building.

"3. Bruce Shaw, who had frantically come to look for his wife inside the smoldering building, was told by an ATF agent, 'You won't find any ATF agents in the building because they were warned on their pagers not to come in this morning and they're now in debriefing.' This conversation was corroborated by his boss, who accompanied Bruce to help him find his wife.

"4. Carol Howe, a paid informant for the ATF, has recently come forward to confirm that she informed the ATF that two individuals, Dennis Mahon and Andreas Strassmier, were planning to bomb the federal building in Oklahoma City. She also said that the likely date for the bombing was April 19!"

In addition to the suppressed information concerning the Middle East connection to the federal building bombing, at least one Oklahoma City investigative reporter claimed to have gathered evidence that Osama bin Laden was involved. Jayna Davis, former news reporter for the NBC affiliate in Oklahoma City, KFOR-TV, tried to make public this information several months prior to 9/11.

Davis said she developed information that a Middle Eastern terrorist cell was operating only blocks from the Murrah Building and that Timothy McVeigh on the day of the bombing was in contact with an Iraqi who had served in Saddam Hussein's Republican Guard. This man was the object of an "all-points" bulletin immediately after the bombing that was later inexplicably withdrawn.

Davis said her evidence led her to believe that McVeigh, along with

Terry Nichols (now serving a life sentence without possibility of parole as an accomplice in the bombing) and at least seven men of Middle Eastern ethnic backgrounds were involved in a conspiracy masterminded by bin Laden.

The reporter said she took her evidence, composed of hundreds of court records, twenty sworn witness affidavits and reports from law enforcement, intelligence and terrorist experts, to the FBI but bureau officials refused even to accept the material.

Further clouding the issue of why the FBI refused to even look at the evidence that refuted the Clinton administration's assurance that the bombing was the work of one lone man, McVeigh, plus a friend, was evidence showing that the FBI's top counterterrorism expert checked into an Oklahoma City hotel just after midnight on the morning the federal building was destroyed.

Danny Coulson, then director of the FBI's Terrorist Task Force, checked into the Embassy Suites Hotel at 12:20 am, about nine hours prior to the bombing, according to a hotel receipt obtained by *WorldNetDaily*. The hotel receipt showed Coulson checked out of the hotel on April 27.

Coulson, in a book published in 1999, claimed he was in Fort Worth, Texas, when he received a call from John O'Neill, the FBI counterterrorism expert, informing him of the Murrah Building bombing. The discrepancy of these stories adds support to those who claim the FBI was involved in the case well before the explosion.

One lawsuit alleged that Ramzi Yousef, convicted in the 1993 World Trade Center bombing, was an Iraqi government agent who, prior to his arrest, went to the Philippines, where he recruited Terry Nichols, McVeigh's accomplice in Oklahoma, to join in a plot to blow up several US-bound airliners.

It is a matter of fact that Terry Nichols made more than a dozen trips to the Philippines right up until 1995 but the Yousef connection has not been fully substantiated. Yousef, of course, was the al Qaeda operative with the plans for "Operation Bojinka," the plan to crash planes into prominent structures including the World Trade Center towers.

Author David Hoffman, writing in 1998, stated that FBI reports as well as research by McVeigh's defense attorneys established that in the early 1990s, terrorist leaders met on the Philippine island of Mindanao.

"It was there [according to one informant] that Ramzi Yousef, Abdul Hakim Murad, Wali Khan Amin Shah and several others discussed the Oklahoma City bombing plot," wrote Hoffman.

Further evidence of a connection between McVeigh and the bin Laden network, over and beyond the Philippine meeting, which may have involved Nichols, is the testimony of witnesses at the Sands Motel just outside Oklahoma City.

A co-owner of the motel, who asked for anonymity, told reporter Jim Crogan of *LA Weekly* that he distinctly recalled terrorist leader Mohamed Atta at his motel with Zacarias Moussaoui, the infamous "twentieth hijacker," about August 1, 2001, just six weeks prior to the 9/11 attacks. He identified a third man as Marwan al-Shehhi, reportedly one of the terrorists that was aboard Flight 175.

He said the men asked for a weekly rate on some rooms at the motel but they were told the rooms were all occupied. He said all three men were friendly but that Atta did most of the talking.

"I asked him what they were doing here in the area," the owner said. "And Atta told me they were going to flight school. I thought he meant training in Oklahoma City. But Atta told me no, they were taking flight training in Norman.

"I said I didn't understand why they would want to rent one of my rooms, since we were about twenty-eight miles from Norman and there are a lot of reasonably priced motels a lot closer. But he said they had heard good things about my place and wanted to stay there."

The man explained that there were no weekly rooms available and the trio left. Later, following the 9/11 attacks, the motel owner saw their pictures on the news and called the FBI. But there was never any significant follow-up to his report.

One law enforcement source said he considered the motel owner's story credible and took the information to the FBI but was told, "it probably wouldn't go nowhere." "They were afraid the whole Oklahoma City bombing can of worms would be opened up and the FBI would have to explain why they didn't investigate this material before," the officer told a reporter.

"One reason for the FBI's apparent lack of interest might be this motel's alleged connection to Timothy McVeigh and a group of Iraqis who worked in Oklahoma City," noted reporter Crogan. "According to the motel owner and other witnesses and investigators interviewed by the *Weekly*, McVeigh and several of these Iraqis were motel guests in the months preceding the 1995 bombing. Witnesses also claimed they saw several of the Iraqis moving barrels of material around on the bed of a truck. The motel owner said the material smelled of diesel fuel and he had to clean up a spill. Diesel fuel was a key component of the truck bomb that blew up the Federal Building."

The motel owner was interviewed by the FBI on several occasions but there was no indication that prosecutors in the case of Moussaoui were even notified of the Moussaoui-Atta connection, who was arrested prior to 9/11, and has been characterized as a marginal figure in the plot. But if he was connected to Atta, it makes him much more of a participant than previously thought.

Reporter Crogan wrote, "If this recollection is correct, the entire incident, and its absence from the public record, raises new questions about the FBI investigation of Moussaoui and the 1995 destruction of the Federal Building in Oklahoma City."

There were so many leads and bits of information about the cover-up in the Oklahoma City bombing that it occasionally slipped into the mainstream media.

According to a report in *US News & World Report* in late 2001, McVeigh possessed several Iraqi telephone numbers, which prompted Pentagon officials to suspect that he was some sort of Iraqi agent. Writer Paul Bedard wrote, "Why haven't we heard this before about the case of the executed McVeigh? Conspiracy theorists in the Pentagon think it's part of a coverup."

Since there is such compelling evidence of Iraqi involvement in the Oklahoma City bombing, one might well ask why this was not brought out by the Bush administration to rally support for their invasion of that nation. The only answer would seem to be that to admit that FBI- and CIA-backed Iraqis were involved in that terrorist event might prompt speculation about the true culprits behind the 9/11 attacks.

WHY DID THE US MILITARY RUSH INTO BAGHDAD?

The record shows that plagiarized papers, secret pre-planning, a lack of post-war planning, distortion of evidence, fear-mongering, and outright lies have permeated the Bush administration's effort to win support for the invasion of Iraq. No wonder so many other US allies declined to back the US effort before and after the war.

Support among the American public consistently spiraled downward, resulting in poll numbers in early 2006 that showed less than 30 percent support.

But in the run up to the invasion, there was scant coverage of dissenting voices, such as the march by 100,000 to 150,000 people in Washington on Sunday, October 27, 2002. Led by celebrities such as musician Patti Smith and actress Susan Sarandon, the protests were hailed as some of the largest in the nation since the Vietnam War. Jesse Jackson told a crowd gathered by the Vietnam Veterans Memorial, "If we launch a pre-emptive strike, we will lose all moral authority. We must have a higher order than a one-bullet diplomacy." The protest marches came following a poll conducted for the *New York Times* and CNN that showed half of those queried were uneasy at the prospect of war with Iraq.

As war approached in early 2003, there were large demonstrations in both America and other nations, and the day of March 15, 2003 witnessed what some called the largest day of anti-war protest ever witnessed on the planet. Protest rallies involving an estimated 30 million people took place in England, Germany, Spain, Belgium, France, Turkey, South Korea, Taiwan, Thailand, and Australia, and other countries—including thousands of arrests. But none of this seemed to sway President Bush, who declared, "If the UN won't act, if Saddam won't disarm, we will lead a coalition to disarm him."

On March 20, 2003, Bush made good on these words by launching US forces across Iraq's borders.

They promptly made a bee-line for Baghdad, failing to follow normal military tactics, which call for a period of consolidating forces in a captured area, after seizing a series of initial objectives. This failure to subdue the countryside brought deadly repercussions long after the initial fighting had ceased.

There may even be more reasons than most people realize that prompted US leaders with secret-society connections to send troops into Iraq, and thereupon to make such a hurried rush into Baghdad. This concerns the many rare antiquities and even ancient technologies that comprise the ancient heritage of Iraq.

According to ABC News, nearly four hundred ancient Sumerian artifacts were discovered in Iraq in 1999 in the southern Iraqi town of Basmyiah, about one hundred miles south of Baghdad. The Iraqi News Agency said the objects ranged from animal and human-shaped "toys" to cuneiform tablets and even "ancient weapons." At least one cylinder seal depicted a tall person thought to represent the ancient king Gilgamesh. The antiquities were dated to about 2500 B.C.E., said excavation team leader Riyadh al-Douri.

Further discoveries in Iraq were made in 2002 and early 2003 by archaeologists from the Bavarian department of Historical Monuments in Munich, Germany using digital mapping technology. According to spokesman Jorg Fassbinder, a magnetometer was utilized to locate buried walls, gardens, palaces and a surprising network of canals that would have made Uruk a "Venice in the desert."

This equipment also located a structure in the middle of the Euphrates River which Fassbinder's team believed to be the tomb of Gilgamesh, the ancient Mesopotamian king who claimed to be two-thirds god and only one-third human. An epic poem describing Gilgamesh's search for the secret of immortality was inscribed on clay tablets more than 2,000 years ago and is thought to be one of the oldest books in history.

Reportedly, other astonishing finds were being made during this time by both German and French archaeological teams given permission to excavate by Saddam Hussein. It may be worth noting that Germany and France were the two nations most opposed to the US invasion.

The new discoveries were added to those stored in the Iraqi National Museum in Baghdad, which had been closed to the public since the first Gulf War in 1991.

McGuire Gibson, of the Oriental Institute of the University of Chicago and president of the American Association for Research in Baghdad, had previously lamented the loss of ancient artifacts and writings due to the 1991 Gulf War and subsequent embargo of Iraq.

"The aftermath of the war witnessed the looting and sometimes the burning of nine regional museums and the loss of more than 3,000 artifacts, only a few of which have been recovered," wrote Gibson. "The loss of the objects, although grave, was not as destructive as the change that the attacks on the museums will have on the future relationship of museums to the people of Iraq. It is unlikely that there will ever again be an effort at public education about archaeology on the scale that was represented by those regional museums."

In addition to the destruction of historical artifacts, such as the American bombing of the giant ziggurat at Ur and the losses due to construction by US troops at Tell al-Lahm, economic conditions caused by the American embargo have caused an increase in the illegal trading of Iraqi artifacts. Gibson added that almost all archaeological research in Iraq came to a halt because of the war and embargo.

The problems with Iraq's antiquities were greatly exacerbated in late April 2003, when more than 50,000 priceless artifacts and tablets were taken from the Baghdad museum by what appeared to be an organized band of looters who targeted the museum's basement. This deliberate thievery was masked from the Western media by chaotic scenes of common looters thought by some to have been hired for this purpose.

Despite prior attempts to alert American military officers of the danger of losing artifacts dating back 7,000 years—especially precious antiquities stored in the museum's lower floor—American authorities failed to prevent the wholesale looting of humankind's most ancient treasures.

"It was my impression that the Department of Defense had made provisions for the safeguarding of monuments and museums," lamented Maxwell Anderson, president of the Association of Art Museum Directors. Anderson was among a group that in January 2003 alerted Pentagon and State Department officials to the importance of these antiquities. Although promised protection for the antiquities, this alert apparently fell on deaf ears.

According to an Associated Press report, the thieves had keys to the museum and its vaults. Gibson said what appeared to be random looting actually was a carefully planned theft. "It looks as if part of the theft was a very, very deliberate, planned action," he said. "They were able to obtain keys from somewhere for the vaults and were able to take out the very important, the very best material. I have a suspicion it was organized outside the country. In fact, I'm pretty sure it was."

"Glass cutters not available in Iraq were found in the museum and a huge bronze bust weighing hundreds of pounds...[that] would have required a fork lift to remove it indicate that well organized professional cultural thieves were mixed in with the mob," noted Christopher Bollyn of the *American Free Press*.

The fact that some display cases were empty without being broken indicated that some of the precious materials may have been taken out prior to the arrival of the looters. "It was almost as if the perpetrators were waiting for Baghdad to fall to make their move," commented a writer for *Business Week*.

When the looting began on April 17, 2003, one Iraqi archaeologist summoned US troops to protect the national museum. Five Marines accompanied the man to the museum and chased out the thieves by firing shots over their heads. However, after about 30 minutes, the soldiers were ordered to withdraw and the looters soon returned. Apparently, the only building in Baghdad to receive full American protection was the Ministry of Oil.

"Not since the Taliban embarked on their orgy of destruction against the Buddhas of Bamiyan and the statutes in the museum of Kabul—perhaps not since World War II—have so many archaeological treasures been wantonly and systematically smashed to pieces," reported British newsman Robert Fisk, who toured the museum shortly after the incident.

The preventable looting prompted three members of the White House Cultural Property Advisory Committee to resign, disgusted that the alerted American military had failed to protect the Mesopotamian treasures. "This tragedy was not prevented, due to our nation's inaction," wrote committee chairman Martin E. Sullivan in his resignation letter.

The theft of ancient artifacts of undetermined value was confirmed by Colonel Matthew Bogdanos in early 2004. Bogdanos headed an investigation of the looting as deputy director for the Joint Interagency Coordination Group originally assigned to seek out weapons of mass destruction in Iraq. After gaining permission from General Tommy Franks, the group probed the museum looting.

In an interview published in the January/February issue of *Archeology*, Col. Bogdanos was asked what is still missing from the Iraqi National Museum. He replied, "You have the public gallery from which originally 40 exhibits were taken. We've recovered 11. Turning to the storage rooms, there were about 3,150 pieces taken from those, and that's almost certainly by random and indiscriminant looters. Of those, we've recovered 2,700. About 400 of these pieces remain missing.

"The final group is from the basement. The basement is what we've been calling the inside job. And I will say it forever like a mantra: it is inconceivable to me that the basement was breached and the items stolen without an intimate insider's knowledge of the museum. From there about 10,000 pieces were taken. We've only recovered 650, approximately."

It has been widely reported that Saddam Hussein believes himself to be the reincarnation of the King Nebuchadnezzar, the Biblical figure who performed wondrous achievements in construction—including the Hanging Gardens of Babylon—in an attempt to communicate with ancient Mesopotamian gods from the heavens. Could the rush to war with Iraq, the hurried rush to Baghdad, and the "inside job" at the Baghdad museum have something to do with gaining control over recently-discovered knowledge, and perhaps even technology, which might undo modern monopolies in religion and science?

Recent scientific studies into heretofore unknown monatomic [single atom] elements have linked this discovery to ancient writings from Mesopotamia and Egypt. Some scientists claim such elements may hold the key to unlocking the secrets of anti-gravity, longevity, limitless free energy, faster-than light propulsion systems, teleportation and even the possibility of inter-dimensional and time travel. [See *Rule by Secrecy* for further information concerning the significance of these ancient Mesopotamian artifacts.]

After a lop-sided fight, victorious Americans celebrated the "liberation" of Iraq, never realizing that well into 2006 almost two American soldiers a day would still be dying there. By 2006, US military deaths in the Iraqi occupation topped 2,500, the majority of these counted after Bush stood under the "Mission Accomplished" sign. Meanwhile, the US Treasury was paying out more each month to sustain the war in Iraq than

WHY DID THE US MILITARY RUSH INTO BAGHDAD?

it did during the Vietnam War.

An odd sidelight to this was the comment of evangelist Pat Robertson in October 2004. Robertson, a longtime Bush supporter, told CNN that he urged the president to prepare the American people for the prospect of casualties before launching the war in March, 2003.

Robertson said Bush told him, "Oh, no, we're not going to have any casualties."

White House Press Secretary Scott McClellan was quick to state, "The president never made such a comment." Americans were left to wonder who was telling the truth—the President or the evangelist?

On September 8, 2003, long after the official fighting in Iraq had ended with no weapons of mass destruction in hand, President Bush finally conceded another article of faith concerning that nation's leader. To newsmen who gathered as he met with Congressional members on energy matters, Bush confessed, "We have no evidence that Saddam Hussein was involved with the 11 September attacks."

Yet only the week before Bush's concession, Cheney still refused to rule out such a connection. "We don't know," he said, adding, "[In invading Iraq] we will have struck a major blow right at the heart of the base, if you will, the geographic base of the terrorists who've had us under assault now for many years, but most especially on 9/11."

Washington appeared to be playing a double standard—ignoring the obvious Iraqi ties to the Oklahoma City bombing while placing unwarranted suspicion on Iraq for the 9/11 tragedies.

US COMPLICITY IN THE WORLD DRUG TRADE

The current War on Drugs has been going on for so long that most people have forgotten when it began. Most authorities trace this failed but ongoing war to President Richard Nixon who, in 1970, established the National Commission on Marijuana and Drug Abuse. The commission, under the chairmanship of Raymond P. Schafer, former governor of Pennsylvania, began work the following year.

According to the commission's report, *Marihuana, A Signal of Misunderstanding*, "Soon after funds became available on March 22, 1971, we commissioned more than fifty projects, ranging from a study of the effects of marihuana on man to a field survey of enforcement of the marihuana laws in six metropolitan jurisdictions. Of particular importance in our fact-finding effort were the opinions and attitudes of all groups in our society."

In other words, this was a genuine, objective report. Its conclusions?

After dismissing public approval of recreational drug use as counter to the benefit of society, the commission likewise opposed the option of using criminal penalties to eliminate drug use, stating, "Marihuana's relative potential for harm to the vast majority of individual users and its actual impact on society does not justify a social policy designed to seek out and firmly punish those who use it."

Commission members pointed out that "even during Prohibition, when many people were concerned about the evils associated with excessive use of alcohol, possession for personal use was never outlawed federally and was made illegal in only five States."

The report also stated, "There is a legitimate concern about what the majority of the non-using population thinks about marihuana use and what the drug represents in the public mind. The question is appropriately asked if we are suggesting that the majority in a free society may impose its will on an unwilling minority even though, as it is claimed, uncertainty, speculation, and a large degree of misinformation form the basis of the predominant opinion. If we have nothing more substantial than this, the argument goes, society should remain neutral."

The commission concluded, "We recommend to the public and its policy-makers a social control policy seeking to discourage Marihuana use, while concentrating primarily on the prevention of heavy and very heavy use."

But Nixon said he disagreed with the report, thereupon launching what then came to be an ineffective and indeed counterproductive drug war.

Today the number of US prison inmates held on drug charges is about half a million, greater than the entire jail population of Western Europe. And most of these are persons of color who lived below the poverty line.

Another possible explanation for the never-ending War on Drugs came when Senator Carl Levin, a Michigan Democrat, documented in 2001 how more than $300 billion in drug money moves yearly through

THE TERROR CONSPIRACY

the US banking system.

Levin's estimate, based on a staff investigation lasting more than a year, was augmented by the Brookings Institution in 2001. Brookings spokesman Raymond Baker reported that despite the strictest money-laundering laws in the world, US banks still held an estimated $500 billion a year in money from drug dealers and terrorists.

In one sting operation by US Customs, $7.7 million was deposited in the Citibank account of a Cayman Islands bank. When the money was transferred to a firm called M. A. Bank, it turned out to be a shell company without any physical office.

In the more naive times of the early 1970s, no one foresaw the advent of synthetic cocaine, adulterated hash, rock cocaine, PCP and the recent designer drugs such as Ecstasy. Then, the greatest drug bugaboo was heroin, the drug that placed a "monkey on your back." Interestingly enough, heroin use in the 1970s was reported at about 2 percent of the drug-taking population, a percentage that has remained remarkably stable up until this day. But the heroin business accounts for a higher percentage of the profits in the world's illicit drug trade.

Everyone knowledgeable of the world drug trade knows that the two primary sources of poppies, the flower from which heroin is made, are the Golden Triangle in Southeast Asia and Afghanistan.

The modern Afghan drug trade began with US involvement in Afghanistan in 1979, a provocation that led to the Soviet invasion, as recounted by Alfred McCoy, author of the respected *The Politics of Heroin in Southeast Asia*:

"CIA assets again controlled this heroin trade. As the Mujahedeen guerrillas seized territory inside Afghanistan, they ordered peasants to plant opium as a revolutionary tax. Across the border in Pakistan, Afghan leaders and local syndicates under the protection of Pakistani Intelligence operated hundreds of heroin laboratories. During this decade of wide-open drug-dealing, the US Drug Enforcement Agency in Islamabad failed to instigate major seizures or arrests. US officials had refused to investigate charges of heroin dealing by its Afghan allies 'because US narcotics policy in Afghanistan has been subordinated to the war against Soviet influence there.'

"In 1995, the former CIA director of the Afghan operation Charles

Cogan, admitted the CIA had indeed sacrificed the drug war to fight the Cold War. 'Our main mission was to do as much damage as possible to the Soviets. We didn't really have the resources or the time to devote to an investigation of the drug trade, I don't think that we need to apologize for this. Every situation has its fallout.... There was fallout in terms of drugs, yes. But the main objective was accomplished. The Soviets left Afghanistan.'"

The Taliban were not so lenient on the opium trade.

It was reliably reported that zealous Muslims within the Taliban government had banned the growth of poppies and had succeeded in destroying nearly 95 percent of the crop by the spring of 2001. Britain's *Financial Times* reported in early 2002, "The Taliban's ban on opium poppy two years ago was 'enormously effective' in reducing poppy crops almost entirely in areas under the regime's control. The US estimates that Afghanistan produced 74 tons of opium last year, compared to 3,656 tons the previous year." Anti-Taliban hard-liners in the United States believed this reduction of the poppy crop was merely a "business decision" designed to drive prices up and ensure higher profits to the Taliban. More knowledgeable drug experts have pointed out that the Taliban are not peddling heroin on the streets of LA or New York and that powerful drug distributors must have viewed the poppy loss as a business disaster.

After the US invasion of Afghanistan in 2002, opium production soared again. Under the Taliban no more than 185 tons of opium was produced annually. By the end of 2002, that figure had risen to an estimated 3,400 tons, according to BBC's Central Asian analyst Pam O'Toole. By 2005, *US News & World Report* noted that almost 500,000 acres of poppies were under cultivation.

In fact, following the American occupation of Afghanistan, opium production grew so vast that a government study in 2004 stated that nation was "on the verge of becoming a narcotics state." This White House report was sent to Congress by Secretary of State Condoleezza Rice on behalf of President Bush.

In 2005, despite being occupied by thousands of US and allied troops, Afghanistan earned $2.7 billion from opium exports, amounting to 52 percent of the country's $5.2 billion gross domestic product.

Although the War on Drugs continues unabated, Western military commanders have resisted local pleas to intervene in the Afghan drug trafficking, arguing that they don't have the resources to broaden their mission. "Our primary mission is a combat mission," said Col. Jim Yonts, a spokesman for the US forces in Afghanistan. "We stay focused on our role of defeating the Taliban and al Qaeda."

The post-invasion growth of poppies means that Afghanistan has reverted back to late-1990s levels, when the country produced 70 percent of the world's illicit opium.

To fully explain the politics of drugs would require a separate book, but it must be understood that drugs—particularly opium-based drugs such as heroin—have been the basis for both social control and wealth for centuries. In more recent times, Samuel Russell, second cousin of General William Huntington Russell, founder of the Skull and Bones Order at Yale, founded Russell and Company in 1823 with the intent of smuggling opium to China. He later acquired Perkins and Company, another opium smuggling operation controlled by some of Boston's finest blue blood families. These families were enriched first by the slave trade, and then by opium smuggling in the nineteenth century. Other Boston families integrated Russell's firm into an opium syndicate that include the Cabots, Lowells, Higginsons, Forbeses, Cushings, and Sturgises. An early investor was Joseph Coolidge whose grandson, Archibald, was a founder of the Council on Foreign Relations.

Thus, it may come as less of a surprise to learn that—ever since the Vietnam War—it has been charged that the CIA has imported drugs to support its clandestine operations. Mounds of court papers and news stories attest to this criminal activity yet no one in high authority seems capable of doing anything about it. One former British commando who operated in Afghanistan during the Soviet occupation has stated that both American and British military officers tolerated opium smuggling by the Mujahideen as the profits were used to support their actions against the Russians. Tom Carew said after debriefing sessions in both London and Washington, he quickly became aware that both British and American authorities turned a blind eye to the Mujahideen drug smuggling.

What becomes clear in all this is that anyone desiring to profit from the drug trade would be opposed to the destruction of the poppy crop. The facts also call into question the sincerity of US Government officials and their dedication to the War on Drugs.

More recent allegations of US involvement with the illicit drug trade reach all the way to the top. Indeed, at least five books and many Web sites have connected both President George W. Bush and his father with the drug trade.

The most prominent anecdote involves a colorful assassinated drug dealer and DEA informant named Barry Seal. Daniel Hopsicker, formerly executive producer of a business news television show aired on NBC, published a book on Seal in 2001 entitled *Barry & 'the boys': The CIA, The Mob and America's Secret History.*

In this book, Hopsicker details how Seal, who was at the same time one of America's most successful drug smugglers and a CIA agent, became angry at George H. W. Bush when he was Reagan's vice president. Seal felt Bush had betrayed him by not getting him out of legal problems concerning drugs. Seal had been implicated in the CIA drug smuggling connected to the airport at Mena, Arkansas. These covert operations were in turn linked to Bill Clinton during his tenure as that state's governor, when at least one Arkansas lawman publicly stated that it was then-Governor Clinton who squashed a state investigation into the drug smuggling activities at Mena.

In retaliation for the apparent betrayal by Bush, Seal reportedly arranged for a DEA "sting" at a Florida airport in 1985. But instead of nabbing ordinary drug dealers, the operation caught Bush's sons, Jeb and George W., accepting a shipment of cocaine. Both were already prominent political leaders at that time. According to Hopsicker, "Seal then stepped in and 'took care' of things. The Bushes were now supposedly in his debt. Plus he hung on to the videotape shot of the sting for insurance."

This same story was echoed in a book by former air force intelligence officer and CIA asset Terry Reed, along with former *Newsday* prize-winning investigative reporter John Cummings. In *Compromised*, Reed asserts that Seal told him, "It seems some of George Bush's kids just can't say no ta drugs, ha, ha, ha, ha. Well, ya can imagine how valuable information like that would be, can't ya? That could get you out of almost any jam, it's like a get-out-of-jail-free card. I even got surveillance videos catchin' the Bush boys red handed. I consider this stuff my insurance policy."

Seal's "insurance policy" lapsed quickly. He was machine-gunned in

Baton Rouge, Louisiana, on February 19, 1986, less than a year later and whatever tapes he may have had disappeared.

His death inspired a lengthy letter to then attorney general Ed Meese from the Louisiana attorney general, William J. Guste Jr., stating, "I, for one, was shocked when I learned of his death. In October, as chairman of the Subcommittee on Narcotics and Drug Interdiction of the President's Commission on Organized Crime, I had presided over a seminar at which Barry Seal had testified. His purpose there was to inform the commission and top United States officials of the methods and equipment used by drug smugglers."

According to investigator Hopsicker, three boxes of documents, including audio/videotapes, which Seal had kept with him at all times, were taken from the scene of his murder by an FBI special agent from the Baton Rouge office. The agent arrived at the crime scene less than ten minutes after the shooting.

Was Barry Seal's murder just another drug-related street shooting or did someone not want him to reveal what he knew? Hopsicker did discover that the very plane Seal claimed was used to fly cocaine to the 1985 sting ended up as the property of George W. Bush sometime after Seal's death. The writer also found in tracing the ownership of the turboprop King Air 200 that the trail led to several persons connected to either the Iran-Contra or the savings and loan scandals of the 1980s. Hopsicker also found FAA records that showed that Seal had flown aircraft connected through a Phoenix firm to Southern Air Transport, a known CIA proprietary company.

Voters might recall that the younger Bush never actually denied using cocaine when the issue came up in his 2000 campaign for president. He simply brushed the allegation aside with a claim of youthful foolishness. Some of the thousands still serving prison sentences for possession of cocaine must wish their convictions could be overturned and excused as the foolishness of youth.

Cheney also has had questions raised about drug running through Halliburton's subsidiary KBR as well as the firm's connection to a suspect Russian oil company.

At least one of the fat loans given by the US Export-Import Bank in 2000 after being lobbied by Halliburton was to the Tyumen Oil Co., controlled by the Alfa Group conglomerate. The loan was approved in April 2002. A Center for Public Integrity investigative report stated, "It guaranteed $489 million in credits to a Russian oil company whose roots are imbedded in a legacy of KGB and Communist Party corruption, as well as drug trafficking and organized crime funds, according to Russian and US sources and documents."

In 1997, the Russian equivalent of our FBI presented Russia's lower House of Parliament a report alleging both organized crime and drug running involving Tyumen's parent company, the Alfa Group. The report stated that two Alfa entities, Alfa Bank and the trading company Alfa Eko, in the early 1990s were deeply involved in laundering both Russian and Colombian drug money and in importing drugs from the Far East into Europe. A former KGB officer said Alfa Bank was founded with Communist Party and KGB funds and utilized former government agents who had served in anti-organized crime units under the communist regime. He said heroin was often disguised as flour and sugar shipments bound for Germany.

Russian reports showed that in 1995 a Siberian railroad worker stole a sack of sugar from a rail car leased to Alfa Eko and that shortly afterward many people in his town became "poisoned" after eating the heroin-laced sugar. This incident prompted official raids on Alfa Eko that turned up "drugs and other compromising documentation."

Even Alfa Group's 1998 takeover of Tyumen Oil prompted allegations of impropriety and connections to Moscow's Solntsevo crime family. Despite all this evidence of drug smuggling, Cheney's Halliburton prevailed and US taxpayers supported the loans.

More heavy political pressure may have come from Tyumen's lead attorney, James C. Langdon Jr., a managing partner of the worldwide law firm of Akin Gump Strauss Hauer & Feld. Langdon was one of George W. Bush's "Pioneers," a group of fund-raisers that gathered at least $100,000 each for the 2000 campaign. Another helpful person was Halliburton's top lobbyist, Dave Gribbin, who served as Cheney's chief of staff when he headed the Pentagon under the elder Bush.

Drugs, oil, politics, intelligence agencies, and shady and complicated business dealings all found a focal point in 2001. It was in the wayward son of a prominent Saudi family named Osama bin Laden.

BIN LADEN, THE MADE-TO-ORDER ENEMY

As in the JFK assassination, authorities on the day of the 9/11 attacks had a suspect even before anyone knew for certain what had happened. He was identified as Osama bin Laden, the son of a wealthy Saudi Arabian family and a man who during the Russo-Afghan War of the 1980s received arms and financing from the US government.

Despite the fact that bin Laden repeatedly denied knowledge of the attacks, he was presumed guilty by both the government and the press. No other interpretation of the attack was allowed in the corporate mass media. Bin Laden was a made-to-order enemy. He is the man blamed for the 1993 WTC attack, and the bombing of American embassies in Africa in 1998, and had been a fugitive from US justice for more than a decade. Nobody might ever have heard of Osama bin Laden if President Bill Clinton had not fired missiles indiscriminately into Afghanistan in an attempt to kill him in 1998.

Bin Laden's history is relatively nondescript yet fascinating as an example of a piously religious man being drawn into a world of geopolitics and murder.

A lengthy biography of bin Laden was presented by PBS's *Frontline* and it relied in part on a document that the show's editors said came from an anonymous source close to bin Laden. They added that while some of the information could not be independently verified and even ran contrary to other sources, the document nevertheless was "a very useful source of information." The document seemed to be a fairly accurate and somewhat sympathetic biography of bin Laden.

According to this document, bin Laden was born in 1957 to a Syrian mother. He was the seventh son of more than fifty brothers and sisters. His father, Mohammed Awad bin Laden, had immigrated to Saudi Arabia in about 1930, where he worked as a laborer in the port city of Jeddah on the Red Sea. During the post-World War II reign of King Ibn Saud, the founder of modern Saudi Arabia, the elder bin Laden gained a fortune by constructing the king's palaces. He impressed the king and began to build good relations with the royal family, especially Faisal, who took the throne when his brother, King Saud IV, was forced to abdicate in 1964.

The elder bin Laden reportedly played a role in convincing Saud IV to step down in favor of Faisal. For his trouble, Faisal issued a decree that all construction projects would go to bin Laden. This included contracts to restore the holy mosques in Mecca and Medina, the most venerated of Muslim shrines.

According to the PBS document, the elder bin Laden was a stern disciplinarian who kept his children in one location and instilled in them strict business and religious mores. To his credit, the father reportedly showed no difference in the treatment of his vast brood. During the Haji holy season, the elder bin Laden spent his construction company wealth on funding the travels of many Islamic leaders and scholars. Through the father's generosity, the son made many long-lasting friendships.

Mohammed Awad bin Laden died in a 1968 plane crash when Osama bin Laden was still a teenager. By age seventeen, bin Laden had married a young Syrian relative and had completed his early education. In 1981, he received a degree in public administration from the King Abdul-Aziz University in Jeddah. During this time, bin Laden followed many other educated Arabs in joining the Muslim Brotherhood. As early as the first two weeks of the Soviet invasion of Afghanistan in December 1979, bin Laden was taken to Pakistan to meet leaders of the anti-Soviet forces and to witness the pitiful columns of refugees. Returning to Saudi Arabia, he began collecting for the Afghan cause. He made several short trips to Pakistan during the next couple of years, taking with him an immense amount of money and materials.

In 1982, bin Laden finally entered Afghanistan to meet with the Mujahideen fighters, taking along construction machinery and even a few of the bin Laden construction workers. He also reportedly established a "guesthouse" in Peshawar on the Afghan-Pakistan border that became a way station for Arab fighters, sent by him to various Afghan factions fighting the Soviets. By 1988, he had established more than six camps of his own in Afghanistan and his own force, the Maktab al-Khidimat (MAK), which soon was engaging the Soviets. Composed primarily of devout Muslims, these fighters came from Egypt, Lebanon, Syria, Turkey, Saudi Arabia and other Middle Eastern nations.

From 1984 through 1989, he spent more than eight months out of each year in Afghanistan, where he participated in several major battles and numerous smaller skirmishes. His relations with the Taliban were warm because they both saw themselves as devout practitioners of Islam. Theirs was a bonding of religion, not of politics.

Returning to Saudi Arabia in late 1989 as the Soviets were withdrawing from Afghanistan, bin Laden found himself trapped by a royal ban on his travels. He had angered the Saudi royals by announcing his intention of spreading his holy war into South Yemen and warned of invasion by Saddam Hussein, who then had warm relations with the Saudis. When Saddam Hussein invaded Kuwait in 1991, he saw it as a sign of his prophecy come true and proposed to the Saudis that he bring in his Arab Mujahideen to protect the kingdom. Before a decision was made on his suggestion, bin Laden was shocked to learn that American troops had arrived in Saudi Arabia.

It was a transforming moment, as the presence of any foreign troops on Saudi soil was considered intolerable by many Muslims. He had much earlier stated that the next great battle would be against America. His virtual house arrest in Jeddah and an armed raid on his suburban farm by the national guard caused his relations with the Saudis to sour. Bin Laden convinced a brother to arrange for him to visit Pakistan on business, but once he arrived there in the spring of 1991 he sent back a letter stating he would not return and apologized for his perfidy.

Heading immediately for Afghanistan, he tried unsuccessfully to mediate between the various factions there. His devout demeanor endeared bin Laden to fellow Muslims. He was considered a truthful person, a simple person with good manners and a humble and generous personality. Despite his frail appearance and bland speeches, his followers saw him as an inspirational leader and showed him great respect. He also evinced a cunning caution, to the point of avoiding electronic devices, including wristwatches, which he believed might be used to track him.

During his stay and later in Sudan, the Saudis with the aid of Pakistani intelligence and perhaps their close associates, the CIA, reportedly tried to kill him but his many friends within the Pakistani establishment tipped him off each time. Apparently, the forces of the status quo desired to eliminate this religious fanatic who heeded neither bribes nor Western reasoning. By 1994, the Saudis publicly renounced bin Laden, withdrawing his citizenship and freezing his assets, estimated at between $200 million and $300 million. But this was only money traceable to him through the bin Laden Group. Millions more are tied up in bin Laden family money and their complex joint ventures with the royal Saudi family, including King Fahad.

During a stay in Sudan, there were anti-American incidents in Somalia and South Yemen, followed in 1995 by a car bombing in the Saudi capital of Riyadh. Although bin Laden was blamed in each of these incidents, the PBS document claimed he had no direct knowledge of them. They reportedly were carried out by Arabs who had trained with bin Laden in Afghanistan and had been imbued with anti-American feelings. There was no indication of who truly was behind them and they may not have known themselves.

Sought by both the Americans and the Saudis, bin Laden returned to Afghanistan, where he was granted sanctuary by the ruling Taliban. Shortly after arriving back there in mid-1996, the Khobar Towers on an American base in Saudi Arabia was bombed, killing nineteen American soldiers. Although no one claimed responsibility for the attack, once again Arab Afghan fighters who had been connected to bin Laden were blamed.

But no one was paying much attention to the diminutive "freedom fighter," so bin Laden issued what may have been his first public anti-American message, a twelve-page declaration of war against America. At that time his only demands were that American troops leave Saudi Arabia.

Reportedly, American Special Forces planned to attack his residence in 1997 but canceled the plan when an Arab newspaper in London published a report on the operation, again apparently provided by leaks from the sympathetic Pakistani military and intelligence personnel. By now, bin Laden was completely caught up in his own war against what he considered "infidels." He utilized every resource at his command, including the media. He even allowed an ABC television interview in April 1998, warning at that time that attacks would come within weeks.

An attack was expected inside Saudi Arabia. Instead American embassies in Kenya and Tanzania were bombed on August 7, 1998, provoking outrage all around the world.

President Clinton responded by ordering missiles fired at bin Laden's

Afghan camp in Khost. About 250 Arabs were killed but bin Laden was not there. A plant in the Sudan, suspected of producing chemical weapons, also was targeted by sixteen cruise missiles. Later it was found that the plant, owned by Saudi businessman Saleh Idris, actually was producing medicine, not chemical weapons.

The Taliban government of Afghanistan offered to put bin Laden on trial on condition that the US government supply sufficient evidence of his guilt in the bombings. Nothing came of this offer. By then, some members of the US intelligence establishment were saying that bin Laden was training Islamic fighters for action in Chechnya and other areas of Russia, through an organization called al Qaeda.

In fact, the al Qaeda network is quite different from World War II "fifth columnists" and traditional insurgent movements in that its far-flung groups of operatives are not closely connected and do not have a clear command structure. It is a loose conglomeration of dedicated fighters operating across continents. Such an organization would be susceptible to penetration by any number of national security forces, in fact, almost anyone.

At least one intelligence insider has suggested that al Qaeda—translated as "the base"—does not mean a central headquarters but rather a CIA database of Arab mercenaries available for missions at a price. If this is the case, al Qaeda could well be following orders from someone other than bin Laden or his god.

However, the PBS document stated that bin Laden's followers are not true mercenaries but religious zealots who do not require much money. "Explosives and weapons are very cheap in some parts of the world," it stated. "In Somalia, TNT, for example, is cheaper than sugar. In Yemen, you can buy an RPG [Rocket Propelled Grenade] for less than a TV set. The role of money here is over-exaggerated by many writers."

According to this document, bin Laden was nearly forgotten by his Arab followers until the African bombings that killed twelve Americans, about three hundred Kenyans and Tanzanians and wounded five thousand. President Clinton told the public, "Our target was terror. There is convincing evidence from our intelligence community that the bin Laden terrorist network was responsible for these bombings. Based on this information, we have high confidence that these bombings were planned, financed and carried out by the organization bin Laden leads."

With bin Laden's name bantered about by the news media, his notoriety rose once again. The PBS document stated, "People's reaction, however, was mixed. While many felt triumph for scaring the Americans, many others felt upset by the picture of hundreds of civilians killed and injured in the attack. They felt this can never be justified.

"After the American [missile] attack on Sudan and Afghanistan, it became almost shameful to criticize bin Laden. The American strike with associated remarks by Clinton and American officials proved that bin Laden is a big challenge to America. In the minds of the average Arab and Muslim, bin Laden appeared as the man who was able to drive Americans so crazy that it started shooting haphazardly at unjustified targets. Their view was that while bin Laden or others can make 'executive' mistakes because of their difficult circumstances, logistics and communication, America is not supposed to [make] mistakes unless it is done on purpose."

BIN LADEN REPLIES TO BUSH

What did the primary suspect have to say about the 9/11 attacks? A great deal—but one had to know where to look.

Early on, the Bush administration asked the major news media not to report on what bin Laden had to say, arguing that he might use the opportunity to pass secret messages along to his al Qaeda network. Next, White House spokesman Ari Fleischer instructed the press to censor any future tape-recorded messages from bin Laden, although he didn't actually use the word "censor." Fleischer spent some time arguing with the media representatives, saying only, "we have the power but this is only a request." In the end, the sycophantic corporate media agreed to self-censor any word from bin Laden. However, the European media and alternative outlets in America, especially on the Internet, made no such agreement.

In an interview on September 28, according to the Pakistani newspaper *Ummat*, bin Laden stated, "I have already said that I am not involved in the 11 September attacks in the United States. As a Muslim, I try my best to avoid telling a lie. I had no knowledge of these attacks, nor do I consider the killing of innocent women, children and other humans as an appreciable act. Islam strictly forbids causing harm to innocent women, children and other people. Such a practice is forbidden even in the course of battle. It is the United States, which is perpetrating every maltreatment on women, children and common people."

In this interview, largely unreported in the United States, bin Laden unsurprisingly blamed the attacks on Israel, claiming, "All that is going on in Palestine for the last eleven months is sufficient to call the wrath of God upon the United States and Israel, (and) what had earlier been done to the innocent people of Iraq, Chechnya and Bosnia."

Bin Laden went on to state, "we are not hostile to the United States. We are against the [US government] system which makes other nations slaves to the United States or forces them to mortgage their political and economic freedom."

One cannot, of course, take bin Laden at face value, but then the same could be said for the US government, which in the past has been caught in so many lies and misstatements that it is surprising that anyone pays serious attention to official pronouncements.

In the late fall of 2001, a videotape of Osama bin Laden was offered to the public by the CIA and proclaimed by President Bush as a smoking gun, "a devastating declaration of guilt" in the 9/11 tragedies.

Immediately, voices rose criticizing the tape. Bin Laden's mother, Alia Ghanem, told a British newspaper, "There are too many gaps and the statements are very unlike him. Osama is too good a Muslim and too good a person to say or do what the script of the video suggests." Ghanem, who still lives in Saudi Arabia, said the tape was "doctored." Ghanem also denied reports that her son had called her prior to September 11 and told her he would be out of touch for some time because something big was about to happen. Some days later, his mother's claim was supported by Arabic language experts, who claimed that the Pentagon's translation of the tape was incorrect, taken out of context and that incriminating words had been put in bin Laden's mouth.

Two independent translators and an expert on Arabic culture reported their findings on the German state television program *Monitor*, which broadcast on December 20, 2001, over Germany's Channel One, *Das Erst*, often compared to NBC or the BBC. Dr. Abdel El M. Husseini stated, "I have carefully examined the Pentagon's translation. This translation is very problematic. At the most important places which have been presented as proof of bin Laden's guilt, it is not identical with the Arabic."

In the Pentagon translation given great publicity by the United States corporate media, bin Laden was quoted as saying, "We calculated in advance the number of casualties from the enemy." But, according to Dr. Murad Alami, "The words 'in advance' are not even heard on the tapes. This translation is wrong. When we take the original Arabic from the tape there are no misunderstandings which would allow for us to read this into the original."

At another point in the Pentagon translation, bin Laden was reported saying, "We had notification since the previous Thursday that the event would take place that day." But Alami stated, "'Previous' is never said. The following sentence that the event would take place on that day is not heard in the original Arabic." Alami said the sentence "We ordered each of them to go to America" was in the active voice while the original Arabic was in the passive voice, "they were ordered to go to America." He added the translation with the word "we" was simply wrong. The expert said the sentence translated by the Pentagon as "they didn't know anything about the operation" is not understandable on the original tape.

Another of the experts interviewed, Gernot Rotter, a professor of Islamic and Arabic studies at the University of Hamburg, after studying the Pentagon's translations, stated, "The American translators who listened and transcribed the tapes have apparently written a lot of things into the text that they wanted to hear, which are actually not heard on the tape no matter how many times you listen to it."

This was somewhat supported by a December 20, 2001 *USA Today* article that described how the tape was hurriedly translated in twelve hours by a Lebanese and an Egyptian who "had difficulties with the Saudi dialect that bin Laden and his guest used in the tape. Regardless of whether bin Laden or his organization was involved in the attacks or not, this tape is of such bad quality, in some places it cannot be understood at all, and those parts which can be understood are torn out of context so that the tape cannot be used as evidence to prove anything."

After a hiatus of three years, a bin Laden tape was suddenly produced in January 2006. Parts of an audiotape purportedly of bin Laden were played on Al-Jazeera television and later a full version was published on its website. CBS News styled the tape as "chilling" and reported that bin Laden threatened more attacks on the United States. The news agency also reported that the CIA had verified the authenticity of the tape and that it proved bin Laden was still alive.

As in 2001, independent researchers once again questioned the authenticity of the latest bin Laden tape.

Internet columnist and Washington insider Wayne Madsen noted, "What's not right about the Osama Bin Laden audio tape? One thing that the Bush administration does well is manage perceptions of the public. Amid protests over the NSA wiretapping, the extension of the Patriot Act, and the nomination of neo-Fascist Samuel Alito to the Supreme Court, an audio tape on Osama Bin Laden is sent to Al Jazeera. On the tape, Bin Laden suddenly veers from being a traditional right-wing Wahhabi fanatic to the right of the House of Saud to a leftist progressive. The tape by Bin Laden was quickly verified as 'authentic' by a CIA that is now firmly in the grasp of neo-cons under Porter Goss. However, the tape is an obvious fake being used by the Bush administration to scare Americans into believing 'al Qaeda' is making plans for another attack and an attempt to link Bin Laden to Democrats.

"The reason the tape is as phony as Niger yellowcake documents and Saddam's weapons of mass destruction is as plain as day. 'Bin Laden' allegedly quotes from the introduction of a book written by long-time Washington, D.C. progressive author and journalist and a friend of mine, Bill Blum. Bill was once an editor and contributor to *Covert Action Quarterly*, a magazine devoted to exposing CIA operations like the arming, funding, and training of Bin Laden and his Mujaheddin guerrillas during the Afghan-Soviet war. The Bush perception managers are either incredibly stupid or are trying to ensnare liberal journalists as aiders and abettors of al Qaeda, something that is certainly within their scope.

"Bin Laden allegedly quotes the following passage from Blum's book, *Rogue State*: 'If you [Americans] are sincere in your desire for peace and security, we have answered you. And if Bush decides to carry on with his lies and oppression, then it would be useful for you to read the book *Rogue State*, which states in its introduction: 'If I were president, I would stop the attacks on the United States: First I would give an apology to all the widows and orphans and those who were tortured. Then I would announce that American interference in the nations of the world has ended once and for all.'

"However, this quote is not from *Rogue State*, again, pointing to a very bad forgery of the Bin Laden audiotape. No sooner had the alleged Bin Laden tape been released, neo-con activist Cliff Kincaid was already spinning nonsense about Blum and his publisher, Common Courage Press of Monroe, Maine, being part of some sort of pro-bin Laden progressive and liberal 'Fifth Columnist' grouping in the United States.

"Bin Laden might not be so eager to quote Blum if he was aware of his other work, *Killing Hope*, an expose of the CIA's covert wars. In it, Blum defends the Soviet occupation of Afghanistan as self-defense against the CIA-backed Islamist guerrillas, including bin Laden's forces that were backed by the CIA. Now, why would bin Laden plug an author like Blum who backed bin Laden's hated enemies, the Soviet Communists and their Afghan allies? Because the bin Laden tape and his purported oratory are frauds."

Even the staid BBC saw the obvious connection between President Bush's troubles and the release of the bin Laden tape by stating, "The commander-in-chief has been under intense pressure in recent weeks, accused of trampling on civil liberties in pursuit of terror suspects. His defence has been that America is a nation at war. So Bin Laden's latest threats to launch new attacks on the US will only serve to underline this argument."

THE BIN LADEN FAMILY AND FRIENDS

Osama bin Laden as well as many of his al Qaeda operatives are Saudis. And this makes for a very troublesome aspect to the War on Terrorism.

To understand the problem, one must understand that the United States, and perhaps most of the industrialized world, is immeasurably dependent on the eight major oil fields of Saudi Arabia. Loss of even a significant portion of this petroleum could mean unthinkable consequences to the economy of both America and the world.

Control over this much-needed energy source is concentrated in one ruling family, a family with longstanding and well-documented ties to major oil players including the Bush family.

Media reports to the contrary, Osama bin Laden still receives financial support from his family even if they do not agree with his views and actions.

According to the PBS biography, most of the bin Ladens are faithful Muslims, who are taught that it is a sin to keep something that is not rightfully yours. Whether they agree with their sibling or not, they sincerely believe that bin Laden's share of the family fortune rightfully belongs to him and they see that he receives his due.

So, while the bin Laden assets are held by other family members, who can rightfully argue that bin Laden owns none of it, his share of the family profits continue to go to him. Some family members support bin Laden because they feel it is their religious duty. Others are more circumspect, not wishing to offend the Saudi royals, while others still make no effort to hide the fact that they send bin Laden money.

Of all the nations that are the most probable sponsors of bin Laden, first place must go to Saudi Arabia, home of bin Laden, the fundamentalist Wahhabi sect, and the Saudi royal family, primary business partners of the Bush family. This may go far in explaining the dearth of reporting on the Saudis in the mainstream media.

In fact, Defense Secretary Donald Rumsfeld tried to suppress a mid-2002 special report by the Defense Department naming Saudi Arabia as the "kernel of evil" and stating that Saudi funds support most of the Middle East's terrorist groups because the Saudis have a vested interest in perpetuating tension in the region. According to federal whistle-blower Al Martin, "It has always been a guideline of Republican administrations, starting with Richard Nixon, to suppress the truth about Saudi Arabia."

Likewise, as reported previously, by mid-2004, the Bush administration continued to drag its feet in supplying White House intelligence briefing documents to the 9/11 Commission. In July 2003, the Bush administration asked Congress to withhold 28 pages of its official 9/11 report. It was reported that the pages claimed there were ties between the

Saudi government and the hijackers. The connection was through Saudi financiers Omar al Bayoumi and Osama Brassman, both of whom conducted business with Saudi government officials.

As previously noted, individual Saudis also became the defendants of a $1 trillion lawsuit filed on behalf of more than six hundred families of 9/11 victims in 2002. Since then, many more families have joined the suit raising the total number of persons involved to about 4,000. Yet to date this story has received scant mention in the mainstream media. The suit was filed by attorney Ron Motley of Charleston, South Carolina, best known for his landmark $350 billion settlement from the tobacco industry in the late 1990s.

"This has become a true mission for me," said Motley. "The individuals that we've sued facilitated the events of September 11." Liz Alderman of Armonk, New York, whose son Peter died in the WTC attack, said she joined the suit because "there is no other way for the truth to come out. I've learned and I believe that an awful lot of the funding that enabled the terrorists to attack America was provided by Saudi Arabia," she said.

Two of the most prominent Saudis named in the suit were Prince Sultan bin Abdul Aziz al-Saud, Saudi Arabia's defense minister, and Prince Turki bin Faisal, a former intelligence chief and ambassador to Britain. The Saudi embassy in Washington had no comment on the suit, but, according to the *New York Times*, a State Department source said, "The Saudis have made their concerns known at a senior level [of the US government]."

The *Times* also reported that the Bush administration might well move to dismiss or delay the suit because it might damage the already strained relationship between the two countries. The paper made no mention of the close business relationships between the Saudis and the Bush family nor the fact that victims families have implored Bush not to block the suit.

In August 2003, Motley cleared his first major legal hurdle when a federal judge in Washington, D.C., refused to dismiss a Saudi bank, two large Muslim charities and two other defendants from the suit. The suit continued.

Lawyers for the Saudi defendants had argued that the charges against their clients was "guilt by association" but Motley countered by pointing out that under the new US anti-terrorism laws there is no demand to show a direct link to a crime. He said if a person or organization knowingly gives money to a terrorist group, that person or organization can be sued. Motley presented evidence that the chairman of the Al Rajhi bank had connections to Osama bin Laden's former personal secretary.

The stonewalling and obfuscation of the Bush administration toward 9/11 in general and the 9/11 Commission's emphasis on the Saudi funding of al Qaeda in particular proved too much for one victim's relative.

On November 26, 2003, Ellen Mariani, the whose husband, Louis Neil Mariani, was killed when Flight 175 struck the South Tower of the WTC, filed a $911 million plus damages class action civil suit in the United States District Court of the Eastern District of Pennsylvania. Defendants included President Bush, Vice President Cheney, Attorney General Ashcroft, Secretary of Defense Rumsfeld, CIA Director George Tenet, Transportation Secretary Mineta, National Security Adviser Rice and former President George Herbert Walker Bush. The suit was brought under the Racketeer Influenced and Corrupt Organizations Act (RICO), usually reserved for organized crime figures.

Interestingly, another defendant in the suit was Peter G. Peterson, chairman of the Council on Foreign Relations (CFR). The suit claims CFR members "are believed to have provided Defendant [Bush], et. al., while acting under color of federal law with critical national security advice not believed to be in the best interests of the Plaintiff [Mariani] and the American public." In the conclusion to the suit, Mariani's attorney, Philip J. Berg wrote, "Defendants must be held to account for their actions prior to and after 9/11 for the good of our nation and our security. Anything less will render the United States Constitution and out leaders' ritual vows 'to preserve and protect our Constitution against all enemies, foreign and domestic' meaningless."

By 2005, personal conflicts had caused Mariani to withdraw from the suit which was then resubmitted by Berg, this time naming World Trade Center worker and rescue hero William Rodriguez as the plaintiff. (Rodriguez's eyewitness account of bombings in the basement levels of one of the towers is covered in Part I of this book.)

In yet another 9/11 legal development, on November 28, 2004 a group of New York City citizens including 9/11 family members and survivors formally submitted a Citizens Complaint and Petition to New York State Attorney General Eliot Spitzer. The complaint demanded that Spitzer's office open a criminal inquiry and/or grand jury investigation into "the many still unsolved crimes of 9/11, over which he has jurisdiction," urging him to address "previously suppressed or ignored areas of inquiry identified by the 9/11 Family Steering Committee, 9/11 CitizensWatch and many independent researchers." Spearheading the effort were activists from within the grassroots 9/11 truth movement, led by a national organization noted earlier called 911truth.org.

The lead complainants included Bob McIlvaine, who lost his son Robert in the World Trade Center collapse; Patricia Perry, who lost her son John, a New York City Police officer; William Rodriguez, the WTC maintenance worker and rescue effort hero mentioned previously; numerous other 9/11 family members and survivors; and a variety of activist organizations.

With such suits and complaints, and considering the quarrels between the 9/11 Commission and the Bush administration, it now seems probable that any state sponsorship of the 9/11 terrorists, outside or the US, must have come from Saudi Arabia.

US News & World Report quoted an unnamed government official who had read the congressional report as saying, "There is so much more stuff about Saudi government involvement, it would blow people's minds."

This statement was clarified in that same issue by Florida Senator Bob Graham, co-chairman of the report committee. "The reality is that the [Saudi] foreign government was much more directly involved in not only the financing but the provision of support— transportation, housing and introduction to a network which gave support to the terrorists." He added, "They were not rogue agents, [but] were being directed by persons of significant responsibility within the government."

According to writer Craig Unger, who investigated the elder Bush's role in both the Iran-Contra and Iraqgate scandals, the estranged sister-in-law of Osama bin Laden, Carmen bin Laden, said she thought family members might have provided funds for Osama.

Saudi Arabia has long profited from its cozy relationship with American leaders. That nation profited most from the 1991 Gulf War. According to London's *Financial Times*, "Saudi Arabia oil revenues have tripled since mid-1990 because of the closure of production in Iraq and Kuwait."

Interestingly enough, it was the elder Bush's own secret society—the Council on Foreign Relations (CFR)—that blew the whistle on his business partners and friends in Saudi Arabia. In a report issued in October 2002, a CFR task force reported that Saudi Arabian officials for years have ignored countrymen and Muslim charities that provided major funding for the al Qaeda network and that US officials had systematically refused to acknowledge this connection.

"Saudi nationals have always constituted a disproportionate percentage of al Qaeda's own membership; and al Qaeda's political message has long focused on issues of particular interest to Saudi nationals, especially those who are disenchanted with their own government," stated the CFR report. Such connections are so numerous and documented that by late 2002 even the mass media began to question the Saudi role.

In his recent and widely noted book *House of Bush, House of Saud: The Secret Relationship Between the World's Two Most Powerful Dynasties* (Scribner: March 2004), author Unger argues that the seeds for 9/11 were planted nearly thirty years ago in a series of savvy business transactions that subsequently translated into a long-term political union between the Saudi royal family and the extended family of George H. W. Bush.

Unger's book begins with a single question: "How is it that two days after September 11, 2001, even as American air traffic was tightly restricted, a Saudi billionaire socialized in the White House with President George W. Bush as 140 Saudi citizens, many immediate kin to Osama Bin Laden, were permitted to return to their country?"

According to Unger's account, a potential treasure trove of intelligence was allowed to flee the country—including an alleged al Qaeda intermediary who was said to have foreknowledge of the 9/11 attacks. Unger asks: "Why did the FBI facilitate this evacuation without questioning these people? Why did Saudi Arabia, the birthplace of most of the hijackers, receive exclusive and preferential treatment from the White House even as the World Trade Center continued to burn?"

Saudi Arabia is not only in conflict over the politics but there are serious schisms within its religious community too. There is a serious division in the Muslim faith between the followers of the prophet Mohammed and its most extreme sect, the Wahhabi. The Wahhabis are taught that Jews are sub-humans who should be killed, while Muslims who have studied the *Hadith*, or Traditions, know that Mohammed married a Jewish woman and stated that faithful Jews would join Muslims in Paradise.

The most vicious opponents of Israel are the Wahhabis and there is one very good reason for their fear and anger. Statistics tell the tale. Literacy in the Arab world is below 50 percent. "Wahhabis are functionally illiterate, they cannot read about this conflict on their own. Typically, they memorize a few passages of the Koran taken out of context, and never read the accompanying *Hadith* for explanation," noted author John Loftus.

Loftus said Muslim scholars and leaders do not speak out against the "primitive Wahhabi apostasy" because most Muslim mosques are impoverished and depend on Saudi subsidies. To the Saudi royalty, literacy and knowledge would mean an end to their domination, so for years they have funded anyone who might aid their cause.

Why? Israel's literacy rate is 97 percent and it is the only nation in the Middle East that allows Arab women to vote. "To the Saudis, a democratic Palestinian nation would be a cancer in the Arab world, a destabilizing example of freedom that would threaten Arab dictators everywhere," explained Loftus, an attorney who has represented a number of federal whistle-blowers within the US intelligence community.

As information slowly leaked to the public, more and more attention was drawn to the role of the Saudis in supporting terrorism. In early October, the congressional committee investigating the 9/11 attacks was shocked to hear testimony from FBI special agent Steven Butler concerning the bureau's knowledge of Saudi money going directly to two of the accused hijackers.

Butler said one of his confidential informants, Abdussattar Shaikh, rented rooms in San Diego to Khalid al-Midhar and Nawaf al-Hazmi, both accused of hijacking American Airlines Flight 77. Two other Saudi nationals, Osama Basnan and Omar al-Bayoumi, also aided the hijackers by paying their rent, helping to open a bank account and arranging flight training, despite the fact that both had been charged with visa fraud.

Agent Butler also said he alerted his superiors in the FBI about this money flow but it went nowhere. Perhaps this inaction was due to evidence that at least some of the funding of the two terrorists came from the Saudi embassy. It was reported that Princess Haifa bint Faisal, wife of the Saudi ambassador, wrote cashier checks to Bayoumi, which were believed to have been passed along to the hijackers al-Midhar and al-Hazmi.

The worldwide banking connections of the Saudis—including banks controlled by globalist financiers—make untangling their funds difficult. For example, The National Commerce Bank in Saudi Arabia maintains a correspondent bank relationship with JP Morgan Chase as well as the Bank of America, according to the worldwide bank database, bankersalmanac.com. Correspondent banks act like branch banks, offering a variety of services including payments, wire transfers and stock trades. US officials charged that National Commerce Bank was used by wealthy Saudi businessman Yasin al-Qadi to funnel money to the al Qaeda network through a charity called the Muwafaq Foundation.

Jeff Hershberger, a spokesman for Bank of America, declined to say if the bank had a relationship with the Saudi bank, but Kristin Lemkau, speaking on behalf of JP Morgan, confirmed that her bank had a correspondent relationship with the Saudi bank.

The business circles involving the Saudis have grown to include the Bush family in Texas.

"The famous Saudi family [bin Laden] and the Bushes of Texas moved in similar financial circles down in Houston," noted the *Austin American-Statesman* in late 2001. In 1973, the oldest son of the bin Laden clan, Salem bin Laden—though at the time he spelled it Binladen or Binladin—came to Texas to recruit his father's former pilot to fly the family's corporate jet. Soon, Salem became involved in a number of Texas businesses, including ownership of a small Houston airport, a San Antonio aviation services company and a home in a San Antonio suburb called Enchanted Valley.

Under a policy of primogeniture [the first born gains the inheritance], only the oldest bin Laden son has control of the family fortune. This is the same method with which the European Rothschilds have managed to maintain their immense wealth over the centuries. Salem bin Laden then represented his family's fortune.

When Salem found that his father's old pilot, Gerald Auerbach of San Antonio, did not want to leave Texas, he established Binladen Aviation at San Antonio International Airport and put Auerbach in charge. Salem also purchased a lot from Auerbach in Kingsland, Texas, and built a house there. "I had owned [the lot] for several years, but I couldn't afford to build a house myself," Auerbach told a news reporter. "I really think he did it for me. He let us use it when he wasn't there." He added that Salem would jet into Texas for brief stays two or three times a year.

After 9/11, just up the road from the house once used by Salem bin Laden, there were clumps of American flags with a sign reading, "Bomb bin Laden!"

According to a Texas news article, "Had it not been played out in the Middle East, the bin Laden family story could have been pure Texas—a business dynasty linked to power, politics and big money. Besides its business ties to the Lone Star state, the family acquired holdings that range from waterfront condos in Boston to property in California to holdings in medical research firms and a US private investment firm to which former President Bush serves as an adviser [the Carlyle Group].

"The family's high-level connections were longstanding and well-known: The former President visited the bin Laden family in Saudi Arabia in 1998 and 2000."

Incredibly, the evidence also indicates that George W. Bush was put into the oil business by bin Laden money.

According to several published reports, Bush family friend James R. Bath used money from Osama bin Laden's brother to open a partnership with George W. Bush in Arbusto Energy, a West Texas drilling company.

Bath and the younger Bush had served together in the Texas Air National Guard. Later, according to *The Houston Chronicle*, Salem bin Laden named Bath his business representative in Texas shortly after the senior Bush was named CIA director by appointed President Gerald Ford in 1975. According to Texas court and financial records, Bath, a Houston entrepreneur, represented Salem bin Laden in such business deals as the $92 million customization of a Boeing 747 jet for use by the Saudi royal family and the purchase of the single-runway Houston Gulf Airport.

In 1992, Bath came under investigation by federal authorities for lobbying illegally for Saudi interests but nothing came of the inquiry. But, in sworn depositions, Bath acknowledged he represented four prominent Saudis, including Salem, as a trustee and used his name on their investments in return for a 5 percent commission on each deal. Bath, whose resume stated he handled all North American investments and operations for Sheikh Salem bin Laden, has consistently declined to discuss his business dealings for the record.

"Throughout Salem bin Laden's dealings in Texas, he cloaked himself in third parties and offshore companies that gave few clues to his identity," wrote Mike Ward of the *Austin American-Statesman*. "Other Texas investments were listed in the names of trustees, not Salem." Documents that are normally public, such as aviation, registration and other records that might provide more detail about the bin Laden family connections in Texas, have been denied to the public on the orders of Attorney General John Ashcroft in the wake of 9/11.

Salem bin Laden had a keen interest in aviation and it proved his undoing. On May 29, 1988, the forty-two-year-old flying enthusiast went up in an ultra-light craft that suddenly and inexplicably veered into power lines. He was pronounced dead after being rushed to San Antonio's Brooke Army Medical Center.

Another prominent Saudi represented by Bath was Sheikh Khalid bin Mahfouz, former CEO of National Commerce Bank, Saudi Arabia's largest bank and the one most closely associated with the royal family. It has already been noted that this bank is one that US authorities have identified as a conduit to the al Qaeda terrorist network. Sheikh Khalid bin Mahfouz was one of several Saudi defendants named in the one trillion dollar lawsuit filed in 2002 by attorney Motley, representing more than six hundred families of 9/11 victims.

Mahfouz was described by author J.H. Hatfield as a "deal broker whose alleged associations run from the CIA to a major shareholder and director of the Bank of Credit & Commerce International (BCCI). BCCI was closed down in July 1991, amid charges of multibillion-dollar fraud and worldwide news reports that the institution had been involved in covert intelligence work, drug money laundering, arms brokering, bribery of government officials and aid to terrorists."

The wealthy Saudi also reportedly paid $200 million for Dallas's Texas Commerce Bank Tower in 1985, which cost only $140 million to build. This deal not only helped cash-strapped Texas oilmen at the time but also benefited the founders of Texas Commerce Bank, the family of James Baker, former Secretary of State under President George H. W. Bush. Mahfouz, Bath and former Texas Governor John Connally were also partners in Houston's Main Bank, according to *Time* magazine reporter Jonathan Beaty.

In the early 1980s, Bath was listed as a $50,000, 5 percent investor in two limited oil exploration partnerships controlled by George W. Bush. This venture, Arbusto Energy, evolved into Harken Energy. The Bush White House has consistently argued that the money invested in Arbusto Energy belonged to Bath, not bin Laden. However, several researchers have maintained that Bath at the time could not have had this kind of money to invest. This was supported by Bath's former business partner, Charles W. White of Houston.

White said, based on his knowledge of Bath's finances at the time coupled with Bath's financial records filed during a divorce, that Bath had no substantial money of his own at the time the investment was made. In an interview with Beaty, White described a variety of backroom business deals with Bath, rich Arabs, Texas wheeler-dealers and the now defunct Bank of Credit & Commerce International (BCCI).

"You have to understand that they thought I was one of them," White explained. "Bath told me he was in the CIA. He told me he had been recruited by George Bush [Sr.] himself in 1976, when Bush was director of the agency. This made sense to me, especially in light of what I had seen once we went into business together. Bath and George, Jr., were pals and flew together in the same Air National Guard unit, and Bath lived just down the street from the Bush family when George, Sr., was living in Houston. He said Bush wanted him involved with the Arabs, and to get into the aviation business.

"That's how Bath, who didn't know anything about the aviation business, became one of the biggest jet aviation dealers in the country within a couple of years. Look, here's a Boeing he's leasing to the Abu Dhabi National Oil Company. That's a multimillion-dollar jet. That's how he became a representative for Sheikh Khalid bin Mahfouz, whose family controls the National Commerce Bank of Saudi Arabia."

White also said Bath was investigated by the DEA in the 1970s. He was suspected of flying currency to the Cayman Islands. Nothing came of the investigation when no evidence of drug involvement was found.

It was at this same time that Main Bank, according to Beaty, "made the news when a bank examiner discovered that it was purchasing $100 million in hundred-dollar bills each month from the Federal Reserve, an amount that dwarfed its minuscule asset base."

While representing Mahfouz's business interests in Texas, Bath had racked up more than $12 million in contract overruns by overcharging for aviation fuel at his Southwest Aviation Services company at Houston's Ellington Field.

According to an October 28, 1991, report in *Time* magazine, Southwest Aviation in 1990 was charging government military aircraft—including then President Bush's *Air Force One*—anywhere from twenty-two to more than forty cents per gallon more than the Air National Guard base at Ellington was paying for jet fuel. The article pointed out that each time Bush's government-owned jet landed at Ellington, it was serviced by Bath's company rather than the lower-priced government facility. *Houston Post* reporter John Mecklin estimated that between 1985 and 1989, the Department of Defense paid Mahfouz's agent Bath more than $16.2 million for fuel under government contracts that should have cost $3.6 million.

In 1990, the same year Southwest Aviation was overcharging the government and Bush for fuel, the President drew a "line in the sand" to block Iraqi intrusion into Saudi Arabia. It is interesting to note that this line was located between the Iraqi forces and the Harken oil interests owned by his son, then soon-to-be Texas Governor George W. Bush.

The president's eldest son was a $50,000-a-year "consultant" to and a board member of Harken Energy Corp. of Grand Prairie, Texas, near the home of the Texas Rangers baseball team of which Bush was a managing general partner.

It should be noted that while connected to Harken in the late 1980s, the younger Bush received low-interest loans from the company while he served as a director and most certainly benefited from insider transactions. Ironically, Bush denounced similar shenanigans in mid-2002 following the scandals of Enron and WorldCom. One Bush official explained, "Corporate officers should not be able to treat a public company like their own personal bank."

According to filings with the Securities and Exchange Commission, the low-interest Harken loans totaled more than $180,000 and allowed Bush to purchase 105,000 shares of stock through a stock option program for senior company officials.

In January 1991, just days before Desert Storm was launched, Harken shocked the oil industry by announcing an oil-production agreement with the small island nation of Bahrain, a former British protectorate and a haven for international bankers just off the coast of Saudi Arabia in the Persian Gulf. Harken Energy, of which President Bush was a director from 1986 to 1993, formed an offshore subsidiary in September 1989 in the Cayman Islands. The subsidiary, Harken Bahrain Energy Company, was set up in anticipation of the company's venture drilling for oil off the coast of Bahrain.

Veteran oilmen wondered aloud how unknown Harken, with no previous drilling experience, obtained such a potentially lucrative deal. Furthermore, it was reported that "Harken's investments in the area will be protected by a 1990 agreement Bahrain signed with the US allowing American and 'multi-national' forces to set up permanent bases in that country."

Through a tangled web of Texas oilmen, wealthy Saudi sheiks and unscrupulous bankers connected to BCCI, the younger Bush eventually gained a sizable interest in Harken Energy. Two months before Saddam Hussein sent Iraqi troops into Kuwait, Bush sold two-thirds of his Harken stock, netting himself nearly a one-million-dollar profit. The stock dropped when the Iraqi invasion began.

In October 1990, the younger Bush told *Houston Post* reporter Peter Brewton that accusations that his father ordered troops to the area to protect Harken drilling rights was "a little far-fetched." He further claimed he sold his Harken stock before the Iraqi invasion but Brewton could find no record of the sale in the files of the Securities and Exchange Commission (SEC).

Records of Bush's Harken stock sale finally turned up in March 1991, eight months after the July 10, 1990, SEC deadline for filing such disclosures. One week after Saddam's troops entered Kuwait, Harken stock had dropped to $3.03 a share. The tardy SEC records revealed that by some good fortune, Bush had sold 66 percent of his Harken stock on June 22, 1990—just before the Iraqi invasion of Kuwait on August 2—for the top-dollar price of $4 a share, netting him $848,560.

Common business interests brought the Bush and bin Laden families a special closeness. An *Austin American-Statesman* article detailed both the financial and social connections between the two families, stating "Binladens traveled in same financial circles as Bush." It should be remembered that from 1989 to 1993, it was the Bush family, particularly Jeb and Neil, who were involved in the savings and loan debacle that cost taxpayers more than $500 billion.

It also should be noted that during the Persian Gulf War, it was Binladen Brothers Construction [now the Binladen Group] that helped build airfields for US aircraft. The bin Laden brothers were then described as "a good friend of the US government."

Later the bin Laden firm continued to construct an American air base in Saudi Arabia despite the fact that Osama bin Laden had already been blamed for terrorist acts such as the truck bombing of the Khobar Towers at the Dhahran base that killed nineteen Americans. A *WorldNetDaily* writer commented, "So let's get this straight. Bin Laden blows up our facilities, and his family gets the contract for rebuilding them. Do you get the feeling there is more going on than meets the eye?"

The Bank of Credit & Commerce International (BCCI)—another joint business endeavor of the Bushes and bin Ladens—was closed by federal investigators in 1991 after suffering some $10 billion in losses. BCCI was a Pakistani-run institution with front companies in the Cayman Islands that used secret accounts for global money laundering and was used by US intelligence to funnel money to bin Laden and the Mujahideen in Afghanistan fighting against the Soviet-backed government. During this struggle in Afghanistan, the Binladen Group joined other wealthy Saudis in an effort that came to be known as "the Golden Chain," which helped create the al Qaeda network.

Kahlid bin Mahfouz, mentioned earlier as a major player with well-to-do Texas oilmen, owned a controlling interest in BCCI. It has been called the most corrupt financial institution in history. The interconnections between BCCI and Bush's Harken Energy prompted a *Wall Street Journal* writer in 1991 to comment, "The number of BCCI-connected people who had dealings with Harken—all since George W. Bush came on board—likewise raises the question of whether they mask an effort to cozy up to a president's son."

Another close connection between bin Laden and the Bush family is a private international investment firm known as the Carlyle Group, which in 2006 boasted the management of more than $34 billion. Although it has renovated its website since the September 11 attacks, it is known that Carlyle directors include former Reagan Secretary of Defense Frank Carlucci, former Bush secretary of state James Baker and former Reagan aide and GOP operative Richard Darman. The *New York Times* reported that former President Bush was allowed to buy into Carlyle's investments, which involve at least 164 companies around the world.

In fact, two years after Bush Sr. left public office in 1993, he signed on as a senior counselor with the Carlyle Group. He was later joined by former British Prime Minister John Major and soon the pair was jetting off to Saudi Arabia to meet with the royal family, the bin Ladens and the Mahfouzes. Mahfouz's two sons soon became investors in the Carlyle Group although one, Abdulrahman bin Mahfouz, was a director of the Muwafaq Foundation, designated by the US Treasury Department as "an al Qaeda front."

According to the September 28, 2001 *Wall Street Journal*, "George H. W. Bush, the father of President Bush, works for the bin Laden family business in Saudi Arabia through the Carlyle Group, an international consulting firm." It has been confirmed by the senior Bush's chief of staff that Bush sent a thank-you note to the bin Laden family after a social visit in early 2001.

But it has been reported that after the attacks of 9/11, the Carlyle Group distanced itself from the family by buying out substantial bin Laden holdings in the firm.

Perhaps the closest Saudi friend to the Bush family was Saudi Arabian Ambassador to the United States Prince Bandar bin Sultan, the man who arranged the secretive flight of the bin Ladens in the days following 9/11.

The $1 trillion lawsuit filed against the Saudis alleges that Prince Bandar's father, who serves as the Saudi defense minister, contributed at least $6 million to four charities known to finance Osama bin Laden and al Qaeda.

Prince Bandar's relationship with the Bush family goes back to the days of the Reagan administration when Bush Sr. and Bandar would lunch regularly. "After Bush became president in 1989," wrote journalist Craig Unger, "Bandar acted as an envoy between him and Saddam Hussein, assuring Bush that the US could count on Saddam to provide a bulwark against extremist Islamic fundamentalism." Unger further stated that after the 2000 election, Bandar joined Bush Sr., former National Security Advisor Brent Scowcroft and General Norman Schwarzkopf for a hunting trip in Spain.

With such connections and his son as a sitting president of the United States, the senior Bush's Carlyle involvement was questioned by Larry Klayman, chairman and general counsel of Judicial Watch, who said, "Any foreign government or foreign investor trying to curry favor with the current Bush administration is sure to throw business to the Carlyle Group. And with the former President Bush promoting the firm's investments abroad, foreign nationals could understandably confuse the Carlyle Group's interests with the interests of the United States government."

After detailing some of the Carlyle/bin Laden investments in several businesses, including aerospace industries as well as the tremendous defense buildup since 9/11, writer Michael C. Ruppert commented, "In other words, bin Laden's attacks on the WTC and Pentagon, with the resulting massive increase in the US defense budget, have just made his family a great big pile of money."

There is evidence that President Bush and his father tried to block past efforts to find and prosecute Osama bin Laden. According to a special BBC investigation reported in the November 10, 2001, issue of the *Times of India*, a "secret FBI document, numbered 1991 WF213589" emanating from the FBI's Washington field office, blamed the recent terrorist attacks on "connections between the CIA and Saudi Arabia and the Bush men and bin Ladens."

The British newspaper, the *Guardian* wrote apparently of another document, marked "Secret" and coded "199 (national security)," concerning two of bin Laden's relatives. These two documents allege that the FBI had been told to "back off" an investigation of his brother, Abdullah bin Laden, who along with another brother, Omar, lived in Falls Church, Virginia just outside Washington. Abdullah was the United States director of the World Assembly of Muslim Youth (WAMY) until 2000. Although listed in FBI files as a "suspected terrorist organization," WAMY was not placed on the Bush administration's terrorist list, which would have frozen its assets. Despite several grand jury probes, no charges have been brought against the organization, which claims to be dedicated to guarding Muslim youth against "destructive ideologies."

Yet according to journalist Greg Palast, in mid-2002 Pakistan expelled several WAMY operatives, and officials in both India and the Philippines have accused WAMY of funding militant Muslim groups. Furthermore, in 2003, an unnamed security official who served under George W. Bush told journalist Craig Unger, "WAMY was involved in terrorist-support activity. There's no doubt about it."

Documents disclosed that the FBI file on the two bin Laden brothers was closed in 1996. According to Palast, "High-placed intelligence sources in Washington told the *Guardian*: 'There were always constraints on investigating the Saudis.'" The source said restrictions became worse after Bush took office and added, "There were particular investigations that were effectively killed."

The Saudis' attempts to lobby in Washington brought several Muslim organizations into the far-flung web of post 9/11 investigations. According to the *Washington Post*, federal agents since the mid-1990s had sought to track an estimated $1.7 billion that moved between these organizations. Investigators said the groups were created in the 1970s by the al-Rajhi family, one of Saudi Arabia's primary banking dynasties. Collectively, the organizations own or control a number of businesses worldwide. A spokesman for the al-Rajhis denied any wrongdoing on their part.

In late March 2002, federal agents raided sixteen homes and offices in northern Virginia believed to be involved in a nexus of Saudi-backed organizations with connections to terrorist groups. The after-the-fact and sweeping raids infuriated Muslims and non-Muslims alike.

Grover Norquist, a Republican Party activist who shared offices with the one of the raided organizations and was a board member of the Islamic Institute, said the groups existed "to promote democracy and free markets. Any effort to imply guilt by association is incompetent McCarthyism." Norquist, along with Islamic Institute chairman Khaled Saffuri, helped arrange meetings between Islamic leaders and senior Bush administration officials.

Then there is the case of a former employee at the US Consulate in Saudi Arabia who took bribes to provide fake visas. Abdullah Noman, fifty-four, a citizen of Yemen, worked at the consulate from September 1996 until November 2001. He admitted to taking bribes of both money and gifts worth thousands of dollars in exchange for visas for entry into the United States, making it appear that the bearers were members of legitimate trade delegations. "They would come in with everybody else and then disappear," noted Assistant US Attorney Lee Vilker.

Vilker said there was no known connection between Noman and al Qaeda terrorists but he admitted that authorities had not been able to locate all those who obtained visas from Noman, who was arrested in Las Vegas in late 2001 while accompanying a Middle Eastern trade delegation. He faced a prison term of fifteen years and a $250,000 fine plus deportation after serving time.

But even more ominous revelations came in 2002 from Michael Springman, a twenty-year veteran of the US Foreign Service and former chief of the American visa bureau in Jeddah, Saudi Arabia, who told of suspicious behavior there many years ago.

In a *BBC News* interview, Springman said, "In Saudi Arabia, I was repeatedly ordered by high level State Department officials to issue visas to unqualified applicants. These were, essentially, people who had no ties either to Saudi Arabia or to their own country. I complained bitterly at the time there. I returned to the US, I complained to the State Department here, to the General Accounting Office, the Bureau of Diplomatic Security and to the Inspector General's office. I was met with silence.

"What I was protesting was, in reality, an effort to bring recruits, rounded up by Osama bin Laden, to the US for terrorist training for the CIA. They would then be returned to Afghanistan to fight against the then-Soviets.

"The attack on the World Trade Center in 1993 did not shake the State Department's faith in the Saudis, nor did the attack on the American barracks at Khobar Towers in Saudi Arabia three years later, in which nineteen Americans died. FBI agents began to feel their investigation was being obstructed."

With the information above in hand, it is now clear that if there was a state sponsor behind the 9/11 attacks, as argued by the Bush administration to justify the invasions of Afghanistan and Iraq, that state would have to be Saudi Arabia. And considering the close business and social connections between the Saudi royals and bin Ladens with the Bush family, much closer scrutiny of this connection is fully justified.

Either the Bushes were too stupid to see what is happening right under their very noses or their resistance in revealing evidence about the Saudis' role is guided by something more sinister. Few people have ever accused the Bushes of being merely stupid

PART III - THE 9/11 BACKLASH

"In order to make sure that we're able to conduct a winning victory, we've got to have the best intelligence we can possibly have. And my report to the nation is we've got the best intelligence we can possibly have."

—President George W. Bush
in a September 26, 2001 speech to the CIA.

Fear mongering has always been a favored tool of despots and tyrants. After all, why would a free and prosperous population willingly give up their rights and liberties? Ever since 9/11, the Bush administration has gained increasing social control by holding the threat of terrorism over the heads of the American people.

A recent example of the use of this age-old device came in early 2006, when President Bush—under fire for the unresolved wars in Iraq and Afghanistan, the torture of terrorist suspects, and unconstitutional spying on Americans—played the fear card yet again, declaring: "We cannot let the fact that America hasn't been attacked in four and a half years since September 11 lull us into the illusion that the threats to our nation have disappeared." He then went on to detail what he described as a thwarted terrorist attack on Los Angeles in 2002. Bush revealed that the California strike was planned by a man named Hambali, reportedly a key lieutenant of Khalid Sheikh Mohammed, the alleged mastermind of the 9/11 attacks. Both Hambali and Mohammed were reported captured in 2003.

Bush said these al Qaeda leaders recruited Asian men who were to use shoe bombs to blow open the cockpit door of a commercial airliner, which then would be crashed into the US Bank Tower in Los Angeles. Bush mistakenly referred to this building as "Liberty Tower," but was quickly corrected that its original name had been "Library Tower." Bush said the plot was foiled when a key Asian al Qaeda member was arrested but declined to name the suspect or his nationality.

Soon, this story filled the mass media airwaves with some stations airing scenes from the Hollywood alien invasion film *Independence Day* as graphic representation of the destruction of the US Bank Tower.

But even before Americans could heave a collective sign of relief at being spared this carnage, serious questions arose over Bush's statement. Many thoughtful persons wondered why Bush had not called attention to the saving of Los Angeles early in 2003 when such news might have blunted the large and numerous anti-war demonstrations conducted prior to the invasion of Iraq.

Concern increased when Los Angeles Mayor Antonio Villaraigosa told newsmen he knew nothing of such an attempt and felt "blindsided" by Bush's announcement of the 2002 attack. He said communication regarding such an attack with the White House had been "nonexistent" despite at least two requests by him to meet with Bush regarding security issues.

"I'm amazed that the president would make this [announcement] on national TV and not inform us of these details through the appropriate channels," Villaraigosa told newsmen. "I don't expect a call from the president, but somebody."

Others were even less considerate in their characterization of Bush's sudden story of the 2002 Los Angeles attack. Doug Thompson, a writer for *Capitol Hill Blue*, the oldest political news site on the Internet, said he was contacted by members of the US intelligence community, who disputed Bush's claim. Thompson said he was able to confirm the intelligence credentials of at least four of the persons who contacted him. All asked not to be identified for fear of reprisals.

"The President has cheapened the entire intelligence community by dragging us into his fantasy world," Thompson quoted a longtime CIA operative as saying. "He is basing this absurd claim on the same discredited informant who told us al Qaeda would attack selected financial institutions in New York and Washington."

Indeed, in August 2004, during the heat of the Presidential election, the Bush White House had sought to increase the terror alert level by claiming attacks were imminent on major financial institutions. This alert was later withdrawn after officials admitted it was based on old information from a discredited source.

Thankfully, the siege mentality of some American leaders was not always as strong as those espoused by President Bush in 2006.

In prophetic testimony before joint hearings of the Senate Armed Services Appropriations and Intelligence committees in the spring of 2001, Secretary of State Colin Powell explained why Americans should not give up their freedoms for the hope of security. "If we adopted this hunkered-down attitude, behind our concrete and our barbed wire, the terrorists would have achieved a kind of victory," he declared.

But the rhetoric was to change completely as new and constitutionally questionable laws and regulations were put into effect later that year.

Within days of the 9/11 attacks, President Bush declared a "War on Terrorism." He initially called it a "crusade," but that term was quickly dropped when it was pointed out that Muslims, both within and without the Middle East, still remember the bloody history of that word and would take offense.

To initiate a war, there first must be a perceived enemy. That one grand enemy was now claimed to be Osama bin Laden and his al Qaeda network. As previously noted, the FBI announced a list of suspected hijackers with unbelievable speed, while at the same time acknowledging that the men used false identity papers. But this list was questioned in many quarters, including government agents.

"There are people within the US intelligence community who doubt that the hijacker list from 9/11 has much truth in it," said one unnamed intelligence source as quoted by author Jon Rappoport. "They see it as a more-or-less invented list. They know that if you start with men showing false passports (or no passports) to get on four planes on 9/11, you can't assemble a correct list of nineteen suspects within a few days—especially since all those men are presumed dead and missing, untraceable.

"Al Qaeda is being used as a term to convince people that these terrorists are all connected in a vast, very well-organized network that is global in reach, that has a very sophisticated and far-flung communication setup, that issues orders from the top down to cells all over the world," stated the intelligence source. "There are a number of people inside the US intelligence agencies who know this is a false picture. They know that false intelligence is being assembled in order to paint a picture which is distorted, so that the American people will have a single focus on one grand evil enemy."

In October 2004, the BBC in England broadcast a documentary entitled *The Power of Nightmares: The Rise of the Politics of Fear*, which challenged the Bush administration's concept of al Qaeda as a multi-faceted globe-spanning octopus of terrorism. The three-hour documentary by writer/producer Adam Curtis raised some pertinent questions such as:

- Why has the Bush administration, despite the roundup of hundreds of suspected terrorists and the use of torture, failed to produce any hard evidence of al Qaeda activities?
- Of the 664 persons detained in Britain on suspicion of being terrorists, why have only 17 been found guilty of crimes and of these, none were proven members of al Qaeda?
- Why has the administration prompted so much frightening speculation concerning "dirty" radioactive bombs when experts have stated that public panic will kill more people than radioactivity?
- Why did Defense Secretary Rumsfeld claim on *Meet the Press* in 2001 that al Qaeda controlled massive high-tech cave complexes in Afghanistan, when none were later found following the military invasion?

While acknowledging that groups of disaffected terrorists do exist around the world, the BBC documentary nevertheless argued that, "the nightmare vision of a uniquely powerful hidden organization waiting to strike our societies is an illusion. Wherever one looks for this al Qaeda organization, from the mountains of Afghanistan to the 'sleeper cells' in America, the British and Americans are chasing a phantom enemy."

According to *Los Angeles Times* columnist Robert Scheer, "...the film, both more sober and more deeply provocative than Michael Moore's *Fahrenheit 9/11*, directly challenges the conventional wisdom by making a powerful case that the Bush administration, led by a tight-knit cabal of Machiavellian neoconservatives, has seized upon the false image of a unified international terrorist threat to replace the expired Soviet empire in order to push a political agenda." He pointed out that everything we know about al Qaeda comes from only two sources, both with a vested interest in maintaining the concept of a well-financed and deeply entrenched enemy: the terrorists themselves and military and intelligence agencies. "Such a state of national ignorance about an endless war is, as *The Power of Nightmares* makes clear, simply unacceptable in a functioning democracy," Scheer added.

The documentary also noted this was not the first time that American political figures had hyped a foreign enemy to achieve their own goals—in fact, by many of the same neoconservatives responsible for today's fear mongering.

Their goal was to cut short President Richard Nixon's efforts at "détente" with the Soviet Union in the early 1970s, and the leaders of this faction were none other than Secretary of Defense Donald Rumsfeld and Chief of Staff Dick Cheney in the Gerald Ford administration. Both Rumsfeld and Cheney claimed that reconciliation with the Soviets was impossible because they were hiding weapons of mass destruction (WMDs), a new generation of nuclear submarines that were undetectable by current technology. This claim was firmly denied by the CIA at the time, which called it "complete fiction." The charge ultimately proved false, but not before trillions were spent on the biggest peace-time military build up in American history during the subsequent Reagan administration.

In Britain it has been suggested that al Qaeda is not a real organization but rather a computer list of Arab mercenaries—freedom fighters/terrorists for hire.

"Bin Laden...was armed by the CIA and funded by the Saudis to wage jihad against the Russian occupation of Afghanistan. Al Qaeda, literally 'the database,' was originally the computer file of the thousands of mujahideen who were recruited and trained with help from the CIA to defeat the Russians," noted British commentator Robin Cook.

Often supposed enemies prove to be mirror images of each other. Noted author Thom Hartmann pointed out that both Bush's neocons and Muslim terrorists operate from the same ideology—both believe the end justifies the means and that people must be frightened into accepting religion and nationalism for the greater good of morality and a stable state.

A HISTORY OF UNCONSTITUTIONAL ACTIONS

If the idea of strong federal protection during times of terrorist threats seems comforting, picture this: A pimple-faced 18-year-old dressed in camouflage and armed with a fully loaded M-16 arrives at your door and informs you that you must leave your home and come with him because the authorities fear a biological attack in your city. If you protest and say you'll stay and take your chances, you are in violation of the law and subject to arrest, fine and imprisonment. After seeing his armed companions, you decide to join your neighbors in a military truck destined for a "relocation camp" situated many miles from your home. At the camp, you are instructed to stand in line for a vaccination against smallpox, anthrax or whatever the latest threat might be. If you refuse the inoculation, recalling that in past years so many such vaccines were proven to be tainted, you are again subject to fine and jail.

If this sounds like some paranoid's view of an Orwellian nightmare, you should know that laws authorizing such action had already been passed in 16 states and the District of Columbia by the end of 2002. Maine, New Hampshire, Maryland, Virginia, South Carolina, Georgia, Tennessee, Florida, Missouri, Oklahoma, Minnesota, South Dakota, Utah, Arizona and New Mexico had passed all or parts of the model law. The other states had either rejected or stalled the legislation.

And don't take comfort if your state is not among these as most of this overreaching law was incorporated into the Homeland Security legislation.

Many states modified or outright rejected this legislation, which was drawn up as a model law for the federal Centers for Disease Control and Prevention following the anthrax attacks that occurred in the Capitol on the heels of 9/11.

One might have noticed that not much has been mentioned in recent years about these attacks. Perhaps this is because investigation showed that the anthrax pathogens involved were military grade and unavailable outside the United States. To date, no one has been charged with those attacks.

The Model State Emergency Health Powers Act was then sent to each state legislature with a federal endorsement for its passage. Federal officials claimed the laws were needed to provide local authorities the legal right to make quick decisions in an emergency involving contagious or deadly pathogens.

One advocate, Attorney Gene Matthews with the Department of Health and Human Services argued, "We have not used emergency powers in probably 50 years. This is something we need to attend to."

Under this act, authorities would be able to federalize all medical personnel, from EMTs to physicians, and enforce quarantines. They would have the right to vaccinate the public, with or without their consent, seize and destroy private property without compensation and ration medical supplies, food, fuel and water in a declared emergency.

"[This act] goes far beyond bioterrorism," said Andrew Schlafly of the Association of American Physicians and Surgeons. "Unelected state officials can force treatment or vaccination of citizens against the advice of their doctors."

The Federal Emergency Management Agency (FEMA), designated as the lead agency under the Department of Homeland Security, also has plans in its files for the evacuation of cities and the use of sprawling temporary camps to house their residents.

Under the pretext of planning for the War on Terrorism, FEMA has dusted off and augmented contingency plans to counter the effects of nuclear, biological and chemical attacks.

By mid-2002, FEMA was notifying its vendors, contractors and consultants to envision the logistics of millions of displaced Americans forced to leave cities that come under attack. The firms were given a deadline of January 2003, to be ready to establish such displaced person camps. FEMA made it known that it already had ordered significant numbers of tents and trailers to be used for housing.

History has provided proof that traditional American openness and fairness will not necessarily be supported by the nation's highest authorities.

During the War Between the States, President Abraham Lincoln suspended the writ of habeas corpus, that mainstay of American justice, which demands that the accused has the right to face his accusers. This action was later overturned by the US Supreme Court, but only because Lincoln had not sought approval from Congress.

During World War I, that same court upheld the right of the president to seize the property of enemy aliens without a hearing, stating, "National security might not be able to afford the luxuries of litigation and the long delays which preliminary hearings traditionally have entailed." And, of course, the Supreme Court upheld the rounding up, incarceration and property seizure of Japanese Americans following the attack on Pearl Harbor.

Many Americans, from leading academics to the man on the street, wondered aloud what would become of traditional American liberties in the War on Terrorism.

Frank Serpico, the former New York policeman who turned in corrupt officers in the 1960s and was the subject of a popular film, spoke at a July 4, 2002, reading of the Declaration of Independence in Chatham, NY:

"It is my opinion that never before have we, as a nation, stood in greater danger of losing our individual liberties as we are today," he told the audience. "We, the people of this great nation, are being punished for the transgressions of our leaders and their consorts...When I still have the freedom to speak, I'll always use it." Ironically, several in the audience there to hear Serpico read the Declaration of Independence booed his remarks.

Even former Attorney General Janet Reno, under whose leadership the tragedies at Ruby Ridge and Waco unfolded, expressed concern. "I have trouble with a war that has no endgame and I have trouble with a war that generates so many concerns about individual liberties," she told an audience at Old Dominion University in Norfolk, VA, in 2002.

Reno asked Americans to remember the lessons learned from the unjust imprisonment of Japanese-Americans during World War II, adding that she believed the government would be hard pressed to find a legal basis to prosecute many of the Taliban and al Qaeda prisoners detained at Guantanamo Bay Naval Base in Cuba.

Indeed, horror stories had begun to leak out about the degrading treatment of prisoners who had been captured "on the battlefield" in the War on Terror, and held thereafter at the Guantanamo prison as "enemy combatants." The Bush administration's response was that since the prison was not on American soil, the legal protections provided by the US Constitution did not apply, and that secret military tribunals would be convened.

But for months and then years, hundreds of men languished in the naval prison without trial, in apparently cruel conditions. By 2005, a wide variety of human rights organizations—including Amnesty International, Physicians for Human Rights, and even the United Nations—had charged that the conditions in Guantanamo were in violation of international conventions to which the US is a party.

Regardless, in early 2006, at least 556 persons still remained indefinitely detained at Guantanamo. A FOIA request brought by the Associated Press revealed their names for the first time only on April 20, 2006. The roster indicated that the prisoners came from 41 countries, with the largest groups from Saudi Arabia, Afghanistan, and Yemen. Over 200 had been transferred to other facilities and a few released, but many had been held for over four years; only a handful had ever faced formal charges.

From the outset, such unconstitutional incarceration prompted cries of outrage from civil libertarians and even some congressmen. Senator Patrick J. Leahy of Vermont said the use of military tribunals could send "a message to the world that it is acceptable to hold secret trials and summary executions without the possibility of judicial review, at least when the defendant is a foreign national."

Initially, most Americans gave little thought to the jailing of terrorism suspects in Cuba. It was only after the prosecutions that followed the revelations of the horrors at Abu Ghraib Prison in Iraq that the average American began to question the American military's methods.

Democratic Senator Richard J. Durbin, a member of the Senate Judiciary Committee, tried for more than two years to conduct hearings on the treatment of the Guantanamo prisoners—Durbin had himself spent six-and-a-half years as a prisoner in North Vietnam. "This is not a new question," he said. "We are not writing on a blank slate. We have entered into treaties over the years, saying this is how we will treat wartime detainees. The United States has ratified these treaties. They are the law of the land as much as any statute we passed. They have served our country well in past wars. We have held ourselves to be a civilized country, willing to play by the rules, even in time of war.

"Unfortunately, without even consulting Congress, the Bush administration unilaterally decided to set aside these treaties and create their own rules about the treatment of prisoners."

Durbin pointed out that President Bush and his appointees had unilaterally created a new detention policy claiming that prisoners in the War on Terrorism have no legal rights—no right to a lawyer, no right to see the evidence against them, no right to challenge their detention. In fact, the Government has claimed detainees have no right to challenge their detention, even if they claim they were being tortured or executed.

"For example," he explained, "they have even argued in court they have the right to indefinitely detain an elderly lady from Switzerland who writes checks to what she thinks is a charity that helps orphans but actually is a front that finances terrorism."

Senator Durbin shocked his colleagues and angered Bush supporters in June, 2005, when he cited an FBI account of how Guantanamo prisoners had been chained to cells in extreme temperatures and deprived of food and water and stated, "If I read this to you and did not tell you that it was an FBI agent describing what Americans had done to prisoners in their control, you would most certainly believe this must have been done by Nazis, Soviets in their gulags, or some mad regime—Pol Pot or others—that had no concern for human beings. Sadly, that is not the case. This was the action of Americans in the treatment of their prisoners."

The Democratic whip in the Senate some days later was forced to issue an apology. A tearful Durbin told his fellows, "Some may believe that my remarks crossed the line. To them, I extend my heartfelt apologies."

It was a clear example of the pitfalls of speaking one's true feelings in the midst of patriotic hysteria.

POSSE COMITATUS IGNORED

L ess than a month after the 9/11 attacks, Tom Ridge, a former governor of Pennsylvania, arrived in his new office only steps away from the Oval Office of President Bush, the man who created his job. Ridge's new job was chief of the Department of Homeland Security. Here was the man who was to coordinate 46 different federal government agencies in an effort to protect the American people from terrorists, a position designed from its inception to become a permanent government department.

It was announced that Ridge would work in conjunction with Bush's deputy national security advisor, Army General Wayne Downing, indicating that the military would play a prominent role in counterterrorism activities. Few thought to ask if this was a violation of the Posse Comitatus Act (PCA), the law prohibiting the US military from conducting law enforcement duties against the American public.

The PCA has never really been challenged in this nation's history because it addresses a concern dating back to one of the grievances that caused the American Revolution. The act embodies the traditional principle of separation of military and civilian authority, one of the fundamental precepts of our form of government and a cornerstone of American liberty.

The early colonists were distressed at being placed at the mercy of King George's troops plus being forced to feed and quarter them. But Posse Comitatus, Latin for a support group of citizens for law enforcement, i.e. a posse, was passed in 1878 as a direct result of the outrage over Reconstruction in the South following the War Between the States. Following that war, the Southern states were at the mercy of military authorities, many of whom proved inept or corrupt.

Yet, in recent years this act has been slowly shredded, beginning at least in 1981 when Congress allowed an exception to be made for the War on Drugs. The military was allowed to be used for drug interdiction along the nation's borders. This small and what appeared to be sensible action at the time soon grew out of proportion. Congress, still unable to come to grips with the true social causes of drug abuse, in 1989 designated the

Department of Defense as the lead agency in drug interdiction.

In the tragedy at Waco on April 19, 1993, military snipers were on hand and tanks were used to bulldoze the burning Branch Davidian church. The use of the Fort Hood tanks under the command of General Wesley Clark was authorized because federal officials used the pretext that the Davidians were involved with drugs. But no evidence of drugs was ever found.

On April 19, 1995, when the Murrah Federal Building in Oklahoma City was bombed, President Clinton proposed yet another exception to the PCA, this time to allow the military to aid civilian investigators looking into weapons of mass destruction. About this same time Congress considered but did not pass legislation to allow troops to enforce customs and immigration laws at the borders.

During the 1996 presidential campaign, Bob Dole promised to heighten the military's role in the War on Drugs while another primary contender, Lamar Alexander, suggested that a new branch of the military be formed and substituted for the INS and Border Patrol.

In 2005, President Bush announced that he would use military troops in the event of a national pandemic.

"The need for reaffirmation of the PCA's principle is increasing," wrote legal scholar Matthew Hammond in the *Washington University Law Quarterly*, "because in recent years, Congress and the public have seen the military as a panacea for domestic problems."

He added, "Major and minor exceptions to the PCA, which allow the use of the military in law enforcement roles, blur the line between military and civilian roles, undermine civilian control of the military, damage military readiness, and inefficiently solve the problems they supposedly address. Additionally, increasing the role of the military would strengthen the federal law enforcement apparatus that is currently under close scrutiny for overreaching its authority."

Yet in the wake of 9/11 and prior to the creation of the Transportation Security Administration (TSA), military troops were seen patrolling airports and the streets of Washington and New York with no outcry from a citizenry apparently appreciative of perceived new security. Such scenes were a brief glimpse of life under martial law.

Even after the creation of the TSA, problems persisted.

Eighty-year-old Fred Hubbell, a retired engineer from Texas visiting in Connecticut, was arrested and handcuffed at Bradley International Airport in August 2002, for mentioning one word. Cranky after enduring repeated searches at the airport, the World War II veteran observed a security guard poking through his wallet, "What do you expect to find in there, a rifle?" Hubbell asked sarcastically. "Do you think that was an appropriate remark?" responded the guard. "I do," replied Hubbell, who was promptly arrested.

Judy Powell, a 55-year-old tourist from Britain, bought a GI Joe toy soldier in Las Vegas and packed it in her bag for her return flight home. But she was refused boarding privileges when an airport security officer spotted GI Joe's tiny plastic rifle. "I was simply stunned when I realized they were serious," said Mrs. Powell. "I was really angry to start with because of the absurdity of the situation. But then I saw the funny side of it and thought this was simple lunacy." A spokesman for Los Angeles International Airport defended the action, saying, "We have instructions to confiscate anything that looks like a weapon or a replica. If GI Joe was carrying a replica then it had to be taken from him."

This excuse, of course, carried echoes of Sgt. Schultz from TV's *Hogan's Heroes* explaining, "I vas chust following orders." It is such unthinking responses to orders based on hastily passed laws that so trouble civil libertarians.

If there was any doubt that planning for martial law did not start with the terrorist attacks on 9/11, just ask the residents of Kingsville, TX.

Beginning on the night of February 8, 1999, a series of mock battles using live ammunition erupted around the 25,000 inhabitants of the town, located near Corpus Christi. In a military operation named "Operation Last Dance," eight black helicopters roared over the town. One nearly crashed when it hit the top of a telephone pole and started a fire near a home. Soldiers of the elite 160th Special Operations Aviation Regiment, known as the "Night Stalkers," ferried by the choppers, staged an attack on two empty buildings using real explosives and live ammunition. During the action, an abandoned police station was accidentally set on fire and a gas station was badly damaged when one or more helicopters landed on its roof.

Citizens of Kingsville were terrified during the drill as only the Police

Chief Felipe Garza and Mayor Phil Esquivel were notified of the attack in advance. Both men refused to give any details of the operation, insisting they had been sworn to secrecy by the military. Only Arthur Rogers, the assistant police chief, would admit to what happened. "The United States Army Special Operations Command was conducting a training exercise in our area," he said but refused to provide any details.

Local emergency management coordinator for FEMA, Tomas Sanchez, was not happy with the frightening attack and the lack of information and warning. Sanchez, a decorated Vietnam veteran with 30 years service in Naval Intelligence, was asked what the attack was all about. He replied that based on his background and knowledge, the attack was an operational exercise based on a scenario where "Martial law has been declared through the Presidential Powers and War Powers Act, and some citizens have refused to give up their weapons. They have taken over two of the buildings in Kingsville. The police cannot handle it. So you call these guys in. They show up and they zap everybody, take all the weapons and let the local PD clean it up."

One resident told a reporter, "This is total BS. If we don't stop it now it's going to get worse."

Asked for comment, then Texas Governor George W. Bush said he was not his job to get involved in the concerns over the Night Stalkers using live ammunition in a civilian area of his state.

Sanchez and other military experts told *World Net Daily* that the night attack indicated the use of Presidential Decision Directive (PDD) 25, a Top Secret document that apparently authorizes military participation in domestic police situations. Some speculated that PDD 25 may have surreptitiously superceded the 1878 Posse Comitatus Act.

The events in Kingsville may date as far back as 1971 when plans were drawn up to merge the military with police and the National Guard. (State Guards were gradually eliminated during the past two decades.) In that year, Senator Sam Ervin's Subcommittee on Constitutional Rights discovered that military intelligence has established an intricate surveillance system to spy on hundreds of thousands of American citizens, mostly anti-war protesters. This plan was code named "Garden Plot." Britt Snider, who worked for the subcommittee, said the plans seemed too vague to get excited about. "We could never find any kind of unifying purpose behind it all," he told a reporter. "It looked like an aimless kind of thing."

Four years later Garden Plot began to come into sharper focus. "[C]ode named Cable Splicer [and] covering California, Oregon, Washington and Arizona, under the command of the Sixth Army, [it] is a plan that outlines extraordinary military procedures to stamp out unrest in this country," reported Ron Ridenhour and Arthur Lubow in *New Times* magazine. "Developed in a series of California meetings from 1968 to 1972, Cable Splicer is a war plan that was adapted for domestic use procedures used by the US Army in Vietnam. Although many facts still remain behind Pentagon smoke screens, Cable Splicer [documents] reveal the shape of the monster that the Ervin committee was tracking down."

During the time of Cable Splicer, several full-scale war games were conducted with local officials and police working side by side with military officers in civilian clothing. Many policemen were taught military urban pacification techniques. They returned to their departments and helped create the early SWAT (Special Weapons and Tactics) teams.

Rep. Clair Burgener of California, a staunch Reagan Republican who had attended the Cable Splicer II kickoff conference, was flabbergasted when shown Cable Splicer documents. "I've read *Seven Days in May* and all those scary books…and they're scary!…This is what I call subversive."

Subcommittee Chief Counsel Doug Lee read through the documents and blurted, "Unbelievable. These guys are crazy! We're the enemy! This is civil war they're talking about here. Half the country has been designated as the enemy." Snider agreed, stating, "If there ever was a model for a takeover, this is it."

The War on Terrorism has provided the pretext for the activation of plans such as Cable Splicer, a clear violation of the Posse Comitatus Act. In June 2002, despite promises by the Bush Administration that it would not initiate any new intelligence reforms until after the joint congressional committees had completed their inquiry into the 9/11 attacks, the Pentagon quietly requested permission to create a powerful new position—Under Secretary of Defense for Intelligence. This request for yet another layer of authority was inserted into a Senate defense bill slated for Congressional approval.

Stephen A. Cambone was confirmed by the US Senate as the Under

Secretary of Defense for Intelligence on March 7, 2003, and sworn in four days later.

"The Pentagon's gambit has been such a brilliant stealth attack that many members of Congress aren't even aware it is happening, let alone what it means," noted reporter Linda Robinson. "No hearings have been held, and Pentagon officials portray it as merely an internal managerial matter with few broader implications. But intelligence officials and experts say that could not be further from the truth. The new under secretary position is a bureaucratic coup that accomplishes many Pentagon goals in one fell swoop."

Insiders thought this slippery move served to circumvent the Posse Comitatus Act and deliver even more power into the hands of top Bush Administration officials Dick Cheney and Donald Rumsfeld. Initially, the new under secretary for intelligence was to have been Richard Haver. Haver had been Rumsfeld's special assistant for intelligence and was Cheney's very first assistant secretary of defense for intelligence in the elder Bush's administration. The new job eventually went to Cambone, himself a neo-con who had served under Rumsfeld and one of the participants in the 2000 PNAC report which foresaw the need for a catastrophic attack to gain support for an increased US military presence in the Middle East.

Fears of secretive, overreaching agencies with military connections that might violate the Posse Comitatus Act appeared to find substantiation in January, 2005, when news outlets reported that, since 2002, the Pentagon's Defense Intelligence Agency (DIA) had operated an intelligence-gathering and support unit called the Strategic Support Branch (SSB) with authority to operate clandestinely anywhere in the world where it is ordered to go in support of antiterrorism and counterterrorism missions. The SSB previously had been operating under an undisclosed name.

The defense official confirmed that the SSB reports to Vice Admiral Lowell Jacoby, director of the DIA, but that policies are set by Undersecretary of Defense Cambone, one of Rumsfeld's most senior aides.

A QUESTIONABLE MILITARY RECORD

f the Posse Comitatus Act is rewritten or eliminated, the recent history of the Defense Department has done little to inspire confidence that traditional American liberties will be respected.

For example, following the 9/11 attacks, the Pentagon announced the creation of an Office of Strategic Influence designed to present a more favorable view of the US military to foreign news media. The new unit provoked an immediate controversy when it was learned that it planned to influence international opinion by planting false stories in the foreign media. Critics felt such phony stories might find their way back to the domestic media. This, of course, was nothing new. The CIA had done the same thing for decades but this was too blatant. Even the major media, including the *New York Times*, were stirred to action.

In a rare step backward, the government announced in early 2002 the office would be closed. Rumsfeld, while arguing that criticism of the office was "off the mark," nevertheless admitted that, "the office has been so damaged that...it's pretty clear to me that it cannot function."

However, the defense secretary refused to let the matter lie. At a November 18, 2002, press briefing, Rumsfeld brought up the controversial office, defiantly stating, "And then there was the Office of Strategic Influence. You may recall that. And 'oh my goodness gracious isn't that terrible, Henny Penny, the sky is going to fall.' I went down that next day and said fine, if you want to savage this thing fine I'll give you the corpse. There's the name. You can have the name, but I'm gonna keep doing every single thing that needs to be done and I have."

Rumsfeld's vow to continue the program of disinformation was not repeated in the corporate mass media.

Causing further anxiety among knowledgeable persons was a plan revealed in late 2002 for the US Army to use computers to investigate hundreds of thousands of law-abiding Americans on the chance one might be a terrorist. The plan called for the Army's Intelligence and Security Command (INSCOM) headquartered at Fort Belvoir, VA, to use high-powered computers to secretly search email messages, credit card purchases, telephone records and bank statements on the chance that one might be associated, or sympathetic to, terrorists. Known as the Pentagon's new Information Awareness Office (IAO), this organization was to create a "vast centralized database" filled with information on the most minute details of citizens private lives.

To add insult to injury in the minds of opponents of this plan was the appointment of former National Security Adviser Vice Admiral John Poindexter to head this new office. Poindexter lost his national security adviser job in 1990 after being convicted of lying to Congress, defrauding the government and destroying evidence in the Iran-Contra scandal during the Reagan administration. That scandal involved the illegal sale of weapons to Iran and the profits being sent illegally to the CIA-backed "Contra" army fighting in Nicaragua, all done in defiance of Congress. But as vice president of Syntek Technologies, Poindexter had worked with the Defense Advanced Research Projects Agency (DARPA) to develop "Genoa," a powerful search engine and information harvesting program. Poindexter's convictions were later reversed on a technicality.

Critics, already suspicious over such an overreaching program so susceptible to abuse, were not assuaged by the DARPA logo, which depicts the occult "all-seeing eye" of knowledge perched on a pyramid overlooking an image of the Earth.

Christopher H. Pyle, a teacher of constitutional law and civil liberties at Mount Holyoke College, wrote, "That law enforcement agencies would search for terrorists makes sense. Terrorists are criminals. But why the Army? It is a criminal offense for Army personnel to become directly involved in civilian law enforcement [the Posse Comitatus Act]. Are they seeking to identify anti-war demonstrators whom they harassed in the 1960s? Are they getting ready to round up more civilians for detention without trial, as they did to Japanese Americans during World War II? Is counterterrorism becoming the sort of investigative obsession that anti-Communism was in the 1950s and 1960s, with all the bureaucratic excesses and abuses that entailed? This isn't the first time that the military has slipped the bounds of law to spy on civilians. In the late 1960s, it secretly gathered personal information on more than a million law-abiding Americans in a misguided effort to quell anti-war demonstrations, predict riots and discredit protesters. I know because in 1970, as a former captain in Army intelligence, I disclosed the existence of that program."

Pyle, in writing two book-length reports on the Army's spying for Senator Sam Ervin's Subcommittee on Constitutional Rights, was struck by the harm that could be done if the government ever gained untraceable access to the financial records and private communications of its critics. "Army intelligence was nowhere near as bad as the FBI [with its infamous COINTEL program], but it responded to my criticisms by putting me on Nixon's enemies list, which meant a punitive tax audit. It also tried to monitor my mail and prevent me from testifying before Congress by spreading false stories that I had fathered illegitimate children. I often wondered what the intelligence community could do to people like me if it really became efficient."

Today the national security apparatus is gaining that efficiency, thanks to the computer, yet the public awareness of the danger is not nearly as great as it was in the pre-computer 1970s.

Many people fear any control over the civilian population by the military, even in times of "national emergency," will lead to draconian measures such as the establishment of large concentration camps.

FEMA's call for contractors to build such camps did little to ease the anxiety of the more extreme conspiracy minded. The Internet is alive with sites detailing a string of concentration camps across America, just primed and waiting for the lines of detainees or dissidents to be herded inside.

For the uninitiated, this undoubtedly sounds like paranoia and most people pay little attention to what they perceive as delusional statements; however the record clearly shows that such camps do exist. Many such camps are in actuality military bases, either reported closed or maintained by skeleton crews. Others are operated by FEMA and some facilities began as World War II camps for Axis prisoners.

Author and retired USAR Lt. Col. Craig Roberts stated, "In actuality, there are two true sets of camps. First is the military, which can use any base at will to house detainees...Fort Chaffee, for instance, has in the past had warehouses full of mattresses, bunks, barbed wire rolls, fence posts, etc. All of these were to be used around empty barracks to provide for a detention facility if needed...Some of the 'closed' military bases have been designated as 'emergency holding facilities' and already have barracks, mess halls, compounds and latrines in place. All they need are guards, administrators, logistics people and they're in business. All this can be accomplished in 72 hours…Operational plans are in existence for the 'handling of civilian prisoners and laborers on military installations, both male and female.

"The second category is FEMA. We know they have let a contract for 1,000 'emergency relocation camps' in case of widespread terrorism, biological or chemical attacks on the cities. Again, this can be speedy. The President can declare a national emergency, evoke [Executive Order] 11490, and take over the country without deferring to Congress or the Constitution. Bingo! New World Order in a couple of days."

Roberts said the most ominous of these potential concentration camps is located at Elmendorf AFB in Alaska. "Millions of acres adjoining this base have been deeded to the federal government by the State of Alaska. Its designated use is for a 'mental health facility.' It is our version of Siberia and the gulag," he added.

The creation and maintenance—even the very existence—of such camps is lost in a bewildering maze of Executive Orders (EO) dating back to World War II. Many EOs can be traced to the Kennedy presidency and were issued under the duress of the Cold War and the Cuban Missile Crisis. Many of the EOs detailed on the Internet are outdated, cancelled, revoked or superceded by others. Even a careful search of the Federal Register fails to clarify this issue.

But it is clear from the FEMA website that that agency has many plans—including tornadoes, hurricanes, flooding in addition to a nuclear or biological strike—that include evacuation of major cities. Where are those people to go? Who will feed them? How will they live? The answers to these questions remain elusive. And in the meantime, dozens of large military installations sit, mutely awaiting future inhabitants.

As the Department of Homeland Security moved closer to reality in 2002, the US military was also reshuffling its command structure to include a new United Command Plan which would include a new combatant command responsible for homeland security called US Northern Command (USNORTHCOM). Headed by at least a four-star general or Flag Officer, USNORTHCOM would control all military efforts in North America, to include Alaska, Canada, the United States and Mexico and out to 500 nautical miles offshore. Conceived as part of the response to the War on Terrorism, an "appropriate" role also was under consideration for USNORTHCOM in the flagging War on Drugs.

Even though the Posse Comitatus Act seems to have been largely ignored in recent years, there were ongoing calls to alter or even abolish the law. In an October, 2001, letter to Rumsfeld, Senator John Warner, a Republican from Virginia and a member of the Council on Foreign Relations, wrote, "Should this law [PCA] now be changed to enable our active-duty military to more fully join other domestic assets in this war against terrorism?"

This cry continued into late 2002 when Rep. Tom Trancredo along with members of the Immigration Reform Caucus and families of victims slain in the course of immigration troubles presented Congress with a petition demanding that military troops patrol the US borders. Jumping on the anti-terrorist bandwagon, Trancredo stated, "As long as our borders remain undefended, we cannot claim that we are doing everything possible to protect the nation from terrorism...It's time to authorize the deployment of military assets on our borders."

Also in 2002, a FEMA official named John Brinkerhoff wrote a paper stating, "President Bush and Congress should initiate action to enact a new law that would set forth in clear terms a statement of the rules for using military forces for homeland security and for enforcing the laws of the United States. Things have changed a lot since 1878, and the Posse Comitatus Act is not only irrelevant but also downright dangerous to the proper and effective use of military forces for domestic duties."

This paper remained on the Homeland Security website well into 2006.

CREATING HOMELAND SECURITY

Well into the year 2002, incremental but significant changes began being made to the American system of government. This movement culminated in hurried passage of the Homeland Security bill in late November. This act, which authorized an entirely new cabinet-level department, was the greatest restructuring of the federal government since the National Security Act of 1947, yet with none of that act's deliberation and review.

In early June, 2002, Bush began urging the creation of a permanent and cabinet-level position for Tom Ridge and his Homeland Security staff, hurriedly created in the wake of the 9/11 attacks. Ridge was calling for bringing myriad government agencies under one central control. And it all needed to be done rapidly, Bush argued, because "we face an urgent need, and we must move quickly, this year, before the end of the congressional session." Thus began the push to create the Department of Homeland Security with Ridge holding a cabinet-level position controlling more than 170,000 federal employees and 22 federal agencies.

But Bush would not allow Ridge to confront Congress directly, claiming his was simply an adviser role, not a policy maker. Congress fumed but, as usual, rolled over and played dead.

"The real losers are the American people..." groused Senator Robert Byrd, a Democrat from West Virginia. "The Congress and the American people are forced to learn about the administration's homeland security efforts in piecemeal, patchwork fashion."

On July 15, 2002, Ridge finally submitted a written statement to the House Select Committee on Homeland Security. In it, Ridge wrote, "We are today a nation at risk to terrorist attacks and will remain so for the foreseeable future. The terrorist threat to America takes many forms, has many places to hide, and is often invisible. Yet the need for improved homeland security is not tied solely to today's terrorist threat. It is tied to our enduring vulnerability."

Ridge indicated that in studying how best to implement Homeland security, it became clear that the federal government would need reorganization, and that "the structure of the federal government must be adapted to meet the challenges before us." He admitted that this new reorganization would result in the most significant transformation of the US government in over a half-century.

"It would transform and largely realign the government's confusing patchwork of homeland security activities into a single department whose primary mission is to protect our homeland," he wrote, adding that the new department must have the "right set of tools to work with" and that undue oversight would be "damaging to the new Department's ability to carry out its mission successfully."

He stated that FEMA would be a leading component of the new Homeland Security Department. "The new Department would build on FEMA to consolidate the federal government's emergency response assets to better prepare all those pieces for all emergencies—both natural and man-made, stated Ridge.

He added that in a national emergency, Homeland Security would "provide a line of authority from the President through the Secretary of Homeland Security to one on-site federal coordinator. The single federal coordinator would be responsible to the President for coordinating the entire federal response to incidents of national significance." In vague generalities, Ridge indicated he sought changes deep within the American infrastructure. "We must therefore promote the efficient and reliable flow of people, goods, and services across borders, while preventing terrorists from using transportation conveyances or systems to deliver implements of destruction," he stated.

How to accomplish this? In writing, Ridge explained that, "the principal border and transportation security agencies—the US Customs Service, the US Coast Guard, the Immigration and Naturalization Service (INS), the Animal and Plant Health Inspection Service, and the Transportation Security Administration—would be unified within a single, powerful division of the new Department of Homeland Security. The new Department also would control the issuance of visas to foreigners through the Department of State and would coordinate the border-control activities of all federal agencies that are not incorporated within the new Department. As a result, the Department would have sole responsibility for managing entry of people and goods into the United States and protecting our transportation infrastructure."

He added that the federal budget for 2003 provided $7.1 billion to the US Coast Guard, and admitted it was "both the largest increase and the highest level of funding in Coast Guard history."

While Ridge paid some homage to the "longstanding principles" of the United States and said he believed that government intrusion into the daily lives of citizens should be strictly limited, he nevertheless noted that the president would serve as the ultimate authority over the control of sensitive intelligence information. "The President, as Commander-in-Chief, must have the ability to make decisions about how the Nation's most sensitive intelligence information is handled in order to carry out his sworn duties. The President will be able to exercise his authority in regard to intelligence distribution through such tools as Presidential Decision Directives and Executive Orders." Ridge explained.

"Therefore the new Homeland Security Department would incorporate the Secret Service and would have its director report directly to the Secretary of Homeland Security. It would also assume all authority for controlling the nation's borders."

"Terrorists are determined, opportunistic, and agile, and the Secretary [of Homeland Security] must build a department that can continually adapt to meet this rapidly changing threat," explained Ridge. "Moreover, even if our adversary were not so devious and nimble, the sheer organizational and management challenge confronting the new Secretary of Homeland Security is enormous. The creation of this new Department is larger and more complex than most corporate mega-mergers. History shows that a governmental reorganization of this magnitude is never easy. Providing the Secretary with the freedom to manage the Department is, therefore, profoundly important to achieving our goal of securing the homeland. Without this authority, an already challenging task will be far more difficult. If the new Department is to be greater than the sum of its parts—if it were not, it would obviously not be worth creating—its leadership must have the flexibility to organize it in the optimal way, create a new institutional culture, motivate and reward an outstanding workforce, and respond quickly to changing circumstances, emerging threats, and emergency situations.

In other words, give me the power and I will protect you.

Just four months after the 9/11 attacks, such power was approved by Congress through the Department of Homeland Security Act of 2002.

By 2006, Homeland Security encompassed more than 87,000 government jurisdictions at both the state and local level. Its directorates included Preparedness, Science & Technology, and Management and Policy.

As requested by Ridge, Homeland Security included FEMA, the TSA, Customs, Border Patrol, the INS, the Federal Law Enforcement Training Center, US Coast Guard and the Secret Service.

Critics have questioned how such a massive restructuring of the US Government has helped protect the nation, especially in light of the dangerously open national borders both north and south. To many thought-ful Americans it would seem to be a common-sense first step in the War on Terrorism to tighten security on the United States borders but this does not appear to have happened. On the southern border, despite an increasing clamor for tighter security, a flood of illegal immigrants continues unabated.

Border security also came into question in the case of Gregory Despres, who on April 25, 2005, arrived at the US-Canadian border at Calais, Maine, carrying a homemade sword, a hatchet, knife, brass knuckles and a chainsaw stained with what appeared to be blood.

Customs agents confiscated Despres' weapons, but then allowed him to enter the United States.

The next day, the decapitated body of 74-year-old Frederick Fulton along with his wife, who had been stabbed to death, was discovered in Despres' hometown of Minto, New Brunswick. Despres, who had a history of violence, was immediately suspected of the crimes and eventually arrested in Massachusetts and deported.

Bill Anthony, a spokesman for US Customs and Border Protection, said the Canada-born Despres could not be detained because he is a naturalized US citizen and was not wanted on any criminal charges on the day in question. "Being bizarre is not a reason to keep somebody out of this country or lock them up. We are governed by laws and regulations, and he did not violate any regulations," explained Anthony.

WAS GEORGE ORWELL RIGHT ABOUT 1984?

None of this is really new. Plans to change America from a Constitutional Republic to an imperial state ironically date back to 1984 when the Reagan National Security Council (NSC) drafted a plan to impose martial law in the United States through FEMA. Helping author this plan was Marine Lt. Col. Oliver North, who later admitted that he lied to Congress about a number of matters but was later rewarded by being hired as a highly-paid talk show host. But in 1987, when the plan leaked to the media, his work inspired a sharp protest from then Attorney General William French Smith.

Arthur Liman, then chief counsel of the Senate Iran-Contra committee, declared in a memo that North was at the center of what amounted
to a "secret government-within-a-government," a term similar to Bush's
"shadow government." Officials at the time said North's involvement
in the proposed plan to radically alter the American government by executive order was proof that he was involved in a wide range of secret
activities, foreign and domestic, that went far beyond the Iran-Contra
scandal.

North's shadow-government plan called for suspension of the Constitution, turning control of the government over to the then-largely unknown Federal Emergency Management Agency (FEMA), appointment
of military commanders to run state and local governments and the
declaration of martial law in the event of a crisis such as "nuclear war,
violent and widespread internal dissent or national opposition to a US
military invasion abroad." At the time he drafted these plans, North was
the NSC's liaison to FEMA.

It is the last two scenarios that bother many people when they view
the national events of today, especially since so many members of the
Reagan administration are back in power at the time of this writing.

North's contingency plan was to be part of an executive order or legislative package that Reagan would sign but hold secretly within the NSC
until such a time as a crisis arose. It was never revealed whether Reagan
had signed the plan.

Could the consolidation of power within Homeland Security be a
continuation of this plan? No one knows for certain as President Bush,
immediately upon taking office, ordered all records of former presidents,
including Reagan, sealed from the public.

Ironically, one of those voicing concern over this loss of access was
former Nixon counselor John Dean, who warned that America was slid-
ing into a "constitutional dictatorship" and martial law.

Further concerns were voiced by Timothy H. Edgar, legislative counsel for the American Civil Liberties Union.

In testimony to various congressional committees, Edgar noted that
the Homeland Security Department would have substantial powers as
well as more armed federal agents with arrest authority than any other
government agency. He questioned whether the new department would

have structural and legal safeguards to keep it open and accountable to the public.

"Unfortunately, [this] legislation not only fails to provide such safeguards, it eviscerates many of the safeguards that are available throughout the government and have worked well to safeguard the public interest," stated Edgar. He went on to enumerate some problems areas within the proposed Homeland Security Department saying it:

- Hobbles the Freedom of Information Act (FOIA) by creating broad new exemptions to the act such as "any information voluntarily submitted to the department about threats to the nation's infrastructure." Edgar pointed out that exceptions to FOIA already include information concerning national security and sensitive law enforcement and confidential business information. "This is a deeply misguided proposal, and it should be rejected," he added.

- Limits citizen input by exempting advisory committees to Homeland Security from the Federal Advisory Act (FACA) passed in 1972 to ensure openness, accountability and the balance of viewpoints in government advisory groups. "By exempting from FACA requirements *any* [emphasis in the original] advisory committees established by the Secretary of the Department of Homeland Security, [this act] severely undermines the openness and public-access goals of FACA," argued Edgar.

- Muzzles whistleblowers protected under the federal Whistleblower Protection Act (WPA) by allowing the Homeland Security secretary to make his own personnel rules. "Title 5 [under the new department] does not guarantee employees of the Department of Homeland Security the protections of the WPA," stated Edgar. "Without such protection, employees who are in the best position to spot problems, violations of the law or dangers to the public are effectively silenced."

- Lacks strong oversight by allowing the Homeland Security secretary to override Inspector General investigations in many areas including intelligence, criminal investigations, undercover operations, identity of confidential sources, protective matters of the Secret Service and any matter considered a threat to national security. "Given the mission of the Homeland Security Agency, it is conceivable that many of the functions performed by this new agency could be said to fall under one of these exempted categories," noted Edgar. "We are concerned that transferring these agencies [FEMA, INS, Animal and Plant Inspection Service of the Agriculture Department, Coast Guard] into a Department whose primary function is to protect the United States against terrorism could erroneously be perceived as elevating their regular duties to those of national security, thereby making such currently non-exempt activities exempt from Inspector General oversight."

- Threatens personal privacy and constitutional freedoms because the vagueness of the wording in the Homeland Security Act does not provide sufficient guarantees.

One huge concern voiced by the ACLU counsel concerned plans to combine the CIA and the FBI under Homeland Security.

"The CIA and other agencies that gather foreign intelligence abroad operate in the largely lawless environment," noted Edgar. "To bring these agencies into the same organization as the FBI risks further damage to Americans' civil liberties."

Edgar urged Congress to resist this move, instead placing clear limits on Homeland Security's ability to retain files on Americans that have no connection to criminal activity but relate to First Amendment freedoms. Congress did not.

He said combining domestic and foreign intelligence gathering under Homeland Security could have "a severe impact on civil liberties potentially leading to widespread spying on Americans constitutionally-protected political and religious activity."

"There is already a danger under the relaxed FBI guidelines for domestic investigations recently announced by Attorney General Ashcroft," Edgar added. "No one wants a repeat of the J. Edgar Hoover era, when the FBI [under the infamous Cointelpro program] was used to collect information about and disrupt the activities of civil rights leaders and others whose ideas Hoover disdained. Moreover, during the Clinton Administration, the 'Filegate' matter involving the improper transfer of sensitive information from FBI background checks of prominent Republicans to the White House generated enormous public concern that private security-related information was being used for political purposes. Congress should not provide a future Administration with the temptation to use information available in Homeland Security Department files to the detriment of its political enemies."

Interestingly enough, President Bush himself had some conflict with Congress over Homeland Security legislation, but it had nothing to do with Constitutional issues. Congress wanted the Department's employees covered by civil service protections and Bush did not.

Many observers believed this objection by Bush was a cover to exempt Homeland Security workers from the whistleblower and Freedom of Information protections. If an employee did not go along with the Bush-Ridge program, they could be summarily fired and replaced with someone who would.

Some Democrats welcomed the new department, such as Senator Joseph Lieberman of Connecticut, an early advocate of the administration change, who said, "In fact, I think it will help us immediately." Others of his party objected to many provisions of the Homeland Security bill, charging that many had nothing to do with security, such as liability protection for vaccine manufacturers and exemptions to the Freedom of Information Act.

Despite misgivings, the Homeland Security Act passed speedily through Congress with little or no revision. In the US Senate, the proposal passed on a 90-9 vote. Apparently Senators were so confident that they were about to do a genuine service for America that on November 13 they voted themselves a pay raise for the fourth consecutive year. This vote was tighter, with 36 senators voting to reject a measure that would have denied them the raise.

President Bush signed the Homeland Security bill into law on November 25, 2002. Noting that the agencies responsible for border, coastline and transportation security were now under the same command structure, Bush remarked, "The continuing threat of terrorism, the threat of mass murder on our own soil, will be met with a unified, effective response."

WAS GEORGE ORWELL RIGHT ABOUT 1984?

But this "unity" quickly was questioned as troubles arose within this new labyrinthine system.

One notorious item that came into existence with the creation of Homeland Security was the listing of names of persons known or just suspected of international terrorist connections. By early 2006, this list had grown to 325,000 names, compiled from more than 26 terrorism-related databases from the intelligence and law enforcement communities.

"We have lists that are having baby lists at this point," commented Timothy Sparapani, legislative counsel for privacy rights at the American Civil Liberties Union. "If we have over 300,000 known terrorists who want to do this country harm, we've got a bigger problem than deciding which names go on which list. But I highly doubt this is the case."

Sparapani and many others voiced concern over such an ever-growing list. Georgetown University Law Professor David D. Cole said, "If being placed on a list means in practice that you will be denied a visa, barred entry, put on the no-fly list, targeted for pretextual prosecutions, etc., then the sweep of the list and the apparent absence of any way to clear oneself certainly raises problems.

In early 2006, Attorney General Alberto R. Gonzales tried to assure members of the Senate Judiciary Committee that "information is collected, information is retained and information is disseminated in a way to protect the privacy interests of all Americans."

But Gonzales might have had a hard time convincing Committee member Senator Edward "Ted" Kennedy, who was prevented from flying five times in March 2004 because a "T. Kennedy" appeared on the secret no-fly list.

In terminals in Washington, Boston and other locations, airline employees refused to issue a boarding pass because his name was on the no-fly list. Kennedy was delayed until supervisors were called and approved his travel. Even after supposedly clearing up the mistake in names, Kennedy was stopped yet again from flying, prompting a personal telephone apology from Homeland Security Secretary Tom Ridge.

"That a clerical error could lend one of the most powerful people in Washington to the list—it makes one wonder just how many others who are not terrorists are on the list," commented Senior ACLU Counsel Reginald T. Shuford. "Someone of Senator Kennedy's stature can simply call a friend to have his name removed but a regular American citizen does not have that ability. He had to call three times himself."

Another ACLU attorney, David C. Fathi, said he was stopped more than seven times at airports, but not on every flight. Once he was led from the counter by armed police and questioned extensively.

Fathi, who is of Iranian ancestry, said it is possible to contact the Transportation Security Administration and obtain a letter of clearance. But his letter didn't help. "By the time I show the letter, it's already too late," he lamented, adding, "There is no rhyme or reason... It illustrates the ridiculousness of the system. If it stops [suspects] because they're on the list they should stop them every time. Not every third time."

And lest anyone think that abuse of such power as wielded by Homeland Security would be tempered by time and experience, consider what happened in Bethesda, MD, in February 2006.

Two uniformed men wearing baseball caps with the words "Homeland Security" emblazoned on them walked into the Little Falls Library and loudly announced that the viewing of pornography was forbidden. They then proceeded to ask that one library Internet viewer step outside.

After complaints were lodged against the two "security" officers, Montgomery County chief administrative officer, Bruce Romer, issued a statement calling the incident "unfortunate" and "regrettable." Romer said the two officers were members of the security division of Montgomery County's Homeland Security Department, an unarmed unit charged with patrolling about 300 county buildings. He added this group was not tasked with seeking out pornography and that the two officers had "overstepped their authority" and had been reassigned.

At least in one incidence, the no-fly listing of an American may have had political overtones. Dr. Robert Johnson, a heart surgeon in upstate New York, was a retired Lt. Colonel in the US Army Reserve who had served during the time of the first Gulf War. But when he arrived at a Syracuse airport for a flight, he was barred and told he was on the federal no-fly list as a possible terror suspect.

"Why would a former lieutenant colonel who swore an oath to defend and protect our country pose a threat of terrorism?" Johnson rhetorically asked a local newspaper. Johnson answered himself by speculating that he was placed on the list because in 2004 he, as a Democrat, had challenged Republican Representative John McHugh. Johnson said he planned to run against McHugh again for his 23rd District congressional seat. The colonel also had been an outspoken critic of the invasion and occupation of Iraq.

Like the growing number of citizens who are finding themselves on the no-fly list, Johnson is demanding answers as to who decides which name goes on the list and what is the mechanism for getting off.

By 2006, even many small suburban and rural counties had their own Homeland Security departments, all answerable to the national department.

To concentrate so much power in one new government department head requires a thorough examination of the man who initially wielded such power. And in the case of Tom Ridge, there were worrisome aspects.

TOM RIDGE AND THE PHOENIX PROGRAM

In the conventional biographies, Ridge is reported to have been a Catholic alter boy who won a scholarship to Harvard and went on to earn a B.A. in 1967. He was drafted into the Army while attending Dickinson Law School in Carlisle, PA. In Vietnam, he was awarded a Bronze Star for leading an action that cleared a small Viet Cong force from an area. This war hero won six consecutive terms in the House before becoming the governor of Pennsylvania. Under that state's term limits, he was due to leave office in 2003.

But there is a disquieting side to this all-American-boy-makes-good story.

According to investigative reporters Jeffrey St. Clair and Alexander Cockburn, "He passed up officer training school because it would have meant an extra year of service. Ridge arrived in Vietnam [where he was given the nickname T-Bone] in November 1969, and joined Bravo Company, First Battalion, 20th Infantry Brigade, Americal Division."

One man who served with Ridge wrote to a veteran's webpage stating, "The last several months I participated in the Pacification program along the Red Ball. My squad consisted of four other US soldiers and up to ten ARVN [Army of the Republic of Viet Nam] What a waste. I was not impressed with Ridge either. He was the squad leader of my squad before I became sergeant. The pathetic SOB would have caused all of us to get killed if we hadn't taken care of him. I was glad when he no longer led us."

But Ridge's leadership ability is not what concerned researchers the most. The "Pacification program" referred to by the Vietnam vet was the infamous "Phoenix Program," in which more than 45,000 Vietnamese were assassinated and many thousands more tortured and abused.

Douglas Valentine, author of *The Phoenix Program*, explained, "During the Vietnam War, under the CIA's Phoenix program—which is the model for the Homeland Security Office—a terrorist suspect was anyone accused by one anonymous source. Just one. The suspect was then arrested, indefinitely detained in a CIA interrogation center, tortured until he or she (in some cases children as young as twelve) confessed, informed on others, died, or was brought before a military tribunal (such as Bush is proposing) for disposition.

"In thousands of cases, innocent people were imprisoned and tortured based on the word of an anonymous informer who had a personal grudge or was actually a Viet Cong double agent feeding the names of loyal citizens into the Phoenix blacklist. At no point in the process did suspects have access to due process or lawyers, and thus, in 1971, four US Congresspersons stated their belief that the Phoenix Program violated that part of the Geneva Conventions guaranteeing protection to civilians in time of war."

Ridge received a medal for a small action during his stint in Vietnam. His Bronze Star citation states, "Sgt. Ridge moved forward and began placing accurate bursts of rifle fire on the insurgents, eliminating one and forcing the remainder of the hostile elements to take evasive action."

Vietnam veterans noticed that the citation did not mention enemy troops but instead "insurgents," a term given to any Vietnamese under suspicion by the US authorities.

So, Tom Ridge, a man who participated in a CIA-sponsored terror program in Vietnam that included arrest without due process, torture and assassination, was brought in to be the first head of our newest federal agency, one that is drawing power from more than 200 existing agencies.

Another man who participated in the CIA Phoenix program was Bruce Lawlor, who after serving in Vietnam went on to became a major general. Author Valentine said Lawlor admitted to his participation in Phoenix during an interview for Valentine's book.

"What Lawlor told me basically confirmed everything," said Valentine. "Except there were some additional, startling details. To begin with, Lawlor told me that he joined the CIA in 1967, while he was getting his BA at George Washington University. The CIA hired him to work the night shift, and after he graduated, he was given the chance to become a regular CIA staff officer. He took the paramilitary course, which included instruction in weapons and military tactics, but he was also trained as a foreign intelligence officer, the kind who manages secret agents. After that he was assigned to the Vietnam Desk at Langley headquarters, where he received specialized training in agent operations in Vietnam, and took a language course in Vietnamese. During this time, Lawlor formed a rapport with the Vietnam Desk officer, Al Seal, and when Seal was assigned as the base chief in Danang, he asked that Lawlor accompany him."

In 1984, after leaving the military, Lawlor was the Democratic Party nominee for Attorney General of Vermont. He listed the Phoenix Program on his political resume that was handed out to the press.

One journalist with a small weekly, *Vermont Vanguard*, published the first critical article about Lawlor and Phoenix. By the time of the state Democratic convention, activist groups in the state had organized and produced signs for convention delegates reading "No Assassins for Attorney General." Lawlor lost the Fall primary despite a visit from former CIA Director William Colby, the CIA official who headed the Phoenix Program.

"Imagine my surprise to learn that the Bruce Lawlor is serving as the Office of Homeland Security's Senior Director for Protection and Prevention!" remarked Valentine. "To get right to the point, I have a sneaking suspicion that Lawlor...is still working for the CIA, and thus poses a major threat to democracy in America. He's someone who has access to Ashcroft's political blacklist, and he has control over the covert action teams that can be used to neutralize...dissidents. One of the reasons I have this crazy feeling, is that nowhere in any of Lawlor's official looking, on-line biographies is there any mention of his CIA service. It's like his biographers are deliberately trying to hide his CIA connection from us."

Yet another ranking first Bush Administration senior official with a checkered background is Richard Armitage, best friend of Colin Powell and unanimously endorsed by the Senate Foreign Relations Committee for the position of Deputy Secretary of State in 2001. He too was a major Phoenix Program operative, according to Valentine and others.

Valentine noted, "HR 19, just introduced [in January, 2001] by Georgia Congressman Bob Barr, would repeal the Executive Orders of Presidents Reagan and Carter prohibiting federal employees, including the military, from carrying out assassinations. This implies that the Bush administration plans to deal harshly with terrorists and other inconvenient persons. Richard Armitage, who was involved in the Iran-Contra deal as well as CIA covert operations in Vietnam, will reportedly head up what's called 'The Terrorist Elimination Act of 2001.' That's our new Deputy Secretary of State."

It should be noted that this was not the first time that Armitage's name has come up in connection with criminal behavior. Once again, the issue of illegal drugs cropped up.

In 1987, Col. James "Bo" Gritz, a much-decorated Vietnam veteran, met with Burmese General Kuhn Sa, the head of the Golden Triangle drug trade, in an effort to locate American POWs. Gritz, in his 1988 book, *A Nation Betrayed*, wrote that General Sa detailed for him the heroin trade and named then Assistant Secretary of Defense for International Security Affairs Armitage as the person who handled the financial end of the US narcotics trade through banks in Australia. Armitage reportedly was involved in a shadowy group of US government officials and mobsters conspiring to import heroin into the United States.

Shocked at this revelation, Gritz asked himself, "How could men sworn before God to defend the Constitution so befoul their office? What form of stand-up sewage would facilitate the movement of deadly addictive narcotics into their own homeland? It took several long moments for the full impact to be realized. Then it was as if someone had turned on a light in my mind. Until that moment my mental and emotional conditioning from a career of military service refused to allow such a contemplation. It was so un-American and alien as to be incomprehensible. But, if true, it explained a train of unexplained events. If Richard Armitage was, as Kuhn Sa avowed, a major participant in parallel government drug trafficking, than it explained why our efforts to rescue POWs had been inexplicably foiled."

But if illegal drugs continued to pour into the United States, more conventional products did not in mid-2002. A labor dispute between the International Longshore and Warehouse Union (ILWU) and the Pacific Maritime Association (PMA) caused a stack up of cargo ships along the West Coast from San Diego to Seattle that threatened to cut deeply into the 2002-03 holiday season profits. The strike was broken in October when President Bush invoked the Taft-Hartley Act, a controversial 1947 union busting law that was passed over President Truman's veto. Under this law, an 80-day "cooling off" period can be ordered during a "national emergency."

Although Bush's action received scant attention in a media focused on the proposed invasion of Iraq, one official of ILWU, Jack Heyman, termed Bush's intervention "a historic juncture in the labor movement." Heyman added, "By invoking Taft-Hartley against the longshore workers, Bush is effectively declaring war on the working class here and the Iraqi people simultaneously."

HOMELAND SECURITY AT WORK

It was not just labor unionists that were feeling the chill in the wake of the hot patriotism after 9/11. Two members of a Chicago group opposed to the sanctions against Iraq were confronted by police when they went to buy some postage stamps.

Daniel Muller, a coordinator for Voices in the Wilderness, along with Andrew Mandell, went to a Chicago post office to purchase a quantity of stamps. They were paying in cash. "We needed 4,000 stamps for a mailing we were doing," explained Muller, "and I asked for one not with the American flag on them." When the clerk asked if Statue of Liberty stamps were acceptable, Mandell replied, "Yes, we love liberty." "She asked us to step aside from the counter and she went to the back, out of view," recalled Muller. "I knew something was up because this was a bit out of the ordinary. And Andrew said, 'She's calling the cops,' but I didn't believe him."

However, about 20 minutes later two policemen entered and asked for the pair's identification. "They asked if we had any outstanding warrants. They ran a check on us. They asked why we had asked for stamps without American flags on them. I said we're very rooted in nonviolent activities and we would rather have the Statue of Liberty than the American flag."

The pair was finally released but had to return to the post office the next day to obtain their stamps and then, only after a further half-hour interview with a postal inspector.

"The fact that they did ask for anything but flag stamps did raise a question for the clerk," explained Silvia Carrier, a public relations officer for the Chicago Postal Inspector's office. "Right now, since September 11, clerks have been told to be cautious, to be looking out for anything suspicious.

The experience of Muller and Mandell shows that it matters little that in mid-July 2002 the US Postal Service stated that it would not participate in a snitch program called Operation TIPS.

TIPS or Terrorism Information and Prevention System was trotted out in mid-summer 2002, and was hailed on its website as "a national system for concerned workers to report suspicious activity." The program was part of the Citizen Corps, a program announced by President Bush in his State of the Union address. It was originally scheduled to be launched by early fall 2002 but eventually was officially dropped following public outrage.

In a statement, the Postal Service stated it had "been approached by Homeland Security regarding Operation TIPS; however, it was decided that the Postal Service and its letter carriers would not be participating in the program at this time." Nothing was said about individual carriers deciding to join and the "at this time" left the final word unsaid.

And the experience of the men and the stamps indicated that some persons within the Postal Service still were reporting anything they viewed as suspicious behavior.

In published material, TIPS advocates said the program was to be administered by the Justice Department and coordinated with FEMA, which would bring it under the Homeland Security Department. It would involve "millions of American workers who, in the daily course of their work, are in a unique position to see potentially unusual or suspicious activity in public places." This, of course, referred to postmen, meter readers, repairmen or anyone who might have an axe to grind against their neighbors.

The TIPS plan was immediately compared to the Nazi Gestapo, the former East German secret police service and to Fidel Castro's Committees for the Defense of the Revolution (CDR) in which Cubans are encouraged to spy on and report any "counterrevolutionary" behavior by their neighbors. An estimated eight million Cubans belong to more than 121,000 committees in the CDR, established by Castro on September 28, 1960.

In October 2000, the CDR held parties across the island nation to celebrate their 40 years of existence. "If we see some sort of attack on society or the government, then that is counterrevolution and you have to root it out," voiced one jubilant CDR member while toasting with a glass of rum at a Havana street party.

The CDR's keep detailed records of all neighborhood inhabitants, not only listing each inhabitant but also keeping files on schooling and work history, spending habits, any potentially suspicious behavior, any contact with foreigners and attendance at pro-Castro meetings. The system has evolved into one that routinely provides an individual's information to prospective employers, medical authorities or any law enforcement official.

Needless to say, the American Civil Liberties Union (ACLU) and other public watchdog organizations reacted negatively to Operation TIPS, saying it would create an atmosphere in which Americans would be spying on each other. "The administration apparently wants to implement a program that will turn local cable or gas or electrical technicians into government-sanctioned Peeping Toms," declared ACLU legislative counsel Rachel King.

John Whitehead, executive director of the Rutherford Institute, said, "This is George Orwell's '1984.' It is an absolutely horrible and very dangerous idea. It's making Americans into government snoops. President Bush wants the average American to do what the FBI should be doing.

In the end, though, nothing is going to prevent terrorists from crashing airplanes into buildings."

Even Homeland Security Chief Ridge was forced to backpedal, saying, "The last thing we want is Americans spying on Americans. That's just not what the president is all about and not what the TIPS program is all about." However, he did not reject the program and most observers felt it will continue albeit with less publicity. "It is not a government intrusion," argued Ridge. "The president just wants people to be alert and aware...We're not asking people to spy on people."

Although Ridge still vouched for the TIPS program, a review of the Citizen Corps website showed a marked softening of both language and details after the program began to make a national stir.

In July, 2002, the website stated Operation TIPS "will be a nationwide program giving millions of American truckers, letter carriers, train conductors, ship captains, utility employees and others a formal way to report suspicious terrorist activity. Operation TIPS, a project of the US Department of Justice, will begin as a pilot program in 10 cities...Operation TIPS, involving 1 million workers in the pilot stage, will be a national reporting system that allows workers, whose routines make them well-positioned to recognize unusual events, to report suspicious activity... Everywhere in America, a concerned worker can call a toll-free number and be connected directly to a hotline routing calls to the proper law enforcement agency or other responder organizations when appropriate."

By early August, the list of occupations had been dropped and "suspicious terrorist activity" and "unusual events... suspicious activity" had changed to "suspicious and potentially terrorist-related activity" and "Potentially unusual or suspicious activity in public places."

The TIPS program was merely an official extension of snooping in America, already so pervasive that author Jim Redden called modern life a "snitch culture." Neighborhood Watch groups already in existence were being brought into Homeland Security. In the spring of 2002, Ashcroft had earmarked almost $2 million in an effort to double the number of Neighborhood Watch groups to about 15,000. He claimed this would "weave a seamless web of prevention of terrorism" across the country.

TV personality Ed McMahon went from pitching for Publishers Clearinghouse Sweepstakes to pitching the War on Terrorism. The National

Neighborhood Watch Institute already had been shipping out rectangular street signs reading, "We Support Homeland Security."

From the school kid Drug Abuse Resistance Education (DARE) program to professional finger pointers such as the Southern Poverty Law Center, more and more Americans were being encouraged to spy and report on one another.

In 1997, informing on fellow citizens was codified, at least for the federal government, when the Supreme Court in *US vs. Singleton* exempted federal prosecutors from a statute prohibiting the bribery of witnesses to testify favorably for the government.

There have been many cases, usually not played up in the media, in which innocent people have had their lives unsettled, ruined or even lost due to egregious snitching. The purchase of "snitch" information continues to be a mainstay of federal law enforcement. In 1994, the DEA spent $31.7 million while Customs spent $16.5 million on thousands of informants. Such practices have prompted protests from civil libertarians and attorneys but in today's fearful society, no one seems too concerned.

If opposition to the TIPS network and the growing "snitch culture" in America seems a bit paranoid, consider the plight of A. J. Brown, a freshman at Durham Tech in North Carolina who received some unwelcome visitors on October 26, 2001.

Answering a knock on her apartment door, Brown found herself face to face with two men in suits. "Hi, we're from the Raleigh branch of the Secret Service," said one of the men flipping out an ID folder. "I was like, 'What?' recalled Brown. "And they say, 'We're here because we have a report that you have un-American material in your apartment.' And I was like, 'What? No, I don't have anything like that.' 'Are you sure? Because we got a report that you've got a poster that's anti-American.' And I said no." The agents wanted to enter Brown's apartment but she asked if they had a warrant. "And they said no, they didn't have a warrant but they wanted to just come in and look around. And I said, 'Sorry, you're not coming in.'"

Standing in her doorway, the agents said they knew she had a poster in her apartment of President Bush hanging himself. Brown denied this and after long minutes opened the door wide enough for the agents to see her poster. It was a picture of Bush holding a rope with the caption,

"We Hang on Your Every Word. George Bush Wanted: 152 Dead." The poster also contained drawings of people being hanged. It was a political poster referring to the number of persons subjected to the death penalty in Texas while Bush was governor.

The agents finally left after about 40 minutes but called Brown back two days later to confirm her name, address, phone number and nicknames. "Obviously, I'm on some list somewhere," she commented.

And it's not all about college students. Katie Sierra, a 15-year-old sophomore at Sissonville High School in West Virginia, wanted to form an Anarchist Club at her school and handed out fliers, stating, "Anarchism preaches to love all humans, not just of one country…" She also wore a tee shirt which read, "Racism, Sexism, Homophobia, I'm So Proud of People in the Land of the So-Called Free."

Sierra was suspended and her fellow students shoved her and posted pictures of the girl with bullet holes in her head. After losing a court battle for reinstatement in the state Supreme Court by a 3-to-2 vote, Sierra said, "I'm really disgusted with the courts right now and with the school. I'm being punished for being myself."

Children were especially susceptible to recruitment through the various programs being dreamed up today. And the US military played it own role. The principal of Mount Anthony Union High School in Bennington, VT, was shocked in the spring of 2002 to receive a letter from military recruiters demanding a list of all students, including names, addresses and telephone numbers. As the school's privacy policy prevented the disclosure of such individual information, the principal told the recruiters no. She was doubly shocked to learn that buried deep within President Bush's new education law passed earlier in 2002, the No Child Left Behind Act, public schools must provide such information to military recruiters or face a cutoff of federal funds.

Republican Rep. David Vitter of Louisiana, who sponsored the recruitment requirement in the education bill, noted that in 1999, more than 19,000 US schools denied military recruiters access to their records. Vitter said such schools "demonstrated an anti-military attitude that I thought was offensive."

"I think the privacy implications of this law are profound," commented Jill Wynns, president of the San Francisco Board of Education. "For the federal government to ignore or discount the concerns of the privacy rights of millions of high school students is not a good thing, and it's something we should be concerned about."

Even journalists and academics have come under fire for not acceding to the mob mentality. Robert Jensen is an associate professor of journalism at the University of Texas at Austin. He published a column in the *Houston Chronicle* on September 14, 2001, pointing out that while the 9/11 attacks were "reprehensible and indefensible," the acts were "no more despicable [than] the massive acts of terrorism, the deliberate killing of civilians for political purposes, that the US government has committed during my lifetime."

Jensen's column was rebutted by the university president, Larry R. Faulkner, who labeled Jensen as "not only misguided but [he] has become a fountain of undiluted foolishness on issues of public policy." "I've been marginalized on this campus," lamented Jensen.

Newspaper writers Dan Guthrie of Oregon's *Grants Pass Daily Courier* and Tom Gutting of the *Texas City Sun* both wrote caustically of President Bush's irregular flight across American on 9/11. "What we are stuck with is a crippled President who continues to be controlled by his advisers. He's not a leader. He's a puppet," wrote Gutting, who said that the day his piece ran his publisher assured him he would not be fired for expressing his opinion. But the publisher printed a front-page apology for Gutting's column and a few days later changed his mind about firing him.

Guthrie, who had won several awards, including best columnist in Oregon, wrote that Bush "skedaddled" on September 11. "The picture of Bush hiding in a Nebraska hole [was] an embarrassment," he wrote. Even though the paper's editor and his city editor had signed off on his piece, Guthrie soon joined Gutting in the ranks of the unemployed.

Still, the reporters got off lighter than Richard Allen Humphreys, who described himself as a religious prophet. He was found guilty in late October 2002, by a Sioux Falls jury of threatening President Bush and faced as much as five years in prison and a $250,000 fine. A bartender at a truck stop overheard Humphreys mention "burning bush" and called police. A search of Humphreys' hotel room yielded a card with President Bush's name on it and the words, "Intimidation in the First Degree." In a transcript of a Internet Chat room conversation, Humphreys had written, "now going to ask Bush for justice, and if I don't get it don't be surprised to see a Burning Bush." Humphreys, who represented himself in court, said he was on a "discipleship journey" and was not threatening the president but merely exercising his right to religious expression.

Apparently not even traditional American activities such as taking pictures around town are exempt from the scrutiny of Homeland Security enforcers. Amateur photographer Mike Maginnis was intrigued by all the activity around Denver's Adams Mark Hotel in early December 2002, which included Denver police, Army rangers and rooftop snipers. Maginnis, who works in information technology and frequently shoots photos of corporate buildings and communications equipment, took a few snapshots. He was then confronted by a Denver policeman who demanded his camera. When he refused to hand over his expensive Nikon F2, he was pushed to the ground and arrested.

After being held in a Denver police station, Maginnis was interrogated by a Secret Service agent. He learned that Vice President Cheney was staying in the area and that he was to be charged as a terrorist under the USA PATRIOT Act. According to Maginnis, the agent tried to make him confess to being a terrorist and called him a "raghead collaborator" and "dirty pinko faggot."

After being held for several hours, Maginnis was released without explanation. When his attorney contacted the Denver police for an explanation, they denied ever arresting Maginnis.

Yet another case involved a kindergarten student who only wanted to play. In May, 2002 Scott and Cassandra Garrick of New Jersey, sued the Sayreville School District after their 6-year-old kindergarten student and three classmates were disciplined for playing cops and robbers. It seems other students saw the youngsters playing on the school-yard while pretending their fingers were guns. They told a teacher and the kindergartners were suspended from school.

US District Judge Katherine S. Hayden dismissed a civil suit filed by the parents, claiming school authorities have the right to restrict violent or disruptive games.

The parents' attorney, Steven H. Aden, commented, "They have the right to be children. The school and the courts shouldn't censor their play [even if] it's politically incorrect."

Such incidents are rarely covered in the corporate mass media and never distributed to a large audience but they worry thoughtful people.

"I'm terrified," said Ellen Schrecker, author of *Many Are the Crimes: McCarthyism in America*. "What concerns me is we're not seeing an enormous outcry against this whole structure of repression that's being rushed into place by the Bush Administration." ACLU President Nadine Strossen also voiced concern. "I've been talking a lot about the parallels between what we're going through now and McCarthyism. The term 'terrorism' is taking on the same kind of characteristics as the term 'communism' did in the 1950s. It stops people in their tracks and they're willing to give up their freedoms. People are too quickly panicked. They are too willing to give up their rights and to scapegoat people, especially immigrants and people who criticize the war."

"Besides being unconstitutional and un-American, snooping on innocent people in a free society is cowardly, divisive and just plan evil," argued Internet columnist Paul Proctor. "Regardless of whether or not President Bush's motives are honorable, the fact remains that in tattle tailing for the federal government, anyone with a personal grievance against another individual or group could literally wreck havoc on them with such powers. Needless to say, the potential for tragedy and abuse is huge.

"How secure do you think you are going to feel in this escalating 'War on Terrorism' burdened with the grim knowledge that you're always going to be watched by someone somewhere reporting your personal activities, conversations and correspondence to an unaccountable hierarchy that, in the interest of 'Homeland Security,' has the legal authority to take from you whatever they want, anytime they want, without so much as a warrant or a knock on the door."

Noting President Bush's claim that terrorism threatens our freedom, Proctor added, "But, you see—terrorists don't want your freedom—they want your life. It is tyrants and dictators that want your freedom."

ENTER THE PATRIOT ACT

The first advice any good lawyer gives his or her client is to not sign anything without first reading and understanding it.

Yet, a panicky House of Representatives, still in shock over 9/11 and the subsequent anthrax attacks, rushed the PATRIOT Act into law by a vote of 339-79.

The Act was 342 pages long and made changes, both great and small, to more than 15 different US statutes, most of them enacted after previous misuse of surveillance powers by the FBI and CIA.

It was hurriedly and enthusiastically signed into law by President Bush on October 26, 2001. The speed with which this legislation was presented to Congress left little doubt in many minds that it had long been prepared and simply needed some provocation as an impetus for action.

According to some congressmen, many lawmakers had not even read the entire document when it was passed. The ACLU also reported that some members of Congress had less than one hour to read the extensive changes of law contained within the act.

Many civil libertarians felt those two facts alone should be cause for wholesale dismissals at the Capitol.

Rep. Dennis Kucinich, a Democrat from Ohio, described the atmosphere in which the PATRIOT Act was passed: "[T]here was great fear in our great Capitol…The great fear began when we had to evacuate the Capitol on September 11. It continued when we had to leave the Capitol again when a bomb scare occurred as members were pressing the CIA during a secret briefing. It continued when we abandoned Washington when anthrax, possibly from a government lab, arrived in the mail…It is present in the camouflaged armed national guardsmen who greet members of Congress each day we enter the Capitol campus. It is present in the labyrinth of concrete barriers through which we must pass each time we go to vote."

Rep. Ron Paul, one of only three Republicans to vote against the House bill, said he objected to how opponents were stigmatized by the name alone. "The insult is to call this a 'patriot bill' and suggest I'm not patriotic because I insisted upon finding out what was in it and voting no. I thought it was undermining the Constitution, so I didn't vote for it—therefore I'm somehow not a patriot. That's insulting."

Paul confirmed rumors that the bill was not read by most members of the House prior to their vote. "It's my understanding the bill wasn't printed before the vote—at least I couldn't get it," he told *Insight Magazine*. "They played all kinds of games, kept the House in session all night, and it was a very complicated bill. Maybe a handful of staffers actually read it, but the bill definitely was not available to members before the vote."

Paul's view of the Patriot Bill was echoed by the only independent in the House, Rep. Bernie Sanders of Vermont, who said, "I took an oath to support and defend the Constitution of the United States, and I'm concerned that voting for this legislation fundamentally violates that oath. And the contents of the legislation have not been subjected to serious hearings or searching examination."

The Electronic Frontier Foundation (EFF) of San Francisco, a donor-supported membership group dedicated to protecting freedom when "law and technology collide," published an overview of the PATRIOT Act. They concluded that, "it seems clear that the vast majority of the sections included have not been carefully studied by Congress, nor was sufficient time taken to debate it or to hear testimony from experts outside of law enforcement in the fields where it makes major changes.

"This concern is amplified because several of the key procedural processes applicable to any other proposed laws, including inter-agency review, the normal committee and hearing processes and thorough voting, were suspended for this bill. The civil liberties of ordinary Americans have taken a tremendous blow with this law, especially the right to privacy in our online communications and activities. Yet there is no evidence that our precious civil liberties posed a barrier to effective tracking or prosecution of terrorists."

In a move to assert some control over the new legislation, Congress tacked on a sunset provision requiring that portions of the act must come under review by Congress or expire by December 31, 2005, unless President Bush decided to extend them in the "national interest." But it was Congress, which extended the "sunset" provisions into 2006 to allow for negotiations with the Bush administration.

In early 2005, Republican supporters of the act attempted to have the legislation reauthorized in accordance with the Bush administration's desire to make all powers permanent, but a series of hearings in both House and Senate were held instead. Various reforms to the act were submitted in both chambers, but were blocked by the partisan leadership.

Still, efforts to make the PATRIOT Act permanent met with strong opposition from across the political spectrum and included such groups as the American Conservative Union and Americans for Tax Reform. It appeared that congressional leaders feared the proposed reforms would pass if brought to a full and fair vote.

According to the ACLU, "The House and Senate passed different versions of legislation to reauthorize the PATRIOT Act. Since they were not the same bill, the differences were resolved in a 'conference committee' with representatives from both chambers, but critical compromises were made while excluding Democrats from negotiations. The ensuing conference report failed to include the most important civil liberties protections included in the Senate version of the bill. A final bill and a small amendments package have now passed both houses of Congress.

"The amended Patriot Act continues to fail to adequately protect the privacy rights of innocent, ordinary people in this country."

But the debate over the PATRIOT Act is not over as several organizations have vowed to seek further reforms in the legislation.

The official title of the bill originally was the "Uniting and Strengthening America by Providing Appropriate Tools Required to Intercept and Obstruct Terrorism Act"—USA PATRIOT Act. The name was reminiscent of Hitler's 1933 legislation passed hurriedly following the burning of the *Reichstag* in 1933, which evolved into the Third Reich. It was called "The Law To Remove the Distress of the People and State."

This act, which clearly abridges the rights of Americans, was built upon the little-known Foreign Intelligence Surveillance Act of 1978 (FISA) which cracked the door open to secret government searches. FISA was passed in the contingencies of the Cold War and in the wake of revelations of misused surveillance by the FBI and CIA.

The FISA law created the secret federal Foreign Intelligence Surveillance Court (FISC), which meets in total secrecy to routinely approve covert surveillances on non-Americans by intelligence agencies. The attorney general must approve all applications to the court. Either federal prosecutors are extremely efficient and effective in their work or the seven federal judges who make up this secret court are not picky about the Constitution because out of the some 12,000 requests for secret surveillances and physical searches made during the first 23 years of the FISC, not one application was denied until four in 2003.

"Then came the USA PATRIOT Act," wrote journalist Walter Brasch, "drafted by the Bush Administration and fine-tuned in secret by the House and Senate leadership following the September 11 terrorist attacks. The PATRIOT Act, which incorporates and significantly expands FISA to include American citizens, was overwhelmingly approved by the Congress, most of whom admit they read only a few paragraphs, if any at all..."

"The intent behind the passage of the FISA legislation was to impose limits and a review process upon warrantless surveillance and searches conducted for 'national security' purposes in light of the numerous abuses by federal agencies against US citizens," wrote Patrick S. Poole in a treatise on both the FISA and the FISC. "But the politicization and present use of the FISA process [now expanded through the PATRIOT Act and its revisions] has resulted in the erosion of numerous Constitutional rights and basic legal procedures that have their roots in free societies dating back to the Magna Carta."

The act also greatly expanded law enforcement power into areas that have little to do with terrorism. One provision provides for the collection of DNA from terrorists, then expands this to include anyone suspected of "any crime of violence." Both the scope and penalties under the Computer Fraud and Abuse Act were increased along with the use of wiretaps.

In fact, the act was so broad and subject to abuse that the Foreign Intelligence Surveillance Court took the unprecedented move of forcing then Attorney General Ashcroft to modify Justice Department guidelines concerning FBI terrorism searches and wiretaps. The FISC, for the first time in nearly two decades, rejected some of Ashcroft's guidelines as "not reasonably designed" to safeguard Americans' privacy.

Ashcroft's instructions came in March, 2002, and were addressed to FBI Director Robert Mueller and senior Justice Dept. officials. They were intended to make it easier for investigators in espionage and terrorism cases to share information from searches or wiretaps. The FISC ruled that his guidelines could cause misuse of information in criminal cases, which traditionally required higher legal standards to procure searches and wiretaps.

Ashcroft had cited the USA PATRIOT Act as the justification for expanded guidelines used in wiretaps and searches. "The attorney general seized authority that has not been granted to him by the Constitution or the Congress," noted Marc Rotenberg, head of the Washington-based Electronic Privacy Information Center.

The Electronic Frontier Foundation said Internet users particularly should be concerned about provisions of the act which expand government surveillance while reducing checks and balances, the forced handing over of records by Internet Service Providers (ISP), new and vague definitions of "terrorism," and surveillance without a court order.

Provisions of the original PATRIOT Act that most concerned civil libertarians were that:

- The federal government may now monitor religious and political institutions without suspecting criminal activity to assist terrorism investigations (a violation of the First Amendment right of association).
- The feds now can close to the public once-open immigration hearings and secretly detain hundreds of people without charge while encouraging bureaucrats to resist Freedom of Information requests (a violation of the 5th and 6th Amendments guaranteeing due process, speedy trials and freedom of information).
- The government may prosecute librarians or other keepers of records if they tell anyone that the government subpoenaed information related to a terrorism investigation (a violation of the First Amendment right of free speech).
- The government now may monitor conversations between federal prisoners and their attorneys and may even deny access to lawyers to Americans accused of crimes (a violation of the 6th Amendment right to have legal representation).

■ The government now may search and seize individual and business papers and effects without probable cause to assist an antiterrorism investigation (a violation of the 4th Amendment right against unreasonable searches and seizures).

■ The government now may jail Americans indefinitely without a trial or charges (a violation of the 6th Amendment right to a speedy trial and to be informed of the charges against them).

Despite some slight reforms passed in 2006, these same provisions continue to concern civil libertarians.

And lest anyone think that the government will hold in abeyance any power given to it, many worrisome incidents of application of the draconian law were quickly reported.

In March 2002 John Ashcroft's Justice Department, announced that it planned to use secret evidence to justify financial sanctions against a Chicago-area Muslim charity as part of its effort to stop the funding of terrorists.

Attorneys for the Global Relief Foundation filed a lawsuit claiming the government violated the Constitution when it froze the charity's assets in December 2001. The government said it would share its evidence with the judge but not with the charity or its attorneys. Legal experts said that this may be the first time the government has tried to use secret evidence in a trial, citing the PATRIOT Act as its authority.

Global Relief, along with two other charities—Benevolence International and the Texas-based Holy Land Foundation for Relief and Development—had their assets frozen by the government pending an investigation of their links to terrorism.

"It's completely contrary to anything that's ever happened in this country. This country was founded on the idea of confronting your accuser. If they submit secret evidence or present it to the judge in such a way that we can never see it, we can't cross examine and we can never rebut," said Global Relief attorney Roger Simmons, adding that such government action set "a very dangerous legal precedent."

THE PATRIOT ACT AT WORK

S uch concern takes on even more substance when viewed against the government's track record in such cases even before the 9/11 attacks. Following the WTC bombing in 1993, a Palestinian named Hany Kiareldeen living in New Jersey was held after being secretly accused of meeting with one of the men convicted of the bombing. Kiareldeen suspected the information came from someone with a personal axe to grind.

A federal judge, after reviewing the case, questioned not only the evidence against Kiareldeen but the manner in which it was presented. He wrote, "The [Immigration and Naturalization Service's] reliance on secret evidence raised serious issues about the integrity of the adversarial process, the impossibility of self-defense against undisclosed charges, and the reliability of government processes initiated and prosecuted in darkness."

Niels Frenzen, a University of Southern California law professor, agreed with the judge, stating, "Without exception, when the government uses this one-sided evidence, it's gotten it wrong. Why should anyone think they are going to get it right now?"

Another example of what to expect under the new expanded powers of the federal government, already under fire for its questionable actions in the 1990s at Ruby Ridge and Waco, came at 5 am in San Antonio, Texas, the day after 9/11 when heavily-armed federal agents raided the home of Dr. Al-Badr Al-Hazmi. Al-Hazmi was a 34-year-old radiology resident at the University of Texas Health Science Center who had been working in Lackland Air Force Base's military hospital in the days before September 11.

According to news reports, Al-Hazmi's home was ransacked by agents without a search warrant, his wife and young children held at gunpoint and later the doctor was thrown naked into a cold FBI holding cell without being charged with any crime. He was then flown to a New York prison where Al-Hazmi said he was beaten repeatedly during FBI interrogations. After a week, he was finally allowed to speak to his attorney and discovered the cause of his problems was that his name, a common name in the Middle East, was similar to that of two of the suspected 9/11 hijackers. Another week passed before Al-Hazmi was released and allowed to return home, still without having been charged with any crime.

In 2005, David Banach of Parsippany, NJ, was arrested and held under provisions of the PATRIOT Act. He was accused of using a laser beam to temporarily blind the pilot and co-pilot of a jet plane passing over his house. Banach denied any evil intent, claiming he was simply using the laser to point out stars for his seven-year-old daughter.

If convicted, Banach faced the possibility of 25 years in prison and a $500,000 fine even though the craft landed safely and without incident and the FBI acknowledged that while Banach's actions were "foolhardy and negligent," they found no connection to terrorism. Banach was eventually released after posting $100,000 bail.

To add further to this laser story, research revealed that at the same time as the laser arrest, the government was testing a laser system in the area. This prompted one Internet commentator to write, "The article announcing [Transportation Secretary Norman] Mineta's request to pilots that they begin reporting incidents of lasers being shone into their cockpits was posted on January 12, 2005 the same day that technical testing of the laser warning system was completed. That is to say: the US government allowed the public to believe that terrorists were testing laser beams to bring down aircraft when, in fact, the government was testing lasers to bring down aircraft."

And don't think that arrests such as those above could only happen to someone with a Middle Eastern name or using lasers. Robert Lee "Bob on the Job" Lewis is a fervent Christian who has spent decades researching government scandals. He worked with airline lawyers during the investigation of the bombing of Pan Am Flight 103 over Lockerbie, Scotland.

In April 1998, Lewis was in a restaurant in Houston, Texas, regaling waiters with his knowledge of government skullduggery, including little-reported information on former President George H. W. Bush. Lewis admitted he made a remark about Bush along the lines of, "I'll have his ass."

Sitting in the restaurant was Secret Service Agent Tim Reilly who promptly placed Lewis under arrest for threatening the former president. The next day, in a short hearing, federal Magistrate Marcia Crone avoided any First Amendment issue and instead accepted the hearsay testimony of Agent Reilly. The impecunious Lewis was held for nearly a year in federal custody. His ordeal included being sent to the Fort Worth Federal Correctional Institution where he was placed in the same cell where Whitewater scandal figure James McDougal reportedly committed suicide. Lewis knew full well who McDougal had been and felt his placement there was a form of intimidation. Some months later, Lewis was transferred to a federal hospital in Springfield, MO, where he was involuntarily drugged until letters from some journalists and academic contacts protesting his drugging gained him a release. There was never a court trial or even an adversarial hearing in the case.

Secret evidence, closed trials, false imprisonment, warrant-less searches, involuntary drugging, the seizing of private property all seem like something out of the Nazi era, but fear has pushed many Americans into a passive and accepting mode.

Congressman Paul when asked what was wrong with the PATRIOT Act, replied, "The worst part of this so-called antiterrorism bill is the increased ability of the federal government to commit surveillance on all of us without proper search warrants." Paul was referring to Section 213 of the Act entitled, "Authority for Delaying Notice of the Execution of a Warrant," also called the "sneak-and-peek" provision that allows authorities to search personal property without warning.

Insight Magazine reporter Kelly Patricia O'Meara wrote that, "With one vote by Congress and the sweep of the president's pen, say critics, the right of every American fully to be protected under the Fourth Amendment against unreasonable searches and seizures was abrogated."

Paul pointed out the obvious flaw in the idea that the government would act in a restrained and responsible manner when given this authority. "I don't like the sneak-and-peek provision because you have to ask yourself what happens if the person is home, doesn't know that law enforcement is coming to search his home, hasn't a clue as to who's coming in unannounced...and he shoots them. This law clearly authorizes illegal search and seizure, and anyone who thinks of this as antiterrorism needs to consider its application to every American citizen."

By early 2006, the controversy over surveillance and privacy reached new heights when it was reported that President Bush had instructed the secretive National Security Agency (NSA) to electronically monitor Americans for signs of terrorism.

The potential for "Big Brother" surveillance had been there all along. As far back as 1975, Senator Frank Church, who performed a study of the NSA, warned, "That [the NSA] capability at any time could be turned around on the American people and no American would have any privacy left, such is the capability to monitor everything: telephone conversations, telegrams, it doesn't matter. There would be no place to hide."

Church's warning proved true 30 years later when the news media reported an outcry over Bush's order to turn the NSA against Americans without seeking warrants from the special intelligence court (FISA) or any other court. It was also revealed in 2006 that the NSA had been secretly collecting phone call records of tens of millions of Americans using data from AT&T, Verizon and BellSouth, the three largest phone companies in the US. Moreover, the program was overseen by the new director of the CIA, General Michael Hayden, during his tenure heading the NSA.

Attorney General Gonzales publicly argued that such spying was within the legal rights of a wartime president, again demonstrating that the 9/11 attacks and subsequent War on Terrorism continue to be the foundation for the events of today.

When members of the Senate Judiciary Committee asked to see how the Bush administration arrived at this argument, the White House denied requests for classified legal documents that were behind Gonzales' defense.

Opponents to NSA warrantless spying—including some Republicans—claimed it not only was intrusive and a violation of constitutional safeguards on privacy but ineffective by overloading law enforcement agencies with bad leads. They also saw the surveillance program as a serious step to consolidating power in the executive branch. "The history of power teaches us one thing," said former Reagan administration attorney Bruce Fein, "if it's unchecked, it will be abused."

It was seen as ironic by knowledgeable persons that the 1978 Foreign Intelligence Surveillance Act, bypassed by Bush's orders, was passed in the wake of revelations of how President Nixon used the NSA to spy domestically on political enemies.

Even some of the 2006 revisions of the PATRIOT Act failed to correct portions that concerned both libertarians and congressmen. Rep. C. L. "Butch" Otter of Idaho was one of the three Republicans who found the entire act potentially unconstitutional from the onset. "Section 215 authorizes the FBI to acquire any business records whatsoever by order of a secret US Court. The recipient of such a search order is forbidden from telling any person that he has received such a request. This is a violation of the First Amendment right to free speech and the Fourth Amendment protection of private property," commented Otter, adding, "[S]ome of these provisions place more power in the hands of law enforcement than our Founding Fathers could have dreamt and severely compromises the civil liberties of law-abiding Americans. This bill, while crafted with good intentions, is rife with constitutional infringements I could not support."

The issue of penalties against persons who simply reveal that government intrusion is taking place was a cornerstone of controversy over renewal of the PATRIOT Act in late 2005.

Section 215's "gag order" was retained by Congress after a compromise on the wording so that it remained effective only for a year after a secret search was conducted. One year, obviously, is too long for any American to wait to learn that their government is spying on them.

According to a *New York Times* editorialist, "The compromise also fails to address another problem with Section 215: it lets the government go on fishing expeditions, spying on Americans with no connection to terrorism or foreign powers. The act should require the government, in order to get a subpoena, to show that there is a connection between the information it is seeking and a terrorist or a spy."

One feature of the Act as approved in 2001 had actually been introduced much earlier, in 1998, only to be struck down after a public outcry.

In this case during the Clinton administration, there was a brief furor over proposed new federal banking regulations that would require all banks to report to the government any large deposits or withdrawals or unusual activity on the part of the banking public. Euphemistically called the "Know Your Customer" program, it heralded a new era wherein law-abiding citizens might have to defend their financial matters before government agents. Under this program, banks would be required to create a profile of each customer and report any deviation from the profile to the feds. For example, consider a citizen who sold an unneeded car and deposited the cash in his bank account. Under this program, the bank computer would flag the transaction because this was an unusually large deposit based on the person's previous deposit record. Federal authorities would be notified and soon agents would be sent to interrogate the customer on the chance he or she might be a drug dealer or terrorist.

Rep. Ralph Paul in 1998 had planned to introduce legislation to stop this intrusive program but an irate citizenry saved him the trouble. The schemers behind the proposal, the Federal Deposit Insurance Corp; the IRS and other agencies quickly backed off. Paul said quite prophetically, "Somehow, though, I imagine such action will not stop them, only slow them down."

Paul was right. Almost all of the provisions of the "Know Your Customer" program can be found in the PATRIOT Act.

A clear example of the danger of such intrusive legislation came in early 2006 when Rhode Island retired schoolteacher Walter Soehnge and his wife tried to pay down an excessive credit card bill with a JC Penney MasterCard. They sent in a check for $6,500 to pay down their debt.

When the Soehnges found the money had not been credited to their account, they began to make inquires. They were told that when a payment is much larger than usual, Homeland Security must be notified and that the money is held until a threat assessment is made.

The couple's money was eventually freed although they never found out how making a large credit card payment posed a threat to national security.

"If it can happen to me, it can happen to others," Soehnge noted dryly.

Another of those who actually read the PATRIOT Act and were appalled at its unconstitutional provisions was Nadine Strossen, a professor of law at New York Law School and president of the American Civil Liberties Union. Her main complaint was that the sweeping changes codified by the act have little or nothing to do with fighting terrorism.

"There is no connection between the September 11 attacks and what is in this legislation," Strossen argued. "Most of the provisions related not just to terrorist crimes but to criminal activity generally. This happened too, with the 1996 antiterrorism legislation where most of the surveillance laws have been used for drug enforcement, gambling and prostitution."

By 2005, the PATRIOT Act provisions had been expanded into cases far beyond terrorism.

According to Pittsburgh *Star-Ledger* writer Mark Mueller, "While the Justice Department says it does not uniformly track the Patriot Act's use in such cases, a reading of government reports and congressional testimony shows it has been used hundreds of times against the likes of drug dealers, computer hackers, child pornographers, armed robbers and kidnappers. In Washington State, investigators invoked the law to surreptitiously bug a tunnel that had been bored beneath the US-Canadian border by drug runners. In Las Vegas, prosecutors used it to seize the financial records of a strip-club owner suspected of bribing local government officials.

Reporter O'Meara noted that a similar antiterrorist act in England allows government investigators to obtain information from Internet Service Providers (ISPs) about their subscribers without a warrant. The British law is now being applied to minor crimes, tax collection and public health measures.

The ACLU has already filed a number of lawsuits trying to make the government accountable for its law enforcement activities under the PATRIOT Act. An ACLU press release stated the organization believed "it is critically important that the public learn how [the Justice Department] is using the vast new surveillance powers granted the government." In their suits under the Freedom of Information Act, the ACLU wanted to know among other things:

- The number of times the FBI used pen registers [the numbers that a person has called is kept in a register] or trap and trace devices against US citizens or permanent residents as provided in Section 214 of the PATRIOT Act.
- The number of times the FBI has ordered libraries, bookstores or newspapers to divulge records or other tangible things as provided in Section 215 of the act.
- The number of United States citizens or permanent residents who have been subjected to new surveillance orders since the enactment of the PATRIOT Act.

The ACLU stated that it did not believe that the release of such aggregate, statistical information would jeopardize national security or any other legitimate government interest.

ACLU President Strossen said her overriding concern with the PATRIOT act is the power that is being concentrated in the presidency. "The concern here is about the third branch of government," she explained. "One of the overreaching problems that pervades so many provisions is reduction of the role of judicial oversight. The executive branch is running roughshod over both of the other branches of government. I find it very bothersome that the government is going to have more widespread access to email and websites and that information can be shared with other law enforcement and even intelligence agencies. So again, we're going to have the CIA in the business of spying on Americans…"

Strossen, Paul, Otter and others were pointed but polite in their criticisms of the PATRIOT Act. Others were not so courteous. "In light of the egregious evisceration of the Bill of Rights that this law undertakes, those who blindly supported and signed this blatantly unconstitutional act into law should be collectively condemned and charged with high treason to the Constitution and the people of the United States," wrote columnist Doreen Miller for *YellowTimes*, an online publication of alternative news. "The USA PATRIOT Act creates and allows for a virtual police state with little to no judicial oversight. We, as a nation, are literally treading the razor's edge when it comes to flirting with the grave dangers inherent in giving up our rights for the empty promises of 'safety' and 'national security' masquerading under the guise of a 'patriotic' PATRIOT Act. Once we fall off that edge, reclaiming and reinstating our rights, authority and power as 'We The People' of this great nation might prove very difficult."

Karen G. Schneider, writing for the American Library Association website, wrote, "First of all, I'm a hawk. I believe we should be in Afghanistan, I'd like to see bin Laden oh, say, six feet under, and behind my bifocals, this middle-aged veteran cheers her colleagues in the armed forces defending our nation. However, the USA PATRIOT Act is treason pure and simple, and you need to know how and why, because it presents particularly pernicious issues for the users who rely on your Internet services. The Patriot Act is not antiterrorism legislation; it's anti-speech legislation, and is no more a direct response to the September 11 attacks than the Children's Internet Protection Act is a direct result of sincere concern by members of Congress about the safety of minors. The cold, cynical reality is that the Patriot Act is a bloated hodgepodge of speech-chilling law that lurked in congressional corridors not only before September 11 but in large part before the Bush administration. It was hustled into reality in the post 9/11 environment so quickly, secretively, and un-democratically that our Bill of Rights had been clocked with a one-two punch well before any of us realized it was under attack."

Schneider's concern was clearly illustrated in an incident in which FBI agents showed up some time back at a Bloomsburg, PA, bookstore owned by Arline Johnson. The agents weren't tracking criminals, they were asking which customers bought copies of the Tom Clancy book, *The Hunt for Red October.*

Johnson, who has been challenged for selling books on everything from Karl Marx to gay rights to dinosaurs, said she tells the "book police" that "it's important that people learn and read about everything, whether they believe it or not...It's not the government's job to tell me or anyone what they can read...I once lived and taught in Bulgaria and I don't like totalitarian regimes."

Booksellers do indeed seem most vulnerable to the PATRIOT Act. In November of 2001, the American Booksellers Foundation for Free Expression (ABFFE) sent a letter to its members stating, "Dear Bookseller, it begins. Last week, President Bush signed into law an antiterrorism bill that gives the federal government expanded authority to search your business records, including the titles of the books purchased by your customers...There is no opportunity for you or your lawyer to object in court. You cannot object publicly either. The new law includes a gag order that prevents you from disclosing 'to any person' the fact that you have received an order to produce documents...because of the gag order...you should not tell ABFFE that you have received a court order...you can simply tell us that you need to contact ABFFE's legal counsel."

Marsha Rummel of the Rainbow Bookstore Cooperative in Madison, WI, commented, "[T]he danger to booksellers is just one small part of this new landscape. We must collectively take a stand to defend our democratic rights, including the right to protest our government and oppose the war, and the right to read whatever we like."

THE PATRIOT ACT AT WORK

According to *Newsweek*, the ACLU has been searching for "Conan the Librarian," some librarian who would be willing to serve as a test case against the PATRIOT Act, with little success. The act was being used by the FBI as an excuse for broad new powers to check library records, Internet use, business records and anything else that they claim might lead them to terrorists. "This statute trumps protections in place in 49 of 50 states," observed Gregory T. Nogeim of the ACLU.

By mid-2003, some librarians were flexing their freedom muscles by daily shredding library records to prevent federal agents from obtaining records of what books were being checked out. In a 2002 survey sent to libraries across the nation by the Library Research Center at the University of Illinois, the staffs of 219 libraries said they would cooperate with requests for information about patrons. But 225 said they would not.

"The effect of the USA PATRIOT Act upon businesses that loan, rent or sell books, videos, magazines and music CDs, is not to find and incarcerate terrorists—there are far more ways to investigate threats to the nation than to check on a terrorist's reading and listening habits—but to put a sweeping chilling effect upon constitutional freedoms," wrote *Online Journal* writer Walter Brasch.

James R. Elwood, executive vice president of the International Society for Individual Liberty, an umbrella organization representing individuals and groups in more than 80 countries, stated that the "rule of law—enshrined in the Bill of Rights—which protects the innocent—must be strictly upheld and that the new 'antiterrorist' laws be repealed."

According to Section 112 of the act, a "suspected terrorist" may be determined solely by certification by the attorney general on "reasonable ground" that he "believes" someone to be such.

"Section 236A gives the Attorney General unprecedented powers untouchable by any court, whereby he may detain a suspect in increments of up to six months at a time if he believes the suspect's release would threaten national security or the safety of the community or any person," wrote columnist Doreen Miller, noting that the act states, "At the Attorney General's discretion, no court shall have jurisdiction to review, by habeas corpus, petition, or otherwise, any such action or decision."

INTERNMENT CAMPS IN PLACE

For such power to be concentrated in the hands of one man in the early 2000s brought up the question of the Attorney General's integrity, ambition and philosophical outlook. A brief look at former Attorney General John Ashcroft reveals some disturbing facts. These facts were conveniently ignored or downplayed by a mass media cowed in the patriotic furor following the 9/11 attacks.

In 2000, the Democratic governor of Missouri, Mel Carnahan, was battling Ashcroft for a US Senate seat. Carnahan died in a small plane crash. His wife, Jean, was not with him. Jean agreed to fill the seat for her late husband should he win it and Missouri voters delivered a blow to Ashcroft by casting their votes for a dead man, a clear indication of the respect held for Ashcroft in his home state.

A distinct warning about Ashcroft and what was to come came long before the 2001 terror attacks. In testimony opposing the nomination of John Ashcroft as attorney general given on January 16, 2001, Dr. Debra H. Freeman warned the Senate Judiciary Committee that Ashcroft would bring under the guise of "crisis management" a "form of brutal bureaucratic fascism on the United States that bears striking similarities to the conditions under which Adolf Hitler seized power in Germany in 1933."

Until the 9/11 attacks, Ashcroft who had been most noticeable to the American public when he ordered an exposed breast covered on the statue called The Spirit of Justice that stands in the Justice Department's Hall of Justice, rapidly patched together a spate of antiterrorism laws, most of which would never have made it through Congress under normal circumstances. He was already warping US laws beyond recognition by detaining without trial as many as 1,200 persons, most in violation of immigration laws. Many were later released without charges being filed against them.

But at least one vision of Ashcroft was absolutely outrageous. In a little publicized announcement in August 2002, Ashcroft said he wanted the power to strip American citizens of their constitutional rights, including access to the court system, and indefinitely imprisoned them in interment camps on his word that they were "enemy combatants."

"The proposed camp plan should trigger immediate congressional hearings and reconsideration of Ashcroft's fitness for this important office," declared Jonathan Turley, a professor of constitutional law at George Washington University Law School who actively supported Ashcroft during his contentious nomination hearing. "Whereas al Qaeda is a threat to the lives of our citizens, Ashcroft has become a clear and present threat to our liberties."

An example of the unevenness of Ashcroft justice was seen in the treatment of two Americans captured while fighting for the Taliban in Afghanistan—John Walker Lindh and Yaser Esam Hamdi. Lindh was given a lawyer and a trial where he plea bargained for a reduced prison sentence. Hamdi, a Louisiana-born prisoner captured in Afghanistan and held in the US detention camp at the Guantanamo Bay naval base in Cuba, was transferred to a Navy brig floating off the Virginia coast where he remained indefinitely.

When a federal judge ordered that the Justice Department present evidence justifying Hamdi's treatment, the government simply refused to comply, insisting that the judge could not interfere with the president's "absolute authority in a time of war."

Then there's the case of American citizen Jose Padilla, the "dirty" bomber. Padilla was arrested after federal authorities claimed they learned he was planning to construct a radioactive bomb. However, the Bush Administration some time later quietly admitted they had no evidence that Padilla actually was planning anything like that. "What is clear [in this case] is that Padilla is an American citizen and was arrested in the United States—two facts that should trigger the full application of constitutional rights," said Turley.

"If you think this law applies only to foreign nationals, think again," admonished columnist Doreen Miller. "Jose Padilla, although by no means a model US-born citizen, had his civil rights stripped from him [in May, 2002] just by Ashcroft's uttering the magic words, 'enemy combatant' and 'suspected terrorist.' To this day, no solid evidence has been produced to substantiate Ashcroft's claims—neither bomb parts, nor bomb assembly instructions, nor any plans or maps of intended strike areas."

Padilla was shunted about by the federal government for nearly four years until early in 2005, when a federal judge ruled that Padilla had to be charged with a crime or released. It was only then that Padilla was transferred from military authority to the criminal justice system.

On January 5, 2006, Padilla made a brief appearance before the federal court of the Southern District of Florida. His case appeared likely to stretch into the foreseeable future as both prosecutors and defense attorneys argued over his status.

According to Internet commentator Mike Whitney, "Padilla became the test case for shattering the Bill of Rights with one withering blow. It has succeeded beyond anyone's wildest expectation. There's no chance that the Supreme Court will retry the case and draw more attention to the shocking details of this judicial coup; they already punted once before preferring to pass it along to the lower court. Rather, the meaning of the case will be ignored until the president needs to exercise the newly bestowed powers of supreme leader. That authority is now firmly rooted in the legal precedent established by the Padilla ruling."

"Okay, now let's play a game," wrote columnist Carl Worden. "Replace the name Jose Padilla with Carl Worden. I get picked up and thrown into a military brig where I don't get my call or a visit with my attorney. I am being held without charges as an 'enemy combatant' and the government does not have to appear in open court to present evidence at my arraignment, and they don't have to release me until hostilities have ended—which in the case of the War on Terrorism, that would translate into a life sentence. In the meantime, they can say anything about me they want—but they don't have to prove it. They will probably allege a conspiracy of some sort, which means they don't have to produce hard evidence like illegal weapons or explosives. They will throw in a couple of verifiable facts for credibility purposes, such as my membership in the Southern Oregon Militia and my outspoken 'anti-government,' 'Right Wing Extremist' rhetoric. They will display the weapons I own...they will claim I had bomb-making supplies and equipment in my garage when they searched my premises [common household materials can be construed as bomb-making supplies]. That's right. They found my diabolical [ammunition] reloading bench... Now replace my name with yours and play the same game."

Worden's scenario gets to the heart of cases like Padilla. Such persons

INTERNMENT CAMPS IN PLACE

may be of dark complexion, absolute creeps or religious freaks. But if the American people allow their individual rights to be trampled, then no one is safe. Libertarians clearly see that the only way to guarantee freedom and liberty is to see that laws are applied equally without exceptions, even in deplorable cases.

"We are only now getting a full vision of Ashcroft's America," mused Professor Turley. "Ashcroft [was] a catalyst for constitutional devolution, encouraging citizens to accept autocratic rule as their only way of avoiding massive terrorist attacks. His greatest problem has been preserving a level of panic and fear necessary to induce a free people to surrender rights so dearly won by their ancestors," he added. "Every generation has had Ashcrofts who view our laws and traditions as mere obstructions rather than protections in times of peril. But before we allow Ashcroft to denude our own constitutional landscape, we must take a stand and have the courage to say, 'Enough.' Every generation has its test of principle in which people of good faith can no longer remain silent in the face of authoritarian ambition. If we cannot join together to fight the abomination of American camps, we have already lost what we're defending."

Even the *New York Times* editorialized, "The Bush administration seems to believe, on no good legal authority, that if it calls citizens combatants in the war on terrorism, it can imprison them indefinitely and deprive them of lawyers. This defiance of the courts repudiates two centuries of constitutional law and undermines the very freedoms that President Bush says he is defending in the struggle against terrorism."

Writer Nat Hentoff grumbled, "It bothers me that the executive branch is taking the amazing position that just on the president's say-so, any American citizen can be picked up, not just in Afghanistan, but at O'Hare Airport or on the streets of any city in this country, and locked up without access to a lawyer or court just because the government says he's connected somehow with the Taliban or al Qaeda. That's not the American way. It's not the constitutional way...and no court can even figure out whether we've got the wrong guy."

When asked what the Founding Fathers might say about the Bush-Ashcroft vision for the PATRIOT Act, Congressman Paul laughed and said, "Our forefathers would think it's time for a revolution. This is why they revolted in the first place. They revolted against much more mild oppression."

Troublesome questions also followed Alberto R. Gonzales, who was sworn in as the nation's 80th Attorney General on February 3, 2005. Gonzales, a former White House Counsel to President George W. Bush, immediately played the terror card in his initial remarks to Justice Department employees. He noted they have "a special obligation to protect America against future acts of terrorism. We will continue to make that our top priority while remaining consistent with our values and legal obligations. That will be the lodestar that guides us in our efforts at the Department."

Prior to serving in the White House, he served as a Justice of the Supreme Court of Texas. Before his appointment to the Texas Supreme Court in 1999, he served as Texas' 100th Secretary of State from December 2, 1997 to January 10, 1999. Among his many duties as Secretary of State, Gonzales was a senior advisor to then Governor Bush, chief elections officer, and the governor's lead liaison on Mexico and border issues.

Upon taking up his new office, Gonzales was immediately assailed for a series of questionable decisions as White House Counsel.

In August 2002, following meetings between Gonzales and other Bush administration officials, a Justice Department memo was issued explaining that laws prohibiting torture of prisoners do "not apply to the President's detention and interrogation of enemy combatants." The memo added that only "injury such as death, organ failure or serious impairment of body functions…constitute torture."

Earlier that year, Gonzales had written a memo arguing that al Qaeda and Taliban prisoners were not subject to the provisions of the Geneva Convention because "the war against terrorism is a new kind of war" which "renders obsolete Geneva's strict limitations on questioning of enemy prisoners and renders quaint some of its provisions." Many members of the military, including Secretary of State Colin Powell, warned that ignoring the Geneva Convention might well prove dangerous to future US soldiers captured by the enemy. In fact, a federal judge ruled, "President Bush had both overstepped his constitutional bounds and improperly brushed aside the Geneva Conventions."

INTERNMENT CAMPS IN PLACE

Gonzales' lack of concern over the rights of prisoners may have begun in the days when he served as chief legal counsel for then-Texas Governor George W. Bush. In his official capacity, it was Gonzales who sent Bush memos concerning the facts of all death penalty cases. Bush would then decide who lived and who died. Note that it was during this time that Texas gained national notoriety for the number of death penalties. According to a study of Gonzales' memos, *Atlantic Monthly* concluded, "Gonzales repeatedly failed to apprise the governor of crucial issues in the cases at hand: ineffective counsel, conflict of interest, mitigating evidence, even actual evidence of innocence." According to this study, Gonzales' memos "seemed attuned to a radically different posture, assumed by Bush from the earliest days of his administration—one in which he sought to minimize his sense of legal and moral responsibility for executions."

Gonzales also caused controversy in 1996 when as counsel to Texas Governor Bush he helped keep Bush from jury duty, a service which would have required Bush to disclose his then-secret 1976 conviction for drunken driving in Maine. Gonzales suggested to the judge and defense lawyer that if Bush served, then as governor, he would not be able to pardon the defendant in the future.

Like others in the Bush administration, Gonzales came under fire for his close relationships with energy corporations, including the failed giant, Enron. According to The Center for American Progress, a nonpartisan research and educational institute, Gonzales accrued about $100,000 from the energy industry in 2002, the same year that he authored a Texas Supreme Court opinion, which "handed the energy industry one of its biggest Texas legal victories in recent history."

After entering the White House with Bush, it was Gonzales who worked hard to keep secret the meetings held by Cheney's energy task force.

Persons with a secretive and conspiring mindset, when they are allowed in positions such as US Attorney General, are especially worrisome when considered within the rapid growth of eavesdropping and surveillance technology available today.

BIG BROTHER'S TECHNOLOGY

I n light of recent legislation, the only factor required today to turn the United States into the type of dictatorship described in the novel *1984* is the technology to do so. Such technology was largely unavailable in 1984 but it is today.

Consider the gradual encroachment made by the government in assigning each and every member of the United States a computer or identity number:

- 1935—Social Security initiated.
- 1936—The current Social Security numbering system began.
- 1962—The IRS started requiring Social Security numbers on tax returns even though Social Security cards plainly stated the number was "Not For Identification."
- 1970—All banks were required to have your Social Security number.
- 1971—Military ID numbers were changed to Social Security numbers.
- 1982—Anyone receiving any sort of government largess was required to obtain a Social Security number.
- 1984—Any person being declared a dependent for IRS tax purposes required a Social Security number. Within two years, even new-born babies were required to have a Social Security number under penalty of fine.

A national identification card has been talked about for years but civil libertarians have consistently cooled the public's receptivity to such a concept—until now.

In mid-2002, even as the initial fear over 9/11 began to subside, Rep. Jim Moran of Virginia, citing increased concerns over terrorism, introduced legislation in Congress called the Driver's License Modernization Act of 2002 (H.R. 4633). This bill was styled as a law, which would set uniform standards for drivers' licenses in all 50 states and the District of Columbia.

But it also included provisions to establish a national database and identification system. This bill codified a plan previously sent by Congress to the Department of Transportation urging the development of electronic "smart" drivers' licenses that contain embedded programmable computer chips that could be checked by law enforcement authorities across the nation.

"So it's more of a national ID *system* [emphasis in the original], a linking of Department of Motor Vehicles—and the records they keep on you—across state lines, with some extra on-card security measures thrown in," wrote Frank Pellegrini of *Time.com*. "The plan, Congress hopes, will be cheaper and easier to implement, and less likely to incur the talk-show ire of civil libertarians and states' rights purists (the same type who squawked in 1908 when the FBI was born). But the approach is mere stealth—50 different state ID cards all linked together is pretty much the same as one national ID card, just as all those new quarters are still worth 25 cents each, no matter which state is on the back."

The House bill also states the new ID card must "conform to any other standards issued by the Secretary [of Transportation]," an open invitation for bureaucrat tinkering.

Libertarians rejoiced when Moran's bill failed to become law but warned that most states now issue drivers' licenses with a magnetic strip capable of carrying computer-coded information.

New York City became one of the first major cities to announce plans to try out micro-chipped identification cards for the city's 250,000 employees. Some 50,000 officers and workers for the NYPD were scheduled to receive ID cards.

The state-of-the-art plastic cards contain microchips, holograms and other security devices to prevent theft and to track employee work hours. On the front of this picture ID is the Statue of Liberty and two chips, one containing fingerprints and handprints and the other filled with personal information, including blood type and emergency telephone numbers. Police officials said eventually the ID cards will used in conjunction with "biometric" hand scanners to ensure the person bearing the card is the correct one. They also hoped to save money in computing pay-checks by using the cards to keep track of employee hours.

Pellegrini and others have warned that the real fight will come over when and where citizens will have to show such IDs. "The average American's driver's license gets a pretty good workout these days. He said, "certainly far more than traffic laws themselves would seem to warrant—but you can only get arrested for *driving* without one. If the US domestic response starts to resemble Zimbabwe's, which passed a law in November [2001] making it compulsory to carry ID on pain of fine or imprisonment, well, that's something to worry about."

According to author Steven Yates, a teaching fellow at the Ludwig von Mises Institute, "The long and the short of it is, the Driver's License Modernization Act of 2002 would bring us closer than ever before to establishing a comprehensive national ID system. The present excuse is that extreme measures are necessary to 'protect us against terrorism.'

"It is a testimony to how much this country has changed since 9/11 that no one has visibly challenged H.R. 4633 as unconstitutional and incompatible with the principles of a free society. The 1990s gave us the obviously corrupt Clinton Regime and a significant opposition to federal power grabs. Now it's Bush the Younger, beloved of neocons [neo-conservatives] who see him as one of their own and believe he can do no wrong... Clearly, the slow encirclement of law-abiding US citizens with national ID technology would advance such a cause [globalism or The New World Order] while doing little if anything to safeguard us against terrorism."

Yates also offered up a vision of the near future that disturbs many thinking people. He noted that if the feds really wanted to stifle dissent, they could 'freeze' the dissident's assets by reprogramming his database information. Scanners would not recognize him and he would become officially invisible, unable to drive or work legally, have a bank account, buy anything on credit, or even see a doctor. "Do we want to trust *anyone* [emphasis in the original] with that kind of power?" he asked.

It is just such a prospect that concerns many Christians, who see government control through computers and identification computer chips as the fulfillment of Biblical prophecy warning that no one will be able to conduct business without the "mark of the Beast." This theme also was the premise of the popular Sandra Bullock film, *The Net*, and the *Left Behind* book series which have sold more than 50 million copies.

Lest anyone think this is naïve or even paranoid nonsense, consider that in late October 2002, Applied Digital Solutions, Inc., a high-tech development company headquartered in Palm Beach, FL, announced the launching of a national promotion for its new subdermal personal veri-fication microchip. Entitled "Get Chipped," the promotion is hyping a device that can be implanted under a person's skin to transmit data to various locations. Describing the "VeriChip," company literature states it is "an implantable, 12mm by 2.1mm radio frequency device...about the size of the point of a typical ballpoint pen. It contains a unique ver-ification number. Utilizing an external scanner, radio frequency energy passes through the skin energizing the dormant VeriChip, which then emits a radio frequency signal containing the verification number. The number is displayed by the scanner and transmitted to a secure data stor-age site by authorized personnel via telephone or Internet."

In addition to "VeriChip Centers" in Arizona, Texas and Florida, the firm also fields the "ChipMobile," a motorized marketing and "chipping" vehicle. The new "Get Chipped" campaign was launched just days after the Food and Drug Administration ruled that the chip is not a regulated medical device.

Uses for the chip include controlling access to non-public facilities such as government buildings and installations, nuclear power plants, na-tional research laboratories, correctional institutions and transportation hubs, either by itself or in conjunction with exiting security technologies such as retina scanners, thumbprint scanners or face recognition devices. Company officials envision the chip will come to be used in a wide range of consumer products including PC and laptop computers, personal ve-hicles, cell phones, homes and apartments. They said the implanted chip will help stop identity theft and aid in the war against terrorists.

By early 2006, fears of the chip became reality when a Cincinnati video surveillance firm, CityWatcher.com, began to require its employees to implant the VeriChip device in their arm.

Several members of Congress seemed quite at home with the idea of a national ID card or chip. Rep. Jane Harman of California said, "I think this issue must be looked at. We don't automatically have to call it a na-tional ID card, that's a radioactive term, but we can certainly think about smart cards for essential functions, but we need the database to support that."

This need for a national database was addressed in the USA PATRIOT Act, Which authorized $150 million in tax money for the "expansion of the Regional Information Sharing System [to] facilitate federal-state-local law enforcement response related to terrorist acts."

Asked if she thought the public was ready for such measures, Harman replied, "I think most people are really there. Keep in mind that if we have a second wave of attacks. The folks who are raising objections will probably lose, totally."

Others agree, such as District of Columbia Mayor Anthony A. Williams, who only added to the fear factor when he warned, "We are in a new...really dangerous world now, and we have to maintain a higher level of security."

Williams' plan for increased security was to emulate such cities as London and Sydney by installing hundreds of video cameras throughout the city of Washington, all linked to a central command office. Williams predicted that Washington eventually will have such a surveillance system as England which boasts more than two million cameras in airports, train stations, streets and neighborhoods.

Asked if such a scheme would seriously impact individual civil rights, Williams admitted, "There will be trade-offs."

The Nevada Supreme Court in spring 2002 ruled it was okay for police to hide electronic monitoring devices on people's vehicles without a warrant for as long as they want. The court ruled that there is "no reasonable expectation of privacy" on the outside of one's vehicle and that attaching an electronic device to a man's car bumper did not constitute unreasonable search or seizure. In early 2004, a Louisiana court ruled it was permissible for police there to make warrantless searches of homes and business even without probable cause.

Then there must be some consideration of eavesdropping technology, which includes the two greatest electronic threats to privacy and individual freedom: "Echelon" and "Tempest."

"The secret is out," wrote Jim Wilson in *Popular Mechanics.* "Two powerful intelligence gathering tools that the United States created to eavesdrop on Soviet leaders and to track KGB spies are now being used to monitor Americans."

Echelon, the previously discussed global eavesdropping satellite network and massive super computer system, is operated from the Maryland headquarters of the National Security Agency. It intercepts and analyzes phone calls, faxes and email sent to and from the United States, both, with or without encryption. Encrypted messages are first decrypted and then joined with clear messages. The total is then checked by software known as "Dictionary" for "trigger words." Such terms as nuclear bomb, al Qaeda, Hamas, anthrax, etc. are then shuttled to appropriate agencies for analysis.

Although speculation and warnings about Echelon were circulating on the Internet for a number of years, it was not until 2001 that the US Government finally admitted to its existence. This came about because of high-profile investigations in Europe where it was discovered that Echelon had been used to spy on Airbus Industries and Thomson-CSF, two European companies. In actuality, the government had been using an early version of Echelon even as it was evolving into the futuristic tool of today. In the late 1960s and 1970s, Presidents Lyndon Johnson and Richard Nixon used National Security Agency (NSA) technology to gather files on thousands of American citizens and more than 1,000 organizations, mostly those opposed to the Vietnam War. In a program called "Operation Shamrock," the NSA collected and monitored nearly every international telegram sent from New York.

Although paid for primarily by US taxpayers, Echelon is now multinational, involving overseas clients such as the United Kingdom, Canada, Australia, New Zealand and even Italy and Turkey. Information gleaned from Echelon flows mostly to the CIA. According to investigator Jim Wilson, "Based on what is known about the location of Echelon bases and satellites, it is estimated that there is a ninety percent chance that NSA is listening when you pick up the phone to place or answer an overseas call. In theory, but obviously not in practice, Echelon's supercomputers are so fast, they could identify Saddam Hussein by the sound of his voice the moment he begins speaking on the phone."

Amazing as all this may sound to those unfamiliar with Echelon, the sheer fact that the government now acknowledges it may indicate that it already has become obsolete, largely due to burgeoning Internet traffic. Researchers now believe that Echelon may be phased out in favor of a ground-based technology known as "Tempest," which secretly reads the displays on personal computers, cash registers, television sets and automated teller machines (ATMs).

Jim Wilson said documents now available from foreign governments and older sources clearly show how these systems are used to invade our right to privacy. "We think you will agree it also creates a real and present threat to our freedom," he added.

In September 2002, the *Associated Press* obtained US government documents showing that the Bush administration was considering the creation of a fund that would combine tax dollars with funds from the technology industry to pay for "Internet security enhancements." The documents, one under the title "Executive Summary for the National Strategy to Secure Cyberspace," discussed "sweeping new obligations on companies, universities, federal agencies and home users" to make the Internet more secure, presumably from terrorists.

This new Internet strategy was being headed up by Richard Clarke, formerly a top counterterrorism expert in both the Bush and Clinton administrations, and Howard Schmidt, a former senior executive at Microsoft Corp. The plan, when released in 2003, offered up more than 80 recommendations to tighten Internet security.

The *Associated Press* also wrote about a "key-logger" device, which, during the new "sneak and peek" incursions by federal agents, can be secreted inside a computer using a virus-like program. The device, coded named "Magic Lantern," records every key stroke on the computer, allowing authorities to capture passwords and use them to access encrypted data files. The FBI has acknowledged using such a device in a recent gambling investigation.

William Newman, director of the ACLU in Western Massachusetts, said the use of such technology could easily spread to all Americans. He pointed out that federal law enforcement agencies now are permitted "the same access to your Internet use and to your email use that they had to your telephone records." He said this could lead to agencies overstepping their authority. "The history of the FBI is that they will do exactly that."

Other high-tech items to be employed in the War on Terrorism include a program being developed by the CIA called "Fluent," which searches foreign websites and displays an English translation back to Langley. This may be used in conjunction with "Oasis," a technology, which transcribes worldwide radio and TV broadcasts.

The FBI and some police departments are now using a software program called "dTective" to trace financial transactions by dramatically improving the grainy video of surveillance cameras at banks and ATMs.

The feds are even working on techniques for restoring videotapes and computer disks that have been destroyed, cut up or tossed in water. One software program entitled "Encase" can recover deleted computer files and search for incriminating documents on any computer. This was used by the FBI to examine computers seized in the wake of the 9/11 attacks.

The numbering of individual humans is already in place. A tracking system will be next. And don't count on government watchdog organizations to maintain your privacy rights.

In late 2002, the American Civil Liberties Union gave its stamp of approval to an electronic tracking system utilizing Global Positioning System (GPS) satellites to track suspects and criminals. This "VeriTracks" system is offered by the Veridan company of Arlington, VA. Such GPS tracking not only keeps tabs on convicted criminals but also suspects and can even correlate their position with high-crime areas or crime scenes. Law enforcement agencies can create "electronic fences" around areas they deem off-limits to wearers of a cell-phone-size GPS receiver. The module that records its exact position is carried on the waist while an electronic bracelet worn on the ankle acts as an electronic tether to the GPS receiver.

The module is placed in a docking system at night to recharge batteries and upload its data to a central headquarters which checks to see if the wearer has been at any crime scenes.

How do you get someone to agree to this monitoring system? Sheriff Don Eslinger of Seminole County, FL, answered, "It's either wear the GPS device or go to jail. Most of them find this much more advantageous than sitting in a cold jail cell, and it also saves us between $45 and $55 a day." Eslinger said his county had equipped 10 pre-trial suspects with the GPS device as a condition of making bond and that county officials hoped to expand the program to include non-violent probationers and parolees.

And such surveillance technology is not being limited to felons and probationers. In Texas, some 1,000 drivers allowed an insurance company to place a transponder in their vehicles to keep track of teenaged drivers and their speed.

The firm Digital Angel was developing a wrist band that allows parents to log on to the Internet and instantly locate their children while another company, eWorldtrack, is working on a child-tracking device that will fit inside athletic shoes. The German firm Siemens has tested a seven-ounce tracking device that allows constant communication between parents and their children. Author Joe Queenan quipped, "Fusing digital mobile phone technology, a satellite-based global positioning system and good old-fashion insanity, the device can pinpoint a child within several yards in a matter of seconds."

Such GPS devices reminded civil libertarians of the 1987 film *The Running Man*, in which Arnold Schwarzenegger is equipped with a collar, which will blow his head off if he leaves a prescribed area. They also note that the difference between a suspect and an innocent man is often unclear.

All this technology leads to scary scenarios such as this one envisioned by *Village Voice* writer Russ Kick: "You just got a call that your sister is in critical condition in the hospital. So you jump in your car and hit the gas. Trouble is, the speed limit is 30 miles per hour and your car won't let you drive any faster. Or maybe you're lucky enough to have a vehicle that still lets you drive at the speed you choose. A cop pulls you over and demands a saliva sample, so he can instantly match your DNA to a data bank of criminals' genes. You refuse and are arrested. After booking you, the authorities force you to submit to 'brain fingerprinting,' a technology that can tell if memories of illegal events are in your mind.

"By this point, you're thinking this is a worst-case scenario, a science-fiction dysphoria. Well, wake up and smell the police state, because all this technology—and more—is already being implemented."

GOVERNING BY SECRECY AND DECREE

While waging its War on Terrorism, the Bush Administration has expanded government secrecy in ways hardly imaginable just a few years ago. Information has been sequestered away from the public and the Congress while law enforcement agencies have been allowed to operate in the shadows.

And this was not all in response to the 9/11 attacks. Well before September 11, Bush kept secret some 4,000 pages related to presidential pardons granted by President Clinton as he was leaving office. The administration shielded Vice President Cheney by keeping secret the members and minutes of an energy policy task force headed by Cheney.

Shortly after 9/11, as previously noted, Bush held up the release of presidential papers from the Reagan Administration in which his father played such a big role.

Among President Bush's many secrets was the fact that he has gathered around him one of the most wealthy circle of government officials in the history of the United States, earning mention in the *Guinness Book of World Records, 2000.*

According to *Guinness*, "George W. Bush (inaugurated as the 43rd US president on January 20, 2001) has assembled the wealthiest cabinet in American history by appointing more multimillionaires to the top rank of his government than any of his predecessors. Of the 16 full government members at the heart of the Bush administration, 13 are multimillionaires, seven of them own assets more than $10 million. His cabinet has acquired the nickname 'tycoon's club.' Defense Secretary Donald Rumsfeld and [then] Treasury Secretary Paul O' Neill each have declared assets of at least $61 million, while [then] Secretary of State Colin Powell has at least $18 million."

Information such as this seeped into the public's consciousness during 2001 despite the distraction of the terrorist attacks and the subsequent bombing of Afghanistan and the war talk against Iraq. A mid-2002 poll by the *New York Times* and *CBS News* found that out of 1,000 adults polled by telephone, 58 percent—a clear majority—thought that big business had too much influence on government and Bush himself. The poll also showed that a majority of respondents felt Bush was hiding some things about his own corporate past and that the national economy was in its worst shape since 1994. By more than two to one, respondents said the Bush Administration was more interested in protecting the interests of large companies than those of ordinary Americans.

And Bush was only slightly ahead of Cheney when it came to belief in their word that they had not done anything wrong while in the business sector. Of those surveyed, only seventeen percent thought Bush was telling the truth about his dealings at Harken Energy, while only eleven percent thought Cheney was truthful about the accounting practices of Halliburton while under his control.

Of course, this means that the majority in both cases thought the two top national leaders were hiding something or outright lying about their business dealings. And no one was asked about Halliburton's under the table dealings with Iraq despite US sanctions.

The poll respondents' concern over big business exerting undue influence over the government is fully supported by a brief survey of Bush's top first administration leaders and their connection to multinational corporations, especially oil companies. This survey was conducted by the Center for Responsive Politics, a Washington-based non-profit research group.

Defense Secretary Donald Rumsfeld had close ties to both multinational drug companies such as G. D. Searle, now a subsidiary of Pharmacia, as well as defense giants like General Dynamics and Motorola. He served on the boards of Gilead Sciences, Amylin Pharmaceutical, Kellogg, Sears and Allstate and the Tribune Company, which owns the *Los Angeles Times* and the *Chicago Tribune*.

Former Secretary of State Colin Powell had tight connections to Gulfstream Aerospace and General Dynamics as well as the Media giant Time Warner. His son Michael was the only commissioner on the Federal Communications Commission that advocated allowing the AOL-Time Warner merger to go through without scrutiny. It was estimated that Powell's stock in the company increased in value by $4 million, although the merger subsequently proved disastrous for Time Warner shareholders.

Former National Security Adviser (now Secretary of State) Condoleezza Rice so impressed her fellow board members at Chevron that they named a 130,000-ton oil tanker after her. She also served on the board of the multinational brokerage firm of Charles Schwab and the insurance giant Transamerica Corp.

Former Attorney General John Ashcroft had connections, through campaign contributions during his time as a Missouri senator, to AT&T, Microsoft, Schering-Plough, Enterprise Rent-A-Car and Monsanto. Microsoft was hoping Ashcroft would dismiss the anti-trust suit against the computer giant.

Former Director of the Office of Management and Budget Mitch Daniels Jr. was a former senior vice president of the pharmaceutical giant Eli Lilly. Daniels also had stock holdings of up to $100,000 in Citigroup, General Electric and another drug company, Merck.

Former Chief of Staff Andrew Card had been chief lobbyist for General Motors for more than year before joining the Bush White House.

Former Secretary of Veterans Affairs Anthony Principi, formerly with the Federal Network and president of QTC Medical, also had significant holdings in Lockheed Martin, Microsoft, Schering-Plough, Ford Motor Co. and Qualcomm Inc.

Former Treasury Secretary Paul O'Neill, had been former CEO and chairman of Alcoa, the world's largest manufacturer of aluminum, which was represented by the Texas law firm of Vinson & Elkins. This firm managed to find a loophole in Texas' environmental regulations that brought Alcoa to the top of the list of lead Texas polluters. Vinson & Elkins also happened to be George Bush's third largest campaign contributor. O'Neill was also a past president of International Paper and served on the boards of Lucent Technologies and Eastman Kodak.

Former Transportation Secretary Norman Y. Mineta, the only Democrat in the Bush cabinet, nevertheless has a solid background in aerospace and aviation. He resigned his 21-year seat in the House to take a job with Lockheed Martin. He also has corporate connections to Northwest Airlines, Greyhound, United Airlines, Union Pacific and Boeing.

Former Labor Secretary Elaine Chao served as CEO of United Way and worked for the Peace Corps. But she also sat on corporate boards, including Dole Food, Clorox, and the health care companies C. R. Bard and HCA. She also was an executive at Bank of America.

Former Interior Secretary Gale Norton's selection by Bush was a disappointment to environmentalists as she had represented several corporations in suits charging environmental and health hazards. Her corporate connections include Brownstein, Hyatt & Faber, Delta Petroleum, NL Industries, BP Amoco and Ford Motor Co.

Former Health and Human Services Secretary Tommy G. Thompson, a former Wisconsin governor, reportedly sold his stock in pharmaceutical giants Merck and Abbott Laboratories when he signed on with the Bush Administration but he retained his holdings in Time Warner and General

Electric. While serving as governor, Thompson received privileges, trips and contributions from the Philip Morris tobacco company.

Former Energy Secretary Spencer Abraham, a one-term senator from Michigan, was the primary recipient of automotive industry campaign contributions, having received more than $700,000 from General Motors, Ford Motor Company, Lear Corp. and DaimlerChrysler.

Former Agriculture Secretary Ann M. Veneman worked in the US Dept. of Agriculture under the former President Bush and was head of California's Department of Food and Agriculture in 1995. In 1994, she was on the board of directors of Calgene, Inc., the first company to bring genetically engineered food—the Flavr Savr tomato—to the public. Calgene was bought by Monsanto, the nation's leading biotech company, which in turn was bought by Pharmacia in 2000. She also served on the International Policy Council on Agriculture, Food and Trade, a group funded by Cargill, Nestle, Kraft and Archer Daniels Midland.

Former Commerce Secretary Donald L. Evans, an old buddy of Bush's early days in the oil business, was chairman and CEO of the Denver-based oil and gas company Tom Brown, Inc. He also sat on the board of another oil and gas firm, TMBR/Sharp Drilling. Evans broke all previous contribution records when he garnered more than $100 million for Bush's presidential campaign. As chief of the National Oceanic and Atmospheric Administration, Evans will have control over the nation's coastline, the source of about 25 percent of US gas and oil.

Rice, O'Neill, Powell and Chao remain members of either the Council on Foreign Relations or The Trilateral Commission, groups that are avowed proponents of globalism or top-down one world government. And the Bush first term officials who subsequently left office were replaced mostly by able administrators perfectly willing to follow the policies of their predecessors.

The evidence is clear. The idea that America today is run by corporate executives for corporate executives is no conspiracy theory; it is a fact. And they are doing their best to see that it all operates in secrecy.

In Nazi Germany, the state took over the corporations. In modern America, the corporations have taken over the state. The end result is the same.

And while Bush has claimed meager experience with the corporate world, his 2000 campaign contributions list tells a different story. According to *Sierra Magazine*, the President received almost $1.9 million from the gas and oil industry, $203,000 from the mining industry and $300,000 from the timber and forest-products industry. The Republican Party got more than $20 million from the gas and oil industry, $4.7 million from the mining industry and $5.4 million from the timber and forest-products industry.

Enron's former CEO, Kenneth Lay, along with another officer, Jeffrey Skilling, was convicted on May, 25, 2006, of conspiracy, securities fraud and wire fraud. Lay, a "Bush Pioneer," personally raising more than $550,000 for the Bush 2000 campaign. Lay was also convicted in a separate non-jury trial of bank fraud and making false statements to banks—charges related to his personal finances.

On July 5, 2006, a little more than a month after Lay's conviction, at a time when he must have been pondering whether to serve his time or implicate others in the Enron scandal, he suddenly died of a massive heart attack. Some researchers claimed that the unaccounted for millions missing from Enron were used to pay operatives to manipulate the 2000 presidential election in favor of Bush.

More than 30 former energy executives, lobbyists and lawyers now serve in high-level jobs for the Bush Administration. "The people running the United States government are from the energy industry," acknowledged Peabody Energy executive Fredrick Palmer. If the close corporate connections aren't enough to raise questions about conflict of interest, some have even raised the specter of nepotism, a word apparently forgotten by today's "watchdog" media.

Although apparently a non-issue to the corporate mass media, George W. Bush's first administration was filled with family and relatives.

In late February 2002, Elizabeth Cheney, the vice president's daughter, was named as a deputy secretary of state. Within about a week, her husband, Philip Perry, became chief counsel for the Office of Management and Budget where he joined Director Mitchel Daniels, whose sister is an assistant attorney general.

"That's just the beginning," noted *Washington Post* reporter Dana Milbank, describing nepotism in Bush's first administration. "Among Deborah Daniels' colleagues at Justice is young Chuck James, whose mother,

Kay Coles James, is the director of the Office of Personnel Management, and whose father, Charles Sr., is a top Labor Department official. Charles James Sr.'s boss, Labor Secretary Elaine L. Chao, knows about having family members in government: Her husband is [Kentucky] Senator Mitch McConnell and her department's top lawyer, Labor Solicitor Eugene Scalia, is the son of Supreme Court Justice Antonin Scalia.

"Everybody knows the Bush administration is famously loyal. One reason Bush aides are like family is because some of them *are* family. Ken Mehlman, the White House political director, regularly calls his younger brother Bruce, an assistant commerce secretary, to get his input. "He's a great adviser—I trust him like a brother," quipped Ken."

"Secretary of State Colin L. Powell is the father of Michael Powell, chairman of the Federal Communications Commission," added Milbank. "The director of the Federal Trade Commission's office of policy planning, Ted Cruz, is married to a senior official in the US Trade Representative's office, Heidi Cruz. 'It's a little bit like having adjoining booths at the county fair,' she says.

The *Post* article went on to name numerous familial connections between members of the Bush administration, but argued that there is no nepotism involved and that all office holders are qualified in their own right.

Another troublesome aspect of both Bush terms is the president's contention that he must defend his office from the loss of power. This is blatantly untrue. The American president today carries far more power than ever imagined by our Founding Fathers or even more modern chief executives like Franklin D. Roosevelt.

Bush's secretive manner of drawing ever more power unto himself by issuing "signing statements" drew criticism from credible legal sources by 2006.

Jennifer Van Bergen, a journalist with a law degree, explained that "signing statements" are statements by the President issued upon signing a bill into law. Van Bergen noted that from 1817 until the end of the Carter administration in 1981, only 75 "signing statements" were issued. From the Reagan administration until the end of the Clinton administration, this number had grown to 322. But in the first term alone, Bush issued at least 435 "signing statements, many noting his concept of a "unitary executive."

Such "signing statements" convey a President's view toward the law and his own power. Bush's use of the term "unitary executive," according to Van Bergen, is merely a code word for a doctrine "that favors nearly unlimited executive power."

"In his [Bush's] view, and the view of his Administration, that doctrine gives him license to overrule and bypass Congress or the courts, based on his own interpretations of the Constitution—even where that violates long-established laws and treaties, counters recent legislation that he has himself signed, or (as shown by recent developments in the Padilla case) involves offering a federal court contradictory justifications for a detention," Van Bergen wrote on an Internet legal site.

She took particular note of Bush's "signing statement" while signing into law legislation curtailing torture on prisoners. "When President Bush signed the new law, sponsored by Senator [John] McCain, restricting the use of torture when interrogating detainees, he also issued a Presidential signing statement," said Van Bergen. "That statement asserted that his power as Commander-in-Chief gives him the authority to bypass the very law he had just signed."

Civil libertarians historically have heeded the statement of patriot Thomas Paine, who wrote in *Common Sense*, "In America, the law is king. For as in absolute governments the King is law, so in free countries the law ought to be king; and there ought to be no other."

Yet, Bush argues that such actions, allowing him to ride roughshod over the Congress, the courts and the Constitution are somehow necessary to preserve the presidency.

"I have an obligation to make sure that the presidency remains robust and that the legislative branch doesn't end up running the executive branch," Bush argued in mid-2002. He either ignored or didn't realize that by preparing an attack on Iraq, he was preempting the power of Congress. When he and his appointees rammed the USA PATRIOT Act through a Congress, which had had little or no input, he likewise took powers from the representatives of the people.

Bush's first press secretary Ari Fleischer, also failed to study recent history when he stated that presidential powers have been diminished "in multiple ways" as part of a "long-standing, gradual process."

Perhaps this effort to take power away from legislators was the reason that Bush announced his legal advisers had told him he did not need to consult Congress before ordering a strike on Iraq, despite the fact that war-making powers are explicitly granted to the Congress by the US Constitution.

"What the president is claiming is legally and historically absurd and politically stupid," stated Bruce Fein, a former Justice Department official who worked for several past Republican administrations. "[The US] has never had a more imperial presidency, at least since Roosevelt during his conduct of World War II."

Bush argued that he must work in secrecy to regain open dialog with his advisers and various experts. Bush-appointed chairman of the Republican National Committee, Mark Racicot, explained that, "the ability of the president to carry on communications and get unvarnished advice has eroded over a period of time."

Many Washington insiders, including Fein, scoffed at this argument. "I've been around this town a long time, almost 30 years, and I've never encountered one individual who told me he's not going to the Oval Office unless he's promised confidentiality. It's the biggest hoax in the world. Why he's making up all this stuff is utterly and completely baffling."

Since taking office in January 2001, President Bush has wrapped the Oval Office in more secrecy than any previous president. President Bill Clinton's White House looked absolutely transparent compared to Bush's.

But in the matter of executive privilege, Bush was two faced: documents which placed President Clinton in a bad light were released with impunity, while documents which might have put Clinton in a more favorable light were withheld using executive privilege. For example, in summer 2001, congressional investigators requested transcripts of three discussions between Clinton and Israeli Prime Minister Ehud Barak concerning a Clinton pardon for Marc Rich, the financial wizard who stiffed the IRS for $48 million and claimed citizenship in the US, Israel and Spain. The Bush White House promptly turned them over with the explanation that they were not classified.

"Given the secrecy that the Bush-Cheney administration has pursued, it's inconceivable that they would turn this information over if it affected President Bush," commented Democratic staff director for the House Government Reform Committee Phil Schiliro.

On November 1, 2001, with the nation still in turmoil following the 9/11 attacks, Bush signed an executive order "reinterpreting" the 1978 Presidential Records Act, which provided for the public release of former presidents' documents after they left office. Bush claimed the executive privilege to veto the release of any such documents and thereby establish a "process that I think will enable historians to do their job and at the same time protect state secrets."

Historians were so unimpressed with Bush's logic that before the month was out a group had filed a lawsuit to stop his executive order. Parties to the suit included the American Historical Association, the National Security Archive at George Washington University, the Organization of American Historians, Public Citizen, the Reporter's Committee for Freedom of the Press and history professors Hugh Graham and Stanley Kutler.

"The Presidential Records Act of 1978, which specified that after January 20, 1981, all official presidential and vice presidential records became the property of the federal government, was meant to shift power over White House documents from former presidents to professional government archivists, and ultimately, to the public," said Thomas Blanton, director of the National Security Archives. "But the Bush order attempts to overturn the law, take power back, and let presidents past and present delay public access indefinitely."

Joan Claybrook, president of Public Citizen, charged that Bush's decree "violates not only the spirit but the letter of the law." "We will not stand by while the administration tramples on the people's right to find out about their own government," she added.

The group's attorney Scott Nelson summed up the feeling of many people when he said, "It's interesting that the first beneficiary of this new doctrine would be the father of the man who announced it." He referred, of course, to Bush's father who served as vice president and virtually ran the government for some time after Ronald Reagan was seriously wounded in March 1981.

"This administration is the most secretive of our lifetime, even more secretive than the Nixon administration," said Larry Klayman, chairman of Judicial Watch, the conservative group that sued the government for release of the names of Cheney's energy task force. "They don't believe the American people or Congress have any right to information."

Just after the 9/11 attacks, Attorney General Ashcroft sent a memo to all government agencies urging them to turn down more Freedom of Information requests in favor of "institutional, commercial and personal privacy interests."

This represented a dramatic reversal of decades of open government. "We are moving from a right to know to a need to know society," observed Gary Bass of OMB Watch, a private group that monitors government spending and legislation.

Since 9/11, thousands of pages of documents have vanished from the Internet. Some that might have a direct impact on security measures are understandable, others less so. But the new heightened security has proven a boon to corporate despoilers who would like their sordid track records on safety and environmental pollution kept from the public. Activists and newsmen can no longer gain information on polluting chemical plants or locate hazardous waste dumps.

"There is a pattern of secrecy that is a defining characteristic of the Bush Administration," noted Steven Aftergood, who heads government secrecy research for the Federation of American Scientists. "It resists even the most mundane requests for information."

By 2006, with the wars in Iraq and Afghanistan still raging with no end in sight, the economy slumping and multiple charges of domestic spying, President Bush saw his approval rating dip as low as 35 percent, one of the lowest in recent history.

In February 2006, Vice President Cheney shot a companion while hunting for birds in Texas. Hunting accidents are not that unusual. What was unusual was the day and a half lag time between the shooting and Cheney's appearance before authorities.

Even though the local sheriff ruled the shooting an accident, rumors began to fly. According to Doug Thompson of *Capitol Hill Blue*, a written report from Secret Service agents guarding the vice president stated that Cheney was "clearly inebriated" when he shot Texas lawyer Harry Whittington on the hunting outing. The report stated that agents observed several members of the hunting party, including the Vice President, consuming alcohol before and during the hunting expedition and that Cheney exhibited "visible signs" of impairment, including slurred speech and erratic actions. Thompson concluded that the time lag offered all members of the hunting party time to sober up.

Even the conservative *US News & World Report* voiced concern over this time lag and the secrecy surrounding the incident. Addressing the time lag between the shooting and Cheney's appearance, editors asked, "Would the average Joe have gotten such a pass?"

One editorial noted, "Cheney has constructed something very unusual for a vice president: a world that is almost beyond public and media scrutiny, with little accountability. He hasn't held a full-fledged news conference for nearly four years. He doesn't talk about his advice to the president, even though his influence is by all reports extraordinary. He travels without letting people outside his orbit know what he's up to. He doesn't even disclose his travel expenses, arguing that the law applies to heads of agencies, and he isn't one...He has done an amazing thing—creating a 'zone of privacy' unique in the modern era. President Bush has adopted many of his ideas, presiding over one of the most secretive White Houses in recent history. It sure makes things easier that way. And since the public doesn't seem to care, future leaders are likely to follow Cheney's example."

Taking a cue from President Clinton, Bush turned to executive orders, many activated without fanfare or publicity, to strengthen his rule.

THE SHADOW GOVERNMENT KNOWS

Then there is the issue of the "shadow government." On March 1, 2002, well after the 9/11 attacks, President Bush announced that the American public needn't worry about the survival of vital federal government functions because a "shadow government" made up of unelected bureaucrats were working in underground bunkers stocked with supplies of food, water and electric generators to preserve the government. Many people found little consolation in the idea that while their cities might be devastated by biological, chemical or nuclear terrorism, the Agriculture Dept. and the IRS would still be there for them. Plans for

COG, or Continuity of Government, have been in place since the beginning of the Cold War but were only revved up by the Bush Administration in the wake of the 9/11 attacks.

Actually, authors and commentators have spoken out about a shadow government that runs the country in secret for many years. Col. L. Fletcher Prouty called it the "Secret Team," while Bill Moyers called it the "Secret Government."

The shadow government made public by President Bush was only about the bureaucrats that would try to continue government services in the event of a massive attack or emergency. There was no mention of the shadow or parallel government that has operated since the signing of the National Security Act of 1947 and, according to a growing number of researchers, was behind the assassination of President Kennedy in 1963.

The federal shadow government could well have been named the "Secret Government." The Republican Speaker of the House Dennis Hastert said he only had a vague idea of this sub-rosa government and he is third in line to assume the presidency.

Although, in the event of a crisis, reportedly some 100 senior government managers would escape to one of two secret East Coast underground destinations, according to the *Washington Post*, "only the executive branch is represented in the full-time shadow government."

Following a catastrophic attack, these shadow bureaucrats would try to contain national disruption of food, water, transportation, energy and telecommunications, then move on to reconstitute the federal government. But this is all hush-hush. Participants cannot reveal the whereabouts of these underground retreats even to their own families, who are not allowed to join them.

And the shadow government has now been tied to the Homeland Security apparatus, which refused to reveal any details on its cost or budget.

This prompted a threat from former Senate Majority Leader Tom Daschle that he might issue a subpoena to former Homeland Security Secretary Tom Ridge in order to find out what all these secret preparations are costing the American taxpayer. Bush had even refused to allow Ridge to testify to the Congress about his plans and their costs. Ridge finally was allowed to send a written statement to a joint meeting of several committees.

Daschle said secrecy about the shadow government was so tight he had not learned about it until he read about it in the *Washington Post*. "We have not been informed at all about the role of the shadow government or its whereabouts or what particular responsibilities they have or when they would kick in," groused Daschle.

The executive director of Judicial Watch, the group that criticized President Clinton so doggedly, stated, "This is a case of where left and right agree…True conservatives don't act this way."

"We see an unprecedented secrecy in this White House that…we find very disturbing," said Larry Klayman of Judicial Watch.

Michael Ventura of the *Austin Chronicle* wrote, "Without an active free press (especially the *New York Times*, the *Washington Post* and the *Los Angeles Times*) our elected representatives in Congress would know virtually nothing of most of the major steps the Bush Administration has taken… If America means to you a republic governed according to a Constitution that carefully stipulates checks and balances among the White House, Congress, and the judiciary—a system in which none can overwhelm the others, and in which each is responsible to the others—then you no longer live in America.

"This is not some dire warning about the future. This has happened and is happening. A free press is noting the process step by step: braver members of Congress, Republican and Democrat, have voiced alarm and are attempting legal measures to exercise their constitutional duties (so far to no avail); watchdogs on the right and left agree on the urgency of the situation…while most citizens say and do nothing, giving tacit approval to a new (yes, new!) de facto system of government that recognizes no obligation to obey or enforce the letter or spirit of the Constitution."

The Bush administration is packed with men and women who claim to be conservatives. But what is it they wish to conserve? It would appear not to be the conservation of a constitutional republic.

"[Conservative] does not describe the Bush Administration at all," added Ventura. "They ignore Congress almost completely on crucial issues; they feel no obligation to inform American citizens of the White House's deliberations or even its policies, whether or not national security is at stake; they concentrate tremendous power among the very few. That is not conservatism. There is only one word that adequately describes the bent and preference of George W. Bush's White House: Totalitarianism."

PART IV – HISTORICAL PRECEDENTS

"But as the result of evil, there's some amazing things
that are taking place in America."

—President George W. Bush,
Daytona Beach, FL, January 30, 2002

Historical precedents that may provide insight into the events of 9/11 are so numerous that there is not enough space to present them all. But for the close student of history, there is a clear pattern governing such events. It is based on a Machiavellian manipulation of the well-tried dialectic of the German philosopher Georg Wilhelm Friedrich Hegel.

In theory, the doctrine of the Hegelian dialectic—or the study of opposing forces over time—maintains that thesis encountering antithesis results in synthesis. But some of the early students of Hegel, which included the Bavarian Illuminati and other secret societies, realized that they need not wait for a problem to present itself through the natural course of the dialectic. They could secretly create the problem or a provocation, and then offer their own solution. In other words, in the world of ruthless power politics, one can apply the Hegelian dialectic in a perverse manner. Simply offer a draconian solution to a problem you have engineered, which, after compromises, still advances the secret agenda of those who created the problem in the first place.

The attacks of 9/11 certainly fit this mold. If they were not simply the result of a handful of Muslim fanatics armed only with small blades who miraculously hijacked four separate airliners simultaneously, then they were deliberate provocations instigated for the purpose of advancing a hidden agenda.

Consider a few cases of such provocations and responses from the last century.

THE REICHSTAG FIRE

In January 1933, Germany was a free Republic with one of the most educated and cultured populations in the world at that time. Germany was at peace and enjoying a blossoming of democratic freedom under a coalition government of the Weimar Republic. But on February 27, 1933, the German *Reichstag* or Parliament building was destroyed by fire. In those slower, gentler times, this act was as great a shock to the German people as the destruction of the World Trade Center was to Americans.

As we have noted before, German Chancellor Adolf Hitler and his Nazis blamed the destruction on communist terrorists. They even caught one, a retarded Dutch youth named Marinus van der Lubbe who carried a Communist Party card. After some time in custody, the youth confessed to being the arsonist. However, later investigation found that one person could not have started the mammoth blaze and that incendiaries had been carried into the building through a tunnel which led to the offices of Hitler's closest partner, Hermann Goering, head of the German Air Force, the *Luftwaffe.*

Despite misgivings in many quarters about the official explanation of the fire, it was announced, "the government is of the opinion that the situation is such that a danger to the state and nation existed and still exists." Law enforcement agencies quickly moved against, not only the communists, but also pacifists, liberals and democrats.

Less than a month later, on March 24, 1933, at Hitler's urging, a panicky German Parliament voted 441 to 94 to pass an "Enabling Act" which was the starting point for Hitler's dictatorship. As noted earlier, this sequence of events may sound eerily familiar to Americans living today under the PATRIOT Act.

As a result of this act, Germans soon saw national identity cards, racial profiling, the equivalent of a national homeland security chief (SS Commander Heinrich Himmler), gun confiscation and later, mass murders and incarcerations in concentration camps. In fact, according to Jews for the Preservation of Firearms Ownership (JPFO), a close examination of the US Gun Control Act of 1968 (Public Law 90-618) revealed it to be nearly word for word the gun legislation passed in Germany under Hitler.

"When Germany awoke," wrote British reporter Douglas Reed, "a man's home was no longer his castle. He could be seized by private individuals, could claim no protection from the police, could be indefinitely detained without preferment of charge; his property could be seized, his verbal and written communications overheard and perused; he no longer had the right to foregather with his fellow countrymen, and his newspapers might no longer freely express their opinions."

With the German population firmly under control due to massive propaganda and fear of government retaliation, Hitler was free to launch pre-emptive strikes in former German territories, as well as Poland. World War II ensued.

When the war in Europe ended, an immense amount of loot accumulated by the Nazis was missing. It appeared that by late August 1944, many top Nazi officials saw the handwriting on the wall. When the French town of St. Lo, center of the German defense line facing the Normandy beachhead, had fallen on July 18, opening all of southern France to Allied armor and infantry, Nazi leaders knew the end of the war was only a matter of time.

According to captured medical records, Hitler was on a roller coaster ride of euphoria and depression due to large daily doses of amphetamines, and had increasingly lost contact with reality. However, the second most powerful man in the Reich, Hitler's Deputy Martin Bormann, was not so incapacitated. On August 10, 1944, Bormann called together German business leaders and Nazi Party officials. They met in the Hotel Maison Rouge at Strasbourg. Bormann explained the purpose of the meeting to one attendee: "German industry must realize that the war cannot now be won, and must take steps to prepare for a postwar commercial campaign which will in time insure the economic resurgence of Germany."

These "steps" came to be known as *Aktion Adlerflug* or "Operation Eagle Flight." It was nothing less than the perpetuation of Nazism through the massive flight of money, gold, stocks, bonds, patents, copyrights and even technical specialists from Germany. As part of this plan, Bormann, aided by the black-clad SS, the central *Deutsche Bank*, the steel empire of Fritz Thyssen and the powerful I.G. Farben combine, created 750 foreign front corporations—58 in Portugal, 112 in Spain, 233 in Sweden, 214 in Switzerland, 35 in Turkey and 98 in Argentina.

Bormann's efforts were substantially helped by close connections with foreign banks and businesses begun long before the war. According to former US Department of Justice Nazi War Crimes prosecutor John Loftus, much of the wealth was passed out of Germany by German banker Thyssen through his bank in Holland, which, in turn, owned the Union Banking Corporation (UBC) in New York City.

Two prominent US business leaders who supported Hitler and served on the board of directors of Union Banking Corporation were George Herbert Walker and his son-in-law Prescott Bush, father of George Herbert Walker Bush and grandfather of President George Walker Bush.

Attorneys for these dealings were the brothers John Foster and Allen Dulles. John was later to become secretary of state under Eisenhower while Allen became one of the longest-serving CIA directors. Both were deeply involved with the Council on Foreign Relations.

On October 20, 1942, the US Alien Property Custodian, operating under the "Trading With the Enemy Act," seized the shares of UBC and said the bank was financing Hitler. Also seized were Bush's holdings in the Hamburg-America ship line which had been used to ferry Nazi propagandists and arms. Another company essential to the passing of Nazi money was the Holland American Trading Company, a subsidiary of UBC. It was through Fritz Thyssen's Dutch bank, originally founded by Thyssen's father in 1916, that Nazi money was passed. This Dutch connection connected the Bush and Nazi money directly to former SS officer and founder of the Bilderbergers, Prince Bernhard of the Netherlands.

The leading shareholder in UBC was E. Roland Harriman, son of Edward Harriman, the person who had been a early and important mentor to Prescott Bush. All had been members of the Yale secret society Skull and Bones and all were closely connected to the globalists at the Council on Foreign Relations.

On November 17, 1942, US authorities also seized the Silesian-American Corporation, managed by Prescott Bush and his father-in-law George Herbert Walker, and charged the firm with being a Nazi front company supplying vital coal to Germany.

But, according to government documents that have recently come to light and were published by the *News Hampshire Gazette* in 2003, "the grandfather of President George W. Bush, failed to divest himself of more than a dozen 'enemy national' relationships that continued as late as 1951. The newly-released documents also showed that Bush and his associates routinely tried to conceal their business activities from government investigators and such dealings were conducted through the New York private banking firm of Brown Brothers Harriman.

"After the war," according to the *Gazette* report, "a total of 18 additional Brown Brothers Harriman and UBC-related client assets were seized under the Trading with the Enemy Act, including several that showed the continuation of a relationship with the Thyssen family after the initial 1942 seizures.

"The records also show that Bush and the Harrimans conducted business after the war with related concerns doing business in or moving assets into Switzerland, Panama, Argentina and Brazil—all critical outposts for the flight of Nazi capital after Germany's surrender in 1945."

Why was Prescott Bush not more openly and aggressively prosecuted for his Nazi dealings? This may be due to the fact that the patriarch Bush was "instrumental in the creation of the USO in late 1941," according to a news release from the United Service Organization in 2002. After all, how would it have looked during wartime to publicly prosecute as a Nazi asset the man who helped create the USO, so beloved by US servicemen in all subsequent conflicts?

"The story of Prescott Bush and Brown Brothers Harriman is an introduction to the real history of our country," said publisher and historian Edward Boswell. "It exposes the money-making motives behind our foreign policies, dating back a full century. The ability of Prescott Bush and the Harrimans to bury their checkered pasts also reveals a collusion between Wall Street and the media that exists to this day."

"It is bad enough that the Bush family helped raise the money for Thyssen to give Hitler his start in the 1920s, but giving aid and comfort to the enemy in time of war is treason," declared Nazi prosecutor Loftus. "The Bush's bank helped the Thyssens make the Nazi steel that killed Allied soldiers. As bad as financing the Nazi war machine may seem, aiding and abetting the Holocaust was worse. Thyssen's coal mines used Jewish slaves as if they were disposable chemicals. There are six million skeletons in the Thyssen family closet, and a myriad of criminal and historical questions to be answered about the Bush family complicity."

Illustrating other interconnecting business associations of this time was ITT's German chairman Gerhardt Westrick, a close associate of John Foster Dulles, who was a partner to Dr. Heinrich Albert, head of Ford Motor Co. in Germany until 1945. Two ITT directors were German banker Baron Kurt von Schroeder and Walter Schellenberg, head of counterintelligence for the Nazi Gestapo.

Rockefeller-owned Standard Oil also came under investigation during World War II for a series of complex business deals, which resulted in desperately-need gasoline reaching Nazi Germany.

Nazi-American business connections were further buttressed by the 1936 partnership between the J. Henry Schroeder Bank of New York and Rockefeller family members. According to author Charles Higham, "[An entity called] Schroeder, Rockefeller and Company, Investment Bankers, was formed as part of an overall company that *Time* magazine disclosed as being 'the economic booster of the Rome-Berlin Axis.' The partners in Schroeder, Rockefeller and Company included Avery Rockefeller, nephew of John D., Baron Bruno von Schroeder in London, and Kurt von Schroeder of the Bank of International Settlements and the Gestapo in Cologne...Their lawyers were John Foster Dulles and Allen Dulles of Sullivan and Cromwell. Allen Dulles (later CIA director and Warren Commission member) was on the board of Schroeder. Further connections linked the Paris branch of (the Rockefeller) Chase National Bank to Schroeder as well as the pro-Nazi Worms Bank and Standard Oil of New Jersey's interests in France. Standard Oil's Paris representatives were directors of the Banque de Paris et des Pays-Bas, which had intricate connections to the Nazis and to Chase."

It is interesting to note that throughout the war, Chase maintained its financial connections with the Nazis through its Paris bank and that I.G. Farben chief Hermann Schmitz served as Chase president for seven years prior to the war and eventually held as much stock in Standard Oil of New Jersey as the Rockefellers. "Schmitz's wealth—largely I.G. Farben bearer bonds converted to the Big Three successor firms, shares in Standard Oil of New Jersey...General Motors, and other US blue chip industrial stocks, and the 700 secret companies controlled in his time by I.G., as well as shares in the 750 corporations he helped Bormann establish during the last years of World War II—has increased in all segments of the modern industrial world. The Bormann organization in South America utilizes the voting power of the Schmitz trust long with their own assets to guide the multinationals they control, as they keep steady the economic course of the Fatherland," wrote journalist Paul Manning, who added, "The Bormann organization is not merely a group of ex-Nazis. It is a great economic power whose interests today supersede their ideology."

These long-standing banking and business connections coupled with the Schmitz business network allowed *Reichsleiter* Bormann to forge a formidable Nazi-controlled organization for postwar activities.

Jim Keith, author of numerous conspiracy books, wrote, "...in researching the shape of totalitarian control during this century, I saw that the plans of the Nazis manifestly did not die with the German loss of World War II. The ideology and many of the principal players survived and flourished after the war, and have had a profound impact on postwar history, and on events taking place today."

Being so closely connected to the Nazis, patriarch Bush must have taken notice of Hitler's method for gaining unwarranted power—fabricate a crisis, call for sweeping powers to protect the population and take totalitarian control.

Luftwaffe chief Goering verbalized this method clearly when he spoke at the Nuremberg War Crimes Trials following the war: "Naturally, the common people don't want war; Neither in Russia, not in England, nor for that matter in Germany. That is understood. But, after all, it is the leaders of the country who determine the policy and it is always a simple matter to drag the people along, whether it is a democracy, or a fascist dictatorship, or a parliament, or a communist dictatorship. Voice or no voice, the people can always be brought to the bidding of the leaders. That is easy. All you have to do is tell them they are being attacked, and denounce the peacemakers for lack of patriotism and exposing the country to danger. It works the same in any country."

Since the *Reichstag* fire, the Bush family and their associates in the Council on Foreign Relations, Trilateral Commission and Bilderbergers have often mimicked Hitler's tactics gained from the philosopher Hegel of creating a problem, offering a draconian solution and advancing their agenda through any resulting compromise. Public notice of such methods is now widespread, particularly in modern Germany.

In mid-2002, when German Justice Minister Herta Daubler-Gmelin commented on President Bush's threats against Iraq, she noted, "Bush wants to distract attention from his domestic problems. That's a popular method. Even Hitler did that." She was quickly forced to resign for calling attention to this aging but effective ploy.

PEARL HARBOR

In its immediate aftermath, the 9/11 attacks were compared to the attack on Pearl Harbor that launched America into World War II. This comparison was quite appropriate—but not for the reason most people thought.

Controversy has raged for years over the question of Franklin Roosevelt's foreknowledge of the December 7, 1941, attack on Pearl Harbor and it is now clear that certain elements in Washington, D.C. knew of the Japanese attack in advance.

While few journalists and some Republicans accused the Roosevelt administration of foreknowledge, government spokesmen and establishment historians blamed the attack on the failure of US intelligence and incompetence within the naval high command.

Today, the accumulation of available information has now caused wide acceptance of the idea that the devastating attack on Pearl Harbor was tolerated, even encouraged, in an effort to galvanize public support for America's participation in the war.

Roosevelt was quite open in his allegiance to England. While proclaiming neutrality, he had sent war ships and ammunition to Britain just as proposed by the Century Group, a foreign policy think-tank composed of CFR members. He ordered the occupation of Iceland, closing it off to the Germans, and authorized attacks on U-boats. He openly approved loans to Japan's enemy, nationalist China, and quietly approved the recruitment of well-paid American "volunteers" for Chiang Kai-shek's famous "Flying Tigers." Much of this was in violation of international war rules and was guaranteed to provoke the Axis powers.

"Roosevelt was himself a prototypic Wall Streeter," wrote CFR researcher James Perloff. "His family had been involved in New York banking since the eighteenth century. His uncle, Frederic Delano, was on the original Federal Reserve Board." Roosevelt's son-in-law, Curtis B. Dall, wrote, "Most of his [Roosevelt's] thoughts, his political 'ammunition,' as it were, were carefully manufactured for him in advance by the CFR-One World Money group." Dall, of course, was referring to the New World Order long before George Herbert Walker Bush popularized the term.

Those who accept the idea that Roosevelt and a few other insiders knew that Pearl Harbor was to be attacked point to these facts:

- During Pacific naval exercises in 1932 and 1938, and with Japanese military attachés closely observing, US Navy officers theoretically destroyed the Pacific Fleet at Pearl Harbor both times.
- Roosevelt ordered the Pacific fleet moved to the exposed position at Pearl Harbor over the vigorous objections of Admiral James O. Richardson, who was replaced for refusing to issue the order.
- Roosevelt, Secretary of State Cordell Hull and other high-level officials knew that war was inevitable and that negotiations with Japan's Kichisaburo Nomura were hopeless because the broken Japanese code revealed Nomura was instructed not to yield to Hull's harsh demands.
- They also knew that a large Japanese task force, including six aircraft carriers, had dropped from sight after moving towards America.
- This prompted US Army Chief of Staff George C. Marshall, a close associate to many CFR members, to send an oddly-

worded message to Pearl Harbor commanders on November 27, 1941, "Hostile action possible at any moment. If hostilities cannot, repeat CANNOT, be avoided, the United States desires that Japan commit the first overt act. This policy should not, repeat NOT, be construed as restricting you to a course of action that might jeopardize your defense." Despite this clear warning, with its accompanying suggestion not to attack any attackers, Pacific Fleet ships remained at anchor and aircraft were bunched into clusters of "sitting ducks" as "security" against saboteurs.

- During the first week of December, Americans intercepted the Japanese diplomatic "Purple" code ordering the Washington embassy to destroy all secret papers and prepare to evacuate.

- On December 4, Australian intelligence reported sighting the missing Japanese task force moving toward Pearl Harbor but Roosevelt dismissed it as a rumor begun by pro-war Republicans.

- A Dutch submarine tracked the Japanese fleet to Pearl Harbor and radioed this news to headquarters, prompting a warning from Col. F.G.L. Weijerman, the Dutch military attaché in Washington.

- A British agent named Dusko Popov learned of Japan's plans from German sources but his warnings to Washington were ignored.

- According to John Toland, author of *Adolf Hitler*, separate warnings regarding a pending attack on Pearl Harbor, though varying as to a specific time, came from US Ambassador to Japan Joseph Grew; FBI Director J. Edgar Hoover; Senator Guy Gillette; Rep. Martin Dies; and Brig. Gen. Elliot Thorpe in Java.

- Dutch naval officer, Capt. Johan Ranneft, said sources in US Intelligence told him on December 6 that the Japanese carriers were only 400 miles northwest of Hawaii.

- During investigations after the attack, Marshall and Navy Secretary Frank Knox both testified they could not recall their whereabouts the night of December 6. It was later revealed that they were both in the White House with Roosevelt.

■ Then there is the issue of the aircraft carriers. In 1941, the American public, as well as a few hidebound military officers, still believed that the battleship was the ultimate weapon. But anyone who had been paying attention knew that Gen. Billy Mitchell had proven in the mid-1920s that a single bomb-laden airplane could destroy a battleship. Battleships were obsolete. Victory in any Pacific war would go to the side with the strongest air power and that meant aircraft carriers. Not one aircraft carrier was present when Pearl Harbor was attacked.

On November 25, 1941, Secretary of War Henry Stimson had a conversation with Roosevelt, after which he wrote in his diary, "The question was how we should maneuver them into the position of firing the first shot without too much danger to ourselves...It was desirable to make sure the Japanese be the ones to do this so that there should remain no doubt in anyone's mind as to who were the aggressors." The answer to this dilemma came on December 7.

The most damning evidence yet of Roosevelt's foreknowledge of an attack came from the 1948 interrogation of Germany's Gestapo chief Heinrich Mueller. In a 1995 book by Gregory Douglas, based on previously secret files, Mueller stated that on November 26, 1941, the Germans in Holland had intercepted a private trans-Atlantic telephone conversation between Roosevelt and British Prime Minister Churchill.

Churchill informed Roosevelt of the movements of the missing Japanese fleet and stated, "I can assure you that their goal is the (conversation broken) fleet in Hawaii, at Pearl Harbor." "This is monstrous," exclaimed Roosevelt, "Can you tell me...indicate...the nature of your intelligence?" "Reliable," answered Churchill, who mentioned agents within the Japanese military and foreign service as well as their broken code.

"The obvious implication is that the Japs are going to do a Port Arthur on us at Pearl Harbor. Do you concur?" asked Roosevelt. Churchill replied, "I do indeed unless they add an attack on the Panama Canal to this vile business." Port Arthur, today called Pinyun Lu-shun, was a strategic

Russian port on China's Liaotung Peninsula. The Japanese launched a surprise torpedo attack against the port, which began the 1904-05 Russo-Japanese War.

Roosevelt then said, "...I will have to consider the entire problem...A Japanese attack on us, which would result in war between—and certainly you as well—would certainly fulfill two of the most important requirements of our policy." Roosevelt speaks about absenting himself from the White House on some pretext, adding, "What I don't know, can't hurt me and I cannot understand messages at a distance."

Addressing the unlikely proposition that US military officers would have knowingly allowed American units to be attacked, author Douglas explained, "[T]he warning did not come to Roosevelt from below but on a parallel level and from a foreign intelligence source which was far better equipped to decode and translate the Japanese transmissions."

THE GULF WAR

Most people accept the idea that the Gulf War was all about oil—from the accusation that Kuwait was slant-drilling into Iraq's southern Rumaila reserves, to the destruction of the oil fields at its finish. Here we found a new enemy in Saddam Hussein, a former ally who had been armed and financed by the CIA, an agency whose top officials have long been connected to oil men and Council on Foreign Relations globalists.

The allied victory in the Persian Gulf War of 1991 was loudly trumpeted by the American mass media, but the actions leading to this conflict were sparsely reported throughout the coverage. These machinations involved elites in secret societies and indicated a very different rationale for the war than the one presented to the public.

No one can argue that the United States military, with some assistance from British, French and Arab forces, did not perform magnificently during this brief conflict. It only took between January 17 and February 28, 1991, for the coalition of Operation Desert Storm to soundly defeat the Saddam Hussein's well-armed Iraqi forces, then representing the fifth largest army in the world. This astounding military success was due primarily to the allied forces' superiority in both weaponry and training as opposed to Saddam's conscripts who, though veterans of combat against Iran, had limited training and low morale.

This created a lop-sided war, which resulted in more than 300,000 Iraqi casualties, (both military and civilian) and 65,000 prisoners, compared to the extraordinary low allied losses of 234 killed, 470 wounded and 57 missing.

Of course, the prime mover of that war was President Bush's father, George Herbert Walker Bush, an oilman, former CFR member, and former CIA director, as well as a Trilateralist and Skull & Bonesman.

Both Bush and then Secretary of State James Baker had been deeply involved in the oil business. Any Bush policy that increased the price of oil meant more profit to his companies, those of his oil-men supporters and, of course, to the Rockefeller-dominated oil cartel.

An added bonus was that any conflict which divided the Arab world would only strengthen the hand of the US, Britain and Israel in the region, while the act of creating a coalition of countries fighting for the United Nations could only advance the globalists' plan for a one-world military force. This "battle of the New World Order was some kind of manufactured crisis with a hidden agenda," concluded researchers Jonathan Vankin and John Whalen after careful study of the events leading to this conflict.

The war was a drastic reversal of fortune for Saddam Hussein, who previously had enjoyed a close relationship to the senior Bush. In his role as CIA Director, and then as Vice President, the elder Bush along with the Agency, had supported Hussein through his eight-year war against Iran, following the surprise ouster of the Shah in 1979. This included looking the other way when Hussein gassed Iraq's uncooperative Kurds. The US had supplied Iraq with the crop-dusting helicopters used in Hussein's 1988 gassing attacks.

But by 1990, Hussein's Iraq had become a primary threat to the balance of power between Israel and its Arab neighbors and Hussein was now strapped for cash due to the Iraq-Iran War and couldn't pay his bills. Under pressure from the international bankers for slow repayment of loans and from the Organization of Petroleum Exporting Countries (OPEC), which refused to allow him to raise oil prices, Saddam needed a quick source of cash. He therefore turned his eyes to Kuwait—the third largest producer of oil next to Iraq and Saudi Arabia.

Few Americans know that Kuwait was once a possession of Iraq, having long since been carved out of Iraq by Britain. In 1899 the British took control of Kuwait's foreign policy under an agreement with the dictatorial Sabah family; the Sabahs had produced a series of ruling Sheikhs since assuming control of the area's nomad tribes in 1756. Kuwait then became a British Protectorate in 1914 when German interest suddenly gave the area strategic importance. British dominance was solidified by sending British troops to the area in 1961 after Iraq sought to reclaim it.

The Pentagon had known that Iraqi troops were massing along the Kuwait border since mid-July 1990. On July 25, Saddam sought advice from the United States on his intentions to reclaim Kuwait. He met with US Ambassador April Glaspie, who told him, "I have direct instructions from President Bush to improve our relations with Iraq. We have considerable sympathy for your quest for higher oil prices, the immediate cause of your confrontation with Kuwait....

"I have received an instruction to ask you, in the spirit of friendship not confrontation, regarding your intentions: Why are your troops massed so very close to Kuwait's borders?"

According to transcripts released long after the war, Hussein explained that, while he was ready to negotiate his border dispute with Kuwait, his design was to "keep the whole of Iraq in the shape we wish it to be." This shape, of course, included Kuwait, which Hussein considered still a part of Iraq. "What is the United States' opinion on this?" he asked.

"We have no opinion on your Arab-Arab conflicts, like your dispute with Kuwait," replied Glaspie. "Secretary Baker has directed me to emphasize the instruction, first given to Iraq in the 1960s, that the Kuwaiti issue is not associated with America."

In other words, the USA had no particular interest in Saddam's intention to reclaim Kuwait.

"Shortly after this, April Glaspie left Kuwait to take her summer vacation, another signal of elaborate American disinterest in the Kuwait-Iraq crisis," noted authors Webster Griffin Tarpley and Anton Chaitkin in *George Bush: The Unauthorized Biography*. On July 31, Bush met with GOP congressional leaders but said nothing about the Gulf situation.

The crisis escalated on August 2, when Iraqi troops moved into Kuwait. Bush froze all Iraqi assets in the United States, adding to Saddam's money woes, which had worsened in 1990 after international bankers refused him further loans. Glaspie was prohibited from speaking out by the State Department, so the American public could not learn of Bush's duplicity.

In later testimony before the Senate Foreign Relations Committee, Glaspie pointed out that the July 25 conference was her first and only meeting with Hussein, who had not met with any foreign ambassador since 1984, the mid-point of his war with Iran.

But if Hussein had not met with US diplomats, the same could not be said of American businessmen. Economist Paul Adler noted, "...it was known that David Rockefeller met with the Iraqi leader on at least three known occasions after the Chase Manhattan consortium became the lead banker in a number of major Iraqi credit syndications." It was also reported that Alan Stoga, a vice president of [Henry] Kissinger Associates met with Iraqi leaders during the two-year period preceding the Gulf conflict.

"Saddam began to realize that he could not get what he wanted from the striped-pants set. He began doing business with the people who mattered to him—foreign businessmen, defense contractors, technologists and scientists, occasionally even visiting newsmen," reported the Washington newspaper, the *Spotlight*, now the *American Free Press*.

Following the money trail of such non-diplomatic contacts that led to the Gulf War, Rep. Henry Gonzalez, then chairman of the House Committee on Banking, Finance and Urban Affairs, discovered that almost $5 billion in loans had been passed to Saddam Hussein in the 1980s through the Atlanta, GA, branch of Italy's government-owned bank, Banca Nazional del Lavoro (BNL). The branch manager, Christopher Drogoul, was finally brought into federal court where he pled guilty to approving this huge cash transfer without the approval of BNL's head office in Italy. However, the whole investigation was put on hold during the Gulf War.

Most observers disbelieved that Drogoul could have conducted such a massive transaction without the knowledge of his superiors. Bobby Lee Cook, one of Drogoul's several defense attorneys, argued that his client had been made the patsy in "a scheme orchestrated at the highest levels of the US Government."

In court, BNL official Franz Von Wedel testified that his boss Drogoul had acted on the advice of the bank's consultants, Kissinger Associates.

In both 1989 and 1990, the Bush Justice Department had quashed indictments against BNL by the Atlanta Attorney General's office following an FBI raid on the bank on August 4, 1989. Action against the bank managers was held up for more than a year. Indictments were finally handed down one day after Bush declared a cease-fire in the Gulf War. This scandal—dubbed "Iraqgate"—prompted Gonzalez to prepare a House resolution calling for the impeachment of Bush Attorney General William Barr for "obstruction of justice in the BNL scandal." House Judiciary Committee Chairman Rep. Jack Brooks called on Barr to appoint a special prosecutor in the case.

In a classic case of who-will-watch-the-watchers, Barr said he could find no evidence of wrongdoing on his part and refused to appoint a special prosecutor. It was one of the only times that an attorney general had failed to appoint a special prosecutor when asked to do so by Congress.

The clincher of this sordid story of financial scheming and official malfeasance was that not only had most of the $5 billion been used by Hussein to buy weaponry to be used against American servicemen, but that US taxpayers picked up the tab.

Gonzalez said $500 million of the loans to Hussein came through the government-backed Commodity Credit Corporation (CCC) and had been intended to purchase grain from US farmers. However, grain shipped through the port of Houston had gone to then-Soviet bloc nations in exchange for weapons, while the remainder of the grain purchase had freed Hussein's limited cash reserves to buy more military materials. The Bush administration had pledged taxpayer guarantees should Hussein default on the loans, which he did after sending troops to Kuwait. According to at least one public source, more than $360 million in American tax money was paid to the Gulf International Bank in Bahrain, which was owned by seven Gulf nations including Iraq. This amount was only the first of an estimated $1 billion to be paid to ten banks by the CCC to cover the $5 billion of Hussein's defaulted loans.

"The $1 billion commitment, in the form of loan guarantees for the purchase of US farm commodities, enabled Saddam to buy needed food on credit and to spend his scarce hard currency on the arms buildup that brought war to the Persian Gulf," wrote Russell S. Bowen, author of *The Immaculate Deception*.

Even after the Iraqi invasion began on August 2, Bush publicly appeared strangely non-committal. Asked by reporters if he intended any intervention in the Gulf crisis, Bush said, "I'm not contemplating such action..."

His attitude apparently changed drastically that same day after meeting with British Prime Minister Margaret Thatcher, a regular attendee of Bilderberg meetings who had been implicated with Bush in both the Iran-Contra and October Surprise scandals.

After meeting with Thatcher, Bush began to describe Hussein as a "new Hitler" and said, "the status quo is unacceptable and further expansion [by Iraq] would be even more unacceptable." Despite assurances from Hussein that Kuwait was his only objective and with no concrete evidence to the contrary, Bush nevertheless personally telephoned the leaders of Saudi Arabia and warned that they would be the next target of this "new Hitler."

Panicked, the Saudis handed over as much as $4 billion to Bush and other world leaders as secret payoffs to protect their kingdom, according to Sabah family member Sheik Fahd Mohammed al-Sabah, chairman of the Kuwait Investment Office.

Long after the Persian Gulf War, when audits found this money had been diverted into a London slush fund, anti-Sabah elements in Saudi Arabia criticized the payoff. They were told by al-Sabah, "That money was used to buy Kuwait's liberation. It paid for political support in the West and among Arab leaders—support for Desert Storm, the international force we urgently needed."

Whether this money played any role or not, Bush soon drew a "line in the sand" to block further Iraqi intrusion, then launched Desert Storm, an offensive that drove Iraqi troops from Kuwait.

Yet, even as America's patriotic soldiers closed in on Hussein, the whole war was suddenly stopped. George H. W. Bush's old business partner remained in power and the "Great Game," the continuing maneuvering for control of the oil as mentioned in Part III, continued.

THE GULF WAR

Even through the ensuing years of the Clinton administration, periodic air forays into Iraq continued, ostensibly to punish Hussein for preventing UN inspection of his development centers for biological and nuclear weaponry. However, this time there was a big difference—probing questions were raised by both a suspicious public and a few less timid members of the news media.

In late 1998, a letter writer to a national news magazine asked, "By using weapons of mass destruction to deter Iraq from manufacturing weapons of mass destruction, would America not be doing the very thing we're warning Iraq not to do?" Others raised the question of why we attacked Iraq for refusing UN inspection of its sensitive military installations when President Clinton also had refused to allow such inspections in the United States—a refusal greeted with general approval by the American public.

Scott Ritter, a member of the United Nations Special Commission (UNSCOM) created just after the Gulf War to locate and eliminate Saddam Hussein's secret weapons caches, resigned in August of 1998 and accused the US Government of using the commission to justify an attack on Iraq. Ritter said before his resignation that he had initially disbelieved Baghdad's minister of defense when he told him the UNSCOM team was being used to "provoke a crisis." But now, though slowly, he had come to agree with the charge. Ritter's superiors scoffed at the allegation, claiming Ritter's knowledge of the situation was "limited."

However, in early 1999 it was reported that Washington had used UNSCOM to plant electronic bugs in the Ministry of Defense (Iraq's Pentagon). Other US officials now confirmed many of Ritter's accusations.

"The relationship between the United States and the inspection commission...has long been a subject of debate," wrote US News reporter Bruce B. Auster. "The issue is sensitive because UNSCOM is an arm of the UN Security Council, not an agency of the United States, although it does rely on the United States for intelligence and personnel."

Again, the hidden hand of the secret society members who both created and in many ways control the UN could be briefly seen manipulating events.

On December 15, 1998, after stockpiling cruise missiles in the Persian Gulf during the fall, the US launched a much-delayed air strike against Baghdad.

But with Christmas nearing, most Americans couldn't get too worked up over civilian casualties halfway around the word. And any doubts about US involvement in the Persian Gulf—except among those many tens of thousands of unfortunate veterans now having to deal with Gulf War Syndrome caused by a lethal combination of oil fires, biological agents and radioactive uranium-tipped artillery and tank shells—had been thrown away, along with the yellow ribbons which had proudly displayed the total support of the uninformed.

WOULD AMERICANS ALLOW ATTACKS ON AMERICANS?

The WTC/Pentagon attacks certainly provided a convenient excuse to launch the pre-laid plans for military action against Afghanistan and Iraq. But were they simply allowed to happen or were they contrived provocations? Again the question arises: Would any American allow an attack on fellow Americans just to further his own business or political agenda?

Unfortunately, the answer is "Yes." A case in point is "Operation Northwoods." Noted earlier in this book, it's time for a closer look at this planned provocation that involved American lives.

This story came to light when, incredibly, 40-year-old government documents thought to have been destroyed long ago recently were made public. They show that the US military in the early 1960s proposed staging terrorist attacks in the United States and blaming them on Fidel Castro. Between the failure of the Bay of Pigs Invasion of Cuba in April 1961, and the Cuban Missile Crisis of 1962, there was a time when the Pentagon was given authority over the ongoing, and mostly secret, war against Fidel Castro's Cuba.

The entire project was known as "Operation Mongoose" and was headed by Gen. Edward Lansdale, then deputy director of the Pentagon's Office of Special Operations. Mongoose was a gathering point for CIA agents, virulent anti-Castro Cubans, gung-ho military operatives and even organized crime figures, all of whom detested President Kennedy and thought him "soft" on communism and a threat to their own preserves.

From this volatile fusion of violent elements came Operation Northwoods, which were to end up with then Defense Secretary Robert McNamara. Today McNamara says, "I never heard of it." However, the then Chairman of the Joint Chiefs had heard of it, for it was Gen. Lyman Lemnitzer who recommended that the Joint Chiefs oversee this plan to turn world opinion against Castro.

The Joint Chiefs of Staff were going along with this pernicious program but President Kennedy rejected Operation Northwoods. Senior military officers ordered the documents destroyed. But someone slipped up and ironically the papers were discovered in the early 1990s by the Assassination Records Review Board, created to look into Kennedy's assassination in the wake of the Oliver Stone film *JFK*.

These Operation Northwoods documents were discussed in a recent book on the National Security Agency (NSA) entitled *Body of Secrets: Anatomy of the Ultra-Secret National Security Agency* by James Bamford. After a careful study of the documents, Bamford concluded that the Joint Chiefs "proposed launching a secret and bloody war of terrorism against their own country in order to trick the American public into supporting an ill-conceived war they intended to launch against Cuba."

Following the ill-fated Bay of Pigs invasion of Cuba, President Kennedy, angered by the inept actions of the CIA, had shifted responsibility for Cuba from that agency to the Department of Defense. Here, military strategists considered plans to create terrorist actions that would alarm the American population and stampede them into supporting a military attack on Cuba.

Under consideration in Operation Northwoods were plans to create "a series of well-coordinated incidents" in or around the US Naval Base at Guantanamo Bay, Cuba, to include inciting riots, blowing up ammunition stores, aircraft and ships.

They also planned to "develop a Communist Cuba terror campaign in the Miami area, in other Florida cities and even in Washington" or to "...sink a boatload of Cubans en route to Florida (real or simulated)...foster attempts on the lives of Cuban refugees in the United States..."

Other highlights of Operation Northwoods included the tactics of exploding bombs in carefully chosen locations along with the release of "prepared documents" pointing to Cuban complicity, the use of fake Russian aircraft to harass civilian airliners and "Hijacking attempts against civil air and surface craft," even simulating the shooting down of a civilian airliner.

One proposed operation detailed in the Northwoods documents may have provided a prototype of the tactics used on September 11, 2001. On page 10 of the Northwoods plan it states: "An aircraft at Elgin AFB would be painted and numbered as an exact duplicate for a civil registered aircraft...At a designated time the duplicate would be substituted for the actual civil aircraft and would be boarded with the selected passengers, all boarded under carefully prepared aliases. The actual registered aircraft would be converted to a drone [remotely-controlled aircraft]... [From a] rendezvous point the passenger-carrying aircraft will descend to minimum altitude and go directly into an auxiliary field at Elgin AFB where arrangements will have been made to evacuate the passengers and return the aircraft to its original status. The drone aircraft meanwhile will continue to fly the filed flight plan. When over Cuba the drone will be[gin] transmitting on the international distress frequency a 'May Day' message stating he is under attack by Cuban MIG aircraft. The transmission will be interrupted by destruction of the aircraft which will be triggered by radio signal."

It seems clear in the aftermath of 9/11 that Operation Northwoods was not forgotten. In fact, it seemed like covert and "black operations" programs might be making a comeback. Further, it appeared that the success of 9/11 as an inside job had opened a Pandora's box of follow-on covert and "black ops" programs.

In addition to the tremendous military buildup following the 9/11 attacks, the military affairs analyst for the *Los Angeles Times* reported "what may well be the largest expansion of covert action by the armed forces since the Vietnam Era."

"The Defense Department is building up an elite secret army with resources stretching across the full spectrum of covert capabilities," wrote William M. Arkin. "New organizations are being created. The missions of existing units are being revised. Spy planes and ships are being assigned new missions in anti-terror and monitoring the 'axis of evil.'"

In summer 2002, Defense Secretary Rumsfeld's Defense Science Board (DSB) conducted a "Summer Study on Special Operations and Joint Forces in Support of Countering Terrorism." The panel recommended "new strategies, postures and organization."

One such new organization would be a super intelligence support activity called the Proactive, Preemptive Operations Group (P2OG), a unit combining the CIA, military covert action, information warfare, intelligence, and cover and deception. One line of the classified study, which was leaked to the public by the Federation of American Scientists called for "preemption/proaction/interdiction/disruption/quick-response capabilities," in other words, dirty fighting.

According to Arkin, the group would, among other things, "launch secret operations aimed at 'stimulating reactions' among terrorists and states possessing weapons of mass destruction—that is, for instance, prodding terrorist cells into action and exposing themselves to 'quick-response' attacks by US forces. Such tactics would hold 'states/sub-state actors accountable' and 'signal to harboring states that their sovereignty will be at risk.'"

Under the reorganized military, responsibility and accountability for the P2OG group would be held by a "Special Operations Executive" within the National Security Council (NSC). According to *Asia Times* writer David Isenberg, "The NSC would plan operations but not oversee their execution in order to avoid comparisons to past abuses, such as Iran-Contra operations runs out of the NSC by Oliver North during the Reagan administration. Under the board's proposal, NSC plans would be executed by the Pentagon or the CIA."

Several commentators could not help but recall the CIA's Phoenix Program in Vietnam and the Operation Northwoods plan of the Pentagon, which followed the disastrous Bay of Pigs Invasion of Cuba, a joint military-CIA activity.

The thought of such past abuses prompted one writer, Chris Floyd, to rail against "...Bush and his cohorts [who] are plunging the world into an abyss, an endless night of black ops, retribution, blowback, deceit, or murder and terror..."

Pulitzer Prize-winning journalist Seymour Hersh, citing sources in both the Pentagon and CIA, in 2005 agreed with previous writers that the Bush-dominated military would continue to expand its operations both at home and abroad.

"George W. Bush's reelection was not his only victory [in 2004]. The President and his national-security advisers have consolidated control over the military and intelligence communities' strategic analyses and covert operations to a degree unmatched since the rise of the post-Second World War national-security state," Hersh wrote. "Bush has an aggressive and ambitious agenda for using that control—against the mullahs in Iran and against targets in the ongoing war on terrorism—during his second term. The CIA will continue to be downgraded, and the agency will increasingly serve, as one government consultant with close ties to the Pentagon put it, as 'facilitators' of policy emanating from President Bush and Vice President Dick Cheney. This process is well under way."

Such are the chilling plans for expanded covert ops, but at least one such homegrown plot directed by the government against Americans may have been uncovered soon after 9/11 itself.

Late on Saturday, May 11, 2002, an astute deputy sheriff in Jacksonville, FL, stopped a speeding late-model pickup truck. The deputy was amazed to find the truck's driver dressed all in black, wearing a pistol in a shoulder holster and plastic pads on his elbows and knees. In the truck also were large knives, a 12-gauge shotgun, shotgun and pistol ammunition, four ammo magazines, a six-volt battery, duct tape, speaker wire and parts of an explosive device. He was further amazed to find the suspect was a soldier from Fort Stewart, GA.

He arrested Army Specialist Derek Lawrence Peterson. The arresting officer recognized Peterson's truck as one seen earlier parked near the main gate of a nearby Florida Power and Light station. Tracking footprints from where the truck had been parked, investigating officers discovered an explosive device beneath power lines.

The 27-year-old soldier explained he was practicing night reconnaissance tactics. A spokesman for Fort Stewart confirmed that Peterson had been stationed there for about a month with B Company, 1st Battalion, 64th Armored Division.

If Peterson were simply an idiot that somehow made it into the Army, one would expect widespread news coverage to demonstrate how seriously authorities were taking attempted bombings. On the other hand, if Peterson were carrying out some undisclosed covert military orders, one would expect the incident to be hushed up. The soldier was held in a Jacksonville jail without visitors in lieu of $5 million bail. Somebody was taking this case quite seriously, yet there was no national news coverage of this incident at a time of heightened fear and excitement over terrorist incidents and the initial court hearing for Peterson was postponed.

Next, consider the case of the man who tried to stop the first World Trade Center bombing.

According to the *New York Times*, in 1992 and early 1993 an FBI informant named Emad Salem was involved with Middle Eastern terrorists connected to Osama bin Laden. They were developing a bomb for use against New York's World Trade Center. Salem, a 43-year-old former Egyptian Army officer, wanted to substitute a harmless powder for the explosive but his plan to thwart the attack was blocked by an FBI official who apparently did not want to expose the inside informant. The attack was allowed to proceed. The February 26, 1993 explosion in the WTC resulted in six deaths, more than 1,000 casualties and damage in excess of a half billion dollars.

Salem said he wanted to complain to FBI Headquarters in Washington but was dissuaded from doing so by another FBI agent. Salem said the agent told him, "I don't think that the New York [FBI] people would like the things out of the New York Office to go to Washington, D.C." It was also reported that the FBI repeatedly attempted to lay blame for the attack on the UN Mission from Sudan.

"[I]n 1992 and 1993, the New York City FBI informant and agent provocateur Emad Salem repeatedly tried to implicate the Sudanese UN Mission in his own 'Islamic terror cell' World Trade Center bomb plot conspiracy," noted author Webster Griffin Tarpley. "Here we see how a false flag terror cell sheep-dips [covers up the true background of] its dupes [and brings them] into contact with a target, which then becomes the object of a police investigation, and possibly later of military attack."

Tarpley also pointed out that when authorities searched the apartment of El Sayyid Nosair, suspected of the 1990 assassination of New York City Rabbi Meir Kahane, they found training manuals from the Army Special Warfare School at Fort Bragg and copies of teletypes going to the Secretary of the Army and the Joint Chiefs of Staff. "Clearly,

[Nosair] had a source in a sensitive position in the US military..." Tarpley wrote. "Much more likely, his terrorist controller occupied a sensitive position in the US military..."

False flag operations, the use of agents provocateur, misdirecting public opinion—we now see that fabricating crises to further political goals is a methodology well understood and utilized in the 20th century. Was this the game on 9/11? Was Osama bin Laden merely substituted for Fidel Castro or some other enemy of the moment?

WAR AS AN ECONOMIC STIMULUS

Even the most cursory examination of past military actions shows a distinct correlation between such warfare and the national economy. Marine Major General Smedley D. Butler, writing in the 1930s, stated, "War is a racket...War is largely a matter of money. Bankers lend money to foreign countries and when they cannot pay, the President sends Marines to get it."

In the same vein, many historians and economists have argued that America's emergence from the Great Depression was made only possible because of World War II.

The controversial *Report From Iron Mountain* is prophetic on this point. This secret 1963 policy paper, leaked to the press and later published as a book in 1967, makes clear that war is not only necessary to maintain societal control but to prop up a sagging financial system. The study that led to this famous white paper reportedly began in 1961 with Kennedy administration officials such as McGeorge Bundy (CFR, Bilderberger and Skull and Bones), Robert McNamara (Trilateralist, CFR and Bilderberger) and Dean Rusk (CFR and Bilderberger). Knowing of Kennedy's goal of ending the Cold War, these men were concerned that there had been no serious planning for long-term peace.

Although denounced as a literary hoax in some circles, *Report From Iron Mountain* is an amazing document, written at the onset of our national experience in Vietnam. It most certainly reflects the elitist views of those who are said to have solicited the study.

According to the report, "War itself is the basic social system, within which other secondary modes of social organization conflict or conspire. It is the system which has governed most human societies of record, as it is today." The report's authors saw war as both necessary and desirable as "the principal organizing force" as well as "the essential economic stabilizer of modern societies."

The report writers concluded, "...we must first reply, as strongly as we can, that the war system cannot responsibly be allowed to disappear until (1) we know exactly what (forms of social control) we plan to put in its place and (2) we are certain, beyond reasonable doubt, that these substitute institutions will serve their purposes..."

Most significantly, the report states, "The elimination of war implies the inevitable elimination of national sovereignty and the traditional nation-state," and added, "The possibility of war provides the sense of external necessity without which no government can long remain in power...The basic authority of a modern state over its people resides in its war powers."

The report goes on to say that war "has served as the last great safeguard against the elimination of necessary social classes"... and war functions serve to control "essential class relationships."

A former high-ranking Pentagon officer, Col. Donn de Grand Pre, who worked for Robert McNamara in the early 1960s, stated in a 2001 interview, "One of the policy makers that I was associated with at the time—for good or for ill—was Henry Kissinger. At that time Henry was an untenured professor at Harvard University and he was also working for the Operations Research Office at the Pentagon, which was paying him a stipend for that work. Simultaneously, Henry was also working for the Council on Foreign Relations under Nelson Rockefeller...Henry would come to the Pentagon and since my boss, General [Robert] York was his contact there, I became Henry's contact [while Gen. York was off on a lengthy study in Vietnam]. It evolved into informal luncheons where Henry would come down from the Hudson Institute, which is close to Iron Mountain, where he and 14 others were working on this study. Henry was a little bit reluctant to talk about this study, but he gave us enough information to enable us to realize that there was such a study going on. It lasted anywhere from eight to 10 months....The Iron Mountain study was not fiction by any means.

"Here was the overall purpose of the study: to analyze different ways a government can perpetuate itself in power, control its citizens and prevent them from rebelling. Their major conclusion was that, in the past, war was the only reliable means to achieve that goal. Remember, this study was in the process of being formulated in early 1963. Kissinger's intellectual buddies from Harvard and also from Yale were already formulating this no-win war in Vietnam."

Regardless of its origin, the tone of the *Report* is certainly conspiratorial and it most certainly reflects the mindset and class-conscious views of men connected to the secret societies. These same men were responsible for the involvement of America in Vietnam in the 1960s and 1970s and their mindset was behind the attempt to foment war in Central America in the 1980s as well as the conflicts of the 1990s in the Middle East and Balkans. Is what we are seeing in Iraq and Afghanistan today merely a continuation of the policies of such men?

Shortly after the 9/11 attacks, the London *Observer* revealed one indication of the behind-the-scenes manipulation that takes place to support an ever-more-centralized world economy. According to this newspaper, a "secretive committee," called the Working Group on Financial Markets, was prepared to coordinate intervention by the Federal Reserve on "an unprecedented scale" when the markets opened a week after the events of 9/11.

Unofficially called "the plunge protection team," this group, made up of bankers and representatives of the New York Stock Exchange, NASDAQ and the US Treasury, was prepared to spend billions of dollars to purchase equities from mutual funds and other institutional sellers if panic selling had taken place. This was a plan in readiness to prevent a replay of the stock market crashes of 1929 and 1987.

The "plunge protection team" was created by a special executive order of President Ronald Reagan in 1989. "It is known to include senior bankers at leading Wall Street institutions such as Merrill Lynch and Goldman Sachs. It has acted before, in the early 1990s and during the 1998...hedge fund crisis," noted *Observer* reporter Richard Wachman.

We've noted that Georgia Democratic Rep. Cynthia McKinney was figuratively eviscerated in the mass media for charging that friends of George W. Bush and other corporate big wigs were profiting from the

War on Terrorism.

Yet on December 20, 2001, when war hero Senator John McCain chided his fellow senators about pork and profits accumulated since 9/11, there was no comparable media reaction. McCain was particularly miffed at a proposal to lease 100 Boeing 767s as refueling tankers for 10 years and then spend $30 million to reconfigure the planes as commercial airliners and return them to Boeing. "This is the wrong thing to do," groused McCain. "We're going to spend $20 billion plus over a 10-year period and 10 years from now are going to have nothing to show for it."

"This kind of behavior cannot go on," he later told the Senate. "You will lose the confidence of the American people. This is called war profiteering."

There was no hand wringing by the mass media about his comments. Only on several Internet sites and in some alternative media were there snickers of understanding. For some time, rumors had flown that Boeing was being offered a sweetheart money package as a bribe to keep quiet about the fatal crash of TWA 800.

Controversy has continued to swirl around the crash, which involved a Boeing 747 passenger jetliner that crashed off Long Island on July 17, 1996. Although hundreds of witnesses reported seeing a streak in the sky prior to the plane exploding and the fact that military exercises were being conducted in the area at the time, the government concluded that a spark had somehow gotten into a central fuel tank and caused the explosion which killed 230 passengers and crew.

Books, magazine articles and the Internet have been filled with speculation that TWA 800 was accidentally shot down when its late departure took it into a weapons testing zone. Boeing officials initially objected to the conclusion that somehow their craft were defective, yet later became strangely silent giving birth to rumors that the aircraft company was being paid off for its silence.

The last minute and little publicized add-on to a defense spending bill which caused McCain such concern only added to such speculation. Apparently McCain and other senators had not heard this speculation. Junior Senator Rick Santorum of Pennsylvania naively asked a colleague why the Air Force could not simply keep the Boeing 767s after they were paid for. He was told, "We can't do that. It will queer the deal."

In the wake of the 9/11 attacks, Americans were asked to give up many things including some Constitutional rights in the War on Terrorism. However, government contractors, especially those delivering military goods, gave up nothing. If fact, they gained plenty, even those companies that had been caught in past scandals.

Take the Lockheed Aircraft Company, for example. In the mid-1970s, Prince Bernhard of the Netherlands was forced to resign from the secretive and exclusive Bilderbergers, which represented the inner core elite of more than one secret society. In London, just after World War II, Lord Rothschild and Dr. Joseph Hieronim Retinger encouraged Prince Bernhard to create the Bilderberger group. The prince personally chaired the group until 1976 when he resigned following revelations that he had accepted large payoffs from Lockheed to promote the sale of its aircraft in Holland. Today, Texaco Inc. has sold its US gas stations to Dutch Shell, drawing yet another American firm into even closer ties with the global economy.

Despite the bribery scandal involving the Dutch prince and other public officials worldwide, Lockheed continued to enjoy the largess of the US government. Despite pledges to institute ethical reforms, Lockheed officials again came under fire in the mid-1990s. The company pled guilty to making payoffs to an Egyptian official to win approval for a deal involving C-130 cargo planes.

Since 1995, Lockheed, which has since changed its name to Lockheed Martin, has been named in 33 more court cases involving charges of overcharging on government contracts, improper technology transfers to China, falsifying the results of nuclear safety tests, job discrimination, environmental pollution and more.

This dismal public record did not deter the US government, from awarding Lockheed Martin a contract in October 2001 to build the nation's newest military jet, the F-35 Joint Strike Fighter. The contract was expected to exceed $200 billion during its decades-long life. It was called "the richest military contract in history."

Lockheed Martin and the previously discussed Halliburton are not alone in repeatedly violating both laws and regulations while continuing to collect vast amounts of public money. According to *US News & World Report*, "In the past dozen years, 30 of the 43 largest federal contractors have racked up more than 400 enforcement cases, resulting in at least 28 criminal convictions, 286 civil settlements, mostly involving their government contracts...Allegations included price fixing, bogus testing, polluting, overcharging, hiding product defects, violating export laws and withholding financial data from the government. They also represent more than accounting quibbles: Company workers have been killed and seriously injured and national security potentially put at risk."

Yet four out of every ten federal procurement dollars go to these same companies. "If it was a food-stamp recipient, they'd go to jail," complained Oregon Democrat Rep. Peter DeFazio. "It's an extraordinary double standard."

In research conducted by *US News & World Report*, it was determined that only one of the government's 30 largest contractors—General Electric Co.—has ever been denied new contracts and that punishment only lasted a few days.

Due to the cost, bureaucratic paperwork and apparent indifference— not to mention undiscovered bribes—no government agency keeps tabs on which company has broken the law. So the fat contracts just keep coming.

Following the trend of the big corporations getting bigger, many defense contractors have merged into huge multinational entities, making it even more difficult for government watchdogs to detect unlawful activities and make cases. No one—either in the major news media or the government—seems capable of determining exactly which individuals are in control of these corporate behemoths.

With the sudden and burgeoning national defense buildup following the 9/11 attacks, no one expects these corporate zebras to change their stripes any time soon.

But perhaps a better way to increase cash flow these days is just to— steal it.

Soon after the events of 9/11, as the dot.com bubble was bursting, and as Americans watched the unfolding of the greatest wave of corporate accounting scandals in the history of the country that were epitomized by the fall of President Bush's friends at Enron, an even larger accounting scandal was somehow lost in the shuffle of egregious corruption in Washington. According to reliable estimates from within the government itself, the Department of Defense (DoD) and other departments of the federal government were unable to account for trillions—yes trillions—in missing funds.

In a January 29, 2002 article entitled "The War on Waste," CBS News quoted Secretary of Defense Donald Rumsfeld as admitting that, "according to some estimates we cannot track $2.3 trillion in transactions."

It seems that on September 10, 2001, Secretary of Defense Rumsfeld had held a press conference to announce the problem. According to CBS, Rumsfeld said that, "the money wasted by the military poses a serious threat. In fact, it could be said it's a matter of life and death."

CBS then got to the punchline: "Rumsfeld promised change but the next day—September 11—the world changed and in the rush to fund the war on terrorism, the war on waste seems to have been forgotten."

One can only imagine that, if there were any problems with defense appropriations in Congress over the missing money on September 10, the events of 9/11 put a quick end to any Congressman's hesitation to authorize fresh new funds for defense contractors.

One of those most responsible for bringing this and other government accounting scandals to light was Catherine Austin Fitts, former managing director of Wall Street investment bank Dillon, Read and former Housing and Urban Development (HUD) assistant secretary in the first Bush administration. Fitts is now a well-known federal whistleblower and economic reformer whose website, whereisthemoney.org, details the missing-money scandal at both the DoD and HUD, including quotes like this from David K. Steensma of the DoD's Inspector General office: "We reported that DoD processed $1.1 trillion in unsupported accounting entries to...DoD financial statements for FY 2000."

Fitts said the figure actually tops $3 trillion: "Total undocumented accounting adjustments for reported periods for the Department of Defense [and HUD for fiscal 1998-2000] amount to a whopping $3.3 trillion, or $11,700 for every American. The Department of Defense has failed to produce independent audited financial statements since the requirement went into effect in 1995."

At least $59 billion was also missing at HUD, said Fitts, as its Inspector General had refused—for starters—to certify HUD's fiscal 1999 financial statements. Characterizing the depths of the scandal, Fitts said that

Americans are "at the mercy of a group of creditors who are our creditors because they are financing us with the money they stole from our public and private pension funds."

At her website solari.com, and in other writings and lectures, Fitts has explained that, beginning with the savings and loan scandal in the 1980's which involved the stripping of nearly $500 billion from banks and government, criminalized insider elites began a rise to power that is now epitomized by their perpetration of 9/11. Now in a greater position of power in the 1990's, "these same syndicates then stripped an estimated $6 trillion of investors' value in pump and dump stock market and mortgage market schemes and an estimated $4 trillion of taxpayer money." Where has the $10 trillion gone? Most likely, says Fitts, into offshore accounts that will be used to buy up assets back on shore once these elites have engineered the destruction of the dollar.

Meanwhile, the grand plan of globalization and centralization of the world's economy as envisioned by the globalists within the Trilateral Commission and Council on Foreign Relations continued.

Following in the footsteps of their successful effort to combine the once sovereign nations of Europe into one union, the globalists today are putting into place a "North American Union," all without any authorization, oversight or funding by the US Congress.

Under a CFR-sponsored unilateral agreement called the Security and Prosperity Partnership, signed by President Bush, Mexican President Vincente Fox and then-Prime Minister of Canada Paul Martin at Waco, Texas, in March, 2005, the United States, Mexico and Canada are being merged into one economic bloc.

Concurrently, public hearings were underway in Texas and other affected states for the construction of a CanaMex or NAFTA [North American Free Trade Area] superhighway stretching from southern Mexico up through the Midwest and into Canada. All this under the supervison of the North American Superhighway Coalition composed of representatives from Texas, Oklahoma, Kansas, Iowa, Missouri, the Ambassador Bridge, various federal agencies and private firms. Two attempts to pass legislation authorizing this unilateral partnership in Congress failed and there has been precious little accounts of this effort in the corporate mass media.

Randy Ghent, one of a growing number of opponents to the CanaMex Superhighway, stated, "I couldn't think of a more disastrous project if I had to think all year."

Critics say the NAFTA Superhighway scheme would add to air pollution, traffic congestion, oil dependence, global warming, roadkill and human death. Local economics and quality of life would suffer, as development moves from town centers to narrow strips along the highway while noting that NAFTA activities already have caused corporate exodus to the south, robbing the United States of more than 600,000 jobs. There is already talk of creating a "North American Parliament" to deal with the new economic union.

NAFTA and the WTO agreements have encouraged companies to move out of the country and social services continued to lag behind demand. Additionally, tremendous amounts of money including criminalized cash flows were flowing through the military-industrial complex and primarily into large corporate accounts, or into the private hands of the cronies and accomplices of the criminalized elites.

Detectives long have used the question of qui bono, who benefits, as the beginning of their investigation. Journalists also use this method, often couching it in the old adage, "Follow the money."

THE MASS MEDIA

B ut don't look to the corporate mass media to seek truth about the War on Terrorism or the missing money. Corporate behemoths— be they media or energy or military contractors—share the same status-quo interests as the government, and for the corporate media to broadcast anything that might depart too far from the official government story about 9/11 and its aftermath is simply not in their interest.

But by 2006, as egregious problems caused by the Bush regime became all too obvious, certain elements within the mass media were willing to question Bush's policies, particularly after his unconstitutional spying and support for turning management of important sea ports over to a nation with known terrorist ties. But early on, the mainstream media stood with the government.

For example, Fairness & Accuracy in Reporting (FAIR) noted that on October 10, 2001, network executives representing ABC, NBC, CBS, Fox and CNN were involved in a conference call with then National Security Adviser and Council on Foreign Relations heavyweight Condoleezza Rice. The executives apparently agreed to limit how and what they would broadcast regarding bin Laden or his al Qaeda group. Bush people even tried unsuccessfully to have al Jazeera, described as the "CNN of the Mideast," tone down its coverage of bin Laden. When this effort failed, al Jazeera was "accidentally" bombed off the air by US military warplanes.

The Bush administration's effort to block any far-reaching inquiry was even more successful with members of Congress. Free speech was curtailed when they threatened to cut off intelligence reports to legislators who spoke offhandedly to the media. Then White House spokesman Ari Fleischer, already on the record saying Americans "need to watch what they say," extended this constraint by contacting major newspapers asking that they not print full transcripts of bin Laden's interviews.

According to a FAIR news release, "The point is not that bin Laden or al Qaeda deserve 'equal time' on US news broadcasts, but that it is troubling for the government to shape or influence news content. Withholding information from the public is hardly patriotic. When the White House insists that it's dangerous to report a news event 'in its entirety,' alarm bells should go off for journalists and the American public alike."

Another small, but insightful, example of the media glossing over 9/11 issues and questions came on April 18, 2002, when Associated Press writer Sheila Hotchkin reported on the relatives of the victims of Flight 93 who were allowed by the government to listen to cockpit audio tapes from the doomed plane. No reporters were allowed in and the relatives were encouraged not to speak to the media.

But a few did, such as Hamilton Peterson, whose father, Donald A. Peterson, had perished in the crash. In an initial version of the story, Hotchkin quoted Peterson as saying "he learned things from the tape he did not know before, but declined to elaborate." By the next day, Peterson's observation regarding things he had not known was deleted from news accounts. What did Peterson learn that the rest of us are forbidden to know? Who is behind this mass media control? As noted earlier, the tape was played once again for the jury at the Zacarias Moussaoui trial in April of

2006. A transcript that included English translations of Arabic statements that were alleged to have been made by the hijackers was made available to the public at that time, but the recording itself was withheld.

Particular attention should be paid to the five major corporations, which dominate the American mass media—GE, The Walt Disney Co., Viacom/CBS, News Corp. and Time Warner. This represents a concentration of media power unthinkable prior to the Clinton years.

One of the few members of Congress to address this monopoly of the news media by an increasingly small number of giant corporations was Rep. Bernie Sanders, an independent from Vermont.

"[O]ne of the best-kept secrets is the degree to which a handful of huge corporations control the flow of information in the United States. Whether it is television, radio, newspapers, magazines, books or the Internet, a few giant conglomerates are determining what we see, hear and read," he said.

During the 1990s, "Telecommunication firms were engaged in the most visible and dramatic drive for corporate alliance and consolidation," wrote author William Greider in *One World, Ready or Not*. "AT&T, Time Warner, TCI, MCI, Ameritech and Nynex, CBS, ABC, Disney and many others—the overlapping deals were stunning as US firms rushed to unite market power and technological assets in cable and telephone systems, broadcasting, film-making, publishing and other media, while simultaneously forging telecom partnerships abroad. US consumers would provide the capital for these huge new conglomerates through the deregulated rates they paid to cable and telephone companies. The winners, it was clear, would be a handful of broad and powerful media combines, as dominant as the railroad and oil trusts were in the 1890s."

In 2005, a Project Censored team researched the board members of 10 major media organizations from newspaper to television to radio. Of these ten organizations, they found there are a mere 118 people sitting on 288 different American and international corporate boards. This study proved the close interlocking of big media and corporate America.

"We found media directors who also were former Senators or Representatives in the House such as Sam Nunn (Disney) and William Cohen (Viacom). Board members served at the FCC such as William Kennard (*New York Times*) and Dennis FitzSimmons (Tribune Company) showing revolving door relationships with big media and US government officials," stated the report, adding, "These ten big media organizations are the main source of news for most Americans. Their corporate ties require us to continually scrutinize the quality of their news for bias. Disney owns ABC so we wonder how the board of Disney reacts to negative news about their board of directors' friends such as Halliburton or Boeing. We see board members with connections to Ford, Kraft, and Kimberly-Clark who employ tens of thousands of Americans. Is it possible that the US workforce receives only the corporate news private companies want them to hear? Do we collectively realize that working people in the US have longer hours, lower pay and fewer benefits than their foreign counterparts? If these companies control the media, they control the dissemination of news turning the First Amendment on its head by protecting corporate interests over people."

Apart from the corporate concentration of media ownership there is a corporate bureaucracy that rewards mediocrity and conformity while stifling initiative and hard-hitting investigative journalism.

"Much of what is reported as 'news' is little more than the uncritical transmission of official opinions to an unsuspecting public," wrote media critic Michael Parenti.

"What [reporters] pass off as objectivity is just a mindless kind of neutrality," said journalist Brit Hume, who added reporters "shouldn't try to be objective, they should try to be honest."

The power of this combined media behemoth is overwhelming.

According to recent studies, the average American spends nearly half of his/her waking hours with some form of the major consumer media—TV, radio, Internet, newspapers, magazines, recorded music, DVDs/VHS tapes, video games and books. It is projected that by the end of 2007 this time spent on media will only increase, mostly on the Net.

Studies in 2006 posted at medialiteracy.com revealed that the typical American spends more than four hours a day watching TV, two and a half hours listening to radio, more than 30 minutes on the Internet, about one hour listening to recorded music and reading newspapers, 20 minutes reading magazines and 17 minutes reading books.

Over and above this increasing consumer usage and ownership consolidation, there is a corresponding decrease in the number of distribution companies, critical to the widespread dissemination of information. *Standard & Poor's* editors noted that for years distribution problems caused by the consolidation of formerly independent distributors "disrupted deliveries and relationships with retail clients...canceled, missed and late deliveries were common occurrences." Authors have complained for years that books on controversial subjects always seem to encounter distribution or publicity problems. With an estimated 800 new magazines added each year to the existing 18,000 or so (most fail within the first year), it is easy to understand the importance of distribution.

Major banks, most controlled by secret society members, own significant amounts of stock in the ever-decreasing number of media corporations. "Through elite policy-shaping groups like the Council on Foreign Relations and the Business Roundtable, they steer the ship of state in what they deem to be a financially advantageous direction," noted authors Martin A. Lee and Norman Solomon in 1990. "GE, CapCities, CBS, the *New York Times* and the *Washington Post* all have board members who sit on the Council on Foreign Relations."

Little has changed today. A cursory glance at the *Standard & Poor's Corporation Records* shows CFR and Trilateral members sit on the boards of the major media corporations.

Corporate ownership intermingled with secret society members, many of whom are employed in the media, may explain why Bilderberg, Trilateral and CFR meetings are not reported by America's "watchdog" media. In fact, the membership lists of these societies read like a "Who's Who" of the mass media.

These members include many past and present media corporate leaders such as Laurence A. Tisch and William Paley of CBS; John F. Welch, Jr., of GE/NBC; Thomas S. Murphy of ABC; Robert McNeil, Jim Lehrer, Hodding Carter III and Daniel Schorr of Public Broadcast Service; Katherine Graham, Harold Anderson and Stanley Swinton of the Associated Press; Michael Posner of Reuters; Joan Ganz Cooney of Children's TV Workshop (Sesame Street); W. Thomas Johnson of CNN; David Gergen of *US News & World Report*; Richard Gelb, William Scranton, Cyrus Vance, A. M. Rosenthal and Harrison Salisbury of the *New York Times*; Ralph Davidson, Henry Grunwald, Sol Linowitz and Strobe Talbott of *Time*; Robert Christopher and Phillip Geyelin of *Newsweek*; Katherine Graham,

Leonard Downie Jr. and Stephen S. Rosenfeld of the *Washington Post*; Arnaud de Borchgrave of the *Washington Times*; Richard Wood, Robert Bartley and Karen House of the *Wall Street Journal*; William F. Buckley Jr. of *National Review* and George V. Grune and William G. Bowen of *Reader's Digest*. Furthermore, sitting on the boards of directors of the corporations, which own the media are multiple secret society members.

Some of the well-known reporters, anchors and columnists who are members of the CFR and/or the Trilateral Commission include Dan Rather, C. C. Collinwood, Diane Sawyer, David Brinkley, Ted Koppel, Barbara Walters, John Chancellor, Marvin Kalb, Daniel Schorr, Joseph Kraft, James Reston, Max Frankel, David Halberstam, Harrison Salisbury, A. Ochs Sulzberger, Sol Linowitz, Nicholas Katzenbach, George Will, Tom Brokaw, Robert McNeil, David Gergen, Mortimer Zuckerman, Georgie Ann Geyer and many others. Small wonder so many researchers see a conspiracy of silence among these media peers.

Then there are "media watchdog" organizations such as Accuracy in Media (AIM). Many persons assume such groups are watching out for the public's interests. Not according to writer Michael Collins Piper, who in 1990 made public that AIM founder Reed Irvine was paid $37,000 a year as an "adviser for the division of international finance" of the Federal Reserve System. Noting that many Fed members also belong to the secret societies, Piper wrote, "To this day, Irvine and AIM never touch on any subject which is sensitive to the interests of the international Establishment: whether it be the Bilderberger group, the Trilateral Commission, the Council on Foreign Relations or the truth about the privately owned Federal Reserve."

There are also choke points within the flow of information, such as the international desk at Associated Press headquarters in New York where one person decides what news from outside the United States makes it onto the wire service. It is important to understand that the real control over the mass media is not direct control over the thousands of hardworking editors, reporters and news directors throughout the nation, but rather the control over the distribution of the information. If one doesn't see or hear about a story, to them it didn't happen.

Then there is the tremendous pressure created by fear of job security and loss of sources. Many national columnists must rely on insider sources to provide juicy information. Much of this information comes from government sources, which would dry up if they published the wrong story. Even the more hard-hitting national reporters still must pull their punches if they want to maintain their insider sources.

The ever-concentrated corporate ownership of the media has meant objective news, long viewed as a public service, flies out the window in favor of bottom-line profits based on ratings. At the time of the JFK assassination, the three major TV networks—ABC, CBS and NBC—supported their news departments with public service funds. Today, these same news departments are funded as programming with a resultant concern over ratings. News today is "a kind of commodity in the marketplace, no longer a holy profession," commented former CBS correspondent Daniel Schorr, "Today, it doesn't matter anymore. You just make your money and to hell with public service."

Veteran newsman Walter Cronkite agreed. Quoted in a professional journal, he said the current state of television journalism is "disastrous and dangerous" and decried "unreasonable profits...to satisfy shareholders." "[I]n demanding a profit similar to that of the entertainment area, they're dragging us all down."

"I challenge any viewer to make the distinction between [TV talk show host] Jerry Springer and the three evening newses and CNN," commented *60 Minutes* correspondent Morley Safer.

The watchdog media in America, as they like to portray themselves, appear to be more like lap dogs to their corporate owners. This can be seen in a quick glance at Project Censored, a yearly posting of stories judged to be of importance to the public but which are ignored, downplayed or "spiked" by the major mass media corporations. Project Censored is conducted through a media research group at Sonoma State University. Nearly 200 members of the faculty and student body reviewed nearly a thousand nominations from national journalists and academics.

According to this study, the top censored stories of 2005-2006 were:

1. Bush Administration Moves to Eliminate Open Government
2. Media Coverage Fails on Iraq: Fallujah and the Civilian Deaths
3. Another Year of Distorted Election Coverage
4. Surveillance Society Quietly Moves In
5. US Uses Tsunami to Military Advantage in Southeast Asia

6. The Real Oil for Food Scam
7. Journalists Face Unprecedented Dangers to Life and Livelihood
8. Iraqi Farmers Threatened By Bremer's Mandates
9. Iran's New Oil Trade System Challenges US Currency
10. Mountaintop Removal Threatens Ecosystem and Economy
11. Universal Mental Screening Program Usurps Parental Rights
12. Military in Iraq Contracts Human Rights Violators
13. Rich Countries Fail to Live up to Global Pledges
14. Corporations Win Big on Tort Reform, Justice Suffers
15. Conservative Plan to Override Academic Freedom in the Classroom
16. US Plans for Hemispheric Integration Include Canada
17. US Uses South American Military Bases to Expand Control of the Region
18. Little Known Stock Fraud Could Weaken US Economy
19. Child Wards of the State Used in AIDS Experiments
20. American Indians Sue for Resources; Compensation Provided to Others
21. New Immigration Plan Favors Business Over People
22. Nanotechnology Offers Exciting Possibilities But Health Effects Need Scrutiny
23. Plight of Palestinian Child Detainees Highlights Global Problem
24. Ethiopian Indigenous Victims of Corporate and Government Resource Aspirations
25. Homeland Security Was Designed to Fail

The censored list clearly shows that the bulk of such stories concern US foreign policy, misdeeds by American businesses or the steady globalization of both government and multinational corporations.

"The first step in liquidating a people is to erase its memory. Destroy its books, its culture, its history. Then have somebody write new books, manufacture a new culture, invent a new history. Before long the nation will begin to forget what it is and what it was," wrote Czech author Milan Kundera about life under communist dictatorship in *The Book of Laughter and Forgetting*.

A DISMAL FOREIGN POLICY RECORD

Osama bin Laden has alleged that US foreign policy attempts to enslave other nations. It this an outrageous lie or could some truth be found in his statement?

A serious study of United States foreign policy since World War II indeed presents a picture that is contrary to the image that the US promotes peace, democracy, and prosperity overseas, as is often envisaged by the American public.

"I don't think we, the American people, deserved what happened [on 9/11]. Nor do we deserve the sort of governments we have had over the last 40 years," said Gore Vidal in a mid-2002 interview. "Our governments have brought this upon us by their actions all over the world... Unfortunately, we only get disinformation from the *New York Times* and other official places. Americans have no idea of the extent of their government's mischief. The number of military strikes we have made unprovoked, against other countries, since 1947-48 is more than 250. These are major strikes everywhere from Panama to Iran. And it isn't even a complete list. It doesn't include places like Chile, as that was a CIA operation. I was only listing military attacks."

As confirmed by the *New York Times* years ago, US foreign policy has been in the hands of the Council on Foreign Relations elite since at least 1939. In addition to the media corporate leaders, mainstream reporters and anchors listed above, this elite and its associates include present and former government officials such as Presidents George H. W. Bush, Bill Clinton, Gerald Ford, Jimmy Carter and Richard Nixon, virtually every CIA director, as well as a considerable number of familiar past and present government officials such as Dick Cheney, Henry Kissinger, Wesley Clark, Strobe Talbott, Alexander Haig, Alan Greenspan, Bruce Babbitt, James A. Baker III, Sandy Berger, Colin Powell, Harold Brown, Zbigniew Brzezinski, Frank C. Carlucci, Richard Darman, John Deutch, Lawrence Eagleburger, Robert McFarlane, Brent Scowcroft, Condoleezza Rice and Casper Weinberger.

Within three hours after the attacks of 9/11, Kissinger, Talbot, Clark and Haig were all prominently seen on both CNN and the broadcast networks. Their message was so similar that one would have thought they were reading from the same CFR script: The attacks were terrible, something must be done, terrorism transcends national boundaries and therefore all the nations must come together under the United Nations to successfully combat this new type of warfare.

This clarion call was seen by some as nothing more than an effort to use the 9/11 tragedy as another reason to perpetuate the disastrous status quo of foreign policy: support for America's ongoing policy of neo-colonialism; the use of the United Nations as a tool in that strategy; the political subjugation and control of other nations through military dictators or wealthy families supported by, and often placed in power, by the US military or intelligence services; and the wholesale stripping away of the native wealth of other nations, including the US itself, through the kind of economic globalization and financial centralization that has been promoted by CFR elites for decades.

But as the very phenomenon of 9/11 itself reveals, the result of this empire-building policy has been dismal at best and catastrophic at worst.

Never mind the historical aggression displayed by American foreign policy in the Mexican War of 1848 and the Spanish-American War of 1898. Consider this selection of our misguided foreign policy adventures just since World War II:

In 1953, a few years after Iran's Prime Minister Mohammed Mossadegh engaged in a gradual and lawful nationalization of the oil industry in that Mideast nation, he and his democratic government were deposed by a coup instigated by the CIA. This brought the Shah to power, with the monarchy assuming complete control in 1963, and turning Iran into a client state of the US. Thousands of Iranians, perhaps millions, died during the repressive rule of the Shah and his brutal SAVAK secret police. The Shah was finally forced out in 1979 by the Ayatollah Khomeini, who quickly became the US's latest foreign enemy despite the fact that he had been on the CIA payroll while living in Paris. The Shah was granted asylum in the United States and a medieval version of Islam took control over Iran.

In Guatemala in 1954, the CIA toppled the popularly elected government of Jacobo Arbenz, which had nationalized United Fruit property. Prominent American government officials such as former CIA Director

Walter Bedell Smith, then CIA Director Allen Dulles, Secretary of State for Inter-American Affairs John Moors Cabot and Secretary of State John Foster Dulles were all closely connected to United Fruit. An estimated 120,000 Guatemalan peasants died in the resulting military dictatorships.

Fidel Castro, with covert aid from the CIA, overthrew the military dictatorship of Fulgencio Batista and instituted sweeping land, industrial and educational reforms as well as nationalizing American businesses. Swiftly labeled a communist, the CIA then organized anti-Castro Cubans resulting in numerous attacks on Cuba and the failed Bay of Pigs Invasion in 1961. The island nation has been the object of US economic sanctions since that time.

More than 3,000 persons died in the wake of an invasion of the Dominican Republic by US Marines in 1965. The troops ostensibly were sent to prevent a communist takeover, although later it was admitted that there had been no proof of such a takeover.

Also in 1965, the US began the bombing of North Vietnam after President Lyndon Johnson proclaimed the civil war there an "aggression" by the north. Two years later, American troop strength in Vietnam had grown to 380,000, and soon after climbed to more than 500,000. US dead by the end of that Asian war totaled some 58,000, with casualties to the Vietnamese, both north and south, running into the millions.

In 1968, General Sukarno, the unifier of Indonesia, was overthrown by General Suharto, again with aid from the CIA. Suharto proved more dictatorial and corrupt than his predecessor. A reported 800,000 people died during his regime. Another 250,000 persons died in 1975 during the brutal invasion of East Timor by the Suharto regime aided by the US Government and Henry Kissinger.

In 1973, the elected government of Salvador Allende in Chile was overthrown by a military coup aided by the CIA. Allende was killed and some 30,000 persons died in subsequent violence and repression, including some Americans. Chile was brought back into the sphere of influence of the US and remained a military dictatorship for the next two decades.

In 1979, the powerful and corrupt Somoza family, which had ruled Nicaragua since 1937, was finally overthrown and Daniel Ortega was elected president. But CIA-backed Contra insurgents operating from Honduras fought a protracted war to oust the Ortega government in which an estimated 30,000 people died. The ensuing struggle came to include such shady dealing in arms and drugs that it created a scandal in the United States called Iran-Contra, which involved persons connected to the National Security Council selling arms to Iran, then using the profits to buy drugs in support of the Contras. All of those indicted or convicted of crimes in this scandal were pardoned by then President George H.W. Bush.

US Marines landed in Lebanon in 1982 in an attempt to prevent further bloodshed between occupying Israeli troops and the Palestine Liberation Organization. Thousands died in the resulting civil war, including hundreds of Palestinians massacred in refugee camps by right-wing Christian forces while Ariel Sharon, then an Israeli General, looked on in apparent approval. Despite the battleship shelling of Beirut, and the destruction of that great Mediterranean city, American forces were withdrawn in 1984 after a series of bloody attacks on them. More than two decades later, the conflict between Israel and the Palestinians remains as intractable and deadly as ever, in large part due to the virtually unconditional support of Israel by the US, which has been institutionalized by the Israel lobby discussed in Part I of this book.

In 1983, US troops invaded the tiny Caribbean island nation of Grenada after a leftist government was installed. The official explanation was to rescue a handful of American students who initially said they didn't need rescuing. The only real damage inflicted in this tiny war was to a mental health hospital partly owned by a White House physician and widely reported to be a CIA facility.

During the 1970s and 1980s, the US Government gave aid and arms to the right wing government of the Republic of El Salvador, which represented the financial interests of a tiny oligarchy, for use against its leftist enemies. By 1988, some 70,000 Salvadorans had died.

More than one million persons died in the 15-year battle in Angola between the Marxist government aided by Cuban troops and the National Union for the Total Independence of Angola, supported by South Africa and the US Government.

When Muammur al-Qaddafi tried to socialize the oil-rich North African nation of Libya beginning with his takeover in 1969, he drew the wrath of the US Government. In 1981, it was claimed that Qaddafi had sent hit teams to the United States to assassinate President Reagan and in 1986, following the withdrawal of US oil companies from Libya, an air attack was launched which missed Qaddafi but killed several people including his infant daughter.

In 1987, an Iraqi missile attack on the US frigate *Stark* resulted in 37 deaths. Shortly afterward, Iraqi officials apologized for the incident. In 1988, a US Navy ship shot down an Iranian airliner over the Persian Gulf resulting in 290 deaths. The Reagan Administration simply called it a mistake.

Thousands of freedom-seeking Chinese were killed in Beijing's Tiananmen Square in 1989 after government hardliners there conferred with former President Richard Nixon on how to deal with the dissidents. Nixon, of course, was the only US president to resign under threat of criminal indictment and was in power during the shooting of students at Kent State University on May 4, 1970.

As many as 8,000 Panamanians died over Christmas 1989, when President George H. W. Bush sent US troops to invade that Central American nation to arrest his former business partner, Manuel Noriega. The excuse was that Noriega was involved in the importation of drugs to the United States. *US News & World Report* noted that in 1990, the amount of drugs moving through Panama had doubled.

We noted previously that Iraqi casualties, both military and civilian, totaled more than 300,000 during the short Persian Gulf War of 1991. It has been estimated that more than one million Iraqis, including women and children, have died as a result of the continued missile and air attacks (not including those killed since the US invasion in 2003) as well as economic sanctions against that nation.

Also in 1991, the United States suspended assistance to Haiti after the election of a liberal priest sparked military action and disorder. Eventually, US troops were deployed. Once again in 2004, the US fomented and backed the toppling of the same democratically elected president and replaced him with an unelected gang of militarists, CIA operatives, and corporate predators.

Other nations that have felt the brunt of CIA and/or US military activity as a result of foreign policy include Somalia, Afghanistan, Serbia, Kosovo, Bosnia, Brazil, Chad, Sudan and many others.

As Dr. Martin Luther King Jr. stated during the Vietnam War, "My government is the world's leading purveyor of violence." He did not say "my country" or "my people"—it is the government, or rather those who control it, that are responsible. Of course, we the distracted and unaware citizens who claim to live in a democracy must take our fair share of the blame as accessories after the fact.

Another American hero, Robert Bowman, flew 101 combat missions in Vietnam and so knows the results of US foreign policy first hand. Bowman rose to a lieutenant colonel (USAF) and later became head of advanced space programs for the Department of Defense. After his retirement he became a Bishop of the United Catholic Church in Melbourne Beach, FL. Bowman noted in 1998, "President Clinton [and later President Bush] did not tell the American people the truth about why we are the targets of terrorism when he explained why we bombed Afghanistan and Sudan. [They both] said that we are a target because we stand for democracy, freedom, and human rights in the world. Nonsense!

"We are the target of terrorists because, in much of the world, our government stands for dictatorship, bondage and human exploitation. We are the target of terrorists because we are hated. And we are hated because our government has done hateful things."

The solution, Bowman said, is to change our ways. "Getting rid of our nuclear weapons, unilaterally if necessary, will enhance our security. Drastically altering our foreign policy will ensure it...In short, we should do good instead of evil. Who would try to stop us? Who would hate us? Who would want to bomb us? That is the truth the American people need to hear."

As noted in Part I, by 2004 Bowman had seen through to the heart of darkness of American foreign policy, going public with the charge that the Bush Administration was behind the 9/11 attacks. "9/11 is based on a pack of lies. It wasn't misjudgment; it was treason..."

If America's dismal and counterproductive foreign policy was simply the result of incautious and insipid blundering, one might expect that occasional mistakes would be made in favor of the American people. But a careful study of the United States' errant policies during the past century clearly indicate a persistent pattern of policies which only enrich the wealthy and further the goals of the globalist elite.

MANUFACTURED ENEMIES

We've seen how so many of our worst enemies of the past were actually created by the US government. Again, the primary question is whether America simply has a penchant for creating Frankenstein monsters or if such creations part of a conscious agenda?

The history of the Vietnam War can be personified in Nguyen Tat Thanh, the son of a lowly Vietnamese rural educator. This man later changed his name to Ho Chi Minh [He Who Enlightens] and became the driving force behind Indochinese nationalism for three decades.

As a young man during World War I, Ho Chi Minh lived in France where he came into contact with French socialists and their Illuminati and Masonic philosophies. In 1919, he spoke before the attendees of the Versailles Peace Conference, calling for expanded rights in Indochina.

In 1930, Ho founded the Vietnamese Communist Party, which later was changed at the urging of Soviet leaders to the Indochinese Communist Party to avoid being perceived as simply a national movement. However, the nationalism of his party was reaffirmed in 1941, when he and others entered Vietnam and created the League for the Independence of Vietnam, or the Viet Minh. When the Japanese overran Indochina in 1945, Ho Chi Minh and General Vo Nguyen Giap began working with the American Office of Strategic Services (the predecessor of the CIA) to oust the occupation forces.

Ho continued to receive American aid after the Japanese withdrew from Vietnam following their surrender on August 14, 1945. "We had a trusted agent to whom we regularly supplied with weapons, radio equipment, operators and medicine. All of it served to reinforce his position and status," wrote journalist Lloyd Shearer. Ho, along with his able General Giap, was then able to force the withdrawal of French troops from French Indochina and soon he was facing the US Army in the south.

There exists a wealth of documentation indicating that the Russian Revolution—indeed the very creation of communism—sprang from Western conspiracies beginning even before World War I. "One of the greatest myths of contemporary history is that the Bolshevik Revolution in Russia was a popular uprising of the downtrodden masses against the hated ruling class of the Czars," wrote author G. Edward Griffin, who said both planning and funding for the revolution came from financiers in Germany, Britain and the United States. Although the revolution began as an uprising, the preponderance of Western support went to the Bolsheviks, emanating largely from Wall Street, as detailed in *Rule by Secrecy*.

In January 1917, Leon Trotsky was living in New York City working as a reporter for the *New World*, a communist newspaper. Trotsky had escaped an earlier failed attempt at revolution in Russia and fled to France where he was expelled for his revolutionary behavior. "He soon discovered that there were wealthy Wall Street bankers who were willing to finance a revolution in Russia," wrote journalist William T. Still.

One of these bankers was Jacob Schiff, whose family had lived with the Rothschilds in Frankfurt. Another was Elihu Root, attorney for Paul Warburg's Kuhn, Loeb & Company. According to the *New York Journal-American*, "[I]t is estimated by Jacob's grandson, John Schiff, that the old man sank about $20 million for the final triumph of Bolshevism in Russia." Root, a CFR member, contributed yet another $20 million, according to the *Congressional Record* of September 2, 1919.

To illustrate the interconnectedness of America's wealthy and powerful elite, another grandson, Andrew Schiff, is married to the daughter of Democratic presidential contender Al Gore.

Author Gary Allen noted, "In the Bolshevik Revolution we have some of the world's richest and most powerful men financing a movement which claims its very existence is based on the concept of stripping of their wealth men like the Rothschilds, Rockefellers, Schiffs, Warburgs, Morgans, Harrimans and Milners. But obviously these men have no fear of international communism. It is only logical to assume that if they financed it and do not fear it, it must be because they control it. Can there be any other explanation that makes sense?"

If there can be identified one single motivating factor behind the horror and tragedy experienced in the 20th century, it is surely anti-communism. The animosity between the so-called democracies of the West and the communism of the East produced continuous turmoil from 1918 through the end of the century. This animosity culminated in the Cold War and massive arms race against the Soviet Union that evolved out of

World War II. This conflict gave the globalists and their military-industrial complex the "perceived enemy" they needed to maintain their rule and their permanent war economy.

As mentioned previously, more recent manufactured enemies—though on a smaller scale—have included Ho Chi Minh, Saddam Hussein, the Shah of Iran, Manuel Noriega, Ferdinand Marcos and many others.

But then such enemies are necessary to convince an otherwise peaceful population on the need for wars and foreign expeditions. It's all part of a formula that has proved quite successful down through the centuries. Create a boogeyman enemy to keep the public distracted but focused, then play both ends against the middle to maintain profits and control.

THE HEGELIAN DIALECTIC

Conspiracy researchers were mystified for years how such high-level capitalists as the Morgans, Warburgs, Schiffs and Rockefellers could condone, much less support, the communists who espoused an ideology which overtly threatened their position and wealth.

To understand this seeming dichotomy, indeed to understand how the secret society members operate, we have noted that one must study the philosopher who most greatly influenced these men—the founder of idealism, Georg Wilhelm Friedrich Hegel.

Coming on the heels of the Age of Reason—the intellectual revolt against the authority of the church—German philosophers Hegel, Johann Gottlieb Fichte and Immanuel Kant inspired future generations with the idea that modern man need not be chained by religious dogma and tradition.

Hegel's unique theoretical method, known as the "Hegelian dialectic," has unfortunately proven to be an exceptional tool for manipulating people and events—that is, when in the hands of ruthless people. Generally it can be said that Hegel identified the universal process by which opposites—which he termed "thesis" and "antithesis"—are always reconciled in a higher-level compromise or "synthesis."

Hegel's dialectic reduced world history and human interaction itself to a simple formula: When one person or group desires one thing (the thesis) around which they organize for power or control, this in turn always evokes a reaction (the antithesis) around which an opposing person or group organizes itself. The confrontation of these two forces moves history forward, as the thesis and antithesis struggle toward a resolution that amounts to a compromise at a new level (the synthesis). This may be achieved through negotiation or some sort of violent battle.

Hegel's dialectic was a mind-boggling effort and a philosophic problem that has not yet been fully completed—adherents and opponents of Hegel may well continue to philosophize into the next millennium. It is therefore easy to understand why such a broadly conceived system has been interpreted in so many ways by Hegel's followers, which have included such opposites as Karl Marx and Adolf Hitler.

The application relevant here is the idea that Western capitalists, along with the Marxist followers of Hegel, created communism on one side (thesis) as a perceived enemy of the democratic nations on the other side (antithesis). The ensuing conflict produced huge markets for finance and armaments and eventually a general blending of both sides (synthesis). Often during the past 50 years it was said that the USA was becoming more like Russia while they were becoming more like the USA.

The members of secret societies traceable to Cecil Rhodes' Round Tables and the Illuminati understood the Hegelian dialectic quite well. Indeed, their predecessors had already for centuries cunningly deployed a version of the dialectic with which to manage events in their selfish interests. These early-day Machiavellis found it was but a small step to the realization that one needn't wait for the crisis and turmoil that Hegel said would naturally unfold in the normal course of history. Instead, these conflicts could be covertly created and then artificially controlled to one's own benefit.

No wonder that in modern times we have witnessed the cycles of financial booms and busts, crises and revolutions, wars and threats of war, all of which were engineered behind the scenes to maintain a "balance of power" in the interests of global elites—the Machiavellians of today.

Social activists and policy-makers alike have learned this both-ends-against-the-middle stratagem well, whether by experience, intuition or study. Demand more than you really need (thesis) from your opposition or employer (antithesis), manipulate the process in your favor wherever possible, and, even after some compromises, you'll usually end up with far more than you would have achieved (i.e., the synthesis) than if you had allowed the natural process of the dialectic to unfold unmolested.

"This revolutionary method—the systematic working of thesis vs. antithesis = synthesis—is the key to understanding world history," declared conspiracy author Texe Marrs.

Russian revolutionaries such as Lenin and Trotsky were being used by the Western elite to get Russia out of World War I, to the benefit of Germany. But at the elite level, communism was being created to stimulate the division of fear and mistrust presented as communism vs. capitalism vs. fascism.

Even Lenin apparently came to understand that he was being manipulated by more powerful forces. "The state does not function as we desired," he once wrote. "A man is at the wheel and seems to lead it, but the car does not drive in the desired direction. It moves as another force wishes."

This other "force" were the members of the secret societies that were behind the birth of communism itself, "monopoly finance capitalists" as Lenin described them.

WHAT DO WE KNOW NOW?

The question now becomes, was 9/11 truly an unprovoked and surprise attack by a handful of Muslim zealots or was it yet another case of the Hegelian method being used to promote a pre-existing secret agenda?

Undoubtedly, the primary groups of conspirators behind 9/11 were: (1) those who perpetrated the actual attack upon the United States, i.e., directed the planning for the many details and contingencies involving the hijackings, worked to hand off essential "match" details to the hijackers, planted bombs at the WTC and Pentagon, and flew or controlled the planes; (2) those who must have acted from the inside to suppress or alter normal defense and security precautions at the moment of crisis, through the confusion caused by multiple simultaneous war games or some other method; and (3) powerful insiders who acted to create and narrate a fraudulent official story, remove evidence through the premature and hasty cleanup of the 9/11 crime scenes, and thwart or slow official investigations, including the blocking of antiterrorism efforts for years within the FBI and CIA.

We've seen that the goal of powerful rogue interests within the US must have been to create this provocation, and then breed an atmosphere of fear behind which to push a predetermined foreign policy and domestic security agendas—including an agenda that amounts to the theft of American civil liberties and even the theft of trillions from the federal treasury—through a confused and panicky Congress. And we have also considered the evidence that covert entities within the governments of Israel, Pakistan, and Saudi Arabia must surely have had foreknowledge of the attacks and may have had a hand in supporting the perpetrators.

If all this is so, how have we reached this dark place in our history?

The record is clear that since the National Security Act of 1947, the United States has slowly been turned into a national security state with more and more power being concentrated in the federal government, particularly the executive branch. Laws are being enacted by presidential orders rather than through reasoned debate and careful study by our elected representatives. And no one seems to notice, especially since the news media has now come under the total control of a mere handful of international corporations. Trained and dedicated newsmen, in the mold of a Walter Cronkite, have been replaced by on-air personalities who are more conscious of ratings than world and national events. Citizens therefore have not choice but to study and learn for themselves, drawing from a variety of non-traditional news sources.

What specifically have we learned from this close examination of the 9/11 attacks and their aftermath?

We know that mere incompetence cannot explain the systematic failure of the normal security protections codified in both the civilian aviation and military sectors and we know that not one single person has yet been reprimanded for this failure. Why did it take a year or more to learn that Cheney's antiterrorism task force was alerted to the problem, that President Bush saw a briefing paper stating bin Laden was preparing to strike in August 2001, and that war game exercises involving the idea of planes crashing into buildings were scheduled for 9/11?

The evidence of foreknowledge of the attacks, particularly within the FBI and CIA, is overwhelming. This raises the question as to who precisely blocked this information and why. Why was there no warning to the public or beefed up security? Who had the power to misdirect and block official investigations?

We also know that actions against the Taliban in general and Osama bin Laden in particular were well under way long before the attacks. How is it that bin Laden remains at large as of this writing despite what we are told are the best efforts of the world's foremost superpower? Does anyone truly believe that the Mossad and the Pakistani ISI, and hence the CIA, have no clue as to bin Laden's whereabouts, especially at a time when every American can be tagged by computer?

It is now clear that the bombing of Afghanistan had more to do with oil and gas pipelines and restoring the poppy fields than with catching bin Laden. And the War on Terrorism shifted from finding those responsible for the attacks to enforcing a "Pax Americana" on the world, exactly as articulated by the neo-cons Cheney, Rumsfeld, Perle and Wolfowitz— even before Bill Clinton was elected. And unlike every past American administration, this group has actually proposed a first-strike use of nuclear weapons in this new war for domination.

We know now that Bush spurned more international treaties than any other world leader and released funds for North Korea's nuclear program at a time when he was preparing to seek war with Iraq, claiming that Saddam Hussein *might* be capable of building a weapon of mass destruction. This issue seemed to indicate a schism within the ranks of the New World Order. The Bush forces pushed hard for an attack while the United Nations worked hard behind the scenes to ensure compliance by Saddam Hussein of UN demands.

Subsequent statements by administration officials including Colin Powell coupled with the now-public Downing Street memo make it clear that the Bush White House knew well that its evidence of Iraq's weapons of mass destruction was weak at best and that the intelligence was "fixed" around a policy of invasion. This could easily fit the definition of a lie.

We now know that plans to circumvent the Constitution were laid as far back as the Nixon years and that the new Department of Homeland Security carries within it concepts and programs which would have been greeted with howls of protests just a few short years ago. And the new technology to identify and classify each individual citizen is now in place. Administration critics cannot be summarily dismissed for using terms like "dictatorship," "1984" and "totalitarianism."

Bush and Cheney consistently fought any truthful investigation into the tragedies of 9/11 and when popular opinion in this matter turned against them, they turned to one of the leading lights of the secret societies—Henry Kissinger, a leading luminary of the Council on Foreign Relations. Again, a groundswell of public opinion as well as the possibility of dredging up old war crime charges prompted Kissinger's resignation even before he began work. Nevertheless, the two men Bush selected to replace Kissinger—Thomas Kean and Lee Hamilton—are both members of the secretive Council on Foreign Relations and elite insiders. The executive director of the 9/11 Commission, Philip Zelikow, was a White House foreign policy insider, and also the principal author of the administration's *National Security Strategy* statement of 2002 that first articulated the concept of preemptive warfare based on the threats posed by 9/11. This was the pre-eminent doctrine that led to the attack on Iraq and the War on Terrorism.

It can also be seen that President Bush is trying to place persons sympathetic to his worldview on the Supreme Court, the place where his father's friends handed him his office. And shifting to a Democrat won't make things better as most of the groundwork for the current "War on Freedom" was laid during the CFR-dominated Clinton administration.

We now know that Bush and most other members of his cabinet are too locked into the monopolies of energy, pharmaceuticals, telecommunications and military/aerospace to allow alternative views to be heard. Bush, Cheney and many others are guilty of the same corporate shenanigans they were forced to criticize in the summer of 2002 following the collapse of Enron, WorldCom and other major corporations.

We now see clearly that the privatization of US industry, energy and institutions to include health care and education does not fulfill the promise of better service at less cost.

If the game plan of the masterminds behind the 9/11 attacks was to curtail American freedom, centralize more power in the federal government and set back the social agenda of the United States in favor of an open-ended military and intelligence buildup, then they succeeded admirably. To many long-time researchers, it all has a familiar ring to it.

In many ways, the aftermath of the 9/11 attacks fit the same template as the assassination of President Kennedy in 1963:

- Within hours, despite a lack of real evidence, one man was blamed for the event along with hints that he was connected to foreign enemies.

- Official pronouncements were widely publicized only to be quietly admitted as errors later on.

- Although within the jurisdiction of the local authorities, the entire case was usurped by the FBI and CIA, both agencies under the control of a president who benefited from the tragedy.

- A group of specialists (medical in the JFK's case and engineers in that of the WTC) was convened but limited in what they could view and study, blocked from conducting an objective probe by federal officials.

- Evidence in the case was hastily removed and destroyed, forever lost to an impartial and meaningful investigation.

- More evidence was locked away in government files under the excuse of "national security."

- Federal malfeasance was excused by claiming lack of manpower and resources and no one was disciplined or fired. Federal agency budgets were increased.

- Any alternative to the official version of events was decried as "conspiracy theory" and "unpatriotic."

- The federal government used the event to increase its own centralized power.

- A foreign war (Vietnam in JFK's case and Iraq and Afghanistan today), which otherwise would have been opposed, was supported by a grieving population.

- A top government leader (then LBJ and now Bush), formerly under suspicion for election fraud and corrupt business dealings, was suddenly propelled to new heights of popularity.

- Many citizens knew or suspected that the official version of events was incorrect but were afraid to speak out.

■ A compliant and sycophantic mass media was content to parrot merely the official version of events and studiously avoided asking the hard questions that might have revealed the truth.

One major difference in the two cases is that following JFK's death, less than 10 days went by before President Lyndon Johnson appointed a special commission to investigate the crime. Well more than a year after the events of 9/11, there was still only talk of creating some sort of investigative body, the time lag due primarily to pressure from President Bush and Vice President Cheney not to convene such an inquiry. It was almost two years before an official 9/11 commission was selected and put to work and by then, most of the primary evidence, such as the steel from the World Trade Center, was long missing or otherwise unavailable.

In the case of the Pearl Harbor attack, the JFK assassination and 9/11, a common denominator was the failure of normal security precautions. This is the tip off.

As Col. L. Fletcher Prouty, former Pentagon-CIA liaison officer, stated in regards to the Kennedy assassination, "The active role is played secretly by permitting it to happen. That was why President Kennedy was killed. He was not murdered by some lone gunman or by some limited conspiracy, but by the breakdown of the protective system that should have made assassination impossible...This is the greatest single clue to the assassination—who had the power to call off or reduce the usual security precautions that are always in effect whenever a president travels? Castro did not kill Kennedy, nor did the CIA. The power source that arranged that murder was on the inside. It had the means to reduce normal security and permit the choice of a hazardous route. It also had the continuing power to cover that crime for...years."

The same question could be asked regarding the tragedies of September 11, 2001:

Who had the power to call off or reduce normal airline and NORAD security procedures and who had the power to deflect any meaningful investigation into the events? This kind of power can only be found at the highest levels of government and corporate control. Today's big time criminals no longer worry about what the government might do to them because they *are* the government. It therefore becomes essential to identify and connect the inner core elite of the world's secret societies, to demonstrate their ownership and interlocking control over the multi-national corporations that dominate our national life.

"Most people prefer to believe their leaders are just and fair even in the face of evidence to the contrary, because once a citizen acknowledges that the government under which they live is lying and corrupt, the citizen has to choose what he or she will do about it. To take action in the face of a corrupt government entails risks of harm to life and loved ones. To choose to do nothing is to surrender one's self-image of standing for principles. Most people do not have the courage to face that choice. Hence, most propaganda is not designed to fool the critical thinker but only to give moral cowards an excuse not to think at all," noted Internet commentator Michael Rivero.

But the time has come for persons of good heart and conscience to stand up and regain the country handed down to them by men and women who not only were discomforted by fighting for a free and democratic republic but risked their very lives and fortunes.

Look to local leaders as they are the ones more likely to care about the public welfare. Our democratic republic, with its Constitution and Bill of Rights, is without a doubt the greatest form of government ever initiated in the written history of this planet. Let's make it work as it was intended.

By the time you read this, there is every likelihood that other major terrorist attacks may be in the offing and that some new war may have broken out in some far corner of the world, most likely Iran. There will be more "experts" brought forward to generate fear and instruct us on the need to curtail freedom to save democracy.

Do not be stampeded.

We all agree that the true culprits, of this or any future tragedy, must be identified and punished. But we must make certain through an objective investigation and cool reasoning that we indeed have the true culprits. We must not be played for suckers as so many times in the past.

The corporate mass media has bombarded the public with facts, statistics, personal opinion and commentary to the point of distraction and confusion.

WHAT DO WE KNOW NOW?

Viewed in its broadest perspective, however, the picture is both clear and appalling:

The United States today is under the control of a dynastic family, blood relatives to virtually all European monarchs, whose patriarch can be shown to have been both in sympathy and in business with Hitler and his Nazis. The Bushes control three of the nation's most populous and powerful states—Florida, Colorado and Texas, as Gov. Rick Perry is considered little more than a surrogate Bush. Considering the close connections between Arnold Schwarzenegger, the Bushes, Karl Rove and other New World Order luminaries, one could argue that they control California.

And the Bushes are blood relatives to the royal family of England, as were Al Gore and John Kerry as documented by the prestigious genealogical publication *Burke's Peerage*. The Windsors originated in Germany and trace their ancestry to many major European royals.

The Bush family has been involved with the CIA since before the time of the 1961 Bay of Pigs invasion, with all that implies regarding covert wars, drug smuggling and assassinations, not mention the creation of Saddam Hussein as well as Osama bin Laden and his al Qaeda network. One would imagine that the public would finally catch on after realizing that the same family financed three major world evildoers—Hitler, Hussein and bin Laden.

And each generation has belonged to a secret college society linked to the Bavarian Illuminati as well as prominent members of other such societies whose avowed purpose is to end United States sovereignty in favor of globalism. The family has even been linked to accused assassins, John Hinckley and Lee Harvey Oswald. What are the odds?

At least two Bush sons were at the heart of the savings & loan debacle, which cost every man, woman and child in the United States thousands of dollars. The eldest son, not elected but selected by a Supreme Court packed by previous Republican presidents including his father, has been linked to Enron, Harken and other shady oil company dealings and has surrounded himself with men of questionable ethics and truthfulness.

Collectively, this family and their corporate cronies are today seeking what amounts to dictatorial powers to combat the proclaimed War on Terrorism, despite the growing evidence that the attacks which launched this war were known in advance and allowed to happen to bring about the erosion of individual rights and the centralization of even more power unto themselves. And that view is putting the very best possible light on the affair. Considering the longstanding connections between this family, its political supporters, the secret societies, the CIA, overseas intelligence agencies, war-profiteering corporations, the energy industry, the bin Laden family, Saddam Hussein and the al Qaeda network, a case can be made that the 9/11 attacks were instigated by persons other than Osama bin Laden.

The nature of public life in the US today has begun to resemble the very despotic societies—Hitler's Third Reich, Stalinist Russia, Communist Eastern Europe and China—that America contested during the last century.

Such totalitarian regimes stemmed from centralized governments that serve themselves rather than the people, that respond more swiftly to policies of the central government than evidence of criminal activities or public need and use every means at their disposal to spy on and intimidate their citizens. Thoughtful observers see much that same trend in the United States today.

These are not conjectures or conspiracy theories. These are the facts.

The questions regarding the 9/11 attacks and their aftermath bring only further questions. These questions concern what the American people intend to do about all this.

Will they continue to be led by a corporate mass media that deceives by omission more than commission and distracts them from the real issues?

Will they continue to reelect politicians who have been in office while all the causes of current problems were put into place?

Will they continue to blindly follow the standards of the two major political parties that have demonstrated that precious little difference exists in their major policies?

Will they continue to support a foreign policy that angers and alienates peoples all across the globe with its thinly-disguised neo-colonialism?

Will they allow the US military to continue enforcing this foreign policy while gaining unwarranted control over their own nation and lives?

Will they continue to permit their nation to be the primary seller of arms to the world and then bemoan the fact that those same arms are used against them?

Will they finally take a look behind the green curtain of media spin to identify the globalists who own and control that media as well as the government and, hence, the military?

Will they stand up and exercise their own individual power or stand idly by, frozen by fear, intimidation or confusion, while their remaining liberties are lost?

Only you, the reader, can answer these questions.

SOURCES

INTRODUCTION

XVIII Scholars for 9/11 Truth: http://www.st911.org/.

XIX Paul Craig Roberts: http://www.prisonplanet.com/articles/february2006/080206towerscollapse.htm

XX Stanley Hilton case: Pat Shannan, "Former Bob Dole Staffer Says Bush Had 9-11 Foreknowledge," *American Free Press* (October 4, 2004); http://www.suetheterrorists.net/

PART I – THE EVENTS OF SEPTEMBER 11, 2001

6 Commission road map questions: Family Steering Committee: http://www.scoop.co.nz/stories/WO0507/S00369.htm

8 Fighters at one-fourth speed: http://911research.wtc7.net/planes/analysis/norad/index.html#otis

8 Intercepts: William Thomas, "Pentagon Says Interceptors Flew: Too Far, Too Slow, Too Late," http://www.thetruthseeker.co.uk/article.asp?ID=1325

9 Stand-down suspicion not removed: David Ray Griffin, *The 9/11 Commission Report: Omissions and Distortions* (Northampton, MA: Olive Branch Press, 2005)

9 War games as true causes: Michael C. Ruppert, *Crossing the Rubicon* (Gabriola Island, Canada: New Society Publishers, 2004)

10 Steganography: Editors, "Digital moles in the White House?" *WorldNet-Daily.com* (2001); www.worldnetdaily.com/news/article.asp?ARTICLE_ID=24594

11 Kleinberg's comments about "luck": www.9-11commission.gov/hearings/hearing1/witness_kleinberg.htm

11 Bush's quote on terrible pilot: David Ray Griffin, *The New Pearl Harbor* (Northampton, MA: Olive Branch Press, 2004)

13 Bush capitulated: Webster Griffin Tarpley, *9/11 Synthetic Terror* (Joshua Tree, CA: Progressive Press, 2006)

14 Lt. Col. Marr: Scott, op. cit.; Col. Deskins: Hart Seely, "Amid Crisis Simulation, 'We Were Suddenly No-Kidding Under Attack'" *Newhouse News Service* (January 25, 2002)

14 William B. Scott: Scott, op. cit.

17 Timothy McNiven: Greg Szymanski, "Army Theorists Crafted Model of 9-11 Attack Back in 1976," American Free Press (March 21, 2005); http://www.codenamegrillfire.com/index.php?n=1&id=1

17 Robert M. Bowman: http://www.prisonplanet.com/articles/april2006/ 040406mainsuspect.htm

18 Cheney and Office of National Preparedness: http://www.washing-tonpost.com/ac2/wp-dyn?pagename=article&contentId=A64420-2001May8&notFound=true

19 Cheney and energy task force: Ruppert, *Crossing the Rubicon*, op. cit.

19 Flying bin Ladens: Jane Mayer, "The House Of Bin Laden," *New Yorker* (November 12, 2001)

20 Bin Ladens flown from US: Craig Unger, "Saving the Saudis," *Vanity Fair* (October, 2003)

20 Tom Kinton: Ibid.

21 No stone unturned: Editors, "They Saw It Happen," *America at War*, (New York: Personality Profiles Presents, 2001)

21 Some identified hijackers still alive: Editors, "Hijack suspects alive and well," *BBC News* (September 23, 2001)

22 Saeed al-Ghamdi: Ibid.

22 Saudi Prince al-Faisal: http://911review.org/Wiki/HijackersAliveAndWell.shtml

22 Arab names similar: Hanna Rosin, "Some Cry Foul As Authorities Cast a Wide Net," *Washington Post* (September 28, 2001)

23 Kristin Breitweiser: Jim Miklaszewski, "US had 12 warnings of jet attacks," NBC, MSNBC, *Associated Press* and *Reuters* (September 18, 2002)

23 Venice Airport, Florida: Daniel Hopsicker, *Welcome to Terrorland*, (Eugene, OR: Madcow Press, 2004)

23 C-130 takes evidence: Ibid.

24 No Arabs on Flight 77: Thomas R. Olsted, M.D., "Autopsy: No Arabs on Flight 77," *SierraTimes.com* (July 6, 2003); www.sierratimes.com/03/07/02/article_tro.htm

24 Hani Hanjour's flight capabilities: http://www.newsday.com/ny-usflight-232380680sep23.story

24 Danielle O'Brien: Griffin, op. cit.

25 Passport found: http://www.cnn.com/2001/US/09/16/gen.america.under.attack/; "Terrorist Hunt," *ABC News* (September 12, 2001)

25 Trail left deliberately: Griffin, op. cit.

26 Flight Data Recorders found: Greg Szymanski, "Black Box Cover-Up," *American Free Press* (December 12, 2004)

26 Terrorists looked for hookers: Editors, "Reports: Hijack Suspects Looked for Hookers in Boston," *Reuters* (October 10, 2001)

27 Atta and cocaine and Chertoff quote: Hopsicker op. cit.

27 Ari Fleischer: www.foxnews.com/story/0,2933,49226,00.html

29 Abu Zubaydah: Gerald Posner, *Why America Slept*, (New York: Random House, 2003); Johanna McGeary, "Confessions of a Terrorist," *Time* (September 8, 2003)

29 Posner quote: Ibid.

29 Sgt. Ali A. Mohamed: John Sullivan and Joseph Neff, "An Al Qaeda operative at Fort Bragg," *Raleigh News & Observer* (November 13, 2001)

30 John Sullivan and Joseph Neff: Ibid.

32 Pentagon survivor's story: Author's interview with April Gallop, April 18, 2004

32 Bombs in Pentagon: http://911review.com/attack/pentagon/witnesses.html

33 Steve Riskus: Thierry Meyssan, editor, *Pentagate*, (London: Carnot Publishing Ltd., 2002)

34 Chris Murray: Griffin, op. cit.

35 Francois Grangier: Meyssan, op. cit.

35 Witnesses: Ibid.

36 Rumsfeld's missile quote: http://www.defenselink.mil/news/Nov2001/t11182001_t1012pm.html

37 Cheney's comments: Secretary Norman Mineta's testimony to the National Commission on the September 11 Terrorist Attacks; www.cooperativeresearch.org/timeline/2003/commissiontestimony052303.html

37 Patently false account of Cheney's whereabouts: David Ray Griffin, *The 9/11 Commission Report*, p. 254.

38 NORAD procedural change: DDOD 3025.15, February 18, 1997; CJCSI 3610.01A, June 1, 2001

38 Jerry Russell: http://www.rumormillnews.com/cgi-bin/forum.cgi?read=46729

40 Controlled implosions: Olivier Uyttebrouck, "Explosives Planted In Towers, N.M. Tech Expert Says," *Albuquerque Journal* (September 11, 2001)

40 Romero reverses himself: John Fleck, "Fire, Not Extra Explosives, Doomed Buildings, Expert Says," *Albuquerque Journal* (September 21, 2001)

40 Louie Cacchioli: Editors, "New York City," *People.com* (September 12, 2001); http://people.aol.com/people/special/0,11859,174592-3,00.html

41 Lt. Paul Isaac Jr.: Randy Lavello, "Bombs in the Building: World Trade Center 'Conspiracy Theory' is a Conspiracy Fact," www.prisonplanet.com/analysis_lavello_050503_bombs.html

41 Teresa Veliz and bombs: Dean E. Murphy, "Teresa Veliz: A Prayer to Die Quickly and Painlessly," *September 11: An Oral History* (New York: Doubleday, 2002)

41 Ross Milanytch: *America at War*, op. cit.

41 John Bussey: http:/www.911truth.org/article.php?story=200601181042231 92

42 Steve Evans of BBC: Christopher Bollyn, "New York Firefighters' Final Words Fuel Burning Questions about 9-11," *American Free Press* (August 19, 2002)

42 Explosion at base of building: Col. Donn de Grand Pre, "Many Questions Still Remain About Trade Center Attack," *American Free Press* (February 11, 2002)

43 Tom Elliott: Peter Grier, "A Changed World – Part 1: The Attack," *The Christian Science Monitor* (September 17, 2001)

44 Mike Pecoraro: Editors, "We Will Not Forget," *The Chief Engineer* (February 10, 2005)

46 William Rodriguez's account: http://www.theconservativevoice.com/articles/article.html?id=7762

46 Rodriguez lawsuit: Pat Shannan, "Trade Towers Hero Files 9-11 Rico Suit," *American Free Press* October 29, 2004

46 José Sanchez: Greg Szymanski, "Second WTC Janitor Comes Forward With Eye-Witness Testimony Of 'Bomb-Like' Explosion in North Tower Basement," *ArcticBeacon.com* July 12, 2005.

48 NYFD taped comments on explosions: http:/www.911truth.org/article.php?story=20060118104223192

48 Special Report: Terrorism in the US," London *Guardian*, September 12, 2001.

48 CNN videotapes smoke from WTC 6: Christopher Bollyn, "Unexplained 9-11 Explosion at WTC Complex," *American Free Press* (July 22, 2002)

50 Ben Fountain and drills: www.unityinamerica.com/stories/survivorStoriee.asp; www.prisonplanet.com/011904wct7.html

50 Securacom and Bush: http://www.utne.com/web_special/web_specials_2003-02/articles/10292-1.html

50 Mayor Giuliani warned: www.prisonplanet.com/eye_witness_account_from_new_york.html; http://physics911.org/net/modules/wfsection/article.php?articleid=15

51 Zarrillo's account: World Trade Center Task Force interview with Richard Zarrillo, October 25, 2001, File No. 9110161

52 Transcripts: www.prisonplanet.com/eye_witness_account_from_new_york.html

52 Firefighters Palmer and Bucca: Bollyn (August 19, 2002), op. cit.

52 A coherent plan: Ibid.

53 Stanley Praimnath. Donovan Cowen and Ling Young: http://globalresearch.ca.myforums.net/viewtopic.php?t=523

54 Kevin R. Ryan: John Dobberstein, "Area Man stirs debate on WTC collapse: South Bend firm's lab director fired after questioning federal probe," *South*

Bend Tribune (November 22, 2004)

54 Peter Tully: Christopher Bollyn, "Seismologists Have Questions About 'Spikes' At Twin Towers," *American Free Press* (February 7, 2005)

55 Loizeaux's speculation: Ibid.

56 Seismic evidence of two shocks: Christopher Bollyn, "Seismic Data Refutes Official Explanation," *American Free Press* (September 9, 2002)

56 Arthur Lerner-Lam and Eric Hufschmid: Ibid; Eric Hufschmid, *Painful Questions* (Goleta, CA, Endpoint Software, 2002)

57 FEMA Study: www.fema.gov/library/wtcstudy.shtm

58 Meridian Plaza fire: Hufschmid, op. cit.

58 Never before: Griffin, op. cit.

59 No collapse observed: FEMA Report (1988) Appendix A

60 Thomas Eager, "clips" and "unzippering": www.worldnewsstand.net/2001/ towers/trusseseager.html

60 Hollow shaft: Editors of the National Commission on Terrorist Attacks Upon the United States, *The 9/11 Commission Report* (New York: W. W. Norton & Company, 2004), page 541, note 1.

60 Enormous lie about WTC steel: David Ray Griffin, *The 9/11 Commission Report: Omissions and Distortions* (Northampton, MA: Olive Branch Press, 2005), page 28.

61 A few tiny fires: Hufschmid, op. cit.

61 Larry Silverstein; Editors, "America Rebuilds," *PBS-TV* (September, 2002)

63 WTC steel sold for scrap: Bill Manning, "Selling Out the Investigation," *Fire Engineering* (January, 2002)

63 Evidence treated like garbage: Francis Brannigan, "WTC 'Investigation'?: A Call To Action," *Fire Engineering* (January, 2002)

64 Corley and Murrah Building: www.fas.org/irp/congress/1998_hr/h980604-corley.htm

64 W. Gene Corley and team complaints: Avery Comarow, "After the fall," *US News & World Report* (May 13, 2002)

65 National Construction Safety Team report: http://www.nist.gov/public_affairs/releases/ncst_first_report.htm

67 Critical mysteries: Jim Hoffman, 911research.wtc7.net

68 Pre-planted explosives: Steven E. Jones, "Why Indeed Did the WTC Buildings Collapse?" See http://www.physics.byu.edu/research/energy/htm7.html

68 Not 'junk science': Elaine Jarvik, "Physics Professor Concludes Bombs, Not Planes, Toppled WTC," KUTV Interview published on *Deseretnews.com* (November 10, 2005)

68 Who set explosives?: http://kutv.com/topstories/local_story_314234334.

html

70 "Inside job": Greg Szymanski, "Bush Insider Claims WTC Collapse Bogus," *American Free Press* (June 27, 2005); http://www.lewrockwell.com/reynolds/reynolds12.html

70 $30 billion: Editors, "The Road to September 11," *Newsweek* (October 1, 2001)

71 Kenneth Katzman: www.washingtonpost.com/wo-dyn/articles/A14120-2001Sep11.html

71 State Dept. Warning: Phillip Matier and Andrew Ross, "State Department Memo Warned of Terrorist Threat," *San Francisco Chronicle* (September 14, 2001)

71 Snider resigns from joint committee: Tabassum Zakaria, "Head of Congressional Probe Into September 11 Quits," *Reuters* (April 29, 2002)

71 Sen. Richard Shelby: Miklaszewski, op. cit.

72 Sen. Bob Graham: Ibid.

72 McCain co-sponsors inquiry: Lisa Stein, "Private Eye," Top of the Week, *US News & World Report* (October 7, 2002)

72 Small teams of investigators: Greg Miller, "Tactics Impede Investigation," *Los Angeles Times* (May 4, 2002)

73 FBI investigates leaks: Christopher Newton, "FBI Asks Lawmakers to Take Lie Detector Test in September 11 Leak Investigation," *Associated Press* (August 2, 2002)

74 Attack seen as inevitable: John Dougherty, "Panel: Attack on US 'Inevitable'," *WorldNetDaily* (September 21, 2001)

74 Terrorists trained to crash airliners: Yossef Bodansky, *Target America: Terrorism in the US Today* (New York: Shapolsky Publishers, 1993)

74 Italian wiretaps: Sebastian Rotella and Josh Meyer, "Wiretaps May Have Foretold Terror Attacks," *Los Angeles Times* (May 29, 2002)

75 Spanish wiretaps: Ibid.

75 Prime Minister warned: Michael Evans, "Spy Chiefs Warned Ministers of al Qaeda Attacks," London *Times* (June 14, 2002)

75 Cayman Islands warning: Chris Hansen, "Warning Signs," *MSNBC* (September 23, 2001)

76 Taliban warning: Kate Clark, "Revealed: The Taliban minister, the US envoy and the warning of September 11 that was ignored," London *Independent* (September 7, 2002); http://news.independent.co.uk./world/politics/story.jsp?story=331115

76 Manila warning: Editors, "Flashback: Airliner terror plan was code-named 'Project Bojinka,'" *WorldTribune.com* (September 25, 2001)

76 Air France Flight 8969: Matthew L. Wald, "Earlier Hijackings Offered Signals

That Were Missed," *New York Times* (October 3, 2001)

76 Philippine warnings: Dorian Zumel Sicat, "Abu's long-standing ties to global terrorism bared," *Manila Times* (February 15, 2002)

77 Terry Nichols and terrorists: Dorian Zumel Sicat, "RP cops aware of long-term rightwing, Muslim connection," *Manila Times* (April 26, 2002); www.manilatimes.net/national/2002/apr/26/top_stories/20020426top6.html.

77 Chinese manual: www.NewsMaxstore.com/nms/showdetl.cfm?&DID=6&Product_ID=886&CATID=9&GroupID=12

77 China enters WTO: http://www.cnn.com/2001/WORLD/asiapcf/central/11/10/china.WTO/

78 Dr. Tatyana Koryagina: www.newsmax.com/archives/articles/201/10/3/212706.shtml

79 Egyptian warning: Patrick E. Tyler and Neil MacFarquhar, "Egypt Warned US of a Qaeda Plot, Mubarak Asserts," *New York Times* (June 4, 2002)

79 Atwan warning: Editors, "Expert: Bin Laden Warned of 'Unprecedented' US Attack," *Reuters*, (September 11, 2001)

80 Arab MBC channel: Editors, "US Airlines May Be a Terror Risk Over Next Three Days," *Airjet Airline World News* (June 23, 2001)

81 Letter to NY Times: http://judiciary.senate.gov/oldsite/childers.htm

82 Internet domain names: Jeff Johnson, "Internet Domain Names May Have Warned of Attacks," *Cybercast News Service* (September 19, 2001); http://www.middleeastwire.com/atlarge/stories/20010919_3_meno.shtml

82 Editor Russ Kick and school kids: Russ Kick, "September 11, 2001: No Surprise," *Everything You Know Is Wrong* (New York: The Disinformation Company, 2002)

83 Willie Brown's warning: Phillip Matier and Andrew Ross, "Willie Brown got low-key early warning about air travel," *San Francisco Chronicle* (September 12, 2001)

83 Pentagon officials won't fly: Evan Thomas and Mark Hosenball, "Bush: 'We're At War'," *Newsweek* (September 24, 2001)

83 Ashcroft uses charter jets: Jim Stewart, "Ashcroft Flying High," *CBS News* (July 26, 2001)

83 David Welna report: www.thememoryhole.org/tenet-9-11.htm

84 Rumsfeld lays off blame: http://www.defenselink.mil/news/Nov2001/t11182001_t1012pm.html

85 Carnivore and FBI memos: Editors, "FBI 'Carnivore' glitch hurt al Qaeda probe," *Reuters* (May 29, 2002). www.cnn.com/2002/US/05/28/attack.carnivore.reut/index.html

86 John O'Neill as most committed tracker: Lawrence Wright, "The Counter Terrorist," *New Yorker* (January 14, 2002)

SOURCES

86 Richard A. Clarke: Ibid.

87 A major attack coming: Ibid.

88 FBI negligence: Wes Vernon, "Agent: FBI Could Have Prevented 9-11," *News-Max.com* (May 31, 2002)

88 Mission jeopardized: Vernon, op. cit.

88 Phoenix suspicions: Editors, "FBI Agent Warned of Suspicious Flight Students Last Summer," *Fox News* (May 3, 2002)

89 Agent Williams' memo: Richard Behar, "FBI's 'Phoenix' Memo Unmasked," *Fortune.com* (May 22, 2002)

89 FBI agents indicted: Alex Berenson, "Five, Including F.B.I. Agents, Are Named in a Conspiracy," *New York Times* (May 23, 2002)

89 Kenneth Breen and Elgindy: Dave Eberhart, "Egyptians Knew of Planned 9-11 Attack Last August," *NewsMax.com* (May 29, 2002)

89 Asst. US Atty. Kenneth Breen: Whitley Strieber, "Is the FBI Penetrated?" *UnknownCountry.com* (May 25, 2002); www.unknowncountry.com/journal/print.phtml?id=95

89 Gary Aldrich: http://www.newsmax.com/archives/articles/2001/12/28/111159.shtml

90 FBI and Clinton White House: James Risen, "C.I.A.'s Inquiry on al Qaeda Aide Seen as Flawed," *New York Times* (September 22, 2002)

90 FBI Agent Ivan C. Smith: Paul Sperry, "Why FBI missed Islamic threat. Agents: Clinton shifted counterterror efforts to fighting 'right-wing' groups," *WorldNetDaily* (July 25, 2002)

90 Commerce Dept. report sanitized: Ibid.

91 FBI Director Robert Mueller: Eric Lichtblau and Josh Meyer, "Terrorist Signs Were Missed, FBI Chief Says," *Los Angeles Times* (May 30, 2002)

92 Randy Glass: John Mintz, "US Reopens Arms Case In Probe of Taliban Role," *Washington Post* (August 2, 2002); Wanda J. DeMaarzo, "Feds reopen probe of Florida arms deal," *Miami Herald* (August 2, 2002)

93 Operation Diamondback: http://www.opednews.com/duncan_011205_NJ_Terrorism_Michael_Chertoff.htm

93 Indicated the World Trade Center: Mintz and DeMaarzo, op. cit.

94 David Schippers: http://www.infowars.com/transcript_schippers.html

94 Sibel Edmonds, Andrew Buncombe, "I saw papers that show US knew al Qaeda would attack cities with aeroplanes," London *Independent* (April 2, 2004)

96 System in need of repair: http://www.911citizenswatch.org/print.php?sid=329

97 Sibel Edmonds comments: http://baltimorechronicle.com/050704SibelEdmonds.shtml; http://www.breakfornews.com/Sibel-Ed-

monds.htm

97 Letter to Kean: http://www.911citizenswatch.org/modules.php?op=modloa
d&name=News&file=article&sid=373

97 Leahy, Grassley letter: www.justacitizen.com/articles_documents/Leahy_
Grassley_letter_to_Ashcroft_7-9-04.pdf

98 Ramzi bin al-Shibh in custody: Lisa Stein, "Man of the hour," *US News &
World Report* (September 23, 2002)

98 FBI docs in Moussaoui's cell: Lisa Stein, op. cit.

99 Harry Samit: Richard A. Serrano, "Agent Faults FBI on 9/11," *Los Angeles
Times* (March 21, 2006)

100 Coleen Rowley: http://www.counterpunch.org/sperry0613.html;
http://www.apfn.org/apfn/WTC_whistleblower1.htm

101 Rowley testimony defused: Steve Perry, "How All the President's Men Buried Coleen Rowley," *CounterPunch* (June 13, 2002)

101 Echelon like vacuum cleaner: Ned Stafford: "Newspaper: Echelon Gave
Authorities Warning of Attacks," *Newsbytes.com* (September 13, 2001)

102 French probe Echelon: Warren P. Strobel, "A fine whine from France," *US
News & World Report* (July 17, 2000)

102 Osama's big news: Ben Fenton and John Steele, "Bin Laden Told Mother to
Expect 'Big News', *Daily Telegraph* (October 2, 2001)

103 Predator strikes: http://en.wikipedia.org/wiki/RQ-1_Predator

103 Osama as Tim Osman: Mike Blair, "Public Enemy No. 1 Was Guest of Central Intelligence Agency," *American Free Press* (January 7 & 14, 2002)

104 Olberg in Durenberger's office: Ibid.

105 Kahlid al-Midhar and Nawaq Al-Hazni: Risen, op. cit.

105 Khalid Shaikh Mohammed: Ibid.

106 Double agents: Ruppert, op. cit.

106 Mohammed identified before 9-11: Risen, op. cit.

107 Able Danger: http://www.foxnews.com/story/0,2933,165414,00.html

107 FBI tracked Mohamed Atta in Germany: Audrey Gillan, Giles Tremlett,
John Hooper, Kate Connolly and Jon Henley, "Dozens detained as net
spreads from US to Europe," London *Guardian* (September 27, 2001)

108 Osama bin Laden in Dubai: Alexandra Richard, "The CIA met Bin Laden
While undergoing treatment at an American Hospital last July in Dubai,"
Le Figaro (October 11, 2001), translation by Tiphaine Dickson; www.glob-
alresearch.ca/articles/RIC111B.html

109 CIA team in Afghanistan: Editors, "Newspaper: Afghans tracked bin
Laden," In brief, *USA Today* (December 24, 2001)

109 CIA's James Pavitt: www.cia.gov/cia/public_affairs/speeches/pavitt_
04262002.html

110 CIA Inspector General's report: Douglas Jehl, "C.I.A. Report Finds Its Officials Failed in Pre-9/11 Efforts," *New York Times* (January 7, 2005)

110 Senior officials warned: Risen, op. cit.

110 Bush warned at Crawford: Michael Hirsh and Michael Isikoff, "What Went Wrong," *Newsweek* (May 27, 2002)

111 Presidential Daily Brief: *Final Report of the National Commission on Terrorist Attacks Upon the United States,* W.W. Norton & Company Ltd., (New York: 2004)

111 Keen on different circumstances: Editors, "September 11 attacks might have been prevented, inquiry chairman says," *AFP Worldwide* (March 22, 2004): www.afp.com/english/home/

111 FAA issued hijack warnings in early 2001: Eric Lichtblau, "9/11 Report Cites Many Warnings About Hijackings," *New York Times* (February 10, 2005)

112 Bush's credibility gap: Hirsh and Isikoff, op. cit.

112 JFK short selling: Jim Marrs, *Crossfire: The Plot That Killed Kennedy* (New York: Carroll & Graf, 1989)

114 Short selling estimates: Kyle F. Hence, "Massive pre-attack 'insider trading' offer authorities hottest trail to accomplices," Centre for Research on Globalisation (April 21, 2002)

114 Richard Crossley: James Doran, "Millions of shares sold before disaster," London *Times* (September 18, 2001)

115 US Treasury notes: Ibid.

115 Dylan Ratigan: Ibid.

115 Michael Ruppert: Kellia Ramares and Bonnie Faulkner, "The CIA's Wall Street connections," *Online Journal* (October 12, 2001)

116 Suspicious trades worldwide: Ruppert, *Crossing the Rubicon*, op. cit.

116 Alex Popovic: Marcy Gordon, "SEC Investigating Trading in Shares of 38 Companies; Asks Brokerages to Review Records," *Associated Press* (October 2, 2001)

116 Harvey Pitt: Ibid.

117 Other suspicious trading: Michael C. Ruppert, "Suppressed Details of Criminal Insider Trading lead directly into the CIA's Highest Ranks," *From The Wilderness Publications* (October 9, 2001)

117 "Buzzy" Krongard: http://www.cia.gov/cia/information/krongard.htm

117 Frightening implications: Rupert (2001), op. cit.

118 Don Radlauer: Christopher Bollyn, "Revealing 9-11 Stock Trades Could Expose The Terrorist Masterminds," *American Free Press* (May 13, 2002)

119 Walter Burien: www.serendipity.li/wot/burien01.htm

119 Jerry Bremer: Elizabeth Neuffer, "Officials Aware in 1998 of Training," *Boston Globe* (September 15, 2001)

120 No conceivable ties: *The 9/11 Commission Report,* op. cit.

121 Germans say US and Israelis warned: Ned Stafford, "Newspaper: Echelon Gave Authorities Warning of Attacks," *Washington Post,* Newsbytes (September 13, 2001)

121 4,000 Israelis reported missing: Editors, "Thousands of Israelis missing near WTC, Pentagon," *Jerusalem Post* (September 12, 2001)

122 Odigo message warnings: Editors, "Instant Messages To Israel Warned of WTC Attack," *Washington Post* (September 28, 2001)

122 CEO Micha Macover: Yuval Dror, "Odigo says workers were warned of attack," *Ha'aretz Daily* (November 3, 2001)

122 Zim American Israeli Shipping Co.: Christopher Bollyn, "Who Knew? Israeli Company Mum About WTC Pullout," *American Free Press* (December 10, 2001)

123 Israeli Lobby controversial study: http://ksgnotes1.harvard.edu/Research/wpaper.nsf/rwp/RWP06-011

123 Israelis film WTC: Editors, "The White Van: Were Israelis Detained on September 11 Spies?" *ABC News* (June 21, 2002)

124 Maps in car: Paulo Lima, "Five Men Detained As Suspected Conspirators," *Bergen* [New Jersey] *Record* (September 12, 2001)

124 Foreign Counterintelligence Investigation: Marc Perelman, "Spy Rumors Fly on Gusts of Truth," *Forward* (March 15, 2002)

124 Stoffer and Berlet: Ibid.

125 DEA report leaked: Ben Fenton, "US arrests 200 young Israelis in spying investigation," London *Telegraph* (July 3, 2002)

125 Guillaume Dasquie: Christopher Bollyn, "120 Spies Deported," *American Free Press* (March 25, 2002)

125 Carl Cameron quotes investigators: Michael Collins Piper, "Israel Knew: Israel Conducts Massive Spying Operation in US," *American Free Press* (December 24, 2001)

126 *Le Monde* on cell phones from vice consul: John F. Sugg, "Israeli Spies Exposed," [Tampa] *Weekly Planet* (April 2, 2002)

126 National Counterintelligence Center warning: Ibid.

126 Military bases and petroleum facilities: Justin Raimondo, 'The 'Urban Myth' Gambit," *Antiwar.com* (March 13, 2002)

126 Served in intel or signal intercepts: Ibid.

127 German paper *Die Zeit*: Rob Broomby, "Report details US 'intelligence failures'" *BBC News* (October 2, 2002)

127 Reversed wiretaps: Charles R. Smith, "US Police and Intelligence Hit by Spy Network," *NewsMax.com* (December 19, 2001); www.newsmax.com/archives/articles/2001/12/18/224826.shtml

128 Pipes and conspiracy theories: Daniel Pipes, "An Israeli spy network in the United States?" *Jewish World Review* (March 11, 2002)

128 Career suicide: Raimondo, op. cit.

129 Lisa Dean and Brad Jansen: Smith (December 19, 2001), op. cit.

129 IASPS "Clean Break" paper: www.israeleconomy.org/strat1.htm

130 Hersh called terrorist: http://transcripts.cnn.com/TRAN-SCRIPTS/0303/09/le.00.html

131 Gen. Hameed Gul: Michael Collins Piper, "Former Pakistani Intelligence Chief Alleges Rogue Spook Agencies Behind Terror Attacks," *American Free Press* (December 5, 2001)

132 Werthebach and von Bülow: Christopher Bollyn, "European Spooks Say Mideast Terrorists Needed State Support," *American Free Press* (December. 24, 2001)

132 Mossad has capability: "US troops would enforce peace under Army study," *Washington Times* (September 10, 2001)

134 Chossudovsky on Pakistani link to 9/11: http://www.globalresearch.ca/articles/CH0111A

134 Global Hawk in Afghanistan: Editors, "Operational debut for Global Hawk," *Jane's Aerospace* (October 8, 2001); www.janes.com/serospace/military/news/misc/globalhawk_ppv.shtml

135 Global Hawk made history: www.dsto.defence.gov.au/globalhawk/releases/parlsec18801.html

135 First flight: News Release, "Global Hawk Completes First Flight," United States Department of Defense (March 2, 1998); www.defenselink.mil/news/Mar1998/b03021998_bt091-98.html

136 Andreas Von Bülow: Joe Vialls, "Home Run' Electronically Hijacking the World Trade Center Attack Aircraft," http://geocities.com/mknemesis/printer.html

136 Joe Vialls: Ibid.

137 NFERS white paper: www.kinetx.com

138 Hijackers flying skills: "Hijackers Suspects Tried Many Flight Schools," *Washington Post* (September 19, 2001)

139 Alhazmi and Al-Mahar: "San Diegans See Area as Likely Target," *Washington Post* (September 24, 2001)

139 Transponder explanation: Vialls, op. cit.

140 Impossible cell calls: Alan Cabal, "Miracles and Wonders," *New York Press* (July 27, 2004)

140 Lyz Glick and Dan Zegart, "Flight 93: What I Never Knew," *Readers Digest* (September, 2004)

140 The biggest known threat: Vialls, op. cit.

141 Objective is loss of national sovereignty: Col. Donn de Grand Pre, "The Enemy Is Inside The Gates," *American Free Press* (February 11, 2002)

142 Glen Cramer: John Carlin, "Unanswered Questions - The Mystery of Flight 93," London *Independent* (August 13, 2002)

142 Cheney acknowledges shoot-down order: Editors, "Cheney Says Military Was Ordered To Shoot Down Planes," *Online NewsHour*, Public Broadcasting Service (September 16, 2001)

142 Paul Wolfowitz: Ibid.

143 Rumsfeld's remark: http://www.Worldnetdaily.com/news/article. asp?ARTICLE_ID=42130

143 Bill Wright: Carlin, op. cit.

143 Wally Miller: Ibid.

145 Commission's "desperate attempt": David Ray Griffin, *The 9/11 Commission Report*, see chapter fifteen.

145 Elaine Scarry: Emily Eakin, "Professor Scarry Has a Theory," *New York Times Magazine* (November 19, 2000)

147 Biblical prophets: Trent C. Butler, gen. ed., *Holman Bible Dictionary*, (Nashville, TN: Holman Bible Publishers, 1991)

147 St. Paul: *The Holy Bible*, 1 Thessalonians 5:20-21 (Living Bible edition)

148 Severely monitored scientific experiment: Ronald M. McRae, *Mind Wars: The True Story of Government Research into the Military Potential of Psychic Weapons*, (New York: St. Martin's Press, 1984)

154 Kissinger's quote and involvement in Chile: Christopher Hitchens, "Regarding Henry Kissinger: A panel discussion on the making of a war criminal," National Press Club (February 22, 2001)

154 Kissinger resigns: Editors, "Kissinger resigns as head of 9/11 commission," *CNN.com* (December 15, 2002); http://www.cnn.com/2002/ALLPOLITICS/12/13/kissinger.resigns/

156 Bush and complaining commission: Editors, "Chairman says commission needs more time," *NBC, MSNBC* and news services, (February 13, 2004)

157 Max Cleland: Greg Pierce, Inside Politics, "9-11 Former Sen. Max Cleland Now Export-Import Bank," *Washington Times* (November 25, 2003)

157 Zelikow equivalent to Cheney or Bush: David Ray Griffin, *The 9/11 Commission Report: Omissions and Distortions* (Northampton, MA: Olive Branch Press, 2005)

158 Zelikow wrote military strategy document: Excerpted from the transcript of Griffin's public lecture delivered March 30, 2006, at Grand Lake Theater in Oakland. Zelikow's authorship of this document is reported in James Mann's *Rise of the Vulcans*.

158 Cacchioli before staffers: Greg Szymanski, "NY Fireman Lou Cacchioli

Upset that 9/11 Commission 'Tried to Twist My Words'" *ArcticBeacon.com*, (July 19, 2005)

158 Rodriguez discounted: Greg Szymanski, "WTC Basement Blast and Injured Burn Victim Blows 'Official 9/11 Story' Sky High," *ArcticBeacon.com* (June 24, 2005)

159 Permitted President to lie: *Benjamin DeMott*, "Whitewash as Public Service: How *The 9/11 Commission Report* defrauds the nation, *Harper's Magazine* (October, 2004)

159 Ashcroft's testimony was deceptive: Center for American Progress daily report, April 12, 2003; http://www.americanprogress.org

160 Ashcroft erroneously claims funds for counterterrorism: http://slate.msn.com/id/2098783

160 Ben-Veniste easy on Ashcroft: http://www.911commission.gov/hearings/hearing10/staff_statement_9.pdf

160 Clarke's claims electrified country: Center for American Progress daily report, April 22, 2003; http://www.americanprogress.org

160 Highly classified program to monitor al Qaeda dropped: Editors, "In the Months Before 9/11, Justice Department Curtailed Highly Classified Program to Monitor Al Qaeda Suspects in the US," *Newsweek* (March 21, 2004)

163 Rice's lies according to Sibel Edmonds: Andrew Buncombe, "I Saw Papers that Show US Knew al-Qa'ida Would Attack Cities With Airplanes," London *Independent* (April 2, 2004)

164 Chertoff cousins: Christopher Bollyn, "Chertoff's Cousin Crafted Smear of 9-11 Researchers," *American Free Press* (March 7-14, 2005)

164 Four tactics: Joel Skousen, "Debunking the Debunkers," *World Affairs Brief* (February 14, 2005); www.worldaffairsbrief.com

164 Skousen: Ibid.

165 Commission failed dismally: Nafeez Mosaddeq Ahmed, "The War on Truth," (Northampton, MA: Olive Branch Press, 2005)

165 Griffin's conclusions: Griffin, 2005, op. cit.

169 Cover up of high crimes: http://911review.com/articles/griffin/commissionlies.html

PART II – WAR FOR OIL AND DRUGS

173 Weekly report: James P. Tucker, Jr., "White House Whitewash: No Justice for Pearl Brass," *American Free Press* (July 8, 2002)

173 Tucker's statement: Ibid.

174 Loans to Russia: G. Edward Griffin, *The Creature from Jekyll Island* (Westlake Village, CA: American Media, 1994)

175 Kuwait "atrocities": Tom Regan, "When contemplating war, beware of babies in incubators," *Christian Science Monitor* (September 6, 2002)

175 Real reason for Gulf War never known: Jonathan Vankin and John Whalen, *Fifty Greatest Conspiracies of All Time* (New York: Citadel Press, 1995)

175 Occupy a hostile land: George Bush and Brent Scowcroft, *A World Transformed*, (New York: Alfred A. Knopf, 1998)

176 CENTGAS: Editors, *BBC NEWS*, (May 13, 2002); http://news.bbc.co.uk/1/hi/business/1984459.stm

177 Khalilzad supports Taliban: Joe Stephens and David B. Ottaway, "Afghan Roots Keep Adviser Firmly in the Inner Circle," *Washington Post* (November 23, 2001)

178 Khalilzad played important part: Mike Fox, "Bush Appoints Afghan Envoy," *BBC News*, (January 1, 2002)

178 French authors quote O'Neill: http://www.rense.com/general17/deal.htm.

179 US aligns with Russians: S. Frederick Starr, "Afghanistan Land Mine," *Washington Post* (December 19, 2000)

179 Pakistani Naik warned: http://news.bbc.co.uk/1/hi/business/1984459.stm (May 13, 2002).

180 Brzezinski's admission: Bill Blum, translator; Zbigniew Brzezinski interview, *Le Nouvel Observateur* (France), (January 15-21, 1998)

181 External threat needed for consensus: Zbigniew Brzezinski, *The Grand Chessboard: American Primacy and its Geostatic Imperatives* (New York: Basic Books, 1997); http://www.foreignaffairs.org/19971101fabook3692/zbigniew-brzezinski/the-grand-chessboard-american-primacy-and-its-geostrategic-imperatives.html

181 Pre-attack meeting: Jonathan Steele, Ewen MacAskill, Richard Norton-Taylor and Ed Harriman, "Threats of US strikes passed to Taliban weeks before NY attack," London *Guardian*, September 22, 2001

183 Naik and American representatives: Ibid.

184 Bombs destroy music cache: Laura Flanders, "'Arab CNN' First Berated, then Bombed by US," *WorkingForChange.com* (November 14, 2001)

184 Colonel Brian Hoey: Jay Tolson, "World Disorder?" *US News & World Report* (October 21, 2002)

185 Bombing a PR fiasco: http://www.zmag.org/flandersarabcnn.htm

185 Gore Vidal's statement on Bush's plea for no investigation: Marc Cooper, "The Last Defender of the American Republic?" *LA Weekly* (July 5-11, 2002)

186 North Korean nuke news withheld: Paul Bedard, "Going Nuclear," Washington Whispers, *US News & World Report* (October 28, 2002)

187 Sen. Robert Byrd: Paul J. Nyden, "Bush's War Plans are a Cover-Up, Byrd Says," *West Virginia Gazette* (September 21, 2002)

187 Rumsfeld notes: Editors, "Rumsfeld Wanted to Hit Iraq Hours After 9-11!" *NewsMax* (September 8, 2002); www.newsmax.com/archive/

187 Bush on IAEA report: Joseph Curl, "Agency disavows report on Iraq arms," *Washington Times* (October 1, 2002)

187 IAEA denies reports: Ibid.

188 1998 IAEA report: Ibid.

188 Powell's UN report: Williams Rivers Pitt, "Blair-Powell UN Report Written by Student," *Truthout* (February 7, 2003); http://truthout.org/docs_02/020803A.htm

189 Powell's cry: http://www.thenation.com/doc/20030922/alterman

190 Lawrence Wilkerson: http://www.pbs.org/now/politics/wilkerson.html

190 Two Democrats argue against war: Editors, "Democrat Congressman Accuses Bush of Lying to Provoke War!" *NewsMax.com* and UPI (September 30, 2002)

191 Lott remark: http://www.cnn.com/2002/ALLPOLITICS/09/29/iraq.debate/.

191 Clinton's remarks: Editors, "Clinton: Get Bin Laden Before Pursuing Saddam," *The Associated Press* (September 5, 2002)

192 Constitution no longer relevant: http://www.rense.com/general32/longer. htm

193 McKinney's remarks: Rep. Cynthia McKinney, "We Come For Peace," *Truthout* (April 20, 2002); www.truthout.org/docs_02/04.24A.McKinney. Peace.htm

194 Grassy knoll in Roswell: Editors, "McKinney implied Bush knew of September 11 plot," *Atlanta Journal-Constitution* (April 12, 2002)

194 Irate columnist: Kathleen Parker, "McKinney's minions march to a different drummer indeed," *Orlando Sentinel* (April 21, 2002)

195 Bush and the Saudi prince: Patricia Wilson, "Bush Celebrates Saudi Ties Before Meeting Envoy," *Reuters* (August 27, 2002)

195 Rand analyst: Ibid.

195 Newspaper poll showed 47 percent believed officials knew of attacks: Michael Davidson, "Kill the Messenger," *From The Wilderness* (May 6, 2002)

195 Zogby International poll: www.911truth.org/article.php?story=200408301 20349841

196 Downing Street Memo: www.timesonline.co.uk/printFriendly/0,,1-523-

1593607-523,00.html

197 Thomas and Beck comments: http://www.csmonitor.com/2005/0517/dailyUpdate.html

197 Philippe Sands and memo: http://politics.guardian.co.uk/print/0,,5390333-111381,00.html

198 Worldwide poll: Ewen MacAskill, "Worldwide Poll Shows 60% Fear Terror Threat Is Worse after War," London *Guardian* (February 28, 2006)

199 Zogby and CBS polls: Demetri Sevastopulo and Edward Alden, "Most Troops Want Swift US Pull-Out from Iraq," *Financial Times* (February 28, 2006)

199 $3.8 billion welfare hog: Knut Royce and Nathanial Heller, "Cheney Led Halliburton To Feast at Federal Trough," Investigative Report, *The Center for Public Integrity* (August 2, 2000)

199 Cheney making policy: Kenneth T. Walsh, "Cheney: Out of the bunker," *US News & World Report* (March 25, 2002)

201 Kellogg Brown & Root: Jeff Gerth and Don Van Natta Jr., "In Tough Times, a Company Finds Profits in Terror War," *New York Times* (July 13, 2002)

201 Halliburton misdeeds: Editors, "Cheney accused of corporate fraud," *BBC News* (July 10, 2002); http://news.bbc.co.uk/1/hi/world/americas/2119981.stm

202 Raad Alkadiri: Carola Hoyos, "A discreet way of doing business with Iraq," *Financial Times* (November 3, 2000)

202 Carola Hoyos: Ibid; www.truthout.org/docs_01/02.23D.Cheney.Circumvented.htm

202 Judicial Watch suit against Cheney, Halliburton: Editors, "Cheney, Halliburton face suit," *CNN Money* (July 10, 2002); http://money.cnn.com/2002/07/10/news/cheney_lawsuit/.

203 GAO pressured: Peter brand and Alexander Bolton, "GOP threats halted GAO Cheney suit," *The Hill* (February 19, 2003)

203 SEC probes Halliburton: Editors, "Suit accuses Cheney, firm of fraudulent accounting," *CNN.com* (July 11, 2002); http://www.cnn.com/2002/LAW/07/10/cheney.suit/.

204 Bunnatine Greenhouse: http://www.truthout.org/docs_05/011905D.shtml

204 Altanmia fuel deal: http://www.corpwatch.org/article.php?id=11664

205 Kickbacks and Laszlo Tibold: http://www.corpwatch.org/article.php?id=11664

206 Halliburton and Iran: Jason Leopold, "Halliburton Secretly Doing Business With Key Member of Iran's Nuclear Team," *CommonDreams.org* (August 6, 2005); www.commondreams.org/cgi-bin/print.cgi?file=/views05/0806-21.htm

207 Iraqi column showed foreknowledge: Larry Neumeister, "Lawsuit: Iraq Knew of 9/11 Attacks," *Associated Press* (September 4, 2002)

207 Iraqis brought to US: Craig Roberts, *The Medusa File*, (Tulsa, OK: Consolidated Press International, 1997; Craig Roberts, "The Bombing of the Alfred P. Murrah Federal Building," Tulsa Police Department report, September 4, 1996)

209 Four reasons for foreknowledge: Rep. Charles Key, "Rep. Charles Key on the Facts of the Oklahoma Bombing," mailed letter, (March 12, 1997)

210 Jayna Davis had evidence rejected: Editors, "Oklahoma City blast linked to bin Laden," *WorldNetDaily.com* (March 21, 2001)

211 Philippine plot: David Hoffman, *The Oklahoma City Bombing and the Politics of Terror* (Los Angeles, CA: Feral House, 1998)

211 Motel witnesses: Jim Crogan, "The Terrorist Motel: The I-40 connection between Zacarias Moussaoui and Mohamed Atta," *LA Weekly* (July 29, 2002)

212 Crogan's comments: Ibid.

212 McVeigh had Iraqi phone numbers: Paul Bedard, Washington Whispers, *US News & World Report* (October 29, 2001)

214 Artifacts in Iraq: Editors, "Artifacts Uncovered in Iraq," *ABC News.com* (December 28, 1999)

215 Loss of antiquities: McGuire Gibson, "The loss of archeological context and the illegal trade in Mesopotamian antiquities," *Culture without Context* (Issue 1, Autumn, 1997)

215 Pentagon alerted to museum importance: Andrew Curry, "History's Loss," *US News & World Report* (April 28, 2003)

216 Looters had keys to vaults: Jocelyn Gecker, "Experts: Looters Had Keys to Iraq Museum," *Associated Press* (April 17, 2003)

216 Glass cutters: Christopher Bollyn, "Iraqis Robbed," *American Free Press* (April 21, 2003)

216 Robert Fisk: Ibid.

216 Martin E. Sullivan: Gecker, op. cit.

218 Robertson quotes Bush: http://www.cnn.com/2004/ALLPOLITICS/10/19/robertson.bush.iraq/

221 Taliban destroyed poppy crop: http://www.whitehousedrugpolicy.gov/publications/international/factsht/heroin.html

221 White House report: http://www.msnbc.msn.com/id/7090585/

222 Primary mission is combat: Philip Shishkin and David Crawford, "In Afghanistan, heroin trade soars despite US aid," The *Wall Street Journal* (January 18, 2006)

222 Opium trading by Boston families: Steven Sora, *Secret Societies of America's Elite*, Destiny Books: 2003.

222 Tom Carew: www.sabawoon.com/articles.asp?id=132&view=detail

223 DEA "sting": Daniel Hopsicker, *Barry & 'the boys': The CIA, The Mob and America's Secret History*, (Noti, OR: Madcow Press, 2001)

229 Osama bin Laden background: Anonymous source, translated document provided to *Frontline*, Public Broadcasting Service; www.angelfire.com/home/pearly/hjtmis1/osama-bio.html

231 President Clinton's address: Transcript of President Clinton's Oval Office remarks on anti-terrorist attacks, United States Information Agency, (August 20, 1998)

232 *Ummat* interview with bin Laden: http://www.americanfreepress.net/10_22_01/al Qaeda_Not_Involved__Says_bi/al Qaeda_not_involved__says_bi.html.

232 Mother claims tape doctored: Editors, "Bin Laden's mother says video 'doctored'," In Brief, *USA Today* (December 24, 2001)

233 German experts rip videotape: Christopher Bollyn, "Bin Laden Tape Dupes Public, Say Experts," *American Free Press* (January 4-14, 2001)

235 Wayne Madsen quote: http://www.thetruthseeker.co.uk/article.asp?ID=4075

235 BBC and tape: Matthew Davis, "Bin Laden threats may boost Bush," BBC News, (January 20, 2006)

236 Republicans suppress Saudi information: http://pub12.ezboard.com/fnuclearweaponsnuclearweaponsforum.showMessage?topicID=282.topic

238 [Motley suit: Tony Bartelme, "September 11 Suit Wins First Major Legal Battle," *The Post and Courier* (August 7, 2003)

239 911 Citizen's Complaint: http://releases.usnewswire.com/GetRelease.asp?id=39128

239 Senator Bob Graham: Linda Robinson, "What's In The Report?" *US News & World Report* (August 11, 2003)

240 Saudi oil production tripled: Michael Field, "Good for business," *Financial Times* (February 21, 1991)

240 CFR report on Saudis: George Gedda, "Report: Saudi Charities Back al-Qaida," *Associated Press* (October 17, 2002); http://story.news.yahoo.com/news?tmpl=story2&cid=513&u=/ap/20021017/ap_on_go_ot/us_saudi_terror_

241 John Loftus explanation: http://www.john-loftus.com/press_release.asp

242 FBI Agent Steven Butler and the Saudis: Gloria Borger, Edward T. Pound and Linda Robinson, "The Road to Riyadh," *US News & World Report* (December 9, 2002)

242 Saudi bank connected to JP Morgan and Bank of America: Martin Mbugua, "Saudi Bank Tied To Terror Has US Banks," New York *Daily News* (November 10, 2001)

242 Jeff Hershberger: Ibid.

242 Salem bin Laden in Texas: Mike Ward, "Bin Laden relatives have ties to Texas," *Austin American-Statesman* (November 9, 2001)

243 Close ties between bin Ladens and Bushes: Ibid.

244 James Bath: Ibid; Jonathan Beaty and S. C. Gwynne, *The Outlaw Bank: A Wild Ride into the Secret Heart of the BCCI* (New York: Random House, 1993); *American Free Press* (October 15, 2001)

244 Ashcroft denies access: Ward, op. cit.

244 Bath's connection to Saudi bank: Pete Brewton, "The Mafia, CIA and George Bush," (New York: S.P.I.Books/Shapolsky Publishers, Inc. 1992)

244 Mahfouz and BCCI: J. H. Hatfield, *Fortunate Son: George W. Bush and the Making of an American President* (New York: St. Martin's Press, 1999)

245 Bill White: Beaty and Gwynne, op. cit.

246 Main Bank: Ibid.

246 John Mecklin's estimates: http://newsandviews9.tripod.com/news/time-line.html.

247 Harken low-interest loans to Bush: Editors, "Bush Received Company Loans He Now Wants Banned," *Reuters* (July 11, 2002)

247 1990 Bahrain agreement for bases: Russell S. Bowen, *The Immaculate Deception* (Carson City, NV: America West Publishers, 1991)

248 Harken stock sale: Bowen, op. cit.

249 George H. W. Bush and Carlyle Group: Michael Ruppert, "Must Read: The Best Enemies Money Can Buy," *Guerilla News Network* (October 11, 2001) ;http://www.guerrillanews.com/newswire/164.html.

250 Bush and Prince Bandar: Unger, op. cit.

250 Larry Klayman of Judicial Watch: http://www.judicialwatch.org/archive/2001/863.shtml.

250 Big pile of money: Ruppert, op. cit.

251 Two documents: Interviews, "Has someone been sitting on the FBI?" *News Night,* BBC News (June 11, 2002)

251 Constraints on investigating Saudis: Greg Palast, "FBI and US Spy Agents Say Bush Spiked Bin Laden Probes Before 11 September," London *Guardian* (November 7, 2001)

251 Al-Rajhi banking family: John Mintz and Tom Jackman, "Finances Prompted Raids on Muslims; US Suspected Terrorism Ties to N. Va. For Years," *Washington Post* (March 24, 2002)

251 Grover Norquist: Duncan Campbell, "FBI Raids pro-Republicans," London *Guardian* (March 25, 2002)

252 Abdullah Noman: Associated Press, "Official Took Bribes for US Visas," *New York Times* (May 21, 2002)

252 Michael Springman: http://www.gregpalast.com/detail.
   cfm?artid=104&row=1.

PART III – THE 9/11 BACKLASH

256 Bush and Los Angeles plot: Deb Riechmann, "Bush Says Cooperation
   Thwarted 2002 Attack," *Associated Press* (February 9, 2006)

256 Los Angeles Mayor: Michael R. Blood, "L.A. Mayor Blindsided by Bush Announcement," *Associated Press* (February 9, 2006)

257 Doug Thompson's blog: www.capitolhillblue.com/blog/2006/02/intel_
   pros_say_bush_is_lying_a.html

257 Powell's comments: Frank Bruni, "Bush Taps Cheney to Study Antiterrorism Steps," *New York Times* (May 8, 2001)

258 Unnamed intelligence source: Jon Rappoport, "Briefing on Al Qaeda,"
   StratiaWire (September 5, 2002)

259 Al Qaeda an illusion: Robert Scheer, "Is Al Qaeda Just a Bush Boogeyman?" *Los Angeles Times* (January 11, 2005)

259 Al Qaeda as CIA database: Robin Cook, "The struggle against terrorism
   cannot be won by military means," London *Guardian* (July 8, 2005)

260 same ideology: Thom Hartmann, "Hyping Terror for Fun, Profit and Power,
   www.commondreams.org/cgi-bin/print.cgi?file=/views04/1207-26.htm

260 Model State Emergency Health Powers Act: Mimi Hall, "Many states reject
   bioterrorism law," *USA Today* (July 23, 2002)

261 FEMA plans tent cities: John O. Edwards, "FEMA Preparing for Mass Destruction Attacks on Cities," *NewsMax* (July 15, 2002)

262 History of repression in emergencies: Pamela Sebastian Ridge and Milo
   Geyelin, "Civil Liberties of Ordinary Americans May Erode—Legally—Because of Attacks," *New York Times* (September 17, 2001)

262 Frank Serpico booed: Editors, "Serpico decries anti-terrorism measures,"
   Associated Press (July 6, 2002)

263 Janet Reno's remarks: Jim Burns, "William Bennett Hopes to Shape Public
   Opinion of War on Terrorism," *Cybercast News Service* (March 12, 2002);
   www.snsnews.com/ViewPolitics.asp?Page=\Politics\archive\200203\
   POL20020312

263 Guantanamo prisoner information released: "US Discloses Names of 558
   at Guantanamo," *Associated Press*, (April 20, 2006)

263 Sen. Patrick Leahy: Matthew Purdy, "Bush's New Rules to Fight Terror
   Transform the Legal Landscape," *New York Times* (November 25, 2001)

264 Durbin's comments: http://www.senate.gov/~durbin/gitmo.cfm

266 Military as panacea for domestic problems: Matthew Carlton Hammond,

"The Posse Comitatus Act: A Principle in Need of Renewal," *Washington University Law Quarterly*, (summer, 1997)

267 WWII vet Fred Hubbell arrested: Paul Marks, "Texan Learns to Rue Remark," *Hartford Courant* (August 3, 2002)

267 GI Joe disarmed: Editors, "Soldier toy disarmed at airport," *BBC News* (August 5, 2002)

268 Attack on Kingsville: David M. Bresnahan, "What happened in Kingsville, Texas, Monday night?" *World Net Daily* (February 10, 1999)

269 Britt Snider and Garden Plot: Ron Ridenhour with Arthur Lubow, "Bringing the War Home," *New Times* (November 28, 1975)

269 Cable Splicer and reactions: Ibid.

270 New under Secretary of Defense for intelligence: Linda Robinson, "Moves that matter," *US News & World Report* (August 12, 2002)

270 Stephen A. Cambone: http://rightweb.irc-online.org/profile/1066

270 SSB and Stephen Cambone: http://www.cnn.com/2005/ALLPOLITICS/01/23/pentagon.intel/

271 Office of Strategic Influence closed: Editors, "US closes 'disinformation' unit," *BBC News* (February 26, 2002)

271 Rumsfeld vows to continue disinformation: http://foi.missouri.edu/osi/osiisgone.html

273 Army plan to spy on Americans: Christopher H. Pyle, "Be afraid, be very afraid, of spying by the US Army," *The Hartford Courant* (December 5, 2002)

274 Detention camps: Author's interview with retired Lt. Col. Craig Roberts, November 4, 2002.

275 John Brinkerhoff: http://www.homelandsecurity.org/journal/Articles/brinkerhoffposseecomitatus.htm

276 Bush's urgent need: news.bbc.co.uk/2/hi/americas/2031255.stm.

276 Real losers are American people: Editors, "Sen. Lashes Out Over Ridge No-Show," *Associated Press* (April 30, 2002)

278 Statements in support of Homeland Security: Tom Ridge, written statement to the House Select Committee on Homeland Security (July 15, 2002)

279 Gregory Despres: http://www.outsidethebeltway.com/archives/2005/06/man_with_bloody_chain_saw_let_in_to_us_/

280 Oliver North's martial law plan: Alfonso Chardy, "Plan called for martial law in US," *Knight-Ridder News Service* (July 5, 1987)

280 John Dean's concern: Ritt Goldstein, "Foundations Are In Place For Martial Law In The US," *Sydney Morning Herald* (July 27, 2002)

283 ACLU objections to Homeland Security: Timothy H. Edgar, Testimony before the House Select Committee on Homeland Security and others (June

25-28, 2002)

283 Sen. Joseph Lieberman: http://www.cnn.com/2002/ALLPOLITICS/11/25/homeland.security/.

284 Timothy Sparapani: Walter Pincus and Dan Eggen, "325,000 Names on Terrorism List," *Washington Post* (February 15, 2006)

284 David D. Cole: Ibid.

284 Alberto R. Gonzales: Ibid.

284 Sen. Kennedy on list: Sara Kehaulani Goo, "Sen. Kennedy Flagged by No-Fly List," *Washington Post* (August 20, 2004)

285 Reginald T. Shuford and David C. Fathi: Ibid.

285 Library incident: Cameron W. Barr, "Policing Porn is Not Part of Job Description," *Washington Post* (February 17, 2006)

286 Dr. Robert Johnson: www.thenation.com/blogs/thebeat?pid=63406

286 Vietnam veteran writes: Jeffrey St. Clair and Alexander Cockburn, "Tom Ridge in Vietnam: Tarnished Star," *CounterPunch* (October 1, 2001)

287 The Phoenix Program: Douglas Valentine, "US Terrorist Attacks: Homeland Insecurity," *Disinformation* (October 9, 2001); http://www.disinfo.com/archive/pages/article/id1631/pg1/index.html

288 Open letter to Gen. Lawlor: Douglas Valentine, "Flight Of The Phoenix—From Vietnam To Homeland Security," *CounterPunch* (August 25, 2002); http://www.counterpunch.org/valentine0824.html

289 Richard Armitage: Ibid.

290 Armitage major participant in narcotics: James "Bo" Gritz, *A Nation Betrayed* (Sandy Valley, NV: Bo Gritz, 1988)

291 Post office incident: Matthew Rothschild, "The New McCarthyism," *The Progressive* (January, 2002)

292 Operation TIPS: Citizen Corps website; www.citizencorps.gov/tips.html.

292 Cuba's Committees for the Defense of the Revolution: Isabel Garcia-Zarza, "Big Brother at 40: Cuba's revolutionary neighborhood watch system," *Reuters* (October 12, 2000)

292 ACLU opposition to TIPS: Randolph E. Schmidt, "Postal Service Won't Join TIPS Program," *Associated Press* (July 17, 2002)

293 John Whitehead: Ellen Sorokin, "Bush Wants Letter Carriers, Meter Readers As Informants," *Washington Times* (July 16, 2002)

293 TIPS website changes: Editors, "Website for Operation TIPS Quietly Changes," The Memory Hole; www.thememoryhole.org/policestate/tips-changes.htm.

294 Neighborhood Watch: Darragh Johnson and David A. Fahrenthold, "Watching the Homeland," *Washington Post* (March 8, 2002)

295 A.J. Brown and the Secret Service: Rothschild, op. cit.

296 Military recruiters denied, Rep. Vitter and Jill Wynns: David Goodman, "No Child Unrecruited," *Mother Jones* (November-December, 2002)

296 Katie Sierra, Robert Jensen, Dan Guthrie and Tom Gutting: Ibid.

297 Richard Allen Humphreys: Robert Wilson, "Man Convicted of Threatening President Bush in Sioux Falls," *KSFY, Dakota First News* (October 22, 2002)

297 Denver photographer Mike Maginnis: Editors, "Photographer Arrested For Taking Pictures Near Cheney Hotel," *2600 News* (December 5, 2002)

298 Kindergartners disciplined: Editors, "'Gun-toting' tot loses suspension suit," *Associated Press* (May 1, 2002)

298 Ellen Schrecker and Nadine Strossen: Ibid.

298 Snooping is Un-American: Paul Proctor, "The War on Freedom," *News With Views* (July 17, 2002); www.newswithviews.com/war_on_terror/war_on_terrorism1.htm.

299 Rep. Dennis Kucinich: Eli Pariser, editor, "Can Democracy Survive An Endless 'War'?" *MoveOn Bulletin* (July 18, 2002); www.moveon.org/moveonbulletin.

300 Rep. Ron Paul: Kelly Patricia O'Meara, "Police State," *Insight Magazine* November 9, 2001)

300 Rep. Bernie Sanders: Ibid.

301 ACLU statement: http://action.aclu.org/reformthepatriotact/whereitstands.html

302 PATRIOT Act expands FISA: Walter Brasch, "The fiction behind national security," *Online Journal* (July 25, 2002)

302 FISC rejects Ashcroft's guidelines: Ted Bridis, "Special Court Rejects Ashcroft's Rules," *Associated Press* (August 22, 2002)

303 Internet users warned: Editors, "EFF Analysis of The Provisions of The USA Patriot Act," *Electronic Frontier Foundation* (October 31, 2001); www.eff.org/Privacy/Surveillance/Terrorism_militias/20011031_eff_usa_patriot_analysis.html

304 Patriot Act provisions that cause concern: Editors, "Overview of Changes to Legal Rights," *Associated Press* (September 5, 2002); www.newsday.com/news/nationworld/wire/sns-ap-sept-11-legal-rights-glance0905sep05.story

304 Global Relief Foundation faces secret evidence: Geoff Dougherty and Laurie Cohen, "US Using New Law on Secret Evidence: Patriot Act invoked to fight lawsuit by Muslim group," *Chicago Tribune* (March 15, 2002)

304 Global attorney Roger Simmons: Ibid.

305 Hany Kiareldeen and Niels Frenzen: Stephen Franklin and Ken Armstrong, "Secret evidence bill raises concerns," *Chicago Tribune* (Sep. 30, 2001)

306 Dr. Al-Badr Al-Hazmi: Editors, "Saudi doctor returns to San Antonio, denounces terrorist attacks as having 'nothing to do with Islam'"

328 Sheriff Don Eslinger: Ibid.

329 Siemens tracking device: Joe Queenan, "Electronic Leashes for Teenagers," *New York Times* (May 24, 2001)

329 Worst-case scenario: Russ Kick, "Machine Age—Gotcha!" *Village Voice* (February 27, 2001)

333 Corporate connections: The Center for Responsive Politics; http://www. opensecrets.org/bush/cabinet.asp.

334 Campaign contributions: Editors, "Did You Know?" *Sierra Magazine* (September-October, 2002)

334 Fredrick Palmer: Ibid.

335 Bush Administration nepotism: Dana Milbank, "In Appointments, Administration Leaves No Family Behind," *Washington Post* (March 12, 2002)

336 Jennifer Van Bergen: http://writ.news.findlaw.com/commentary/20060109_bergen.html

339 Blanton, Claybrook, Nelson and Klayman quotes: Alan Elsner, "Bush Expands Government Secrecy, Arouses Critics," *Reuters* (September 3, 2002)

339 Gary Bass and Steven Aftergood: Ibid.

340 Cheney inebriated: http://prisonplanet.com/articles/february2006/220206_b_drunk.htm

340 Zone of privacy: Kenneth T. Walsh, "Playing by His Own Rules," *US News & World Report* (February 27, 2006)

341 Only executive branch represented: Barton Gellman and Susan Schmidt, "Shadow Government Is at Work in Secret," *Washington Post* (March 1, 2002)

342 Daschle comments: Ibid.

342 True conservatives don't act this way: Michael Ventura, "The Shadow of Totalitarianism," *The Austin Chronicle* (March 22, 2002)

343 Totalitarianism: Ibid.

PART IV – HISTORICAL PRECEDENTS

347 1968 gun law lifted almost verbatim: www.jpfo.org/GCA_68.htm

347 Douglas Reed's comments: Louis L. Snyder, *Encyclopedia of The Third Reich* (New York: McGraw-Hill Book Company, 1976)

348 Operation Eagle Flight: Paul Manning, *Martin Bormann: Nazi in Exile* (Secaucus, NJ: Lyle Stuart, Inc., 1981

349 Bush's Nazi connections: John Buchanan, "Bush-Nazi Link Confirmed," *New Hampshire Gazette* (October 10, 2003)

350 Edward Boswell comment: http://www.georgewalkerbush.net/bushnazidealingscontinueduntil1951.htm

350 Bush family complicity: John Loftus, "The Dutch Connection," Robert Lederman (February 9, 2002); http://baltech.org/lederman/bush-nazi-fortune-2-09-02.html.

350 ITT: Charles Higham, *Trading With The Enemy: An Expose of the Nazi-American Money Plot 1933-1949*, (New York: Delacorte Press, 1983)

350 Dulles brothers and Schroeder: Higham, Ibid.

351 Nazis as a great economic power: Manning, op. cit.

351 Nazis did not die: Jim Keith, *Casebook on Alternative 3: UFOs, Secret Societies and World Control*, (Lilburn, GA: IllumiNet Press, 1994)

352 Goering's quote: G. M. Gilbert, *Nuremberg Diary* (New York: Signet Books, 1947)

352 Bush like Hitler: John F. Dickerson, "Bush's Furor Over Der Fuhrer," *Time* (September 30, 2002)

353 CFR-One World Money group: Curtis B. Dall, *FDR: My Exploited Father-in-Law* (Washington, D. C.: Action Associates, 1970)

353 Admiral James O. Richardson: Robert Anton Wilson, *Everything Is Under Control: Conspiracies, Cults and Cover-ups* (New York: HarperPerennial, 1998)

353 Japanese war preparations known: Carroll Quigley, *Tragedy and Hope: A History of the World in Our Time* (New York: Macmillan, 1966)

354 Marshall's message: Michael Litchfield, *It's A Conspiracy* (Berkeley, CA: Earth Works Press, 1992)

354 Australian intelligence and Popov reports: Vankin and Whaley, op. cit.

354 Toland's names: Perloff, op. cit.

355 Marshall and Knox in White House: Ibid.

355 Stimson's diary entry: Wilson, op. cit.

356 Germans intercept Roosevelt-Churchill conversation: Gregory Douglas, *Gestapo Chief: The 1948 Interrogation of Heinrich Muller* (San Jose, CA: R. James Bender Publishing, 1995)

356 Warning came on parallel level: Douglas, op. cit.

357 Battle of the New World Order: Jonathan Vankin and John Whalen, *Fifty Greatest Conspiracies of All Time* (New York: Citadel Press, 1995)

358 Glaspie and Saddam's conversation: Russell S. Bowen, *The Immaculate Deception* (Carson City, NV: America West Publishers, 1991); Tarpley and Chaitkin, op. cit.; Jonathan Vankin and John Whalen, *Fifty Greatest Conspiracies of All Time* (New York: Citadel Press, 1995)

358 Glaspie's summer vacation: Webster Griffin Tarpley and Anton Chaitkin, *George Bush: The Unauthorized Biography* (Washington, D.C.: Executive Intelligence Review, 1992)

359 Paul Adler: Warren Hough and Lawrence Wilmot, "Saddam: Bush-

Whacked?" *Spotlight* (April 8, 1991)

360 Bobby Lee Cook: Warren Hough, "Iraq Policy No Accident," *Spotlight* (October 5, 1992)

360 Kissinger Associates: Ibid.

360 Barr's impeachment: Mike Blair, "Gonzalez: Impeach Top Cop," *Spotlight* (September 28, 1992)

360 Bush administration repayments: Mike Blair, "You Pay for Bad Loans to Iraq," *Spotlight* (April 27, 1992)

361 Loan guarantees enabled arms buildup: Bowen, op. cit.

361 Bush quote: Tarpley and Chaitkin, op. cit.

361 $4 billion secret payoff: Warren Hough, "Did George Bush Get a Big Payoff?" *Spotlight* (August 30, 1993)

362 "Weapons of mass destruction": Jay Higginbotham, "Letters," *US News & World Report* (January 18, 1999)

362 Scott Ritter and Bruce Auster quotes: Bruce B. Auster, "Inspecting the Inspectors," *US News & World Report* (January 18, 1999)

364 A secret and bloody war of terrorism: Edward Spannaus, "When US Joint Chiefs Planned Terror Attacks on America," *Executive Intelligence Review* (October 12, 2001)

365 "Northwoods documents: Report by the Department of Defense and Joint Chiefs of Staff Representative on the Caribbean Survey Group to the Joint Chiefs of Staff on Cuba Project," March 9, 1962.

365 Elite secret army: William M. Arkin, "The Secret War: Frustrated by intelligence failures, the Defense Department is dramatically expanding its 'black world' of covert operations," *Los Angeles Times* (October 27, 2002)

366 P2OG: David Isenberg, " 'P2OG' allows Pentagon to fight dirty," *Asia Times Online* (November 5, 2002); www.atimes.com/atimes/Middle_East/ DI05AK02.html.

366 Secret operations launched: William M. Arkin, "The Secret War: Frustrated by intelligence failures, the Defense Department is dramatically expanding its 'black world' of covert operations," *Los Angeles Times* (October 27, 2002)

366 NSC to be in charge: Isenberg, op. cit.

366 An endless night of black ops: Chris Floyd, "Global Eye – Into the Dark," *Moscow Times* (November 1, 2002); www.themoscowtimes.com/stories/2002/11/01/120.html.

367 CIA as facilitators: Seymour Hersh, "The Coming Wars: What the Pentagon Can Now Do in Secret," *New Yorker* (January 17, 2005)

368 Spc. Peterson's arrest: Noelle Phillips, "Fort Stewart soldier jailed in Florida on $5 million bond," *Savannah Morning News* (May 16, 2002)

368 Emad Salem: Ralph Blumenthal, "Tapes Depict Proposal to Thwart Bomb

Used in Trade Center Blast," *New York Times* (October 28, 1993)

368 Sheep-dipped dupes: Webster Griffin Tarpley, *9/11 Synthetic Terror* (Joshua Tree, CA: Progressive Press, 2006)

369 El Sayyid Nosair: Tarpley, op. cit.

369 Gen. Smedley D. Butler: www.veteransforpeace.org/war_is_a_racket_033103.htm

370 Iron Mountain quotes: *Report from Iron Mountain on the Possibility and Desirability of Peace*, (New York: The Dial Press, 1967)

371 Iron Mountain Study not fiction: Radio interview transcript of Col. Donn de Grand Pre, "Former Pentagon Official Says 'No-Win Wars' Part of Plan for One World Government," *Spotlight* (April 23, 2001)

371 Plunge protection team: Richard Wachman, "Federal Reserve Ready to Prop Up Wall Street With Billions," London *Observer* (September 17, 2001)

372 John McCain on war profiteering: Julian E. Barnes, "Cashing In on the Defense Buildup," *US News & World Report* (May 13, 2002)

372 Rick Santorum: Ibid.

373 Lockheed bribery scandals: Christopher H. Schmitt, "Wages of Sin: Why lawbreakers still win government contracts," *US News & World Report* (May 13, 2002)

374 Rep. Peter DeFazio: Ibid.

375 $2.3 trillion missing: "The War On Waste," CBS News January 29, 2002, http://www.cbsnews.com/stories/2002/01/29/eveningnews/main325985.shtml

376 Fitts on missing trillions: Catherine Austin Fitts, "The Missing Money: Why the Citizens of Tennessee Are Working Harder and Getting Less," http://www.scoop.co.nz/stories/HL0207/S00031.htm

376 Engineered destruction of the dollar: See solari.com and Catherine Austin Fitts, "A Matter of Life or Death," Foreword to Mike Ruppert's *Crossing the Rubicon*, p. xiii.

376 Security and Prosperity Partnership: http://www.spp.gov; http://www.whitehouse.gov/news/releases/2005/03/20050323-4.html

376 North American Super Highway: www.nascocorridor.com/

377 Concerns over Super Highway: http://www.imaja.com/as/environment/cars/SuperhighwaysThreatenNA.html

378 Engineered destruction of the dollar: See solari.com and Catherine Austin Fitts, "A Matter of Life or Death," Foreword to Mike Ruppert's *Crossing the Rubicon*, p. xiii.

379 Hamilton Peterson learned things: Russ Kick, "Associated Press Story Change: The Flight 93 Tape," *The Memory Hole*; www.thememoryhole.org/911/ap-93tape.htm

380 Project Censored Report: Bridget Thornton, Brit Walters, and Lori Rouse, "Corporate Media Is Corporate America"; www.projectcensored.org/news-flash/C2006_chap6.pdf

380 Uncritical passing of officials' opinions: Michael Parenti, *Inventing Reality: The Politics of the Mass Media* (New York: St. Martin's Press, 1986)

380 Brit Hume: Ibid.

382 CFR media members: *CFR/Trilateral Influence on the Carter/Reagan/Bush/ Clinton Administration*, non-copyrighted material from the Fund to Restore an Educated Electorate, Kerrville, TX; obtained from *The United States Government Manual 1991/92*, Office of the Federal Register National Archives and Records Administration; Standard & Poor's *Register of Corporations, Directors and Executives*, 1991; *Annual Report 1991/92*, Council on Foreign Relations, New York City.

382 Reed Irvine and AIM: Michael Collins Piper, " 'Watchdog' Won't Bite," *Spotlight* (May 7, 1990)

383 Walter Cronkite, Daniel Schorr and Morley Safer: Bill Kirtz, "Disgust within the ranks," *Quill* (a publication of the Society of Professional Journalists) (May, 1998)

384 Top censored stories of 2005-2006: Project Censored Press Release, Sonoma State University (September, 2005); www.projectcensored.org.

384 "Invent a new history": Milan Kundera, *The Book of Laughter and Forgetting* (New York: HarperCollins, 1978)

385 Gore Vidal: Jon Vlements, "Gore Vidal: Oil Behind Bush's Afghan Fiasco," London *Daily Mirror*. Mirror.co.uk (July 10, 2002)

389 Foreign adventurisms listed: Editors, *The New Encyclopedia Britannica* (Chicago: Encyclopedia Britannica, Inc., 15th Edition, 1991)

390 We are hated because of our government: Robert Bowman, "The Security Charade," *National Catholic Reporter* (October 2, 1998)

390 American Free Press, September 16, 2005. http://www.americanfreepress. net/html/9-11_lies_under.html

391 Ho Chi Minh as agent: Lloyd Shearer, "When Ho Chi Minh was an Intelligence Agent for the US," *Parade* (March 18, 1973); *New Encyclopedia Britannica*, Vol. 5.

392 Greatest myth of contemporary history: G. Edward Griffin, *The Creature from Jekyll Island* (Westlake Village, CA: American Media, 1994)

392 Trotsky and Wall Street: William T. Still, *New World Order: The Ancient Plan of Secret Societies* (Lafayette, LA: Huntington House Publishers, 1990)

392 Jacob Schiff's $20 million: Gary Allen, *None Dare Call It Conspiracy* (Seal Beach, CA: Concord Press, 1971)

392 No fear of communism: Allen, op. cit.

SOURCES

395 The key to understanding world history: Texe Marrs, *Circle of Intrigue* (Austin, TX: Living Truth Publishers, 1995)

395 Another force wishes: Still, op. cit.

400 Normal security bypassed: L. Fletcher Prouty, "An Introduction to the Assassination Business," *Gallery* (September, 1975)

401 Michael Rivero quote: Robert Sterling, "Dubya Dubya Three––Are Americans The Victims Of A Hoax?" *Konformist* (October 23, 2001)

402 Bush's blood ties: http://www.guardian.co.uk/uselections2004/story/0,13918,1284632,00.html

APPENDIX

The Pentagon Attack Papers

Sew Hours in September: The Clock that Broke the Lie

Seven Hours in September: The Clock that Broke the Lie

by Barbara Honegger, M.S.

The *San Francisco Chronicle* commemorated the 100th anniversary of The Great Earthquake of 1906 with a series of front-page articles headed by a single icon—a charred clock frozen at 5:12 am, the exact moment "The Big One" hit.[1] A century after that devastating event, the stopped clock serves as both the ultimate evidence and the symbol that "captures it all."

Again, almost 100 years later, clocks frozen in time at the Pentagon on the morning of September 11, 2001 both "capture it all" and are the ultimate evidence that shatters the "Official Lie" of what happened that terrible morning.

The Pentagon was first attacked at 9:32 am, much earlier than the 9/11 Commission and official cover story claim. (In this summary of evidence, the more precise time of 9:31:40 am is "rounded up" for ease of reference.)

The Pentagon and mainstream media first reported 9:43 as the time of alleged Flight 77 impact (some reports, presumably taken from official sources, were as late as 9:48 and 9:47). Over time, the time given by officials for the claimed outside impact on the building has been moved earlier and earlier, down to 9:37 (as of the time of this writing), but has never come close to the actual time of the first violent event at the Pentagon—9:32. Clearly, if the official story that Flight 77 hit the Pentagon at 9:37 were true, Flight 77 could not have been the source of massive damage to the west side of the building a minimum of five minutes earlier at 9:32.

Converging lines of proof of a 9:32 am violent event at the Pentagon on September 11, well before the official story says anything hit the building:

Multiple standard-issue, battery-operated wall clocks on the walls of the area of the Pentagon attacked on 9/11—including one in the heliport just outside the west face—were stopped between 9:31 and 9:32:40 by a violent event, almost certainly a bomb or bombs inside the building and/ or in a truck or construction trailer parked right outside the west face. The first Associated Press report, in fact, stated that the Pentagon had been damaged by a "booby trapped truck." The Navy posted the stopped heliport clock on an official website and another of the stopped clocks is in the 9/11 display at the Smithsonian Institution.[2] These are just some of the west section Pentagon clocks that stopped between 9:31 and 9:32:40 am on September 11.

April Gallop, an Army employee with a Top Secret clearance, was at her desk in the Army administrative offices in the west section of the Pentagon on 9/11, the area of the building most heavily destroyed, when what she said sounded and felt "like a bomb" went off. "Being in the Army with the training I had, I know what a bomb sounds and acts like, especially the aftermath, and it sounded and acted like a bomb. There was no plane or plane parts inside the building, and no smell of jet fuel." Ms. Gallop still has the watch she was wearing that morning, which stopped shortly after 9:30.

The FAA's [Federal Aviation Administration] timeline document "Executive Summary—Chronology of a Multiple Hijacking Crisis—September 11, 2001" reads: "0932: ATC (Air Traffic Control) AEA reports aircraft crashes into west side of Pentagon."[3] The time is the critical fact here, not the claimed cause.

Denmark's soon-to-be Foreign Minister Per Stig Moller was in a building in Washington, D.C. on 9/11 from which he looked out, heard an explosion and saw the smoke first rise from the Pentagon. He immediately looked at his watch, which read 9:32 am. He gave radio interviews in Denmark the next morning in which he stated that the Pentagon had been attacked at 9:32.[4]

On August 27, 2002, then White House Counsel and now Attorney General Alberto Gonzales gave the Secretary of the Navy lecture at the Naval Postgraduate School in which Gonzales explicitly and clearly states that "The Pentagon was attacked at 9:32." A tape of this segment of his talk was played at the 9/11 Emergency Truth Convergence at American University in Washington, D.C. in July 2005, and is on the public record.

The Pentagon was attacked by *bomb(s)* at or around 9:32 am, possibly *followed* by an impact from an airborne object significantly smaller than Flight 77, a Boeing 757.

We have already seen that Army employee April Gallop, whose watch was stopped by the violent event at the Pentagon shortly after 9:30, says that her military training and experience led her to immediately determine the source of the initial explosion was a bomb.

I have interviewed an Army auditor from Ft. Monmouth, New Jersey, who was on temporary duty assignment at the Pentagon before, on and after 9/11. He was in the Army financial management spaces only minutes before the Pentagon explosion on the morning of 9/11. He had just returned to his temporary office on the ground floor of the adjacent south side of the Pentagon by the cafeteria when he heard an explosion and felt the building shake. Immediately afterwards, he said, hundreds of panicked Pentagon personnel ran by him down the corridor just outside his office and out the South Entrance, yelling "Bombs!" and "A bomb went off!" The witness has requested that his name not be used in this summary, but is willing to testify to a grand jury or independent official investigation.

This Army financial management/audit area is part of, or contiguous to, the Army personnel offices, which was one of two main west section offices heavily destroyed in the Pentagon attack, the other being the Naval Command Center. The day before 9/11, September 10, Secretary of Defense Rumsfeld held a press conference at which he acknowledged that the Pentagon was "missing"—could not account for and needed to "find"—2.3 *trillion* dollars. Were the auditors who could "follow the money," and the computers whose data could help them do it, intentionally targeted? It is worth noting that the Pentagon's top financial officer at the time, Dov Zakheim, who also acknowledged the "missing" trillions, had a company that specializes in aircraft remote-control technology. As remnants found in the Pentagon wreckage have been identified as the front-hub assembly of the front compressor of a JT8D turbojet engine used in the A-3 Sky Warrior jet fighter,[5] and as Air Force A-3 Sky War-riors—normally piloted planes—were secretly retrofitted to be remote-controlled drones and fitted with missiles in a highly compartmented operation at an airport near Ft. Collins-Loveland Municipal Airport in Colorado in the months before 9/11,[6] the question further arises as to whether Pentagon auditors and their computerized data were intention-ally targeted on 9/11.

The Ft. Monmouth Army auditor and his two colleagues were also eyewitnesses to multiple teams of bomb-sniffing dogs and their K-9 han-dlers in camouflage uniform at the Pentagon metro station just outside the Pentagon at approximately 7:30 am on 9/11. He said that K-9 bomb squads had not been at the Pentagon metro stop before 9/11, or since, but only that day. Since K-9 dog squads don't usually search for airliners, but bombs, a bomb attack was clearly anticipated. Ms. Gallop said she also saw the bomb sniffing K-9 teams that morning, from the top of the Pentagon metro stop looking down.

Survivor eyewitnesses from inside the west section of the Pentagon reported that the blast caused its windows *first* to expand *out*wards, and then inwards.[7]

Multiple witnesses said they smelled cordite after the initial explo-sion at the Pentagon, an explosive which has a distinct and very different smell from that of burning jet fuel.[8] And as we have already noted, Ms. Gallop said there was no smell of jet fuel inside the most damaged sec-tion of the building shortly after the first violent event that stopped her watch there shortly after 9:30.

Even Secretary of Defense Rumsfeld told Sam Donaldson in an *ABC News* interview shortly after 9/11 that he first thought a bomb had gone off in the building. Donaldson: "What did you think it was?" Rumsfeld: "A bomb? I had no idea..."

It is important to note that bomb explosion(s) at 9:32 am on the ground floor of the west section of the Pentagon are *not* inconsistent with there having *also* been a later, or even near-simultaneous, impact by some airborne object—a piloted plane, unmanned drone, or missile—into the same or nearby section of the building, which may have been the cause of the collapse of the west wall section approximately 20 minutes after the initial violent event. Indeed, if a heat-seeking missile hit the building *after* the bomb(s) went off, the heat from the explosion(s) would become the *target* for the missile. Recall that the A-3 Sky Warrior planes were retrofitted shortly before 9/11, not only enabling them to be remotely controlled but also fitted with missiles. The round-shaped exit hole in the inner wall of the "C" Ring is evidence that a missile or a piloted or pilot-less remote-controlled plane significantly smaller than Flight 77 *also* struck the building *subsequent* to bombs going off and penetrated the inside of the third ring, as bomb detonations would not have resulted in such a near-symmetrical round-shaped opening.

I have interviewed the then Acting Assistant Secretary of Defense for Special Operations on 9/11, Robert Andrews—the top civilian official in charge of special operations under Secretary of Defense Rumsfeld—a former Green Beret whose office was on the second floor of the south section of the Pentagon, adjacent to the west section. While drawing the path that he took that morning on a sketch of the Pentagon, he revealed the following:

Immediately after the second World Trade Center attack of 9:03 am, Secretary of Defense Rumsfeld left his office on the Potomac side of the Pentagon and went (merely) across the hall on the same floor to his Executive Support Center (ESC), which is set up for teleconferencing. There, he joined the teleconference of top government officials run by Richard Clarke out of the White House Situation Room media room. Clarke, in his book *Against All Enemies*, confirms that Rumsfeld was among the first officials on this teleconference shortly after the second WTC tower was hit. Clarke's account and Andrews' confirmation of it are completely at odds with the official cover story and the 9/11 Commission, which claim that no one could locate Secretary Rumsfeld until approximately 10:30 am when he walked into the National Military Command Center (NMCC). The fact that Rumsfeld, the military's top civilian official, was on Clarke's teleconference with the top official of the FAA, Director Jane Garvey, also puts the complete lie to the official cover story that Air Force interceptors weren't scrambled in time because the military and FAA "couldn't talk each other" on 9/11. *The* top-most officials of the Pentagon and FAA were talking to one another *constantly* on Clarke's teleconference from as early as 9:15. This taped Clarke teleconference is the "Butterfield tape" of 9/11. [During the 1970s Watergate scandal, secretly-made tapes of President Nixon's Oval Office conversations revealed by Alexander Butterfield were the "smoking guns" which forced Nixon to resign or face certain impeachment and trial in the Senate.]

Immediately after the second WTC tower was struck at 9:03 am, Andrews and his aide left his office and ran as fast as they could down to the Secretary of Defense's West section *basement* Counterterrorism Center (CTC), beneath the ground-level location of the violent event in the building that morning, arriving at approximately 9:10. While he and his aide were in this west side basement CTC, a violent event caused the ceiling tiles to fall off the ceiling and smoke to pour into the room. Andrews immediately looked at his watch, which read approximately 9:35 am but which was set fast to ensure timely arrival at meetings, so the actual time was closer to 9:32. He and his aide then immediately evacuated the CTC with the goal of joining Rumsfeld in his Executive Support Center (ESC) across the hall from Rumsfeld's main office. He said that Rumsfeld was already on the White House teleconference when they arrived. En route to Rumsfeld's ESC, Andrews said when he and his aide entered the corridor on the *inside* ring of the west section, "we had to walk over dead bodies" to get to the inner courtyard. (Note: This is two rings *further in* towards the center from the *inner most* hole made by whatever allegedly impacted the Pentagon that morning.)

Once in the inner courtyard, Andrews and his aide ran as fast as they could to Rumsfeld's Executive Support Center, where he joined Rumsfeld as his special operations/counterterrorism adviser during Clarke's White House teleconference. Andrews also said that Secretary of Defense Rumsfeld *spoke with President Bush* while in the Pentagon Executive Support Center. Whether this was via the teleconference or by phone or other means was not stated. The fact that Rumsfeld personally communicated with Bush on 9/11 while Rumsfeld was in his Pentagon ESC was published on an official DoD web site.[9]

WTC janitor William "Willy" Rodriguez, the last person to leave the WTC alive on 9/11, has testified that he was in the first *basement* level of the WTC when an immense explosion went off *below* him in the yet-deeper *sub*basement level(s) of the building a few seconds *before* the plane hit the tower high above.[10] As Robert Andrews revealed that the west side *basement* level of the Pentagon was damaged at approximately 9:32 am and as we know that the cause of the 9:32 Pentagon attack was not an impact event but explosives, there are thus eye- and ear witness reports of bombs going off in *both* the Pentagon *and* the WTC *underground* level(s) *before* both buildings were hit by *any*thing from the outside.

As no "outside" terrorist, al Qaeda or otherwise, could have had access to either the Pentagon or the sustained advance access needed to pre-place explosives inside the WTC, *only* domestic insiders could have pre-placed the explosives in *both* the Pentagon *and* the WTC. Further, because the WTC1 deep-basement explosions(s) experienced by Willy Rodriguez happened *before* the tower was hit by a plane; as any incoming plane not controlled by the same party that triggered the sub-basement detonation(s) could have veered off from the building at the last second, ruining the plane-impact-as-cover-story for the later building collapse; and as the sub-basement explosions were necessary for the actual later collapse of the buildings by controlled demolition, *the same domestic-US insiders had to have controlled both the sub-basement detonations and the incoming plane(s)*. Thus, even if al Qaeda hijackers were on the incoming planes, they were *not* in final control of the impact of the planes into the buildings, which had to have been guaranteed by domestic/US insider controllers to ensure the sub-basement bombs didn't go off prematurely and destroy the plane-impact cover story. This fact is critical, as it takes jurisdiction for the mass murders at the WTC away from the Bush Administration's FBI, which oversees crimes committed in the air, and places it squarely with the State of New York, as murder is a State crime and multiple/mass murders are the sum of individual State crimes. Because the controllers of the timing of the basement level explosives had to have also been the controllers of the final approach of the planes, and the former was clearly on the ground and not in the air, a Manhattan grand jury can suddenly pull jurisdiction for the Bush-Cheney Reichstag Fire out of their hands.

Because the *real* modus operandi at the Pentagon and WTC are so similar, it is logical to deduce that the same domestic-US terrorists were responsible for pre-placing and detonating the bombs—both inside the WTC and inside the Pentagon. That is, a single group of US-domestic conspirators—not al Qaeda or any other outside terrorists—must have planned both the WTC and Pentagon attacks *and* controlled both the approaching planes *and* the inside-the-building explosions in real time on 9/11.

In addition to the already legion evidence that Flight 77 did not hit the Pentagon—i.e. the small hole in the west side of the Pentagon being not nearly large enough for the plane's fuselage, let alone wing width; no damage to the lawn where Flight 77 allegedly struck and skidded before hitting the building; wrecked plane parts at the site identified as being from an A-3 Sky Warrior, a far smaller plane than that of Flight 77, a Boeing 757; Pentagon requests to TV media on the morning of 9/11 not to take up-close images, etc.—there is also *official* evidence that Flight 77 did not hit the building:

In the Air Force's own account of the events of 9/11, *Air War Over America*, the North American Aerospace Defense Command (NORAD) general who finally ordered interceptor jets scrambled on 9/11, although too late, Gen. Larry Arnold, revealed that he ordered one of his jets to fly down low over the Pentagon shortly after the attack there that morning, and that this pilot reported back that there was no evidence that a plane had hit the building. This fighter jet—not Flight 77—is almost certainly the plane seen on the Dulles airport Air Traffic Controller's screen making a steep, high-speed 270-degree descent before disappearing from the radar. [When a plane flies low enough to go undetected, it is said to be "under the radar."] Military pilots—like the one sent by Gen. Arnold on 9/11 to report on the Pentagon's damage—are trained to fly 500 feet above ground in order to evade radar detection. In fact, when the Air Traffic Controller responsible for the plane and her colleagues watched the extremely difficult 270-degree maneuver on her screen, they were certain that the plane whose blip they were watching perform this extremely difficult feat *was* a US military aircraft, and said so at the time. It almost certainly was.

Thus, the likely reason the Pentagon has refused to lower the current official time for "Flight 77" impact, 9:37, to 9:32 am—the actual time of the first explosions there—is that they decided to pretend the blip represented by Arnold's surveillance jet approaching just before 9:37 was "Flight 77." As the official cover story claims that the alleged 9:37 impact was the *only* Pentagon attack that morning, yet by the time Arnold's surveillance jet arrived on the scene the violent event had already happened, the Pentagon cannot acknowledge the earlier 9:32 time without revealing an attack on the building *prior* to the alleged impact.

It is significant that the *The 9/11 Commission Report* ignores the testimony of Secretary of Transportation Norman Mineta to its own commission and did this *only* for the testimony of Secretary Mineta. The clear reason for this blatant and targeted censorship is that Mineta's eyewitness testimony is extremely dangerous to the official cover story. The portion of Mineta's testimony that is particularly dangerous is his claim that Vice President Cheney, in charge in the Presidential Emergency Operations Center (PEOC) beneath the White House since before Mineta arrived in the PEOC at 9:20, insisted to an incredulous "young man" that "the orders (given earlier by Cheney to this same individual) still stand" when the man told Cheney that the presumed plane they had been tracking as a blip on a screen was 50, then 30, and finally just 10 miles from Washington—orders which could only have been *not* to shoot down the plane. Otherwise there would have been no reason for the agent to ask Cheney if they "still" stood, despite the plane's being almost upon the capital where Cheney himself was. This is critical because of the timing that can be inferred from Mineta's testimony: As Mineta arrived at the PEOC at 9:20 am, and as Mineta estimated the "still stand?" interaction between Cheney and the agent happened 5 to 6 minutes after that, or about 9:25, it can be inferred based on the officially given speed of the plane represented by the blip of 540 mph that whatever that fast-approaching blip represented, it arrived in the vicinity of the Pentagon at approximately 9:32—nowhere close to the original official cover story time of 9:43, or even the six-minute-earlier time the Pentagon finally settled on for an alleged impact time of 9:37.

All of this also happened at 9:32 am:

- After an inexplicable delay during which they knew that both WTC towers were under attack, the Secret Service suddenly acts as if the attacks are "real," rushing President Bush out of the library at the Florida school where he had been reading to children.
- The firefighters are suddenly ordered out of WTC1.
- The New York Stock Exchange is ordered closed.

- The takeover of Flight 93 begins with the stabbing of a flight attendant and one of the alleged hijackers announcing that there is a bomb on board, picked up by flight controllers.

Other relevant interviews:

I interviewed the famous "lone taxi driver" whose cab is the only car visible still parked on I-395 above the Pentagon lawn looking down at the west face after the other cars have left the freeway. This taxi can be seen in overhead photos taken on the morning of 9/11 and viewable on the Internet. The driver said his was the last car allowed onto that section of I-395 before police put up a barricade and that he decided not to immediately leave the scene like the others "because I realized this was history and I wanted to see for myself." He stated that he saw no evidence of a plane having impacted the building nor any visible plane pieces on the lawn at the time he arrived, which was after the first violent event in the building, as black smoke was streaming up and to the right from inside-the-building fires. The taxi cab driver drew a diagram of what he saw that morning while overlooking the Pentagon's west face from I-395.

I interviewed a Navy public affairs officer assigned to the Naval Command Center, one of the two major Pentagon west section areas destroyed on 9/11, the other being the Army Financial Management/Audit area as mentioned earlier. This officer was not in the building that morning but was quickly assigned as the deputy public affairs officer at the underground "back-up Pentagon" location in Pennsylvania close to the Maryland border, Site R. This eyewitness Navy officer inside Site R said Deputy Secretary of Defense Paul Wolfowitz and later Vice President Cheney were flown to the Site R underground bunker in response to Richard Clarke's officially declaring "Continuity of Government/Continuity of Operations" (COG/COOP) on the morning of 9/11. This is confirmed in Clarke's book, *Against All Enemies*, in which he reports that Rumsfeld chose Wolfowitz to be the designated COG/COOP official at Site R in his stead. Perhaps significantly, Site R and Camp David are not far from the crash site of Flight 93. Details about Site R, on and after 9/11, are also in James Bamford's book, *A Pretext for War*.

On February 4, 2004, I interviewed Air Force General Ralph Eberhart, Commander of NORAD on 9/11. To my knowledge, Gen. Eberhart has granted no other interview since the events of September 11. Before asking questions, I gave Gen. Eberhart copies of all the mainstream press articles published as of that date on the subject of the confusion of his NORAD Northeast Sector (NEADS) personnel who were running NORAD's "Vigilant Guardian/Vigilant Warrior" emergency response war game exercises that morning. As of the date of the interview, therefore, the then head of NORAD was made aware of the initial confusion by his own NEADS "game" players on 9/11 between incoming exercise reports and incoming reports of the actual hijacks.

I first asked Gen. Eberhart if there was any connection between NORAD's "Vigilant Guardian/Vigilant Warrior" exercise being run on 9/11 and the plane-crashing-into-tower emergency response exercise simultaneously being held at National Reconnaissance Office (NRO) headquarters outside Washington, D.C.[11] He replied, "No." I was surprised at this, as a large portion of NRO personnel are from his own agency, the Air Force. I asked for reconfirmation, to which he again said, "No." Laying the ground for the next question, I mentioned that NEADS' "game" director Lt. Col. Dawne Deskins had said that she was confused as to whether initial reports of the hijacked planes on the morning of 9/11 were "real world" or "part of the game." This, I said, showed that the NORAD exercises that morning had to have been on a hijack scenario *at least similar to* the actual attacks, as otherwise there would have been no grounds for confusion. After considering this for a moment, Gen. Eberhart refused to answer any further questions and abruptly ended the interview.

In addition to the already well known and officially acknowledged evidence of Bush Administration foreknowledge of the broad outlines of the September 11 attacks— advance warnings from the intelligence agencies of as many as 11 foreign countries and the content of the now-famous August 6, 2001 presidential daily brief (whose 10-page attachment still has not been made public), etc.—there is strong evidence that Bush administration insiders had near perfect—if not complete—advance knowledge of both the details and the date of the September 11 attack:

(Note: That Bush Administration insiders had advance knowledge of the date and details of an "outside" attack is not inconsistent with these insiders having facilitated and even orchestrated the attacks. That is, the plot behind the attacks of September 11 is similar to that of the Reichstag fire, through which Hitler rapidly consolidated power. Like the Nazi-fa-cilitated Reichstag fire, there was a real though highly-unlikely-to-suc-ceed "outside" plot about which Administration insiders gained advance intelligence. They then secretly protected and enabled this plot to ensure that it not only succeeded, but succeeded *spectacularly* as the psychologi-cal operation needed to justify the entire subsequent Bush-Cheney global and domestic agenda.)

1. Shortly after September 11, *Newsweek* reported that *before* 9/11, the Bush Administration initiated a Foreign Intelligence Surveillance Act (FISA) Court surveillance/tap of "up to 20" suspected al Qaeda-linked terrorists then in the US, but that then FISA Court Chief Justice Royce Lamberth subsequently ordered the then-already-ongoing surveillance stopped. This can only mean one thing—that the Bush Justice Dept./FBI/NSA initiated the tap *before* asking the FISA Court for a warrant for it, as with the now-famous post-9/11 NSA taps initiated by the Bush adminis-tration without first applying for FISA warrants.

As "up to 20" is a clever way of saying "19" without making the link to 9/11 explicit, the Bush Administration Justice Dept/FBI/NSA almost certainly initiated surveillance of all 19, or close to all 19, of the soon-to-be alleged 9/11 hijackers *before* 9/11. Though Judge Lamberth ordered the surveillance ended once the administration filed the formal warrant application, there is evidence that the Bush administration ignored his order to cease the tap and continued the surveillance of the alleged 9/11 hijackers up to and including the day of 9/11. Zacarias Moussaoui—the only person indicted by the Bush Administration for anything even re-lated to 9/11—has stated in court filings that both he "and my (al Qaeda) brothers" then in the US were surveilled by the Bush administration be-fore 9/11 and that the Bush administration knows he can prove it. How could this be the case? If Moussaoui was one of the "up to 20" al Qaeda-linked terrorist suspects they surveilled before 9/11 without an advance FISA warrant as reported by *Newsweek*, then Moussaoui was also one of the "up to 20" whose taps Judge Lamberth ordered stopped. Moussaoui, after all, was originally named as the "20th hijacker" of the 9/11 plot. Amazingly, the FISA Act requires that, if the FISA Court rejects a surveil-lance initiated before a warrant has been applied for, as in this case, the court has to inform the "target" of the surveillance and give him the government's stated reason for the tap in the surveillance application. Moussaoui says that he can "prove" the Bush administration/FBI initiated surveillance on him before 9/11 because, it can be deduced, the FISA Court itself told him so after Lamberth ordered his—and those of the other "up to 20"—surveillance ended.

If this is the case, it opens the very real possibility that the FISA Court likewise informed most or all 19 of the "up to 20" alleged 9/11 hijackers before 9/11 that they were being surveilled by the Bush Administration— and the reason for such surveillance. This also throws new light on the claims by the Pentagon's then-secret data mining task force, "Able Danger," to have tracked lead 9/11 hijacker Mohamed Atta and at least four of the other 19 hijackers beginning in January, 2000, when Atta actually did enter the country according to Daniel Hopsicker in his book, *Welcome to Terrorland*. The FBI falsely claimed, and still falsely claims, that Atta did not enter the US until the summer of 2000, six months later. The likely reason for this intentional lie about when Atta first entered the country is what Atta is known to have done while inside the US between January and the Summer of 2000. Hopsicker reveals that, among other activities, Atta visited Portland, Maine, in March, 2000, and perhaps even earlier. An abiding "mystery" of the official cover story is why Atta drove to Portland, Maine on September 10, the day before 9/11, and then flew from Portland to Boston early on the morning of September 11. The answer to this "mystery," which the FBI clearly already knows, is the link between what Atta was *doing* in Portland before the administration admits he was even in the country, as well as what he was doing there the day before 9/11 and early on the morning of 9/11. This may all have something to do with the fact that the CIA reportedly runs secret flights out of an airport in Portland, Maine, and that "rendition" detainees have said they were flown out of the country on special jets after first stopping at Portland's International *Jet* Port.[12]

2. The FBI's top bin Laden/al Qaeda hunter until shortly before 9/11, John O'Neill, "happened" to be at the same hotel in the same town near Tarragona, Spain in mid-July 2001 *just before* lead hijacker Mohamed Atta and 9/11 plot "coordinator" Ramzi Binalshibh. Some Bush administration officials now also believe that 9/11 "mastermind" Khalid Sheikh Mohammed (KSM) met there for what the 9/11 Commission calls "the

Final 9/11 Planning Meeting." This cannot be—and is not—a coincidence. O'Neill, who was in close contact with German intelligence—recall that Atta led the "German cell" for the 9/11 attacks—and Spanish intelligence, had clearly been alerted to the upcoming meeting and was at the hotel to surveil/tap/bug the room where the meeting was about to be held. O'Neill and his agency, the Bush administration's FBI, thus knew every detail, or nearly every detail, of the planned 9/11 plot *at least two months in advance.*

Perhaps just as significantly, European media reported that bin Laden was in an American hospital in Dubai incapacitated for surgery during precisely this same mid-July, 2001, period of the Spanish "final 9/11 Planning Meeting." Reportedly, bin Laden was visited in the hospital by the area's then CIA station chief. The question naturally arises as to whether bin Laden was telephoned by Atta, Binalshibh, and perhaps also KSM, or visa versa, while the latter were at the "Final 9/11 Planning Meeting" in the hotel that O'Neill had pre-bugged. If so, then O'Neill, the FBI, and the highest levels of the Bush Administration—including O'Neill's then boss, Attorney General Ashcroft, who suddenly stopped flying commercial aircraft about this time—knew not only every detail of the 9/11 plot as of that date, but almost certainly recorded all the key "outside" conspirators plotting their "final plans" including possibly bin Laden himself, *on tape*—clearly another "Butterfield" tape to be demanded by subpoena.

As noted above, on 9/11 *itself* the US military was conducting NORAD/Air Force emergency response exercises on scenarios involving multiple hijacks, and the NRO was conducting an emergency response exercise on the scenario of a plane crashing into one of the towers at its headquarters just outside Washington, D.C.—many NRO personnel being from the Air Force and CIA. It is next to impossible for this to have been the case unless the exercises, also referred to as war games, were intentionally scripted to *mirror* what had been learned from the above-mentioned detailed advance intelligence. That is, the purpose of the war games held on 9/11 was to practice how to defend against the very attacks that John O'Neill's Tarragona meeting surveillance, the Pentagon's "Able Danger" data-mining tracking, and the FBI's FISA-warrant-less surveillance of the "up to 20" ("19"?) suspected al Qaeda terrorists had already revealed.

You don't practice something in a multi-million-dollar set of exercises that you "can't imagine." The date for the actual attacks—September 11—was then chosen to coincide with the Pentagon's exercises, which in turn mirrored the real attack plans (see below).

Perhaps the most burning data point to prove Bush administration complicity in 9/11 is the fact that lead hijacker Mohamed Atta took to the mid-July "final 9/11 planning meeting" in Spain the information that "the date *has been* set" (i.e. set by someone else *other* than Atta), and that he, Atta, didn't yet know it, but would "know it" in five to six weeks, or by late August, 2001.[13] Atta was clearly waiting to learn the date of "his own" attack. This last piece of the puzzle fell into place during the first phase of Zacarias Moussaoui's sentencing trial, in the 58-page transcript of 9/11"mastermind" Khalid Sheikh Mohammed's interrogation "testimony" read into the trial record by the Bush administration prosecution. In this KSM transcript, it is revealed that bin Laden and KSM "allowed *Atta* to choose" both the final targets for the attacks and the attack date."[14] From this, therefore, we know that neither bin Laden nor "mastermind" KSM nor "coordinator" Binalshibh set the September 11 attack date. However, from what Atta said to Binalshibh—and probably also KSM and even possibly bin Laden by phone link—at the "Final Planning Meeting" in Spain, *we also know that neither did Atta*. Atta was *waiting* to *learn* the date of his "own" attack five to six weeks *after* the mid-July "final 9/11 planning meeting," and that date did *not* come from any of his al Qaeda superiors. It must be the case then, despite KSM's claim that he "let" Atta choose the date, that *none* of the top "outside" terrorist conspirators set the date for the September 11 attacks, *including* Atta.

The key and central fact of the entire 9/11 plot is that the attack date Atta was "waiting for" *was* the date of the Bush administration's planned war games, which, in a vicious circle, were scripted to mirror the content of Atta's attack plan gleaned via advance intelligence obtained from O'Neill's surveillance of the "final planning meeting" near Tarragona, the Pentagon's "Able Danger" tracking of Atta, and the FBI's warrantless surveillance of Atta and other of the about-to-be alleged hijackers. Atta was thus the *sole* individual to whom the date the Bush administration finally chose for its war games—9/11—was leaked as soon as it was selected and he bought his one-way ticket as soon as he learned it, in late

August, 2001, just as he had predicted at the "final planning meeting." The No. 1 Bush administration conspirator, therefore, is whoever gave the administration's own war game scenario details and date—9/11—to Mohamed Atta.

Lt. Gen. Mahmoud Ahmed, then head of Pakistan's military intelligence agency ISI, is a prime suspect for the middleman who laundered this No. 1 Bush administration conspirator's insider war game information to Atta. On the morning of 9/11 he was having breakfast with future CIA Director Porter J. Goss and Senator Bob Graham, who co-chaired the joint House/Senate "investigation" of the 9/11 attacks, and had met with CIA Director George Tenet and with top officials at the Pentagon, about to conduct the war games, in the few days leading up to 9/11. He is most likely the person who was told the date and details of the Pentagon's emergency response exercises and communicated them, directly or via an intermediary, to Atta, as Ahmed also approved wiring $100,000 to Atta shortly before 9/11. Atta then confirmed 9/11 as the date for the war games—which *was* the date of the attacks—in his now-famous NSA-intercepted call with KSM of September 10, in which he related "The Match is about to begin. Zero hour is tomorrow." "Match" is a way of saying "exercise" or "war game." This critical September 10 intercept, by the way, was almost certainly made without an advance FISA warrant, putting the lie to now CIA Director and then NSA Director Gen. Michael Hayden's patently false claim that the "first" warrantless taps were initiated in defensive response to 9/11, and thus came *after* the attacks.

Another abiding "mystery" of September 11 is why Gen. Eberhart, the commander of NORAD on 9/11, claimed to the 9/11 Commission that on the morning of 9/11 NORAD was conducting, among others, a preplanned "Soviet-era" emergency response exercise[15] in which US fighter jets were to defend against Russian nuclear bombers. After all, the Soviet Union had ceased to exist *ten years before*. He didn't say "Russian," he said "Soviet." This is very strange until one discovers that, despite repeated official and media claims that September 11 was "completely unique" and that the skies over America had "never before" been cleared of all commercial and private civilian aircraft, NORAD had conducted another emergency response exercise 40 years earlier, which completely cleared the skies over the mainland US. This was on October 14, 1961, in a war game called "Sky Shield II," which was based on a scenario of how to defend against an air attack by *Soviet* bombers on New York City.[16] The main difference between the 1961 exercise and September 11 is that the clearing of the skies was announced in advance to the public in "Sky Shield." This original Soviet-era exercise, which included 1,800 US and 15 Canadian military planes and was billed as "the greatest exercise ever conducted by Western air-defense forces," is mentioned in the Air Force's own account of the events of September 11, *Air War Over America*. In fact, Gen. Larry Arnold, NORAD's commander for the continental US on 9/11 directly under Eberhart who finally ordered interceptor jets scrambled to belatedly meet the hijack threat, made a point of including the eerily similar 1961 Air Force war game in the book. Not only did both the 1961 and September 11 NORAD "Soviet-era" war game scenarios include attacks on New York City, in the 1961 exercise US military planes played the role of Soviet attack bombers. That is, the US military pre-scripted both the defense *and* the "attack" by its own planes pretending to be Soviet aircraft. If Gen. Eberhart's testimony to the 9/11 Commission is correct, NORAD may have been conducting a "Soviet-era" exercise much like the one in 1961, on 9/11.

In this light, it is significant that mainstream press stories contain intriguing reports that point to the possibility that there were *two* American Airlines "Flight 11s," leaving from two different gates at Boston Logan airport within a few minutes of one another on 9/11, as well as emerging evidence of other of the hijacked 9/11 flight numbers possibly being "twinned,"[17] or duplicated. The question thus naturally arises, were these "twin" planes US *military* planes "playing" hijacked airliner "attackers," similar to the 1961 scenario except substituting commandeered airliners for Soviet bombers? And could the 9/11 exercise have included a "trigger" event to clear the skies over the mainland US so that a realistic test of US air defenses could be conducted without interference from the thousands of civilian aircraft normally in the air?

Key quotes from *New York Times* articles during the 1961 NORAD exercise are eerily similar to stories appearing on 9/11 [text in parentheses and *italics* added]: "It is not so much the fear of collisions with military aircraft that has caused civilian planes to be ordered out of the skies, as it is the knowledge that *in*adequate [civilian FAA] electronic flight controls will be available during the exercise to guide them. Strategic Air Command (SAC) bombers, playing the role of the marauding forces, will seek to foul communications and radar. They will drop tinsel-like pieces of metal called "chaff" overhead [like the myriad small pieces of metal scrap found on the Pentagon lawn and Shanksville, Pennsylvania "crash" site on 9/11?]...that will throw radarscopes [including the FAA's] into a confusion of false signals"; "All the bomber missions were laid out ahead of time and fed into the NORAD computer"; "An automated shorthand running display of the entire battle was provided at NORAD combat center and in similar centers at Strategic Air Command headquarters [where President Bush was taken on 9/11] and in the Pentagon [which was attacked on 9/11]"; "A fight plan for every aircraft [private, commercial and military] is fed into the computer's memory beforehand. When a plane shows on the radarscope, a console operator picks up an aluminum electronic gun, points it at the blip, and squeezes the trigger. That brings the flight to the computer's attention. If the flight [plan] is filed in its memory, the computer automatically replies, 'Yes, I am aware of that [plane].' It does this by marking the flight with an F for Friendly. While the computer compares the flight with its memorized data, it marks the flight P for Pending. Finally, it may mark it H for Hostile. 'We have *two minutes* to identify a flight [as Friendly] before we scramble [interceptor jets]...to make a visual identification of an uncertain aircraft or to attack it'; 'We do not train [in exercises like the 1961 'Sky Shield II, or on 9/11] with Hostile symbology [showing on screens]; therefore, the Strategic Air Command's bombers playing the role of the attacking [Soviet Russian] force [on October 14, 1961] were marked K, for Faker'"; and "There are seventeen units of Army Air Defense Artillery with ground-to-air anti-aircraft missiles near New York [in 1961; how many more were there on 9/11, 40 years later, when none were used?]" The 1961 war game was directed by then NORAD commander Air Force Gen. Laurence Sherman Kuter from his combat operations center at NORAD's Colorado Springs headquarters, which in the mid-1960s moved to Cheyenne Mountain, Gen. Eberhart's command center on 9/11. It may also be significant that the Air Force's war games simulation center is at Maxwell Air Force Base in Alabama, which Gen. Kuter had earlier commanded and where lead 9/11 hijacker Mohamed Atta received training.

The Pentagon's "Able Danger" data miners claim that "Department of Defense lawyers"—almost certainly from the National Security Agency, then headed by Gen. Hayden, an officer in the Air Force, the same service that planned the 9/11 war games—blocked planned meetings with the FBI at which they wanted to tell the FBI that they had "tracked" Atta and other of the 9/11 hijackers prior to 9/11 and ask the FBI to initiate additional surveillance on them. The fact that the FBI *did* initiate exactly such a surveillance of the "up to 20 Al Qaeda linked terrorist suspects" before 9/11 is strong evidence that, despite its current claims to the contrary, the Pentagon's "Able Danger" team *did* communicate what they learned from tracking Atta and the others to the FBI before 9/11, and that the FBI then initiated FISA-warrant-less surveillances of Atta and others subsequently ordered stopped by then Chief FISA Court Judge Lamberth—all *prior* to 9/11. The fact that initially-suspected "20th 9/11 hijacker" Moussaoui officially filed claims that he "and my brothers" *were* surveilled before 9/11 is further evidence that the FBI continued to watch all or most of the 9/11 hijackers right up until the attacks, despite Lamberth's order to cease and desist. FBI Headquarters supervisors David Frasca and his deputy Maltbie refused 70— *seventy*—urgent requests by Moussaoui's FBI interrogator for either a FISA Court warrant or an "ordinary" criminal warrant to get into Moussaoui's computer and surveil anyone mentioned therein. Doing so would have clearly stopped the plot, as Moussaoui now claims to have personally known 17—almost all—of the alleged 19 hijackers.[18]

In addition to all the evidence that plane-impacts-plus-fire was the carefully planned cover story for the cause of collapse of WTC 1, 2 and 7, as well as the west façade of the Pentagon, both of which were initially hit by inside-the-buildings bombs, not planes, the other overwhelming line of evidence for 9/11 being an "Inside Job" is the anthrax attacks.

Any evidence linking 9/11 to the anthrax letters—dated September 11 but sent in mid- October and only to Democratic leaders in Congress, no Republicans—is direct evidence of an inside job because that particular type of anthrax is known to have been of the highly controlled "Ames strain" developed by the US Army at Ft. Detrick, Maryland, and at the University of Iowa in Ames, Iowa. It was also high-spore-count, *military*-grade weaponized anthrax refined according to a trade secret reportedly held by William Patrick, former Ft. Detrick bioweapons expert, mentor of Steven Hatfill, the only "person of interest" stalked by the FBI as a suspect in the still "unsolved" anthrax case, and the close friend and colleague of Bush Administration bio-counterterrorism expert Jerry Hauer, a signer of the PNAC manifesto calling for "a new Pearl Harbor."

On September 11, this same Jerry Hauer personally delivered anti-anthrax *Cipro* to Vice President Cheney's staff at the White House. Why? The conservative legal watchdog group Judicial Watch has filed a suit against Vice President Cheney and other Bush Administration officials demanding to know why *Cipro* was delivered to the executive mansion—and only to the executive mansion—on the day of the attacks. So far the response has been deafening silence. On September 10, the day before 9/11, FEMA and other emergency response personnel arrived in New York City for a counter-bioterrorism exercise called "Tripod II," claimed by the Bush administration to have been scheduled to begin September 12. There is reason to believe that the bio-agent this drill was to practice defending against was anthrax, as Jerry Hauer was also a major planner of the New York City exercise. And there is also a strong possibility the true start date for the exercise was September 11, as many "exercise" personnel were already in place in New York City on September 10. As the Air Force's war game scenario had just "come to life" in real attacks on 9/11, were Hauer and Cheney worried that the same thing might be about to happen with their counter-bioterrorism "exercise" Tripod II? Is this why the anti-anthrax drug *Cipro* was distributed to the White House, "just in case"? If so, it would be strong evidence that Tripod II was on the scenario of defending New York City against an anthrax attack. Was the "vector," or delivery vehicle, for that emergency response exercise scenario anthrax attack to have been by air via hijacked plane(s)?

Notably, in their book on bioterrorism, *Germs*, Judith Miller and William Broad claim, apparently from inside sources, that Ramzi Yousef's plans for the first World Trade Center attack in 1993 included explosively pushing large quantities of cyanide out into New York City. Khalid Sheikh Mohammed, the "mastermind" of 9/11, is Ramzi Yousef's uncle. Finally, former New York City mayor Rudolph Giuliani testified to the 9/11 Commission that when WTC7, the location of his emergency operations center, collapsed on 9/11, he moved those operations to the command

and control center set up on Pier 92 for the "Tripod II" bio-terrorism exercise and that it worked even better than the original. Giuliani told the 9/11 Commission, "The reason Pier 92 was selected as a command center was because on the next day, on September 12, Pier 92 was going to have a drill. It had hundreds of people there—from FEMA, from the Federal Government, from the State [Dept.], from the [New York] State Emergency Management Office—and they were getting ready for a drill for biochemical attack. So that was going be the place they were going to have the drill. The equipment was already there, so we were able to establish a command center there that was *two and a half to three times bigger* than the command center that we had lost at 7 World Trade Center. And it was from there that the rest of the (9/11 and subsequent) search and rescue effort was completed."

Conclusion

The US military, not al Qaeda, had the access to plant explosives inside its own most heavily defended world headquarters, the Pentagon. The US military, not al Qaeda, had the access to plant the explosives Willy Rodriguez heard and felt go off deep in the sub-basement of the World Trade Center. The US military, not al Qaeda, had the sustained access weeks before 9/11 to also plant controlled demolition charges throughout the superstructures of WTC1 and WTC2, and in WTC7, which brought down all three buildings on 9/11. The US military, not al Qaeda, had access to the sulfur-enhanced military-grade thermite (thermate) detected in the sub-basement levels of the WTC needed to melt the steel found molten there weeks later. The US military, not al Qaeda, would have chosen the least populated and most reinforced section of the Pentagon—its newly upgraded west wedge—to strike, minimizing casualties. Real terrorists would have maximized them. A US military plane, not one piloted by al Qaeda, performed the highly skilled, high-speed 270-degree dive towards the Pentagon that Air Traffic Controllers on 9/11 were sure was a military plane as they watched it on their screens. Only a military aircraft, not a civilian plane flown by al Qaeda, would have given off the "Friendly" signal needed to disable the Pentagon's anti-aircraft missile batteries as it approached the building. Only the US military, not al Qaeda, had the ability to break all of its Standard Operating Procedures to paralyze its own emergency response system. Only the US military, not al Qaeda, had access to the weaponized, military-grade US Army "Ames strain' anthrax contained in letters mailed only to Democratic Congressional leaders. It is absurd to believe that al Qaeda would target only Democrats, especially as the US leadership at the time of 9/11 was Republican. When he received the anthrax letter dated September 11, then Senate Democratic leader Thomas Daschle was calling for a Congressional investigation of 9/11 and had already been warned off from "looking too closely at" 9/11 by both President Bush and Vice President Cheney. When he received his anthrax letter, another Democratic leader, Senator Patrick Leahy, was leading the Congressional resistance to the PATRIOT Act, the assault on *Americans'* privacy and civil liberties justified by "al Qaeda's" attack, clearly drafted by the Bush Administration *before* 9/11 and "in the can" awaiting its "trigger event."

And who in the US military chain of command and US civilian leadership are among the prime suspects for these acts of High Treason? First and foremost are the signers of the pre-9/11 Project for a New American Century (PNAC) manifesto calling for "a new Pearl Harbor" to catalyze its global domination agenda, including Vice President Dick Cheney; Secretary of Defense Donald Rumsfeld; then Deputy Secretary of Defense Paul Wolfowitz; Richard Perle, then head of Secretary Rumsfeld's Defense Policy Board; Jerry Hauer, the federal government's top bio-terrorism expert who took anti-anthrax *Cipro* to the White House on 9/11; and then National Security Council Middle East adviser Zalmay Khalilzad, soon to be the first US Ambassador to Afghanistan after 9/11 and now US Ambassador to Iraq—the very two countries whose invasions were rationalized as retaliation for the 9/11 attacks. During the Cold War, Khalilzad was a liaison to then CIA "bag man" Osama bin Laden in the CIA's covert war against the Soviets in Afghanistan, the crucible from which al Qaeda emerged.

Another key suspect is Air Force General Michael Hayden, now Director of the CIA and then head of the National Security Agency (NSA), which tapped the calls of lead hijacker Mohamed Atta and 9/11 "mastermind" Khalid Sheikh Mohammed the day *before* 9/11, and surely on many other occasions before 9/11 as well—all almost certainly without FISA warrants as required by law. These pre-9/11 warrant-less NSA taps put the lie to President Bush's claim that he initiated the program of warrant-less NSA taps of al Qaeda suspects because of—and thus only after—9/11. Yet another key suspect is Army Lieutenant General William "Jerry" Boykin, the radical Christian fundamentalist Special Operations commando recently proposed to head the Army's Special Operations Command. Yet another is the Pentagon's POP2 office, reportedly to plan and script "false flag" operations—attacks orchestrated by the US military but made to appear perpetrated by an outside enemy to justify US military "retaliation." Yet another suspect is Defense Intelligence Agency Iran expert Lawrence "Larry" Franklin, who was "loaned" to Perle and Wolfowitz's neocon associate Douglas Feith and arrested for passing national security secrets to Israeli operatives at the American-Israel Public Affairs Committee (AIPAC). Franklin also was and is an officer in the Air Force reserves, which directed NORAD's "Vigilant Guardian/Vigilant Warrior" war game exercises on 9/11.

Scrutiny should also be leveled at the scriptwriters for the NORAD and NRO emergency response exercises planned for and held on 9/11, especially members of their lead "White Teams," which set the content and then oversee both "Red Team attackers" and "Blue Team defenders" on the actual day of an exercise, in this case on 9/11 itself. And every one of the as-yet-to-be-identified "top Pentagon officials" who the day before 9/11, according to *Newsweek*, suddenly cancelled their already-booked flights for September 11.[19] Also National Military Command Center (NMCC) commander Brig. Gen. Montague Winfield, who on that same day, September 10, asked his deputy, Navy Capt. Charles Leidig to take over for him the next morning between 8:30 and 10:30—precisely the time window of the "game" whose details and date had been given to Atta. Further investigation should be directed at the (government) "agency" the 9/11 Commission revealed, without identifying it by name, took out the vast majority of the put options on American Airlines, United Airlines, Boeing and Morgan Stanley Dean Witter in the few days before 9/11. Also, Michael Chertoff, US Attorney for the District of New Jersey during the first 1993 attack on the World Trade Center who, as a private attorney, represented Egyptian-born US resident Magdy Elamir, under investigation for illegally diverting millions of dollars and whose brother, Mohammed Elamir, funded arms smugglers linked to al Qaeda.[20] Significantly, Mohamed Atta's name in his country of birth, Egypt, was *also* Mohamed Elamir. In other words, the very man President Bush put in charge of the entire 9/11 "investigation" and who is now Director of Homeland Security—*the* top official charged with defending the US mainland from an attack by al Qaeda— may have been directly involved with al Qaeda and even with Mohamed Atta himself. And FBI headquarters supervisor David Frasca and his deputy Michael Maltbie, who ignored 70 pleas by Zacarias Moussaoui's FBI interrogator to let him investigate the contents of Moussaoui's computer before 9/11. Attention should also be directed to Philip Zelikow, NSC adviser along with Zalmay Khalilzad to then NSC Adviser Condoleezza Rice before and on 9/11. Zelikow both orchestrated *The 9/11 Commission Report* cover up of the administration's inside job and, at Rice's personal request, rewrote the Bush administration's official national strategic plan draft to better match the global domination agenda of the pre-9/11 PNAC manifesto.

These are just some of the names being knitted into the scroll of the September 11 Truth Revolution.

Barbara Honegger, M.S. is Senior Military Affairs Journalist at the Naval Postgraduate School (1995-present), the Navy's advanced science, technology and national security affairs university. *This research, as with all of Honegger's research and publications on September 11, is solely in her capacity as a concerned private citizen and does not imply official endorsement.* Honegger served as Special Assistant to the Assistant to the President and White House Policy Analyst (1981-83); was the pioneering Irangate author and whistleblower on the October Surprise (*October Surprise*, Tudor, 1989; and Iran-Contra expose documentary film "Cover-Up"); and was called as a researcher/witness at both the October 23, 2004, and August 27, 2005, Los Angeles Citizens 9/11 Grand Jury hearings held at Patriotic Hall in Los Angeles, Calif. Much of the information and analysis contained in this evidence summary was presented at the L.A. Citizens Grand Jury hearings and at the 9/11 Emergency Truth Convergence conference held at American University in Washington, D.C. in July, 2005.

Notes:

1. The clock stopped at the moment the Great Earthquake hit San Francisco on April 18, 1906 is at http://sfgate.com/greatquake/.

2. The clock at the Pentagon heliport just outside the west section, frozen at 9:31:40 am by the violent event at the Pentagon, was posted on an official Navy web site at http://www.news.navy.mil/view_single.asp?id=2480Pentagonclock_BBC. Yet another stopped Pentagon clock is in the September 11 exhibit at the Smithsonian Institution. It was originally posted at http://www.americanhistory.si.edu/september11/collection/record.asp?ID=19.

3. Federal Aviation Administration (FAA) timeline document "Executive Summary Chronology of a Multiple Hijacking Crisis, September 11, 2001."

4. Danish Foreign Minister Per Stig Moller interview with Denmark Radio P3, September 12, 2001, 6:15 am Denmark time. "…I saw smoke and fire rising from the Pentagon at 9:32…My first impression was that a bomb had been detonated at the Pentagon." The audio of this radio interview is in the 9/11 video documentary *Bomberne som Forsvandt* by Danish researcher Henrik Melvang, available at www.unmask.dk and at www.bombsinsidewtc.dk. See also 9/11 timeline by European researcher Jose Garcia in *Reality, Truth and Evil Facts, Questions and Perspectives on September 11, 2001*, Temple Lodge Publications, 2005.

5. *The 9/11 Conspiracy*, Catfeet Press/Open Court, James Fetzer, editor, 2006, chapter by Prof. James Fetzer; and photos of a JT8D turbojet engine and the remnant found at the Pentagon at http://www.simmeringfrogs.com/articles/jt8d.html.

6. Report by two civilian defense contractor employees at "Secret Global Hawk Refit for Sky Warrior," http://portland.indymedia.org/en/2005/05/318250.shtml.

7. "Loud Boom, Then Flames in Hallway: Pentagon Employees Help Rescue Co-workers," *Washington Post*, September 11, 2001. Quoted in Peter Tiradera, *9/11 Coup Against America: The Pentagon Analysis* (Booksurge: 2006), p. 204.

8. Pentagon eyewitness Don Perkal to MSNBC: "Even before stepping outside, I could smell the cordite. I knew explosives had gone off somewhere." Also eyewitness account of Amtrak electrical engineer Samuel Danner who was at the site and said he smelled cordite (American Free Press, July 7, 2006, reporting based on audio report by Republic Broadcasting Network, summary at http://www.total911.info/2006/07/pentagon-eyewitness-ids-global-hawk.html).

9. Author interview with former Acting Assistant Secretary of Defense for Special Operations and Low Intensity Conflict, Monterey, California; summary posted on Naval Postgraduate School web site www.nps.navy.mil, subsequently changed to www.nps.edu. Article no longer posted; hard copy available from the author.

10. Videotaped testimony of William ("Willy") Rodriguez, former World Trade Center janitor and the last person to leave the WTC alive on September 11, in the 9/11 documentary "Loose Change—Second Edition," text in parentheses added:

"All of a sudden we hear 'Boom!' in the basement. I thought it was a generator that blew up, and I said to myself, 'Oh, my God, I think it was a generator. And I was going to verbalize it, and when I finished saying that in my mind I heard (another, second) 'Boom!' right on the top (above), pretty far away. And so it was a difference (in space and time) between coming from the basement and coming from the top...and a person comes running into the office (in the first basement level, from a deeper basement level) saying 'Explosion!'...and he said '(it was from) The elevators!' And there were many (deep basement WTC1) explosions."

11. "Agency (NRO) Planned Exercise on September 11 Built Around a Plane Crashing into a Building," Associated Press, August 22, 2002; by Jonathan Lumpkin; "They Scrambled Jets, but It was a Race They Couldn't Win," *Syracuse Post-Standard*, January 20, 2002, by Hart Seely; "Rome Staff's Efforts on 9/11 Earn Praise, Commission Says Military Did the Best It Could with the Information It Had," *Syracuse Post-Standard*, June 18, 2004, by Hart Seely; Complete 9/11 Military Exercises Timeline, Cooperative Research, at http://www.cooperativeresearch.org/timeline.jsp?timeline=complete_911_timeline&before-9/11=militaryExercises; *Crossing the Rubicon*, by Michael Ruppert, Chapter 19: "Wargames and High Tech: Paralyzing the System to Pull Off the Attacks" and Chapter 20: "Q&A: Many Asked, Some Answered—and a Golden Moment," New Society Publishers, 2004. In the Acknowledgements to *Rubicon*, p. xi, Ruppert credits the author with what he refers to as "the Holy Grail of 9/11 research" (p. 336): "Thanks to Barbara Honegger, who kept hammering on the wargames until we all paid notice... you showed me the most important lead I needed to put it all together."

12. "Detainee's Suit Gains Support from Jet's Log," *New York Times*, March 30, 2005, p. A1. Key excerpt, text in parentheses added: "Mr. Arar (a "rendered" detainee) says he followed the (Gulfstream jet) plane's movements on a map displayed on a video screen (inside the plane), watching it as he traveled to Dulles Airport outside Washington, to a Maine Airport he believed was in Portland (Maine), to Rome, and finally to Amman, Jordan, where he was blindfolded and driven to Syria." Though the FAA claims its records show a plane on that date making the other stops but landing in Bangor, not Portland, Maine, the detainee's account may be accurate, as only Portland's airport is labeled an "International Jet Port," specializing in landings and takeoffs of just such private, corporate and government jets.

13. Ironically, at the final hearing of the Kean Commission, where its report was released to the press and public, commissioner John Lehman responded to the question, *What if anything remained unknown*, by noting that the Commission still wasn't clear as to "how Atta chose the date for the attacks."

14. Summary interrogation of Khalid Shaikh Mohammed, claimed "mastermind" of the September 11 attack plot, read into the Zacarias Moussaoui sentencing trial

record by the prosecution on March 27, 2006; the full text is part of the court proceedings transcript for that date available through Exemplaris.com.

15. *The 9/11 Commission Report*, note 116, p. 458, at http://www.9-11commission.gov/ report/911Report.pdf. Key excerpt: "On 9/11, NORAD was scheduled to conduct a military exercise, Vigilant Guardian, which postulated a bomber attack from the *former Soviet Union.*"

16. *Air War Over America: Sept. 11 Alters Face of Air Defense Mission*, by Leslie Filson, US Air Force account of the events of September 11. Also "Civilian Planes to be Grounded 12 Hours Today in Defense Test," *New York Times*, October 14, 1961, pp. 1 and 4; "Civilian Planes Halted 12 Hours in Defense Test: Joint Maneuvers Fill Air Over Canada and US with Military Craft, Cities 'Hit' by Bombers," *New York Times*, October 15, 1961, pp. 1 and 46; "Computer is Key to Area Defense: Ever-Alert Device in (New) Jersey Joins in Air Exercises," *New York Times*, October 15, 1961, p. 46; and "US-Canada Test of Air Defense Rated a Success: President Receives a Report on Maneuvers, Search is Pushed for Missing B-52," *New York Times*, October 16, 1961, pp. 1 and 16.

17. For example, see "Flight 11: The Twin Flight," by "Woody Box" at http://new.globalfreepress.com/article.pl?sid=04/03/14/212247, and "Flight 11 and Flight 93 'Survived'" at http://inn.globalfreepress.com/modules/news/article.php?storyid=858.

18. "Moussaoui, Undermining Case, Now Ties Himself to 9/11 Plot," *New York Times*, March 28, 2006, pp. A1 and A14.

19. *Newsweek*, September 24, 2001.

20. "Michael Chertoff—Where All the Questions Should Start," January 12, 2005, http://allspinzone.blogspot.com/.

Index

INDEX